# Futures Past

## Studies in Contemporary German Social Thought
Thomas McCarthy, General Editor

# Futures Past

On the Semantics of Historical Time

Reinhart Koselleck

translated by Keith Tribe

The MIT Press Cambridge, Massachusetts, and London, England

This translation copyright © 1985 by the Massachusetts Institute of Technology. This work originally appeared in German under the title *Vergangene Zukunft. Zur Semantik geschichtlicher Zeiten*, © 1979 by Suhrkamp Verlag, Frankfurt am Main, Federal Republic of Germany.

This book was set in Baskerville by The MIT Press Computergraphics Department and was printed and bound by Halliday Lithograph in the United States of America.

Library of Congress Cataloging in Publication Data

Koselleck, Reinhart.
    Futures past.

    (Studies in contemporary German social thought)
    Translation of: Vergangene Zukunft.
    Bibliography: p.
    Includes index.
    1. History—Philosophy—Addresses, essays, lectures. 2. History—Periodization—Addresses, essays, lectures. 3. History—Terminology—Addresses, essays, lectures. 4. Historiography—Addresses, essays, lectures. I. Title. II. Series.
D16.8.K63313  1985     901     85-5195
ISBN 0-262-11100-4

# Contents

## III
## Semantic Remarks on the Mutation of Historical Experience

# Translator's Introduction

The essays collected here were written between 1965 and 1977, chiefly as contributions to symposia or academic occasions, and were first published together under the title *Vergangene Zukunft. Zur Semantik geschichtlicher Zeiten* in 1979. Koselleck's two previous books were his doctoral dissertation, published as *Kritik und Krise* in 1959, and *Habilitationsschrift*, published as *Preussen zwischen Reform und Revolution* in 1967. His chief scholarly activity since the 1960s has been the organization and editing of a massive dictionary of "historical concepts"— *Geschichtliche Grundbegriffe*—which had by the mid-1980s reached the fifth of six volumes. For any other scholar, such facts might lead one to expect a form of writing dominated by pressures of the moment and the less stimulating aspects of occasional literature. Koselleck is an exception. His published work, and indeed his professional career, has depended to a great extent on a curious dialectic of chance and obligation. His writing is, however, marked by an originality and clarity that belie the manner in which it comes into existence. The essays printed here, whether read separately or together, display a combination of scholarship and coherence which transcends the diverse nature of their origins.

One thread drawing these essays together is their coincident relation to the planning and organization of *Geschichtliche Grundbegriffe*. Indeed, some were written expressly for meetings organized in association with the project. As such, the essays can be read as so many variations on the systematic themes being developed by Koselleck and others for this project. Thus, a clearer understanding of these essays requires some knowledge of the project, as well as of the general nature of *Begriffsgeschichte*.[1] What will, however, strike the Anglo-American reader at once is the range of intellectual interests and capacities that these essays display. It would be hard to imagine work of such depth and theoretical diversity being produced today by a senior, English-speaking professor of history. The peculiar combination of historical, political, and theoretical concerns that surfaces in these essays is, at least in part, the result of Koselleck's participation in the postwar resumption of a German academic tradition, and his membership of a postwar generation of students who began their studies in the late 1940s and who now occupy leading positions in the cultural geography of the Federal Republic.

Born in Görlitz in 1923, Koselleck attended the University of Heidelberg from 1947 until 1953, studying history, philosophy, law, sociology, and the history of art and occasionally attending lectures in medicine and theology. In the sociology seminar led by Alfred Weber, he presented papers on the French Revolution and on Hobbes, and around 1950 he began to prepare his dissertation. The philosophy seminar he attended was led by Gadamer and Löwith; under their influence, and, stimulated by the frequent attendance of Heidegger, he developed much of his historical methodology. At this time he considered himself equally active in history, sociology, philosophy, and law (*Staatslehre*); among his fellow students were Hans Robert Jauss, Juri Striedter, and Dieter Henrich—Romanist, Slavicist, and philosopher, respectively. Only one of his fellow students could be termed a historian, and this contact was outside of the university context.

Koselleck's interest in *Begriffsgeschichte* dates from this period and is attributed to the stimulation of Heidegger and Carl Schmitt. Both men were barred from teaching during this period, a consequence of their National Socialist associations.[2] Schmitt was often in Heidelberg at this time, since his wife was seriously ill in hospital there, and Koselleck came to know him through private contacts. Heidegger impressed Koselleck in discussion by his method of tracing concepts back to their roots: isolating the manner in which key categories shifted and transformed over time and highlighting the resonances present in the contemporary vocabulary of sociopolitical language. Schmitt, on the other hand, taught Koselleck how to pose problems and seek proper solutions, reducing the question of method to the posing of good questions that provide a barrier against a drift into generality.

It was under Schmitt's theoretical influence that Koselleck's dissertation on the relation of Enlightenment and Revolution took shape. This is apparent both in the perception of the contemporary world as one characterized by civil war and in the manner in which the structure of the argument develops.[3] Emphasis is placed on the dialectic of the prospect of Enlightenment and the covert development of Enlightenment thought within the lodges of Freemasonry, promoting a tension between the activity of criticism and the absolutist social order that was to result in the crisis and the destruction of this order. The research that went into this dissertation was intended as a preliminary to a larger study of the critical-political potential of Kant; this was never completed, but the reader of the present essays will find traces of this project in the scattered allusions to Kant.

Following the completion of his dissertation, Koselleck spent two years as a Lektor at the University of Bristol, where he devoted what time he could spare to reflections on historical problems and the sociology of literature; here he formulated the idea of history in the "collective singular," which forms a major component in his analysis of the reconstitution of historicity in the early nineteenth century. In 1956 he returned to Heidelberg, first as assistant to Johannes Kühn and then to Werner Conze, who was then engaged in the establishment of a research group in modern social history.[4]

Conze had studied in Königsberg with Ipsen and Rothfels, and while the former had to some extent preserved a German sociological tradition through the period of the Third Reich, it was to Rothfels that Conze felt particularly indebted. Conze continued the studies initiated by Ipsen on demography and Prussian agricultural organization, and it is important to note that the establishment of social-historical research at Heidelberg during the latter 1950s predates the international reception of the *Annales* historians and of English social history.[5] Another important influence at this time was Otto Brunner, Professor of History at Hamburg, whose pathbreaking study of late medieval Austrian politics, *Land und Herrschaft*, was a model for the deployment of conceptual analysis for solving sociopolitical questions.[6]

On taking up his post at Heidelberg, Koselleck began to consider topics for further research leading to *Habilitation*. His first choice was to study the temporal structure linking the Vienna Congress to Versailles, investigating, for example, the temporalities governing decision-making and the perspectives of futurity that were involved. Conze was not keen on this idea, however, and gave him the Prussian reforms to work on instead.

The result was *Preussen zwischen Reform und Revolution*,[7] a social history in the sense that it was a study of the reformation of a social order through the gradual penetration of new distinctions, qualifications, rights, and procedures. This is not, therefore, a social history in the English sense, for which a minimum requirement is a focus on the lived experience of real people, delineating the network of social relations through the medium of social action. Koselleck's account begins with the draft and revised versions of the Prussian Civil Code and examines the relationship of the state to its various elements, be they *Stände*, societies, families, or individuals. 'The social' is thereby explored in terms of sets of categorizations, their mutual relations, and their articulation in the administrative activity of the state (which, in the case of Prussia, was the dynamic element in the process of "modernization"). Emancipation is traced as a dual process: of the state from the monarchy and of the free citizen from the state. This citizen is an individual who owes primary allegiance to the state but who can take a variety of forms—the laborer, the peasant, the landowner, the bourgeois, the poor.

During the period 1956–1965, Koselleck worked on his *Habilitation*, taught intensively, and wrote reviews but had little opportunity to develop other work. It was in this period that he presented to Conze his idea of a lexicon of historical concepts, which was to have been a one-volume work covering all major concepts from Antiquity to the present. Conze encouraged the idea but insisted that the project be limited to the German-language area and focus primarily on the eighteenth and nineteenth centuries. Resulting from this was the characteristic shape marking each contribution: a concentration on a process of transition to modernity in the late eighteenth century (casually nicknamed the *Sattelzeit* by Koselleck, since become a concept in its own right), preceded by a period in which concepts are no longer intelligible to us without interpretation and exegesis, and followed by a "modernity" in which the conceptual structure does not generally require such elaboration. A meeting of Koselleck, Conze, Brunner, and other collaborators in the autumn of 1963 resulted in proposals for development of the lexicon. A programmatic statement based on this meeting appeared under Koselleck's name in 1967.[8]

In 1966, Koselleck became Professor of Political Sciences at Bochum. In the same year he joined the planning commission for the new university at Bielefeld, conceived as a well-endowed modern university which would be a center for advanced research and teaching. Here again, Conze was instrumental in this development. As one of Germany's leading modern historians, Conze had been appointed to the commission, but when he saw that it would be several years before the Faculty of History was to be established, he withdrew and nominated Koselleck to serve in his place. He returned to Heidelberg to occupy a chair in modern history from 1968 to 1973 and in 1974 became Professor for the Theory of History at Bielefeld, a post he still holds.

Although *Geschichtliche Grundbegriffe* appears under the joint names of Brunner, Conze, and Koselleck, Brunner never played a direct role in the actual editorial work, which was shared by Conze and Koselleck. The true nature of the project lies closer to Koselleck's own intellectual interests than to those of Conze. Thus, it is perhaps inevitable that the work be more closely associated with his name than with Conze's, who nevertheless continues to bear a considerable share of the editorial work. As suggested above, the essays included here are in many respects a product of Koselleck's participation in this project, and so a brief consideration of its features will shed some light on their central preoccupations.[9]

The inclination of German historical work toward a form of analysis emphasizing the importance of conceptual distinctions and categorical reorganizations can perhaps be attributed to the place of law and philology in the German academic tradition. This provides a historical background to the development of *Begriffsgeschichte* as a method, and also helps explain why, once such a project was conceived, it was possible to find so many contributors who were both sympathetic and capable of providing material. "Key concepts" of sociopolitical language—such as *Politik, Geschichte, Demokratie, Gesellschaft, Kritik, Adel,* and *Arbeiter*—were selected and subjected to an investigation which charted their shifting usage and the consequent perspectives they created for their users. What counts as a key concept is determined by the project's purpose: to examine "the dissolution of the old world and the emergence of the new in terms of the historicoconceptual comprehension of this process."[10] It is the genesis of modernity, rather than modernity itself, that is at stake; hence the emphasis on the

*Sattelzeit*. The original program aimed at a coverage of 150 concepts, but it was never intended that these should be dealt with uniformly. Some entries would merely register the formation of a neologism (*Faschismus*, for example); others would provide short essays of about thirty pages on terms which became either more or less central during their progress through the *Sattelzeit* (*Polizei* is a good example). Several entries have almost become monographs in their own right, whether written singly or jointly—Riedel's contributions on *Gesellschaft* and Sellin's on *Politik* fall into the first category, while the 123-page entry for *Geschichte, Historie* has sections written by Koselleck, Christian Meier, O. Engels, and Horst Günther.

In his 1967 outline of the project, Koselleck provided a list of questions to be brought to bear on each term: Is the concept in common use? Is its meaning disputed? What is the social range of its usage? In what contexts does the term appear? Is the term articulated in terms of a concept with which it is paired, either in a complementary or adversary sense? Who uses the term, for what purpose, and to address whom? How long has it been in social use? What is the valency of the term within the structure of social and political vocabulary? With what terms does it overlap, and does it converge with other terms over time?[11] It is clear from these questions that the exposition of a concept's meanings was anticipated from the beginning to involve its placement within a hierarchy of meaning, the cumulative effect of the lexicon being to elucidate a complex network of semantic change in which particular concepts might play a varying role over time. Organizing the concepts in terms of such leading categories as "state" or "economy" was regarded as impractical, though desirable; this would in any case involve a form of interpretation that would diminish the usefulness of the project. Instead, the neutrality of an alphabetic arrangement was settled on, with each contribution adhering to a strictly chronological presentation. In the later phases of the preparatory work, three qualities the contributions should assess were emphasized: the term's contribution to the question of temporalization, its availability for ideological employment, and its political function.[12] Such guidelines could be no more than rules of thumb, however; on the whole, a general pragmatism ruled the project's execution, beginning with the identification of key concepts, continuing with the selection of suitable contributors, and affecting space allocation and the evaluation of final contributions.

It is only to be expected that a large collaborative project display inadequacies and uneven coverage. Few of the contributors can match Koselleck's theoretical rigor and command of material; the tendency is for one or the other to predominate, with varied results, depending on the concept at issue. Theoretical criticisms based on the difficulty of rigorously defining the distinction between "word" and "historical concept," and the consequent impossibility of elaborating a method specific to this mode of doing history, ignore the fact that *Begriffsgeschichte* is more a procedure than a definite method. It is intended not as an end in itself but rather as a means of emphasizing the importance of linguistic and semantic analysis for the practice of social and economic history.

Such is the background against which the essays translated here were written. The themes which run through them—historicity, temporality, revolution, modernity—also find expression in Koselleck's contributions to *Geschichtliche Grundbegriffe*, principally in the entries "Geschichte, Historie" and "Revolution." The actual mode of argument, however, owes much to Gadamer and Schmitt and has much in common with that of *Rezeptionsgeschichte* as developed by Jauss.

As noted above, it was in Gadamer's seminar in Heidelberg that Koselleck encountered Heidegger and became interested in the use of concepts to solve historical problems. More generally, there is much common ground between Gadamer's *Truth and Method*, first published in 1960, and the basic, interpretive framework within which Koselleck moves. Shared by *Truth and Method* and these essays is the construction of a hermeneutic procedure that places understanding as a historical and experiential act in relation to entities which themselves possess historical force, as well as a point of departure in the experience of the work of art and the constitution of an aesthetics.[13] Aesthetic experience is elaborated by Gadamer by examining the development of the concept *Erlebnis*, or experience in the sense of the lived encounter.[14] This term was developed as a counter to the rationalism of the Enlightenment and is characteristic of an aesthetics that centers on the manifestation of the "truth" of a work of art through the experience of the subject.

From this point, Gadamer proceeds to the philosophical question of what kind of knowledge is thereby produced. Modern philosophy is perceived as discontinuous with the classical tradition; the development of a historical consciousness in the nineteenth century made philosophy aware of its own historical formation, creating a break in the Western tradition of an incremental path to knowledge.[15] Koselleck takes up this problem and approaches it as a historical question: What kind of experience is opened up by the emergence of modernity?

The dimensions of this experience are charted with respect to time and space, specifically through consideration of the "space of experience" and the "horizon of expectations," terms which form the subject of Koselleck's final essay and which in many ways summarize the themes of the preceding essays. More emphasis is given to the latter notion, combining as it does the spatial extension apparently available to a historical subject with the temporal projections that issue from this space. The perspective that opens up to a historical subject is doubled by the perception of the site occupied by this subject as one characterized by a conjuncture of heterogeneous dimensions—the *Gleichzeitigkeit der Ungleichzeitigen*, or the contemporaneity of the noncontemporaneous.

These ideas have been developed most explicitly by Jauss in the context of literary history conceived in terms of *Rezeptionsgeschichte*.[16] Like Koselleck, he joins historicity and experience, treating the reception of a literary work as a progression through the horizons of expectation of a succession of readers, whose expectations are constituted by both their historical circumstances and the unchanging literary forms they successively encounter.[17] The study of literature thus becomes a study of the ongoing reception of a text, where this text no longer occupies the position of a stable positivity, but rather is transformed by this process of reception, and, in turn, as an element in the transformation or modification of the experience of its readers, is reproduced as a work of literature. As Jauss emphasizes, not only is it necessary to overcome the diachronic emphasis of literary history through the construction of synchronous structures of perception; one must also recognize that it is the junction of synchronic and diachronic orders and the place of the reader at this junction which make historical understanding possible. By its nature, this junction is constituted by a concatenation of diverse elements, of different histories advancing at different rates and subject to varying conditions. Hence was developed the characterization of the moment of experience as a point of contemporaneity in which all that occurs together by no means enters into this moment in a uniform fashion.[18]

In its own way, *Begriffsgeschichte* is a form of *Rezeptionsgeschichte*, charting the course of the reception of concepts and examining the experience that they both contain and make possible. Overlying this is the continuing influence of Carl Schmitt, the man from whom Koselleck learned the merit of posing good questions. As with *Geschichtliche Grundbegriffe*, the essays presented here are concerned more with the modern world's process of formation than with its actual structure. The perception of modernity as a problematic, if not crisis-ridden, condition is, in these essays, not as obvious as in *Kritik und Krise*, but it nevertheless plays a significant organizing role.[19] Enlightenment rationalism raised the prospect of unending progress and human improvement, and this vision was transformed into a future, realizable utopia through its articulation in the political programs of the French, and later, European revolutions. These broke decisively with the closed and cyclical structure of the eschatological world view in which predictions of the coming End of the World and the Final Judgment set the limit to human ambition and hope; instead, society was now perceived as accelerating toward an unknown and unknowable future, but within which was contained a hope of the desired utopian fulfillment. These utopias and the hopes embodied in them in turn became potential guarantees of their own fulfillment, laying the basis for the transformation of modern conflict into civil war. Because the fronts of political conflict run along ideological grounds, conflict becomes endemic, self-generating, and, in principle, endless. In one sense, then, we exist in a modern world traversed by such conflicts, in which permanent civil war exists on a world scale; and which, while it is directly related to the aspirations of Enlightenment rationalism, is a world quite different from the one anticipated. This modern world represents a future which once existed, is now realized, and is perpetually in danger of outrunning the power of its inhabitants to control its course.

## Acknowledgments

I would like to thank Professor Koselleck for his unfailing helpfulness in the preparation of this translation and for supplying biographical information on which this introduction is based. Valuable assistance was given to me by Mon MacLean who in closely reading the draft translation contributed at many points to its clarification and improvement. I would also like to thank Nicola Pike for preparing the index.

## Notes

1. This can be translated as "conceptual history" or the "history of concepts." Koselleck clearly demarcates it from "intellectual history" (*Geistesgeschichte*) and the history of ideas; he suggests that its postwar development is owed especially to a confrontation with the kind of *Geistesgeschichte* practiced by Meinecke, seeking to historicize this approach by taking as a point of departure the sociopolitical experience of particular conjunctures.

2. On Schmitt, see J. W. Bendersky, *Carl Schmitt: Theorist for the Reich* (Princeton, 1983) 274–276.

3. Koselleck's dissertation was accepted in 1954, but it was not published until 1959. It was republished as a paperback by Suhrkamp in 1975, with a new preface.

4. Cf. W. Conze, "Die Gründung des Arbeitskreises für moderne Sozialgeschichte," in H.-D. Ortlieb, B. Molitor, W. Krone (eds.), *Hamburger Jahrbuch für Wirtschafts- und Gesellschaftspolitik (Festgabe für Carl Jantke)* (Tübingen, 1979) 23–32. Shortly before being offered the post in Heidelberg, Koselleck had also been offered a similar position with Ipsen in Dortmund in the Sociology Faculty.

5. The development of recent sociohistorical work in West Germany is influenced more by those, like Wehler and Kocka, who draw on the work of Hans Rosenberg and Eckart Kehr, the former joining the emigration to the United States and the latter dying there in May 1933.

6. O. Brunner, *Land und Herrschaft* (Darmstadt, 1973). First published in 1939, it is subtitled *Basic Questions on the History of Territorial Organization in Medieval Austria*. An important collection of essays by Brunner was published in 1956 under the title *Neue Wege der Sozialgeschichte* (Göttingen, 1956). He died in 1982.

7. This is Koselleck's *Habilitationsschrift* of 1965; it was published under the title *Preussen zwischen Reform und Revolution* in 1967, and the second edition (Stuttgart), which has since been reprinted, appeared in 1975.

8. "Richtlinien für das Lexikon politisch-sozialer Begriffe der Neuzeit," *Archiv für Begriffsgeschichte* 11 (1967) 81–99.

9. Koselleck's own reflections on this can be found in this text, in his essay "Begriffsgeschichte and Social History."

10. Koselleck, "Richtlinien," 81.

11. Ibid., 87–90.

12. Koselleck, "Einleitung," in O. Brunner, W. Conze, R. Koselleck (eds.), *Geschichtliche Grundbegriffe* (Stuttgart, 1975) Bd. 1: xvi–xviii.

13. Koselleck's serious interest in aesthetics and art history led him to develop a comparative project on the commemoration of those killed in European wars of the nineteenth and twentieth centuries: see his essay "Kriegerdenkmale als Identitätsstiftungen der Überlebenden," in O. Marquard, K. Stierle (eds.), *Identität* (Munich, 1979) 255–276.

14. H.-G. Gadamer, *Truth and Method* (New York, 1975) 55 ff.

15. Ibid., xiv, xv.

16. For a general discussion on this, see R. C. Holub, *Reception Theory* (London, 1984).

17. Jauss sought to bridge the gap between literary history and sociological research and to this end introduced the notion of "horizon of expectations" in his *Untersuchungen zur mittelalterlichen Tierdichtung* (1959). This idea was already to be found in sociological literature; cf. K. Mannheim, *Man and Society* (London, 1940) 179 ff. See also H. R. Jauss, "Literary History as a Challenge to Literary Theory," in R. Cohen (ed.), *New Directions in Literary History* (London, 1974) 36.

18. Jauss attributes this notion to Kracauer, who first elaborated it in his contribution to the Adorno Festschrift of 1963. Jauss, "Literary History," 32.

19. The introduction to *Kritik und Krise* (Frankfurt a.M., 1975) begins with the words: "The present world crisis, determined by the polar tension between America and Russia as world powers, is, from a historical point of view, the resultant of European history." Koselleck notes in his preface to the second edition that this orientation had led to a great deal of misunderstanding (p. ix).

# Notes on Translation and Terminology

As with all translation, ambiguities and resonances which might be of significance in understanding the meaning of the text can be wiped away through an accurate but inadequate choice of word or phrase. In this case the problems begin with the title: "Futures Past" has a grammatical feel to it, but "The Bygone Future" might be a more accurate, if flatter, rendering, introducing a slight sense of archaism. Where serious conceptual problems arose in the translation, I have followed the usual practice of inserting the original word in parentheses, or in some cases have placed the original passage in the notes. Koselleck follows two patterns in his use of Latin citations: sometimes he glosses it in the text, and other times he simply cites it. In the latter case, I have inserted a translation in the main body of the text, placing the Latin original in a note. Where a Latin citation occurs in the notes, I have simply replaced it with an English translation.

When translating German sentences into English, a distinct problem arises that is related to technical possibilities of word and sentence construction in these languages. On the whole, it is possible to employ a German stem in a wider variety of verb, noun, adjectival, and adverbial constructions than is usually possible in English. Consequently, when translating into English, one is sometimes unable to replicate a systematic conceptual development, with the result that a line of argument might be obscured. Various strategies have been adopted in such cases and are explained at appropriate points. It might be useful, however, to briefly elaborate some of the more central terms in these notes, so that the reader can anticipate problems that might arise.

*Zeit* and its derivatives and compounds are clearly of importance in these essays. This term can be translated (fairly unproblematically) as "time," but difficulties arise when it is used as an adverb or adjective. *Zeitlicher Unterschied*, for example, refers to a difference in points of time and would be translated as "temporal difference." But it must be borne in mind that in English, "temporal" has a religious connotation which is quite irrelevant in such an instance. It is important to remember this, since so much of the text deals with eschatology and associated conceptions of time. Similarly, the compound *Verzeitlichung* is rendered as "temporalization" but means simply a rendering into the dimension of time. Finally, there is the problem of *Neuzeit*, which means literally "new time" in the epochal sense; this has usually been rendered as "modernity" on the grounds that one talks of "modern history" in this way. The problem is that, when Koselleck wishes to write specifically about "modernity," he uses a word borrowed from the French: "Modernität."

Closely allied with the idea of time is that of space, *Raum*. A "period" in German is a *Zeitraum*, literally a "time space." The possibilities of one blending with the other are emphasized by Koselleck in the way he employs terminology equally relevant to time and space: perspective, location (*Standort*), horizon. The translation seeks to retain such resonances and might at times become complicated in their rendering, given the possibilities of word construction available to the German user.

There are two words in German for "history," *Geschichte* and *Historie*: and in modern German *Geschichte* also means "story." The relation of the two terms was, until the latter part of the eighteenth century, one different from that common today, and this shift forms one of the major themes of the second essay. Where the distinction of *Geschichte* from *Historie* is a material one, the German terms have either been added or used untranslated. Where no such connotations are at stake, "history" is used without comment.

Finally, it might be noted that the term *Wissenschaft* refers to any systematic and scholarly activity or body of knowledge. When Koselleck refers to "historical science," therefore, it would not be correct to interpret this as a polemical or significant usage. The available alternatives, such as "historical knowledge" or "historical discipline," are inappropriate because they preempt the ambiguity of science, either in the direction of thought or of institutional organization.

# Preface

The question of what historical time might be belongs to those questions which historical science has the most difficulty answering. It compels us to enter the domain of historical theory more deeply than is otherwise necessary in the discipline of history. For the sources of the past, informing us of thoughts and deeds, plans and events, provide no direct indication of historical time. Preliminary theoretical clarification thus is necessary to answer a question that is posed constantly in history but which we find elusive, given the evidence that has been passed on to us.

In conducting research related to historical circumstances, the question of historical time does not have to be explicitly confronted. To arrange and recount events, only an exact dating of such events is indispensable. Correct dating is only a prerequisite, however, and does not indicate the content of what may be called "historical time." Chronology—as an auxiliary discipline—can cope with questions of dating, coordinating the countless calendars and forms of temporal measure employed throughout history in terms of a common time calculated on the basis of the physical-astronomical time of our planetary system. This unitary, naturally governed time is equally appropriate for all the people of our globe, taking into account the inverse seasonal cycles of the northern and southern hemispheres and the progressive variation of day and night. In the same fashion, one can assume a limited variability and general similarity in the biological time of human lives, despite medical intervention. Whoever considers the relation of history and time (if there actually is something called historical time) does not think of such natural presuppositions in our division of time.

Whoever seeks an impression of historical time in everyday life may note the wrinkles of an old man or the scars by which a bygone fate is made present; conjoin the memory of ruins with the perception of newly developed sites and ponder the visible change of style that lends to architectural contours their deeper temporal dimension; or contemplate the coexistence, connectedness, and hierarchy of variously modernized forms of transport, through which, from sleigh to airplane, entire eras meet. Finally, and above all, the seeker will think of the successive generations in his or her own family or professional world, where different spaces of experience overlap and perspectives of the future intersect, including the conflicts with which they are invested. Such preliminary observations make clear that the generality of a measurable time based on Nature—even if it possesses its own history—cannot be transformed without mediation into a historical concept of time.

Even the singularity of a unique historical time that is supposedly distinct from a measurable natural time can be cast in doubt. Historical time, if the concept has a specific meaning, is bound up with social and political actions, with concretely acting and suffering human beings and their institutions and organizations. All have definite, internalized forms of conduct, each with a peculiar temporal rhythm. One has only to think (remaining in the everyday world) of the annual cycle of public holidays and festivals, which provide a framework for social life, or of changes in working hours and their duration, that have determined the course of life and continue to do so daily. Therefore, what follows will seek to speak, not of one historical time, but rather of many forms of time superimposed on one another. In the emphatic words of Herder, which were directed against Kant:

In reality, every mutable thing has within itself the measure of its time; this persists even in the absence of any other; no two worldly things have the same measure of time. . . . There are therefore (one can state it properly and boldly) at any one time in the Universe innumerably many times.[1]

If one seeks to investigate historical times, it is certainly not possible to avoid using temporal measures and unities drawn from a nature conceived according to the principles of mathematics and physics; the dates or duration of a life or an institution; the critical moments or turning points in a series of political or military events; the speed (and its rate of increase) of means of transport; the acceleration or retardation of production; and the rapidity of weapons' discharge. All of these, to take only a few examples, can be historically evaluated only when measured and dated by a natural division of temporality.

But an interpretation of the relationships that arise out of these factors immediately transcends temporal determinations derived from natural, physical, or astronomical phenomena. Pressure of time on political decision-making, the reciprocal effect of the speed of means of transport and communication on the economy or on military actions, the durability or mobility of social forms of conduct in a zone of political or economic demands with a specific and limited span: all of these factors (and others), in their mutual interaction or dependence, force the emergence of temporal determinations which, while certainly conditioned by nature, must, however, be defined as specifically historical. Each survey of such interlinkings among events leads to the determination of epochs and doctrines of specific eras which precipitate and overlap in quite different ways, according to the particular areas under consideration. Such questions, saturated sociohistorically, are considered only occasionally in the following volume, even if it would help to focus more consideration on them.

The following essays, written in the last twenty years, have a more modest intention. They direct themselves to texts in which historical experience of time is articulated either explicitly or implicitly. To be more precise, texts that explicitly or implicitly deal with the relation of a given past to a given future were sought out and interrogated.

In this way speak numerous witnesses, from Antiquity to the present: politicians, philosophers, theologians, and poets. Unknown writings, proverbs, lexica, pictures, and dreams are interrogated, and not least historians themselves. All testimony answers the problem of how, in a concrete situation, experiences come to terms with the past; how expectations, hopes, or prognoses projected into the future are articulated into language. Throughout these essays the following question will be raised: How, in a given present, are the temporal dimensions of past and future related?

This query involves the hypothesis that in differentiating past and future, or (in anthropological terms) experience and expectation, it is possible to grasp something like historical time. It is certainly one of the biologically determined human characteristics that, with increasing age, the relation of experience and expectation changes, whether through the increase of the one and decline of the other, through one compensating the other, or through the opening of previously un-perceived interior or metaphysical worlds that help relativize the finitude of personal life. But it is also in the succession of historical generations that the relation of past and future has clearly altered.

A consistent discovery in the following studies is the fact that the more a particular time is experienced as a new temporality, as "mo-dernity,"[2] the more demands made on the future increase. Special attention is therefore devoted to a given present and its coexisting, since superseded, future. If the contemporary in question detects in his subjective, experiential balance an increase in the weight of the future, this is certain to be an effect of the technical-industrial mod-ification of a world that forces upon its inhabitants ever briefer intervals of time in which to gather new experiences and adapt to changes induced at an accelerating pace. This does not, however, establish the importance of long-term conditions that may have receded into the background and a form of oblivion. It is the task of structural history to achieve that, and the following studies are conceived as a contribution to this end.

Methodologically, these studies direct themselves to the semantics of central concepts in which historical experience of time is implicated. Here, the collective concept "History,"[3] coined in the eighteenth cen-tury, has a preeminent meaning. It will become apparent that it is with History experienced as a new temporality that specific dispositions and ways of assimilating experience emerge. Our modern concept of history is the outcome of Enlightenment reflection on the growing complexity of "history in general," in which the determinations of experience are increasingly removed from experience itself. This is true both of a world history extending spatially, which contains the modern concept of history in general, and of the temporal perspective within which, since that time, past and future must be relocated with respect to each other. The latter problem is addressed throughout this book by the category of temporalization.

Numerous concepts which complement that of history, such as rev-olution, chance, fate, progress, and development, will be introduced into the analysis. Similarly, constitutional concepts will be considered for their temporal implications and the changes these undergo. Finally, scientific temporal categories and the classification of epochs by historians will be examined to determine the degree to which they register a transformation of experience and have (occasionally) promoted such a transformation.

These semantic analyses are not generally conceived in terms of a particular purpose in linguistic history. Rather, they should seek out the linguistic organization of temporal experience wherever this surfaces in past reality. Consequently, the analyses continually reach out and take up the sociohistorical context; trace the thrust in the pragmatic or political language of author or speaker; or, on the basis of the semantics of concepts, draw conclusions concerning the historical-anthropological dimension present in all conceptualization and linguistic performance. It is for this reason that I have included in this volume the study on dreams and terror; this essay involves a degree of methodological risk in considering the manner in which language is reduced to silence and the time dimension appears to become reversed.

The titles of the three parts do not imply a stringent train of thought. They are more a matter of emphases that relate to each other and, in various measure, characterize all the studies. Initially, semantic cross sections are contrasted along a diachronic path. In keeping with this, theoretical and historiographic issues take a prominent place. Finally, greater attention is paid to aspects of linguistic pragmatism and anthropology within semantics. The arrangement is not, however, without a certain expediency, for each piece is conceived as independent and complete, so that series of examples, methodological elaborations, and theoretical considerations of the relation of language and historical reality are almost a constant feature. To avoid unnecessary repetition, the texts are brought into line with each other; nearly all are abbreviated or extended by a few sentences and quotations. A few references to literature that has appeared since the original essays were published have been added.

For the most part, these studies emerged out of the planning and organization of the lexicon *Geschichtliche Grundbegriffe*, edited by Otto Brunner, Werner Conze, and myself. Consequently, I would like to refer the reader to this lexicon and its contributors for further information. I would like to thank these same contributors for their numerous suggestions.

I also wish to thank Siegfried Unseld, who waited patiently for the completion of the volume during years of promises. Not to be forgotten is the memory of Frau Margarete Dank, who died quite suddenly after having prepared the manuscript for the press, leaving a painful void in the work of the faculty and lexicon.

R. K.
Bielefeld, January 1979

# I

## On the Relation of Past and Future in Modern History

# Modernity and the Planes of Historicity

In 1528 Duke William IV of Bavaria ordered a series of historical paintings which were to be hung in his newly built summer house at the Royal Stud. Thematically Christian-Humanist, they depicted a series of biblical events, as well as a series of episodes from classical Antiquity. Most well known and justly celebrated of these paintings is Albrecht Altdorfer's *Alexanderschlacht*.[1]

Upon an area of one and a half square meters, Altdorfer reveals to us the cosmic panorama of a decisive battle of world-historical significance, the Battle of Issus, which in 333 B.C. opened the epoch of Hellenism, as we say today. With a mastery previously unknown, Altdorfer was able to depict thousand upon thousand of individual warriors as complete armies; he shows us the clash of armored squadrons of horse and foot soldiers armed with spears; the victorious line of attack of the Macedonians, with Alexander far out at the head; the confusion and disintegration which overtook the Persians; and the expectant bearing of the Greek battle-reserves, which will then complete the victory.

A careful examination of the painting enables us to reconstruct the entire course of the battle. For Altdorfer had in this image delineated a history, in the way that *Historie* at that time could mean both image and narrative (*Geschichte*). To be as accurate as possible, the artist, or rather the court historiographer advising him, had consulted Curtius Rufus to ascertain the (supposedly) exact number of combatants, dead and taken prisoner. These figures can be found inscribed upon the banners of the relevant armies, including the number of dead, who remain in the painting among the living, perhaps even bearing the banner under which they are about to fall, mortally wounded. Altdorfer made conscious use of anachronism so that he could faithfully represent the course of the completed battle.

There is another element of anachronism which today is certainly much more apparent to us. Viewing the painting in the Pinakothek, we think we see before us the last knights of Maximilian or the serf-army at the Battle of Pavia. From their feet to their turbans, most of the Persians resemble the Turks who, in the same year the picture was painted (1529), unsuccessfully laid siege to Vienna. In other words, the event that Altdorfer captured was for him at once historical and contemporary. Alexander and Maximilian, for whom Altdorfer had prepared drawings, merge in an exemplary manner; the space of historical experience enjoys the profundity of generational unity. The state of contemporary military technology still did not in principle offer any obstacle to the representation of the Battle of Issus as a current event. Machiavelli had only just devoted an entire chapter of his *Discourses* to the thesis that modern firearms had had little impact on the conduct of wars. The belief that the invention of the gun eclipsed the exemplary power of Antiquity was quite erroneous, argued Machiavelli. Those who followed the Ancients could only smile at such a view. The present and the past were enclosed within a common historical plane.

Temporal difference was not more or less arbitrarily eliminated; it was not, as such, at all apparent. The proof of this is there to see in the painting of the *Alexanderschlacht*. Altdorfer, who wished to statistically corroborate represented history (*Historie*) by specifying the combatants in ten numbered columns, has done without one figure: the year. His battle thus is not only contemporary; it simultaneously appears to be timeless.

When Friedrich Schlegel came across the painting almost three hundred years later, he was seized "upon sighting this marvel," as he wrote, by a boundless "astonishment." Schlegel praised the work in long sparkling cascades of words, recognizing in it "the greatest feat of the age of chivalry." He had thus gained a critical-historical distance with respect to Altdorfer's masterpiece. Schlegel was able to distinguish the painting from his own time, as well as from that of the Antiquity it strove to represent. For him, history had in this way gained a specifically temporal dimension, which is clearly absent for Altdorfer.

Formulated schematically, there was for Schlegel, in the three hundred years separating him from Altdorfer, more time (or perhaps a different mode of time) than appeared to have passed for Altdorfer in the eighteen hundred years or so that lay between the Battle of Issus and his painting.

What had happened in these three hundred years that separate our two witnesses, Altdorfer and Schlegel? What new quality had historical time gained that occupies this period from about 1500 to 1800? If we are to answer these questions, this period must be conceived not simply as elapsed time, but rather as a period with its own specific characteristics.

Stating my thesis simply, in these centuries there occurs a temporalization (*Verzeitlichung*) of history, at the end of which there is the peculiar form of acceleration which characterizes modernity. We are thus concerned with the specificity of the so-called *frühen Neuzeit*— the period in which modernity is formed. We will restrict ourselves to the perspective we possess from the onetime future of past generations or, more pithily, from a former future.

## I

First, we should clarify the sense of presence and achronological pungency that we have discovered in Altdorfer's painting. Let us try to regard the picture with the eye of one of his contemporaries. For a Christian, the victory of Alexander over the Persians signifies the transition from the second to the third world empire, whereby the Holy Roman Empire constitutes the fourth and last. Heavenly and cosmic forces were participants in such a battle, finding their place in Altdorfer's painting as Sun and Moon, powers of Light and Darkness respectively attributed to the two kings, Alexander and Maximilian: the sun appears over a ship whose mast assumes the form of a cross. This battle, in which the Persian army was destined for defeat, was no ordinary one; rather, it was one of the few events between the beginning of the world and its end that also prefigured the fall of the Holy Roman Empire. Analogous events were expected to occur with the coming of the End of the World. Altdorfer's image had, in other words, an eschatological status. The *Alexanderschlacht* was timeless as the prelude, figure, or archetype of the final struggle between Christ and Antichrist; those participating in it were contemporaries of those who lived in expectation of the Last Judgment.

Until well into the sixteenth century, the history of Christianity is a history of expectations, or more exactly, the constant anticipation of the End of the World on the one hand and the continual deferment of the End on the other. While the materiality of such expectations varied from one situation to another, the basic figure of the End remained constant. The mythical investment of the Apocalypse could be adapted to a given situation, and even noncanonical prophecies presented little variation from the figures that were supposed to appear at the Judgment, such as the Emperor of Peace (*Engelspäpste*), or harbingers of the Antichrist, such as Gog and Magog who, according to oriental tradition (a tradition also then current in the West), remained confined to the Caucasus by Alexander until the time came for their irruption. However the image of the End of the World was varied, the role of the Holy Roman Empire remained a permanent feature: as long as it existed, the final Fall was deferred. The Emperor was the *katechon* of the Antichrist.

All of these figures appeared to enter historical reality in the epoch of the Reformation. Luther saw the Antichrist in possession of the "holy throne," and for him Rome was the "Whore of Babylon"; Catholics saw Luther as the Antichrist; peasant unrest and the growing sectarian militancy of diverse sections of the declining Church appeared to foreshadow the last civil war preceding the Fall. Finally, the Turks who stormed Vienna in the year of Altdorfer's painting appeared as the unchained people of Gog.

Altdorfer, who had assisted in the expulsion of the Jews from Regensburg and had connections with the astrologer Grünpeck, certainly knew the signs. As city architect he applied himself, while working on his painting, to strengthening the fortifications so that they would be secure against the Turks. "If we fight off the Turks," said Luther at the time, "so is Daniel's prophecy fulfilled, and the Final Judgment will be at the door."[2] The Reformation as a movement of religious renewal carried with it all the signs of the End of the World.

Luther frequently referred to the fact that the Fall was to be expected in the coming year, or even in the current one. But as he once added (and recorded for us in his table talk), for the sake of the chosen, God would shorten the final days, "toward which the world was speeding, since almost all of the new century had been forced into the space of one decade."[3] Luther believed that the events of the new century had been concentrated in the decade since the Reichstag at Worms, at the end of which, as we know, the *Alexanderschlacht* was painted. The compression of time indicated that the End of the World was approaching with great rapidity, even if the actual date remained concealed.

Let us stop for a moment and look forward over the three hundred years whose structural change in temporality is the subject of this essay. On 10 May 1793 Robespierre, in his famous speech on the Revolutionary Constitution, proclaimed:

The time has come to call upon each to realize his own destiny. The progress of human Reason has laid the basis for this great Revolution, and the particular duty of hastening it has fallen to you.[4]

Robespierre's providential phraseology cannot hide the fact that, compared with our point of departure, there has been an inversion in the horizon of expectations. For Luther, the compression of time is a visible sign that, according to God's will, the Final Judgment is imminent, that the world is about to end. For Robespierre, the acceleration of time is a task of men leading to an epoch of freedom and happiness, the golden future. Both positions, insofar as the French Revolution descended from the Reformation, mark the beginning and end of our period. Let us try to relate them in terms of visions of the future.

A ruling principle (*Herrschaftsprinzip*) of the Roman Church was that all visionaries had to be brought under its control. Proclaiming a vision of the future presupposed that it had first received the authorization of the Church (as decided at the Fifth Lateran Council, 1512–1517). The ban on the Joachimite theory of the Third Empire; the fate of Joan of Arc, whose determined affirmation of an unlicensed vision led to the stake; the death by fire of Savonarola: all serve as examples of the fate awaiting prophets whose visions were postbiblical in character. The stability of the Church was not to be endangered; its unity, like the existence of the empire itself, was a guarantee of order until the End of the World came.

Correspondingly, the future of the world and its end were made part of the history of the Church; newly inflamed prophets necessarily exposed themselves to verdicts of heresy. The Church utilized the imminent-but-future End of the World as a means of stabilization, finding an equilibrium between the threat of the End on the one hand

and the hope of Parousia on the other.[5] The unknown Eschaton must be understood as one of the Church's integrating factors, enabling its self-constitution as world and as institution. The Church is itself eschatological. But the moment the figures of the apocalypse are applied to concrete events or instances, the eschatology has disintegrative effects. The End of the World is only an integrating factor as long as its politico-historical meaning remains indeterminate.

The future as the possible End of the World is absorbed within time by the Church as a constituting element, and thus does not exist in a linear sense at the end point of time. Rather, the end of time can be experienced only because it is always-already sublimated in the Church. For just so long did the history of the Church remain the history of salvation.

The most basic assumptions of this tradition were destroyed by the Reformation. Neither Church nor worldly powers were capable of containing the energies which Luther, Zwingli, and Calvin unleashed upon the European world. In his old age, Luther himself doubted the possibility of peace; the Imperial Assemblies labored in vain, and he prayed that the final day would come, "asking only that it not be too soon, that there be a little time."[6] The task of the empire in postponing the End of the World echoes through the plea of a man who saw no way out for this world. The empire had failed in its duty.

Shortly afterward, in 1555, the Religious Peace of Augsburg was signed so that "this praiseworthy nation be secured against an ever-threatening ruin," as it says in paragraph 25. The *Stände* agreed that a "stable, secure, unconditional, and eternally lasting peace was to be created."[7] This was to hold even if (and while disputed, this was conclusive) the religious parties should arrive at no settlement and find no unity. Henceforth peace and religious duty were no longer identical: peace meant that the fronts of religious civil war were to be shut down, frozen in situ. Only with difficulty can we today assess quite how monstrous this imposition seemed at that time. The compromise, born of necessity, concealed within itself a new principle, that of "politics," which was to set itself in motion in the following century.

The politicians were concerned about the temporal, not the eternal, as the orthodox among all parties complained. "L'heresie n'est plus auiourd'huy en la Religion; elle est en l'Estat,"[8] retorted a French lawyer and politician during the confessional civil war. Heresy no longer existed within religion; it was founded in the state. This is a dangerous statement, if we repeat it today. In 1590, however, its meaning consisted in formulating orthodoxy as a question set in terms of the jurisdiction of the state (*Staatsrecht*). "Cuius regio, eius religio"[9] is an early formula for the sovereignty of individual rulers, whatever their confessional tendency, over the religious parties within their domains. But it was only after the Thirty Years War had worn down the Germans that they were able to make the principle of religious indifference the basis for peace. Primarily begun as a religious war by the *Stände* of the Holy Roman Empire, the Thirty Years War ended with the peace negotiations of sovereigns, the status to which the territorial rulers had emancipated themselves. While in the West modern states arose from *guerre civile* and civil war, the religious war in Germany transformed itself—thanks to intervention—into a war between states, whose outcome paradoxically gave new life to the Holy Roman Empire. The renewed life was under new conditions, of course: the peace decrees of Münster and Osnabrück had validity, up until the French Revolution, as the legal (*völkerrechtlich*) basis of toleration. What consequences did the new arrangement of politics and religion have for the construction of the modern apprehension of time, and what displacement of the future had this process brought with it?

The experience won in a century of bloody struggles was, above all, that the religious wars did not herald the Final Judgment, at least not in the direct manner previously envisaged. Rather, peace became possible only when religious potential was used up or exhausted; that is, at the point where it was possible to politically restrict or neutralize it. And this disclosed a new and unorthodox future.

This process occurred slowly and had been laid down well in advance. The first shift can be found in the fact that by the fifteenth century, and in part earlier, the expected End of the World was increasingly prorogued. Nicolaus von Cues at one time placed it at the beginning of the eighteenth century; Melanchthon calculated that the final epoch would begin to wane with the passing of two thousand years from the birth of Christ. The last great papal prophecy in 1595, attributed to Malachias, extended by a factor of three the customary list of Popes, so that (reckoning according to the average duration of papal rule) the end of all time could be expected in 1992, at the earliest.

Second, astrology played a role that it is important not to underestimate; during the Renaissance it was at its peak, its effects however persisting undiminished until the natural sciences (which themselves made their beginning thanks to it) slowly brought astrology into discredit. Newton himself prophesied around 1700 that papal rule would end in the year 2000. Astrological calculation of the future pushed eschatological expectations into a constantly receding future. Ultimately, expectations of the End were undermined by apparently natural determinants. A symbolic coincidence is that in the year of the Peace of Augsburg, 1555, Nostradamus published his *Centuries*. He did, of course, complete his visions with a prophecy of the End quite in keeping with the traditional spirit; the intervening period, however, was formulated in terms of an endless array of undatable, variable oracles, such that an immeasurably extended future was disclosed to the curious reader.

Third, with the paling of presentiments of the End, the Holy Roman Empire lost, in a manner distinct from that earlier, its eschatological function. Since the Peace of Westphalia, it had become clear at the very least that the preservation of peace had become the business of the European system of states. Bodin here played a role as historian which was as pathbreaking as his foundation of the concept of sovereignty. In separating out sacral, human, and natural history, Bodin transformed the question of the End of the World into a problem of astronomical and mathematical calculation. The End of the World became a datum within the cosmos, and eschatology was forced into a specially prepared natural history. Working within a cabalistic tradition, Bodin considered it quite possible that this world would end only after a cycle of 50,000 years. The Holy Roman Empire was thus stripped of its sacred task. Human history, considered as such, had no goal, according to Bodin, but rather was a domain of probability and human prudence. The maintenance of peace was the task of the state, not the mission of an empire. If there were any land with a claim to the succession of imperial power it was the Turkish Empire, which spread itself over three continents. The setting free of a *historia humana* which turned away from sacral history, and the legitimation of a modern state capable of subduing salvation-oriented religious factions, are for Bodin one and the same.

This leads to a fourth point. The genesis of the absolutist state is accompanied by a sporadic struggle against all manner of religious and political predictions. The state enforced a monopoly on the control of the future by suppressing apocalyptic and astrological readings of the future. In doing so, it assumed a function of the old Church for anti-Church objectives. Henry VIII, Edward VI, and Elizabeth I all proscribed in strong terms any prediction of this nature. Disobedient prophets could expect lifelong imprisonment. Henry III of France and Richelieu followed the English example so that they could stop up once and for all the source of a steady stream of religious presentiments. Grotius, who as an émigré from religious persecution published *De jure belli et pacis* in 1625, considered the wish to fulfill predictions, *voluntatem implendi vaticinia*, as one of the unjust sources of war. He added the warning: "Protect yourselves, overbearing theologians; protect yourselves, politicians, from overbearing theologians."[10] All in all, it is possible to say that a rigorous politics had succeeded in gradually eliminating from the domain of political consideration and decision making the robust religious expectations of the future that had flourished after the decline of the Church.

This was also apparent in England, where during the Puritan Revolution the old expectations, expressed in prophetic terms, were prevalent once more. But the last great predictive struggle carried out on a political plane, which occurred in 1650 and concerned the monarchy's return (or failure to return) was already being conducted in terms of a critical philology. The republican astrologer Lilly proved that his Cavalier enemies had falsely quoted from their sources. And if Cromwell made his intentions for the coming year popularly available in the form of an almanac, this is to be attributed more to his cold realism than to a belief in revelations. The last widespread millennial prophecy in Germany arose during the Thirty Years War: Bartholomäus Holzhauser's commentary on the apocalypse, which gave the world only a few decades more.

The basic lines of prediction were always limited, although they were formulated creatively well into the seventeenth century. After this point, straightforward copies, such as the *Europäischen Staatswahrsager*, which sought to apply old texts to the Silesian War, become more numerous. The last attempt to revive the theory of the four monarchies was printed in 1728. It was an epilogue.

The course of the seventeenth century is characterized by the destruction of interpretations of the future, however they were motivated. Where it had the power, the state persecuted their utterance, such as in the Cevennes uprising, ultimately driving them into private, local, folkloristic circles or secret associations. Parallel to this developed a literary feud conducted by humanists and skeptics against oracles and associated superstitions. The first well-known people to become involved were Montaigne and Bacon, who revealed the psychology of prophecy in penetrating essays, well before their contemporaries. There appeared also in Germany in 1632 a *Schriftmäßiges Bedenken von Gesichten*.[11] The most significant critique of prophecy was made by Spinoza in 1670. He not only denounced visions as the customary subterfuge of contemporary factions which were either subversive or merely ambitious, but he also went a step further and sought to unmask canonical prophecy as the victim of primitive powers of self-delusion. Fontenelle's *History of Oracles*, published in 1686, represents a peak of stylistic elegance in this literary feud; compared with its confident, rational, underplayed formulas, the scorn Voltaire pours upon prophets is simply the scorn of the victor.

The facility with which anticipations of devout Christians or predictions of all kinds could be transformed into political action had disappeared by 1650. Political calculation and humanist reservations marked out a new plane for the future. Neither the One Big End of the World nor the several smaller ones could apparently affect the course of human affairs. Instead of the anticipated millennium, a new and different perspective of time had opened up.

Here we touch on a fifth point. It was now possible to look back on the past as "medieval" (*mittelalterlich*). The triad of Antiquity, Middle Ages, and Modernity had been available since the advent of Humanism. But these have only fully come into use and have organized the whole of history quite gradually since the second half of the seventeenth century. Since then, one has lived in Modernity and been conscious of so doing. Naturally, this varies according to nation and *Stand*, but it was a knowledge that could be conceived as the crisis of European thought, to use Paul Hazard's phrase.[12]

## II

While until now we have traced the containment, undermining, destruction, or channeling of millennial expectations, the question arises of the actual conceptions of the future that insert themselves into the space occupied by the waning future. It is possible to identify two types, which relate to each other as well as refer back to the expectations of salvation: rational prognosis and the philosophy of historical process (*Geschichtsphilosophie*).

The conceptual counter to prevailing prophecy was the rational forecast, the prognosis. The delicate art of political calculation was first developed in fifteenth- and sixteenth-century Italy and then brought to a peak of finesse during the seventeenth and eighteenth centuries in the cabinets of the European courts. As a motto for this art, we will repeat a classical quotation from Aristotle, which was used by Guicciardini when introducing it into political literature: "De futuris contingentibus non est determinata veritas." ("For future events the truth is indeterminate.") There are people, says Guicciardini, who write treatises on the course of the future. Perhaps such tracts are good to read, but "since each conclusion in these considerations is developed from a previous one, the whole construction collapses if only one is false."[13]

This insight, which Guicciardini had gained in Italy, the land where modern politics originated, led to a particular attitude. The future became a domain of finite possibilities, arranged according to their greater or lesser probability. It is the same plane that Bodin disclosed for the operation of *historia humana*. Weighing the probability of forthcoming or nonoccurring events in the first instance eliminated a conception of the future that was taken for granted by the religious factions: the certainty that the Last Judgment would enforce a simple alternative between Good and Evil through the establishment of a sole principle of behavior.

For a politician, on the other hand, the only remaining moral judgment related to measuring the greater or lesser evil. It was in this sense that Richelieu stated that nothing was more important for a government than foresight: only in this manner was one able to avoid evils that, once encountered, were increasingly difficult to elude. The second consequence of such a position was preparedness for possible surprise, for it was generally not this or that possibility that would be realized, but a third, fourth, and so on. Daily encounters with such uncertainty emphasized the need for enhanced foresight, and Richelieu's claim that it is more important to think of the future than of the present assumes its proper meaning only when viewed in this light.[14] One might suggest that this is the political forerunner of life insurance, which has gained ground, along with the calculability of life expectancy, since the turn of the eighteenth century.

While prophecy transgressed the bounds of calculable experience, prognosis remained within the dimensions of the political situation.

The prognosis is a conscious element (*Moment*) of political action. It is related to events whose novelty it releases. The prognosis itself, then, continually radiates time in a generally predictable but actually uncertain fashion.

Prognosis produces the time within which and out of which it weaves, whereas apocalyptic prophecy destroys time through its fixation on the End. From the point of view of prophecy, events are merely symbols of that which is already known. A disappointed prophet cannot doubt the truth of his own predictions. Since these are variable, they can be renewed at any time. Moreover, with every disappointment, the certainty of approaching fulfillment increases. An erroneous prognosis, by contrast, cannot even be repeated as an error, remaining as it does conditioned by specific assumptions.

Rational prognosis assigns itself to intrinsic possibilities, but through this produces an excess of potential controls on the world. Time is always reflected in a surprising fashion in the prognosis; the constant similitude of eschatological expectation is dissolved by the continued novelty of time running away with itself and prognostic attempts to contain it. In terms of temporal structure, then, prognosis can be seen to be the integrating factor of the state that transgresses the limited future of the world to which it has been entrusted.

Let us take a favorite example from classical diplomacy: the first partition of Poland. The manner in which, and not the reason that it was done, can easily be traced to Frederick the Great. Frederick lived, after the embittering struggles of the Seven Years War, with a dual fear. First, there was the fear of Austrian revenge. To reduce the chances of this possibility, he concluded an alliance with Russia. In doing this, however, he bound himself to a power which he perceived as the greater or more general danger in the long run, and not merely in terms of Russia's rising population. Both prognostications, the short-term Austrian and the long-term Russian, now entered into political action in a fashion that altered the conditions of the prognosis, that is, altered the immediate situation. The existence of a Greek Orthodox population in Poland provided the Russians with a constant pretext for intervention on the grounds of religious protection. The Russian envoy, Repnin, ruled like a governor-general in Warsaw and directly supervised the meetings of the Polish National Assembly. Unpopular representatives were soon dispatched to Siberia. Poland declined de facto into the status of a Russian province, and the bloody civil war promoted by Russia resulted in the intensification of Russian control. This growing threat in the East brought the long-term threat dangerously close. At the same time, Frederick's own objective of integrating West Prussia with his state vanished into unattainable remoteness. In 1770, the situation worsened. Russia was about to swallow up not only Poland but Romania as well, bringing war to Frederick's gates. Austria had no desire to tolerate the situation. It saw in the annexation of Romania a *casus belli*. Thus Frederick, as the ally of Russia, was in addition bound to the second of the feared evils, a war against Austria, which he did not want. The solution to this dilemma, discovered by Frederick in 1772, is quite startling.

As soon as Frederick learned (before the Russians could know) that the Austrians shrank from the prospect of war, he forced Russia, through the pressure of his obligation to assist them in the event of war, to dispense with the annexation of Romania. In compensation, Russia received the eastern part of Poland, which in any case it already ruled; in return, Prussia and Austria gained West Prussia and Galicia — significant territories, but which, more importantly, were thereby removed from Russian influence. Instead of smoothing the way westward for his intimidating ally in the course of war, Frederick had preserved his peace and had strategically blocked Russian intrusion into the bargain. Frederick had made a double gain out of what had seemed mutually contradictory elements.

Such flexible play with a limited (but within these limits almost infinite) number of varied possibilities was clearly possible only in a particular historical situation. What is the nature of this historical plane in which the refinement of absolutist politics could develop? The future was a known quantity insofar as the number of politically active forces remained restricted to the number of rulers. Behind each ruler stood an army and a population of known dimensions whose potential economic power and monetary circulation could be estimated by cameralistic means. In this plane, history was comparatively static, and Leibniz's statement that "the whole of the coming world is present and prefigured in that of the present"[15] can here be applied to politics. In the domain of a politics constituted by the actions of sovereign rulers, though only in this domain, nothing particularly new could happen.

Characteristic of this is the ultimate boundary within which political calculation operated. Hume, who himself made long-term, contingent prognoses, once said that a doctor forecast with confidence no more than two weeks in advance, and a politician a few years at most.[16] A glance at contemporary diplomatic papers confirms this judgment. Certainly there were constant elements which often became components of an increasingly hypothetical future. Character, for instance, was such a constant; it could be estimated, relying, for instance, on the corruptibility of a minister. But above all, the assumed life span of a governing ruler was a permanent feature of the political calculus of probability. The uttermost future that the Venetian envoy in Paris predicted in 1648 for the coming half-century was his certainty that there would be a War of Spanish Succession: it did indeed take place exactly fifty years later. The fact that most of the wars conducted among European rulers in the seventeenth and eighteenth centuries were wars of succession clearly demonstrates the manner in which the dimensions of historical time were measured by natural, human qualities. But all the same, there remained, as our Venetian envoy reported, "space for the play of time and future, for not all that could occur actually does take place."[17] We have only to recall how the death of the Tsarina in 1762 altered the course of the war.

Based as it was on the life and character of acting personages, the European republic of rulers could still understand history in natural terms. It is not surprising that the ancient pattern of cycles put back in circulation by Machiavelli found such general support. This experience of history, founded as it was on repeatability, bound prospective futures to the past.

This certainly makes clear that the distance separating the early modern political consciousness of time from that of Christian eschatology was nowhere as great as it might seem. *Sub specie aeternitatis* nothing novel can emerge, whether the future is viewed in terms of faith or sober calculation. A politician could become more clever or even cunning; he could refine his technique; he could become wiser or more farsighted: but history would hold for him no new, unknown future regions. The reoccupation of a prophesied future by a predicted future had not yet fundamentally ruptured the plane of Christian expectations. That is what harnesses the republic of rulers to the Middle Ages, even if it no longer conceives of itself as Christian.

It was the philosophy of historical process which first detached early modernity from its past and at the same time inaugurated our modernity with a new future. A consciousness of time and the future begins to develop in the shadows of absolutist politics, first in secret, later openly, audaciously combining politics and prophecy. There enters into the philosophy of progress a typical eighteenth-century mixture of rational prediction and salvational expectation. Progress unfolded to the degree that the state and its prognostics were never able to satisfy soteriological demands which persisted within a state whose existence depended on the elimination of millenarian expectations.

What was new about the expectations of the future that typified progress? The prorogued End of the World had been constituted by the Church and then projected in the form of a static time capable of being experienced as a tradition. Political prognostication also had a static temporal structure insofar as it operated in terms of natural magnitudes whose potential repeatability formed the cyclical character of its history. The prognosis implies a diagnosis which introduces the past into the future. This always-already guaranteed futurity of the past effected the closure and bounding of the sphere of action available to the state. To the extent that the past can only be experienced insofar as it contains an element of that which is to come (and vice versa), the political existence of the state remains trapped within a temporal structure that can be understood as static movement. Progress opened up a future that transcended the hitherto predictable, natural space of time and experience, and thence—propelled by its own dynamic—provoked new, transnatural, and long-term prognoses.

The future of this progress is characterized by two main features: first, the increasing speed with which it approaches us, and second, its unknown quality. "Unknown" because this accelerated time, i.e., our history, abbreviated the space of experiences, robbed them of their constancy, and continually brought into play new, unknown factors, so that even the actuality or complexity of these unknown quantities could not be ascertained. This began to be apparent well before the French Revolution.

The bearer of the modern philosophy of historical process was the citizen emancipated from absolutist subjection and the tutelage of the Church: the *prophète philosophe*, as he was once strikingly characterized in the eighteenth century. Present at the baptism of the prophetic philosopher in the role of godfather was a combination of political calculation and speculation on a future liberated from Christian religion. Lessing has described this type for us: he often "takes well-judged prospects of the future," but he nonetheless resembles the visionary, "for he cannot wait for the future. He wants this future to come more quickly, and he himself wants to accelerate it . . . for what has he to gain if that which he recognizes as the better is actually not to be realized as the better within his lifetime?"[18] This self-accelerating temporality robs the present of the possibility of being experienced as the present, and escapes into a future within which the currently unapprehendable present has to be captured by historical philosophy. In other words, in the eighteenth century, the acceleration of time that had previously belonged to eschatology became obligatory for worldly invention, before technology completely opened up a space of experience adequate to this acceleration.

At first, however, there emerged within this acceleration a retardation which promoted the alternation of Revolution and Reaction in historical time. That which was conceived before the Revolution as *katechon* itself became a stimulus to revolution. Reaction, still employed in the eighteenth century as a mechanical category, came to function as a movement which sought to halt it. Revolution, at first derived from the natural movement of the stars and thus introduced into the natural rhythm of history as a cyclical metaphor, henceforth attained an irreversible direction. It appears to unchain a yearned-for future while the nature of this future robs the present of materiality and actuality; thus, while continually seeking to banish and destroy Reaction, it succeeds only in reproducing it: modern Revolution remains ever affected by its opposite, Reaction.

This alternation of Revolution and Reaction, which supposedly is to lead to a final paradise, has to be understood as a futureless future, because the reproduction and necessarily inevitable supersession of the contradiction brings about an evil endlessness. In the pursuit of this evil endlessness, as Hegel said, the consciousness of the agent is trapped in a finite "not yet" possessing the structure of a perennial imperative (*Sollen*). It has been possible since Hegel's time to convey into historical reality fictions such as the thousand-year *Reich* or the classless society. This fixation on an end-state by participating actors turns out to be the subterfuge of a historical process, robbing them of their judgment. There is a need, therefore, of historical prognostication that goes beyond the rational prognoses of the politicians and, as the legitimate offspring of historical philosophy, can moderate the historical-philosophical design.

There is evidence of this before the French Revolution. Predictions of the 1789 Revolution are numerous, although only a few look forward to a succeeding epoch and its nature. Rousseau was one of the greatest forecasters, whether it was a matter of forecasting the perpetual state of crisis or registering the subjugation of Europe by the Russians and of the Russians by the Asians. Voltaire, who never tired of assessing *la belle révolution* in more colorless and thus more favorable terms, consequently denounced his opponents as false prophets who had lapsed into the habits of earlier times.

We will not examine here the variety of wishful or forced prognoses with the aid of which the Enlightenment built up its self-confidence. Among them, however, is to be found one of the greatest predictions, which has remained in the shadows of anonymity and geographical camouflage up to the present. This concerns a prediction for the year 1774, apparently made for Sweden but aimed also at France. It was thrown up by the classical literature on civil war, ancient theories of despotism and historical cycles, and the critique of enlightened absolutism, but its point of departure is modern. The author is Diderot, who wrote:

Under despotism the people, embittered by their lengthy sorrows, will miss no opportunity to reappropriate their rights. But since there is neither goal nor plan, slavery relapses in an instant into anarchy. Within the heart of this general tumult there can be heard but one cry: "Freedom!" But how can this valuable thing be secured? Nobody knows. And soon the people are divided into various factions, eaten up with contradictory interests. . . . After a short while there are only two factions within the state; they distinguish themselves by two names, under which all necessarily have to include themselves: "Royalist" and "Antiroyalist." This is the moment of violent commotion. The moment of plotting and conspiracy. . . . In this, royalism serves as a subterfuge as much as antiroyalism. Both are masks for ambition and covetousness. The nation now is merely an entity dependent upon a collection of criminals and corrupt persons. In this situation only one man and a suitable moment are needed for an entirely unexpected result to emerge. If the moment comes, the man emerges. . . . He speaks to the people, who until this moment believe themselves all: You are nothing. And they say: We are nothing. And he speaks to them: I am the Lord. And they speak as if out of one mouth: You are the Lord. And he says to them: Here are the conditions according to which I am prepared to subject you. And they say: We accept them. . . . What will succeed this revolution? No one knows. *Quelle sera la suite de cette révolution? On l'ignore.*[19]

Diderot reveals a process that was to remain hidden from most of his contemporaries. He proposed a long-term prognosis, assuming the certainty of the as yet unknown beginning of the revolution; and further disclosed the dual watchwords of Good and Evil, Freedom and Slavery, tracing them to the dialectic of liberty; and thence derived the unexpected result. This expressed in modern terminology the full scope of the classical model. But Diderot went further. For, how the process should later proceed remained murky. He therefore formulated the same question that Toqueville was again to take up, and which remains for us to answer today.

In closing, let us glance once again at Altdorfer's painting, which has led us from Reformation to Revolution. That augured man, Napoleon, carried the picture off to Paris in 1800 and hung it in his bathroom at Saint-Cloud. Napoleon was never a man of taste, but the *Alexanderschlacht* was his favorite painting, and he wanted it in his inner sanctum. Did he sense the manner in which the history of the Occident was present in this painting? It is possible. Napoleon saw himself as a parallel to the great Alexander, and more. The power of tradition was so strong that the long-lost, salvational-historical task of the Holy Roman Empire shimmered through the supposedly new beginning of the 1789 Revolution. Napoleon, who had definitively destroyed the Holy Roman Empire, afterward married the daughter of the last emperor, just as two thousand years earlier Alexander had married the daughter of Darius, likewise in a premeditated second marriage. Napoleon made his son king of Rome.

When he was overthrown, Napoleon said that this marriage was the only true mistake he had ever made, that is, to have resumed a tradition that the Revolution, with himself at its head, appeared to have destroyed. Was it really a failure? While still at the peak of his power, Napoleon saw it differently: "Even my son will find it necessary to be my son, in order to be able to be, in all tranquility, my successor."[20]

# Historia Magistra Vitae: The Dissolution of the Topos into the Perspective of a Modernized Historical Process

There is a history in all men's lives,
Figuring the nature of the times deceased;
The which observed, a man may prophesy,
With a near aim, of the main chance of things
As yet not come to life, which in their seeds
And weak beginnings lie intreasured.
Shakespeare (Henry IV, Part Two)

Friedrich von Raumer, known as the historiographer to the Hohen-staufen, reports the following episode from the year 1811, when he was still Hardenberg's secretary:

During counsel in Charlottenburg, Oelssen [section head in the Ministry of Finance] animatedly defended the preparation of a quantity of paper money so that debts could be paid. All argument to the contrary failing, I said with immense audacity (knowing my man): "But Privy Councillor, do you not remember that Thucydides tells of the evils that followed from the circulation of too much paper money in Athens?" "This experience," he concurred, "is certainly of great importance" — and in this way he allowed himself to be persuaded in order that he might retain the appearance of learning.[1]

Raumer made use of a lie in the heated debates on the redemption of the Prussian debt, for he was aware that Antiquity had known no paper money. But he risked a lie since he calculated its effect — appealing rhetorically to the schooling of his opponent. That effect rested on the force of none other than the old topos according to which history is meant to be the great teacher of life. The privy councillor submitted to this formula, not to an argument. *Historia magistra vitae.*

"For that which we cannot ourselves experience, we have to follow the experience of others"—thus Zedler's *Universal-Lexicon* in 1735,[2] where history is presented as a kind of reservoir of multiplied experiences which the readers can learn and make their own; in the words of one of the ancients, history makes us free to repeat the successes of the past instead of committing earlier mistakes in the present.[3] And so this was the function of history for about two thousand years, a school in which one could become prudent without making mistakes.

What does the application of this topos to our example of the Charlottenburg episode tell us? Thanks to his skill in argument, Raumer placed his colleagues in a supposedly continuous space of experience, which he himself treated with irony. The scene testifies to the continuing role of history as the teacher of life, while simultaneously showing how questionable this role had become.

Before pursuing the question of the degree to which this older topos had dissolved itself within a modernized historical process, we need to look back on its persistence. It lasted almost unbroken into the eighteenth century. We have, up until the present, had no account of all the expressions through which historicity has been conceptualized. Accordingly, we lack a history of the formula *historia magistra vitae*, regardless of how much its meaning led historians' own understanding, if not their work, through the centuries. Despite a verbal identity, the coordinates of our formula have varied greatly in the course of time. It was not unusual for the topos to be reduced by historiographers to an empty rubric used only in prefaces. It is accordingly more difficult to clarify the difference that always prevailed between the mere use of a commonplace and its practical effectivity. Aside from this problem, however, the longevity of our topos is instructive enough, indicating the elasticity with which it accommodates the most diverse constructions. We might note the manner in which two contemporaries employed the exemplary functions of history: Montaigne pursued a purpose more or less opposite that of Bodin. For Montaigne, histories showed how every generalization was qualified or destroyed, whereas Bodin used them to uncover general rules.[4] Histories provided, however, for both exempla of life. Thus the idiom is a formal one, as was later expressed in the familiar saying, "One can prove anything with history."[5]

Whatever doctrine our formula serves, each instance of its use is indicative of something. It implies a thorough apprehension of human possibilities within a general historical continuum. History can instruct its contemporaries or their descendants on how to become more prudent or relatively better, but only as long as the given assumptions and conditions are fundamentally the same. Until the eighteenth century, the use of our expression remained an unmistakable index for an assumed constancy of human nature, accounts of which can serve as iteratable means for the proof of moral, theological, legal, or political doctrines. Likewise, the utility of our topos depended on an actual constancy of those circumstances which admitted the potential similitude of earthly events. If there occurred a degree of social change, it took place so slowly and at such a pace that the utility of past examples was maintained. The temporal structure of past history bounded a continuous space of potential experience.

## I

The idiom *historia magistra vitae* was coined by Cicero according to Hellenistic models.[6] It existed in the context of a rhetorical principle that only the orator was capable of lending immortality to a history that was instructive of life, of rendering perennial its store of experience. The usage is, moreover, associated with further metaphors which indicate the tasks of history. "Historia vero testis temporum, lux veritatis, vita memoriae, magistra vitae, nuntia vetustatis, qua voce alia nisi oratoris immortalitati commendatur?"[7] The primary task assigned here by Cicero to a knowledge of history is principally directed toward the praxis in which the orator involves himself. He makes use of historia as a collection of examples—"Plena exemplorum est historia"[8]—that can be employed instructively, and in a more straightforward manner, than had Thucydides, who emphasized the usefulness of his work by delivering up his history as $\chi\tau\eta\mu\alpha$ $\epsilon\zeta$ $\alpha\epsilon\iota$, a permanent possession for knowledge of similarly constituted cases in the future.

Cicero's authority stretched into the Christian experience of history. The corpus of his philosophical works was not infrequently catalogued in monastic libraries as a collection of examples and was quite widely available.[9] Possibility of literal resort to the idiom was therefore always present, even if it at first provoked some opposition against the heathen *historia magistra* by Church fathers upholding the authority of the Bible. In his widely available etymological compendium, Isidor of Seville had made frequent use of Cicero's *De oratore*, but he suppressed the expression *historia magistra vitae* in his definitions of history. The apologists of Christianity had no little trouble passing on as precedents events belonging to a profane history, and a heathen one at that.[10] To employ as the teacher of life such a history, full of bad examples, exceeded the transformatory powers of Church historiography. Nonetheless, even Isidor, somewhat furtively, allowed heathen histories an educational function.[11] Likewise, Bede consciously justified profane history on the grounds that it provided examples that were either intimidating or worthy of imitation.[12] By virtue of their great influence, both clerics contributed to the maintenance, alongside a superior, religiously founded history, of an instructional motif drawn from a profane history, even if it occupied a subordinate position.

Melanchthon too made use of this pairing, according to which both biblical and heathen histories were able to deliver exempla for earthly changes, relating in their different ways but at the same time to God's arrangements.[13] The conception of the task of historical writing derived from antiquity could be brought into line with the Christian experience of history associated with expectations of salvation. Neither did the linear schema of biblical prefiguration and its fulfillment—right up to Bossuet—burst the framework within which one derived lessons for the future out of the past.

As millennarial expectations became more volatile, ancient history in its role of teacher forced itself once more to the fore. Machiavelli's call not only to admire the ancients but also to imitate them[14] lent an edge to the resolution to continually draw benefit from history because it united in a unique manner exemplary and empirical thought. At the head of his *Methodus ad facilem historiarum cognitionem*, Bodin placed the Ciceronian topos: this foremost position was warranted by the fashion in which it indicated the holy laws of history through which men could recognize the present and illuminate the future, and, moreover, in a practical, political, and nontheological way.[15] It would be wearisome to individually enumerate the ceaseless repetition[16] or baroque elaboration[17] of this idea that occurred up until the later Enlightenment and writers such as de Mably.[18] Histories and historians varied our topos from pathetic formulas such as *futurorum magistra temporum*[19] to careless, imitative maxims.

Thus, for instance, Lengnich, a Danzig historiographer, wrote that a knowledge of history opened up to us "all that could be used again under the same conditions."[20] Or, to cite a far less obscure man, Lieutenant Freiherr von Hardenberg instructed his son's tutor not to confuse his charge with dry facts. For

in general all past and present actions appear similar; knowledge of them is broadly dispensable, but nonetheless of great utility if this skeleton is covered with the appropriate flesh, and a young man shown the forces behind great changes or the counsel or means by which this or that objective was achieved, or in what way or why it failed. In this way one preaches more to understanding than to memory; history becomes pleasant and interesting for the pupil, and he is imperceptibly instructed in the prudence of both private and state affairs, and educated in the way of *artes belli ac pacis.*[21]

This testimony concerning the proper education of a son composed by his concerned father has importance in that the pedagogic expectations of an enlightened age coincide once again with the traditional task of history.

Without prejudice to these evident historiographic statements, one should not underestimate the practical, didactic force of early modern historicopolitical literature.[22] Legal process depended directly on historical deductions; the relative eternity within which the law operated at that time corresponded to a history conscious of its implication within a changeless but iterable nature. The increasing refinement of contemporary politics was mirrored in the reflections of memoirists and the doings reported by envoys. But in this way it remained bound to *Kameralistik* and *Statistik* indices: the accounting of domain. It is more than a customary topos that Frederick the Great constantly invokes in his memoirs: history is the school of the ruler, from Thucydides to Commynes, Cardinal Retz, or Colbert. By continually comparing earlier cases, he claimed to have sharpened his powers of deduction. He finally invoked—as a means of explaining his "immoral politics" without apology—the countless examples by means of which the rules of *Staatsräson* had guided him in his political actions.[23]

Irony is certainly mixed with resignation when Frederick claims in his old age that the scenes of world history repeat themselves and that it is necessary only to change the names.[24] In this dictum there might even be seen a secularization of figurative thought, for it is certain that the thesis of iteratability and thence the pedagogy of historical experience remained an element of experience itself. Frederick's prognosis of the French Revolution testifies to this.[25] Within the apprehendable space of the European republic of rulers, with its native state organs and estates, the pedagogic role of history was, simultaneously, surety and symptom of a continuity that connected the past to the future.

Naturally, there were objections to the maxims according to which one could learn from history. For instance, Guicciardini—with Aristotle—always regarded the future as uncertain and consequently denied the prognostic content of history.[26] Or take Gracian, who, on the basis of the doctrine of circulation, affirmed the principle of foreknowledge. But the inevitability inherent in this doctrine emptied it of meaning and ultimately rendered it superfluous.[27] Or take old Frederick himself, who closed his memoir of the Seven Years War by disputing the pedagogy of all examples: "For it is a property of the human spirit that examples are improving for no one. The stupidities of the fathers are lost upon their children; each generation must commit its own."[28]

Of course, the skeptical attitude that fed such views did not break free of the characteristic integrity of our didactic formula, since it was rooted in the same space of experience. For the contention that one could learn nothing from history was itself a certainty born of experience, a historical lesson that could render the knowing more insightful, more prudent, or, to borrow a term from Burckhardt,[29] wiser. Potential otherness was incapable of abolishing constancy from the world and therefore cannot be regarded as an other. "What vanishes is the determinate element, or the moment of difference which, whatever its mode of being and whatever its source, sets itself up as something fixed and immutable."[30] The skeptical current which was still, in the Enlightenment, able to articulate itself in terms of eternal similitude, was not able to fundamentally place the meaning of the topos in question. Nevertheless, at the same time, the content of our idiom was undermined. History in its ancient form was tumbled from its lectern (and not the least by those of the Enlightenment who so gladly made use of its teachings) during the course of a movement that brought past and future into a new relation. It was ultimately "history itself" that began to open up a new experiential space. This new history assumed a temporal quality peculiar to itself, whose diverse times and shifting periods of experience drew its evidence from an exemplary past.

This process will now, at symptomatic points, be investigated in the course of its transformation in our topos.

## II

As a way of characterizing this event—of a newly emergent temporality—we will use a statement from Tocqueville, whose entire work is heavy with the suspense of the modern breaking free of the continuity of an earlier mode of time: "As the past has ceased to throw its light upon the future, the mind of man wanders in obscurity."[31] This dictum refers to rejection of traditional experience. Behind this is concealed a complex process whose course is in part invisible and gradual, sometimes sudden and abrupt, and which is ultimately driven forward consciously.

*Begriffsgeschichte*, as practiced here, serves as a preliminary measure in determining the nature of this process. It can show how shifting semantic relations break up and distort our topos as it is handed on. Only through this process does the idiom gain its own history; but at the same time, this history does away with its peculiar truth.

To begin in the German language area, there first occurred a terminological displacement which emptied the older topos of meaning, or at least encouraged this. The naturalized foreign word *Historie*—which primarily meant a report, an account of that which had occurred, and in a specialized sense identified the "historical sciences"—was rapidly displaced in the course of the eighteenth century by the word *Geschichte*. Since around 1750, the turn from *Historie* toward *Geschichte* is detectable and emphatic enough to be statistically measurable.[32] But *Geschichte* principally signified an event, that is, the outcome of actions either undertaken or suffered; the expression referred more to an incident than to an account of it. To be sure, *Geschichte* had for a considerable time implied such an account, just as *Historie* referred to an event.[33] Each was colored by the other. But this mutual limitation (which Barthold Niebuhr tried in vain to reverse) led to the development of an emphasis peculiar to the German language. *Geschichte* assumed the sense of history and drove *Historie* out of general linguistic usage. As history (*Geschichte*) converged as event and representation, the linguistic basis was laid for the transcending turning point leading to the historical philosophy of idealism. *Geschichte* as the context of action was incorporated into its knowledge. Droysen's formula that history is only knowledge of history is the result of this development.[34] This convergence to a dual meaning led naturally to a change in the meaning of *Historie* as *vitae magistra*.

History as unique event or as a universal relation of events was clearly not capable of instructing in the same manner as history in the form of exemplary account. The scholarly boundaries of rhetoric, history, and ethics were undermined, and thus the old formula gained new forms of experience from the new linguistic usage. Luden, for example, argued that the weight of proof in historical teachings consisted, if anything, in the events themselves. As he wrote in 1811, such proof depended on the fact that "it is really history (*Geschichte*) itself which speaks there. . . . It is up to each person to either make use of its lessons or neglect them."[35] History gained a new dimension which deprived accounts of their coherence; history was always "more" than any account made of it. If, then, history could only speak for itself, a further step was possible which completely flattened the formula and rendered it a tautological shell. "One just learns history from history," commented Radowitz sarcastically, in turning Hegel's phrase back on Hegel.[36] This particular verbal conclusion was not the only one which— not by accident—was suggested by linguistic usage. A political opponent of Radowitz lent the old formula a new and direct sense by making use of the ambiguity of the German word: "The genuine teacher is history itself, not written history."[37] Thus history (*Geschichte*) is instructive only to the degree that one does without its written representation (*Historie*). All three variants demarcated a new experiential space within which the old *Historie* had to revoke its claim to be *magistra vitae*. Although it survived, it lost this claim to *Geschichte*.

This brings us to a second point. We have negligently spoken of history, or of "history itself," in the emphatic singular, without related subject or object. This curious expression, which today is quite usual, dates from the second half of the eighteenth century. To the degree that *Geschichte* displaced *Historie*, so the former assumed a different character. Initially, and in order to emphasize the new meaning, one spoke freely of history in and for itself, of history pure and simple, of history itself—from History. Droysen later resumed this process with the words "beyond histories there is History."[38]

It is not possible to underestimate the linguistic concentration upon one concept that has taken place since about 1770. Since the French Revolution, history has become a subject furnished with divine epithets of omnipotence, universal justice, and sanctity. The "work of history," to employ the words of Hegel, becomes a driving force dominating men and breaking their natural identity. Here as well, the German language had made some preparations. The semantic abundance and contemporary novelty of the *Geschichte* derived from the fact that it concerned a collective singular. Up until the middle of the eighteenth century, the expression *die Geschichte* generally prevailed in the plural. Taking a typical example from 1748, Jablonski's *Allgemeines Lexikon der Künste und Wissenschaften* informs us that "*die Geschichte* are a mirror for virtues and vices in which one can learn through assumed experience what is to be done or left undone; they are a monument to evil as well as praiseworthy deeds."[39] What we hear in this example is the usual definition, which is characteristic; it is bound up with a plurality of additive individual histories, just as Bodin wrote his *Methodus ad facilem cognitionem historiarium* for the better knowledge of *historiarum*, of histories in the plural.

In the German language, then, *Geschichte(n)* — from the singular forms *das Geschichte* and *die Geschicht*[40] — were both plural forms, referring to a corresponding number of individual examples. It is dramatic to follow the imperceptible and unconscious manner in which, ultimately with the aid of extensive theoretical reflection, the plural form *die Geschichte* condensed into a collective singular. It was first lexically noted in 1775 by Adelung, in anticipating the coming development.[41] Just three years later, a reviewer in the *Allgemeine deutsche Bibliothek* complained of the way in which the new *Geschichte*, empty of all narrative or exemplary meaning, had spread: "The fashionable word *Geschichte* represents a formal misuse of the language, since in the text [under review] we find only *stories* (*Erzählungen*) in the main."[42]

This usage, which effectively marked out history and separated it from all iterable exemplary power, was not least due to a shift in the boundary distinguishing history and poetics. Increasingly, historical narrative was expected to provide the unity found in the epic derived from the existence of Beginning and End.[43] Past facts could only be translated into historical reality in their passage through consciousness. This became clear in the dispute on Pyrrhonism.[44] As Chladenius said, only in "rejuvenated images" can *Geschichte* be recounted.[45] As greater representative art was required of *Historie*—whereby it was expected to elicit secret motives, rather than present chronological series, create a pragmatic structure for the establishment of an internal order out of accidental occurrences—so then poetic demands entered into *Historie*. *Historie* became subject to a demand for an intensified reality long before it was able to satisfy such a demand. It persisted in the form of a collection of ethical examples, although with the devaluation of this role, the value of *res factae* shifted with respect to *res fictae*. An unmistakable index of the propagation of the new historical consciousness of reality is the fact that, conversely, stories and novels proclaimed themselves "true histories" (*histoire véritable, wahrhaftige Geschichte*).[46] In this fashion, they participated in the increased claim to truth by real history, a degree of truth which had been withheld from *Historie* from Aristotle to Lessing.[47] Thus the demands of history and poetics folded together; the one penetrated the other so that light could be cast on the immanent meaning of *Geschichte*.

Leibniz, who still conceived historical writing and poetry as arts of moral instruction, could view the history of humanity as God's novel, whose point of departure was the Creation.[48] This idea was taken up by Kant, who used the term "novel" (*Roman*) metaphorically so that the natural unity of general history might be allowed to emerge. At a time when universal history, composed of a summation of singular histories, transformed into "world history," Kant sought the means by which the planless "aggregate" of human actions could be transposed into a rational "system."[49] Clearly, it was the collective singular of *Geschichte* that rendered such thoughts capable of expression, irrespective of whether it was a matter of world history or of individual history. Thus, for example, Niebuhr announced under this title his lectures on the history of the era of the French Revolution, arguing that only the Revolution had lent "epic unity to the whole."[50] It was history (*Geschichte*) conceived as a system that made possible an epic unity that disclosed and established internal coherence.

The centuries-old dispute between history and poetics was finally dissolved by Humboldt when he derived the peculiarity of "history in general" from its formal structure. Following Herder, he introduced the categories of "strength" and "tendency," categories which continually escape their givenness. He thereby denied all naively accepted material exemplarity of past instances and drew a general conclusion for historical writing on any theme: "The writer of history who is worthy of such a name must represent each incident as part of a whole or, what amounts to the same thing, within each incident illuminate the form of history in general."[51] He thus reinterpreted a criterion of epic representation and transformed it into a category of the Historical.

The collective singular permitted yet a further step. It made possible the attribution to history of the latent power of human events and suffering, a power that connected and motivated everything in accordance with a secret or evident plan to which one could feel responsible, or in whose name one could believe oneself to be acting. This philological event occurred in a context of epochal significance: that of the great period of singularization and simplification which was directed socially and politically against the society of orders. Here, Freedom took the place of freedoms, Justice that of rights and servitudes, Progress that of progressions (les progrès, the plural) and from the diversity of revolutions, "The Revolution" emerged. With regard to France, one might add that the central place the Revolution in its singularity occupies in Western thought is, in the German language, assigned to Geschichte.

The French Revolution brought to light the concept of history characteristic of the German Historical School. Both of these smashed the earlier models which they seemed to adopt. Johannes von Müller, still in Göttingen a follower of the pragmatic instructiveness of his teacher, wrote in 1796: "One does not so much find in history what is to be done in specific cases (everything is ceaselessly altered by circumstance) as rather the general resultant, or eras and nations." Everything in the world has its own time and place and one should purposefully carry out the tasks handed down by fate.[52]

The young Ranke reflects the semantic shift by which the given singularity of a universal reality might be subsumed under one concept of history. He wrote Geschichten der romanischen und germanischen Völker in 1824 and expressly added that this concerned "Geschichten, nicht die Geschichte." He did not, however, dispute the existence of the specific uniqueness of history (Geschichte). If an event became the object of and set in motion unique and genuine forces, this set to one side the direct applicability of historical models. Ranke continued: "The task of judging the past for the benefit of future generations has been given to History: the present essay does not aspire to such an elevated task; it merely seeks to show the past as it once was (wie es eigentlich *gewesen).*"[53] Ranke increasingly limited himself to the past tense, and only during a temporary departure from this limitation, when he edited the *Historisch-Politische Zeitschrift*, did he resort to the old topos of *historia magistra vitae*.[54] His conspicuous failure appeared to compromise recourse to the old topos.

It was not the historical view of the world as such that led—above all, in the transmission of our idiom in historiographies founded on natural law[55]—to the abandonment of direct application of its doctrine. It was, rather, that hidden behind the relativization of all events consumed by *historia magistra* was a general experience which was also shared by those in the camp opposing the progressives.

This brings us to a third point. It is no accident that in the same decades in which history as a collective singular began to establish itself (between 1760 and 1780), the concept of a philosophy of history also surfaced.[56] This is the time when conjectural, hypothetical, or alleged histories flourished. Iselin in 1764, Herder in 1774, Köster in 1775, working up the "philosophy of history" for consumption by historical scholars,[57] did, in terms of semantic history, rather limp along behind Western authors. The problems and questions of the latter were substantially assumed or transformed. What was common to all, however, was the destruction of the exemplary nature of past events and, in its place, the discovery of the uniqueness of historical processes and the possibility of progress. It is linguistically one and the same event which constituted history in the sense customary today and on this basis gave rise to a philosophy of history. Whoever makes use of the expression "philosophy of history" must note, wrote Köster, "that this is no special or particular science, as might easily be believed on first sighting the term. For it is, where a complete section of history (*Historie*), or a whole historical science, is dealt with, nothing more than history (*Historie*) in itself."[58] History and the philosophy of history are complementary concepts which render impossible any attempt at a philosophization of history; this is an insight which was to be fundamentally lost in the nineteenth century.[59]

The potential similarity and iteratability of naturally formed histories was consigned to the past, while History itself was denaturalized and formed into an entity about which, since that time, it has not been possible to philosophize in the way one can about nature. Nature and history could now conceptually part; the proof of this is that in precisely these decades the old domain of *historia naturalis* is eliminated from the structure of historical sciences: for the French by Voltaire in the *Encyclopédie*, for the Germans by Adelung.[60]

Behind this separation, which was prefigured by Vico and might seem to belong only to the history of the sciences, exists the decisive registration of the discovery of a specific historical temporality. This involves what one might call a temporalization of history, which has since that time detached itself from a naturally formed chronology. Up until the eighteenth century, the course and calculation of historical events was underwritten by two natural categories of time: the cycle of stars and planets, and the natural succession of rulers and dynasties. Kant, in refusing to interpret history in terms of astronomical data and rejecting as nonrational the course of succession, did away with established chronology on the grounds that it provided a guideline that was both annalistic and theologically colored, "as if chronology were not derivative of history, but rather that history must arrange itself according to chronology."[61]

The exposure of a time determined solely by history was effected by contemporary historical philosophy long before historism made use of this idea. The naturalistic basis vanished and progress became the prime category in which a transnatural, historically immanent definition of time first found expression. Insofar as philosophy conceived history in the singular and as a unitary whole and transposed it in this form into Progress, our topos was inevitably robbed of meaning. With such a history functioning as the solitary source of the education of the human race, it was natural that all past examples lost their force. Individual teachings disappeared into a general pedagogic arrangement. The ruse of reason forbade man to learn directly from history and indirectly forced him toward happiness. This is the progressive conclusion that takes us from Lessing to Hegel: "But what experience and history teach is this—that nations and governments have never learned anything from history or acted upon any lessons they might have drawn from it."[62] Or, in the words of an experienced contemporary of Hegel, Abbot Rupert Kornmann: "It is the fate of states as well as of men to become prudent (*klug*) just when the opportunity to be so has disappeared."[63]

There is, underlying both statements, not only a philosophical reflection on the properties of historical time, but just as directly the forcible experience of the French Revolution, which seemed to outstrip all previous experience. The extent to which this new historical temporality was based on just this experience was quick to show itself with the revival of the revolution in Spain in 1820. Immediately after the outbreak of unrest, Count Reinhard was prompted by Goethe to make an observation which made evident the temporal perspective: "You are quite right, dear friend, in what you say on experience. It arrives for individuals always too late, while for governments and peoples it is never available. This is because past experience presents itself concentrated in a single focus, while that which has yet to be experienced is spread over minutes, hours, days, years, and centuries; thus similitude never appears to be the same, for in the one case one sees the whole, and in the latter only individual parts."[64] It is not only because transpired events cannot be repeated that past and future cannot be reconciled. Even if they could, as in 1820 with the revival of the revolution, the history that awaits us deprives us of the ability to experience it. A concluded experience is both complete and past, while those to be had in the future decompose into an infinity of different temporal perspectives.

It is not the past but the future of historical time which renders similitude dissimilar. Thus Reinhard had demonstrated the processual nature of a modern history whose terminus cannot be foreseen.

This leads us to another variant of our topos which alters itself in the same direction. It frequently occurred in connection with *historia magistra* that the historian did not only have to teach but also had to form opinions and on the basis of these make judgments. This task was taken up with particular emphasis by enlightened *Historie*, and it became, in the words of the *Encyclopédie*, a *tribunal intègre et terrible*.[65] Almost stealthily, a historiography which had been making judgments since antiquity turned into a *Historie* which autonomously executed its judgments. Raynal's work, not the least thanks to the aid of Diderot, testifies to this. The Final Judgment was thereby rendered temporal: "World history is the court of the world." This quickly circulated phrase of Schiller's, from the year 1784, was already stripped of all historiographic traces and addressed itself to a form of justice contained within history itself and which embodied all human actions. "Whatever is left undone stays forever undone."[66]

The prevailing journalistic use of the idea of the chastisement of time, of the spirit of the age to which one had to constantly adjust oneself, recalls the inevitability of the manner in which the Revolution, or rather the history of mankind, faced compulsory alternatives.[67] But this historicophilosophical determination, equivalent to the temporal singularity of history, is only one side from which *historia magistra vitae* is deprived of its possibility. From an apparently opposite direction, another, by no means weaker, attack was launched.

Thus, fourth, consistent Enlighteners tolerated no allusion to the past. The declared objective of the *Encyclopédie* was to work through the past as quickly as possible so that a new future could be set free.[68] Once, one knew exempla; today, only rules, said Diderot. "To judge what happens according to what has already happened means, it seems to me, to judge the familiar in terms of the unfamiliar," deduced Sieyès.[69] One should not lose heart—one should seek for nothing in history which might suit us.[70] Forthwith, the revolutionaries supplied in a dictionary the directive to write no more history until the constitution was completed.[71] The constructibility of history dethroned the older *Historie*,

for in a state like ours, founded on victory, there is no past. It is a creation, in which—as in the creation of the universe—everything that is present is but raw material in the hand of the creator by whom it is transformed into existence.

So crowed a satrap of Napoleon.[72] This was the manner in which Kant's forecast was fulfilled when he posed the question: "How is history a priori possible? Answer: when the soothsayer himself shapes and forms the events that he had predicted in advance."[73]

The irresistibility of history which, paradoxically, corresponds to its constructibility, offers two aspects of the same phenomenon. Since the future of modern history opens itself as the unknown, it becomes plannable—it must be planned. With each new plan a fresh degree of uncertainty is introduced, since it presupposes a lack of experience. The self-proclaimed authority on "history" grows with its constructibility. The one is founded on the other, and vice versa. Common to both is the decomposition of the traditional experiential space, which had previously appeared to be determined by the past, but which would now break apart.

A by-product of this historical revolution was the fact that historical writing now became less falsifiable than manipulable. With the establishment of the Restoration, an 1818 decree forbade history lessons on the period 1789–1815.[74] By denying the Revolution and its achievements, it appeared to implicitly adapt itself to the view that repetition of the past was no longer possible. But it sought in vain to trump amnesty with amnesia.

Behind all that has been said up to now, behind the singularization of history, its temporalization, unavoidable superiority, and producibility, can be registered an experiential transformation that permeates our modernity. In this process, *Historie* was shorn of the objective of directly relating to life. Since that time, moreover, experience seemed to teach the opposite. An unassuming witness to this circumstance, who summarizes it for us, is the modest and intelligent Perthes, who wrote in 1823:

If each party were to take turns at governing and organizing institutions, then all would, through their self-made history, become more reasonable and wise. History made by others, no matter how much written about and studied, seldom gives rise to political reasonableness and wisdom: that is taught by experience.[75]

This assessment, within the sphere of the expressive possibility of our topos, represents its complete inversion. Counsel is henceforth to be expected, not from the past but from a future which has to be made. Perthes' statement was modern, for it took leave of *Historie*, and as a publisher Perthes was able to further it. Historians engaged in a critical reconstruction of the past were at one with progressives who, in agreeing that no further utility was to be gained from the directives of an exemplary *Historie*, consciously placed new models at the forefront of the movement.

This brings us to our last feature, which contains a question. What was common to this new experience, whose uniqueness had previously been determined by the temporalization of history? As Niebuhr, in 1829, announced his lectures on the previous forty years, he shied away from calling them a "History of the French Revolution," for "the Revolution is itself a product of the period. . . . We do indeed lack a general word for the period and in view of this we should like to call it the Epoch of Revolutions."[76] Behind this dissatisfaction was a recognition that a temporality adequate to history first emerges as something internally differentiated and differentiable. The requisite experience for differentiating time in general is, however, that of acceleration and retardation.

Acceleration, initially perceived in terms of an apocalyptic expectation of temporal abbreviation heralding the Last Judgment,[77] transformed itself—also from the mid-eighteenth century—into a concept of historical hope.[78] This subjective anticipation of a future both desired and to be quickened acquired an unexpectedly solid reality, however, through the process of technicalization and the French Revolution. A parallel of the new and the old revolutions was drawn up in 1797 by Chateaubriand in emigration, whence he drew conclusions from the past for the future in the customary manner. But he was soon forced to realize that whatever he had written during the day was by night already overtaken by events. It seemed to him that the French Revolution, quite without previous example, led into an open future. Thus, thirty years later, Chateaubriand placed himself in a historical relation by republishing his outdated essay, without change in substance, but provided with notes in which he proposed progressive constitutional prognoses.[79]

In 1789 a new space of expectation was constituted whose perspective was traced out by points which, at the same time, referred back to different phases of the past revolution. It was Kant who was the first to foresee this modern system of historical experience when he established a temporally indeterminate, but nevertheless ultimate, goal for the repetition of revolutionary attempts. "Instruction through frequent experience" of intelligent ventures perfects the course of the Revolution.[80] Since then, historical instruction enters political life once again via the back door of programs of action legitimated in terms of historical philosophy. Mazzini, Marx, and Proudhon can be named as the first teachers of a revolutionary application. According to party or position, the categories of acceleration and retardation (evident since the French Revolution) alter the relations of past and future in varying rhythms. This principle is what Progress and Historism share in common.

It also becomes comprehensible, against the background of this acceleration, why the writing of contemporary history, *Gegenwartschronik*, was left behind[81] and why *Historie* failed to keep abreast of an actuality which was increasingly changeable.[82] In a social world undergoing emphatic change, the temporal dimensions, within which experience had previously been developed and collected, become displaced. Historism—like the historical philsophy of Progress—reacted to this by placing itself in an indirect relation to *Geschichte*. However much the German Historical School conceived itself as concerned with a science of the past, it did nonetheless fully exploit the dual meaning of the word *Geschichte* and seek to elevate history into a reflexive science. Here, the individual case lost its politico-didactic character.[83] But History as a totality places the person who has learned to understand it in a state of learning which was to work directly on the future. As emphasized by Savigny, history is "no longer merely a collection of examples but rather the sole path to the true knowledge of our own condition."[84] Or, as Mommsen stated in trying to bridge the gulf between past and future: history is no longer a teacher of the art of making political prescriptions, but is "instructive solely in that it inspires and instructs independent creative judgment."[85] No matter how scholarly, every past example is always too late. Historism can relate to history only indirectly.[86] In other words, historism renounces a history which simultaneously suspends the condition of its possibility as a practical-historical science. The crisis of historism coincides with this, but that does not prevent the necessity of its survival as long as *Geschichte* exists.

The first to make a serious attempt at methodically attacking this problem was Henry Adams. He developed a theory of movement which dealt simultaneously with Progress and History and specified them by his question on the structure of historical time. Adams proposed a law of acceleration (as he called it) on the basis of which standards were continually altered because of the manner in which the acceleration of the future constantly foreshortened resort to the past. Population increased at ever-decreasing intervals; technically created velocities were raised by the square of those previously achieved; the increase of production showed similar tendencies and thereby achieved scientific effectiveness; expectations for an increased life span were rising and thus extending the span of generations—from these and many other examples that could be multiplied at will, Adams drew the conclusion that all teachings but one had been superseded: "All the teacher could hope for was to teach [the mind] reaction."[87]

# Historical Criteria of the
# Modern Concept of Revolution

There are few words so widely disseminated and belonging so naturally to modern political vocabulary as the term "revolution." It also belongs, of course, to those strong expressions whose applications are quite diverse and whose conceptual unclarity is so great that they can be called catchwords. Clearly, the semantic content of "revolution" is not disclosed by such sloganistic use and utility. Rather, the term "revolution" indicates upheaval or civil war, as well as long-term change, and therefore events and structures which penetrate deeply into our daily life. Evidently, the platitudinous ubiquity of revolution and its occasionally very concrete meaning are closely related. The one invokes the other, and vice versa. The following semantic outline will address itself to this relation.[1]

The linguistic situation is variable. While practically every newspaper talks of the second industrial revolution, historical science is still arguing about the way in which the nature and inauguration of the first should be defined. This second industrial revolution not only relieves the human world of physical exertion, but also entrusts intellectual processes to automatic machines. Cybernetics, atomic physics, and biochemistry are all included in the concept of the second industrial revolution; the first is left far behind, involved as it is with the extension of human productivity beyond traditional needs through the use of capital, technology, and the division of labor. There is an absence of generally acceptable criteria of differentiation.

Likewise, we can read daily of the Marxist program of world revolution, originally formulated by Marx and Lenin and then, in particular, inscribed by Mao Zedong on the banners of the Chinese Communist Party. More recently, the concept of Cultural Revolution has become a part of the domestic Chinese situation, whereby the convulsion is evidently to be driven right into the Chinese mentality, dictating the revolution into the body of the masses. Everywhere the conditions for the extension of the proletarian revolution around the globe should be taken advantage of or created. Legal and illegal emissaries of the Communists charged with the realization of this program are active in many countries of the world, especially in underdeveloped parts. As is known, the realization of the alternative posed to Russia and China has itself limited the universal program in Asia.

The semantic content of the word "revolution" is thus by no means unequivocal. It ranges from bloody political and social convulsions to decisive scientific innovations; it can signify the whole spectrum, or alternately, one form exclusive of the remainder. A successful technical revolution, therefore, presupposes a minimum of stability, which initially excludes a sociopolitical revolution, even when the latter may be a precondition or consequence of the former.

Accordingly, our concept of revolution can conveniently be defined as a flexible "general concept," meeting worldwide with a certain initial comprehension, but which in a more precise sense fluctuates enormously from country to country and from one political camp to another. It almost seems that the word "revolution" itself possesses such revolutionary power that it continually broadens itself to include every last element on our globe. We would then have a case of a political catchword continually reproducing itself by virtue of its composition, as well as urging a transformation of the situation itself. What is there in the world that could not be revolutionized—and what is there in our time that is not open to revolutionary effects? Posing this question to our concept refers us to modern circumstances.

If one can characterize our modern history as an era of revolution— one which has not yet come to its end—so a certain direct experience is embodied in this formulation. Typical of this experience is the fact that it can be subsumed under the concept of revolution, more indeed than is perhaps generally allowed. The concept "revolution" is itself a linguistic product of our modernity. That it is possible to distinguish political, social, technological, and industrial revolutions has been accepted since the last century. Only since the French Revolution has the term *révolution* (the same whatever the language) gained the kind of ambivalent and ubiquitous semantic potentiality outlined above.

We will trace the history of our concept back before the period of the great French Revolution, so that we can separate out some peculiarities of modern experience and thus be able to recognize them more clearly.

**I**

In 1842, a French scholar made a historically enlightening observation. Haréau recalled what had been forgotten at the time: that our expression actually signified a turning over, a return of the movement to the point of departure, as in the original Latin usage. A revolution initially signified, in keeping with its lexical sense, circulation.[2] Haréau added that in the political sphere, this was understood as the circulation of constitutions taught by Aristotle, Polybius, and their successors but which since 1789 and through Condorcet's influence was hardly comprehensible. According to ancient doctrine, there was only a limited number of constitutional forms, which dissolved and replaced each other but could not naturally be transgressed. These are the constitutional forms, together with their corruptions, which are still current today, succeeding each other with a certain inevitability. Haréau cited a forgotten principal witness of this past world, Louis LeRoy, who had argued that the first of all natural forms of rule was that of monarchy, which was replaced by aristocracy as soon as the former degenerated into tyranny. Then followed the well-known schema in which aristocracy was transformed into oligarchy, which was in turn displaced by democracy, which degenerated ultimately into ochlocracy, or mass rule. Here, in fact, no one ruled any longer, and the way to individual rule was open once more. Hence, the old cycle could begin anew. Here we have a model of revolution which found expression in Greek as μεταβολη πολιτειων or as πολιτειων αηαχυχλωσις,[3] and which subsisted on the experience that all forms of political association were ultimately limited. Each change led to a familiar form of rule within which men and women remained enthralled, and it was impossible to break out of this natural cycle. All variation, or change, *rerum commutatio, rerum conversio*, was insufficient to introduce anything novel into the political world. Historical experience remained involved in its almost natural givenness, and in the same way that the annual seasons through their succession remain forever the same, so mankind *qua* political beings remained bound to a process of change which brought forth nothing new under the sun. In the course of the seventeenth century, the concept of revolution emerged to characterize this quasi-natural experience. LeRoy at that time defined the progression of constitutions as follows: *Telle est la révolution naturelle des polices. . . .*[4] —this is the natural revolution of state constitutions, which continually transforms the condition of the commonality and finally returns to the point of departure.

The naturalistic undertone to this concept of revolution was by no means accidental; it derived directly from the cycle of the stars, among which, since Copernicus, even the earth could be counted. The path-breaking work of Copernicus on the circular movement of celestial bodies, *De revolutionibus orbium caelestium*, appeared in 1543 and opened the way for the concept of revolution which entered politics via the prevalent astrology of that time. Initially, revolution was a "physico-political" concept (Rosenstock-Hüessy). In the same way that the stars run their circular course independent of earthly men, while at the same time influencing or even determining their lives, this dual meaning resonated through the political concept of revolution from the seventeenth century on: revolutions do take place above the heads of their participants, but those concerned (for instance, Wallenstein) remain imprisoned in their laws.

Overtones of this double meaning can without any doubt be heard in our contemporary linguistic usage. But what distinguishes earlier usage from our own is the consciousness of a return, indicated by the syllable "re" in the word *revolutio*. It was in this sense that Hobbes described the twenty-year period, from 1640 to 1660, following the end of the great English Revolution: "I have seen in this revolution a circular motion."[5] He saw a circular movement, leading from the absolute monarch via the Long Parliament to the Rump Parliament, then to Cromwell's dictatorship, and back via oligarchic intermediary forms to the renewal of monarchy under Charles II. One of the victors, Clarendon (who still blamed the stars for the recent disorder), could quite consistently, after the final return of the Stuarts, celebrate the upheaval as a Restoration. That which is to us apparently incomprehensible was then placed together. The termination and objective of the twenty-year revolution was Restoration. Hence, monarchists and republicans stood closer together than they could then admit: it was for both a matter—terminologically—of the restoration of ancient law, of a return to the true constitution.

The naturalistic metaphor of political "revolution" lived on the assumption that historical time was itself of a uniform quality, contained within itself, and repeatable. While it was always debatable at what point in the ebb and flow of a *revolutio* one would place the present or desired constitutional state, this remained, from the point of view of the circulatory process, a secondary question. All political positions remained preserved in a transhistorical concept of revolution.

Quite different expressions were usual for the bloody struggles themselves, and for the blind passion with which conflicts during the sixteenth and seventeenth centuries were conducted.

As in the Middle Ages, so in the century of the terrible confessional confrontations, which successively and simultaneously laid waste to France, the Netherlands, Germany, and England: a range of definitions was employed. These definitions ranged from uprising and revolt to riot, insurrection, and rebellion, and on to *Zweiung*, internal and civil war. Civil war, *guerre civile*, *Bürgerkrieg*—these were the central concepts by which the suffering and experience of fanatical confessional struggles were precipitated, by means of which, moreover, they were legally formulated.

All of these expressions, which could be supplemented by a substantial series, shared a view of social organization based on a society of orders (*Stände*). While the mode of government might alter, the social order itself was seldom directly displaced by civil war; for the most part, the consequences were merely long-term. The legal resort of civil or confessional war was contained in the *ständisch* right of resistance, as claimed, for instance, by the United Netherlands. For the most part, the old civil war remained a war among qualified members of orders, i.e., a *bellum civile*, no matter what the extent of participation by the lower strata might be. The German "Peasant War" also constituted a constitutional analogue of *Bürgerkrieg*; only after 1789 was it dubbed a "revolution" and thus recouped within a philosophy of history. And if in Germany we do not refer to the Thirty Years War as a civil war—as corresponding events in neighboring countries are called—it is because the Imperial constitutional character of this war has altered with the termination of thirty years of struggle. What had begun as a civil war between the Protestant Imperial orders and the Imperial party ended with a peace treaty between almost sovereign territorial states. Our religious civil war could thus be interpreted *ex post* as a war between states.

Thus for the period (to around 1700) we can conclude that the expressions "civil war" and "revolution" were not interchangeable but at the same time were not mutually exclusive. Civil war meant those bloody events whose legal title derived from the wane of feuding, from *ständisch* treaties, or from confessional positions. These legal titles constituted in concrete struggle a mutual exclusiveness, marking the current enemy as a rebel against the law. In this way State became the counterconcept to Civil War, appropriating all title of right claimed by the latter. The State, symbolically elevated in the Baroque era as a person, prohibited *bellum intestinum* by monopolizing the right of force domestically and the right to declare war externally.

Revolution, initially a transhistorical expression bound to natural factors, was consciously employed as a metaphor for long-term or especially sudden political events, to "upheavals." To this extent it could contain elements of civil war. A German dictionary translated this linguistic borrowing in 1728 as follows:

Revolution, the upheaval, alteration or course of time, *Revolutio regni*, the change or overturning of a kingdom or of a land, if such suffers any special alteration in government and police.[6]

The dictionary of the French Academy in 1694 nonetheless gave as the real and primary meaning of this word the planetary *révolution*. It is against this background that the meaning of a revolution still existed. It referred to a model course of political constitutional struggle which remained entirely predetermined. Along with the repeatability of constitutional forms, political revolution could also be conceived as repetition. Social unrest and uprisings were, on the other hand, understood as "rebellion" and put down accordingly. One "possessed no word which could have characterized a transformation in which the subjects themselves became the rulers" (Hannah Arendt, *On Revolution*). Social emancipation as a revolutionary process still lay outside experience. This would change in the course of the eighteenth century, in the epoch of Enlightenment.

With "revolution" the Enlighteners stood on firm ground, and the concept became modish. Everything that was seen and described was conceived in terms of change or upheaval. Revolution covered morals, law, religion, economy, countries, states, and portions of the earth:

indeed, the entire globe. As Louis Sébastian Mercier said in 1772, "Tout est révolution dans ce monde."[7]

The concept, originally naturalistic and as such transhistorical, extended its partially metaphorical meaning: each and every thing was comprehended through it. Movement abandoned its naturalistic background and entered the reality of everyday life. In particular, the sphere of a genuine human history was opened up through its contamination by "revolution."

What was politically notable about this new general concept of movement was its stylization as a concept in contrast to that of civil war. To the enlightened friends of peace, civil wars appeared to be the inheritance of fanatical religious groupings which, with the advance of civilization, one simply left behind. In 1778, Wieland claimed:

The present condition of Europe [approaches] a benign revolution, a revolution that will not be brought about by revolt and civil wars, not by ruinous struggle of force against force.[8]

This touching optimism, shared by many of his contemporaries, was sustained by an alien experience which had provided the basis for a new model: the Glorious Revolution of 1688 in England.[9] It had proved possible to overthrow a hated ruling house without bloodshed and replace it with a parliamentary form of government drawn from the upper stratum and based on the division of powers. Voltaire noted admiringly that a revolution had taken place in England, in contrast to other countries, which had seen only uprisings and inconclusive, bloody, civil wars. In many respects, "civil war" then acquired the meaning of a senseless circling upon itself, with respect to which Revolution sought to open up a new vista.

The further the Enlightenment advanced, the more civil war faded into historical reminiscence. The *Encyclopédie* dealt with war under eight different rubrics, but the concept *guerre civile* was not one of them. Civil wars did not seem possible any longer. In proportion to this, the concept of revolution was stripped of its political rigor, and it was possible for all those utopian hopes that make intelligible the élan of the years after 1789 to stream into it. It was expected, as in England, to be able to pluck the fruits of a revolution without having to undergo the terror of civil war. Should it come to the spilling of blood, then the example of the American independence movement appeared to guarantee a happy conclusion.

Certainly, there was no lack of warnings and prognoses foretelling the awfulness of civil war that lay behind the mask of radiant revolution. Leibniz was the first, in 1704 indicating with extraordinary clarity the character of the coming *révolution générale* in Europe;[10] Diderot delivered the most exact prognosis, depicting the future Napoleon as a dialectical product of fear and freedom; and Rousseau went so far as to prophesy the coming century. In 1762 he wrote: we are approaching the condition of crisis, and the century of revolutions. It is impossible to predict the revolutions singly, and just as impossible to anticipate them. It was certain that the European monarchies would be swept away, but what would follow them, no one knew. Diderot asked a similar question: "What will succeed this revolution? No one knows."[11]

Such questions, posed by the sharpest minds of the Enlightenment, and which are still not possible for us to answer today, opened up a new horizon of expectation. Since then, revolution obviously no longer returned to given conditions or possibilities, but has, since 1789, led forward into an unknown future. The nature of this future is so obscure that its recognition and mastery have become the constant task of politics. As Haréau retrospectively observed, "The word 'revolution' has lost its original sense." Since then, it had supplied a "fond mobile de la science humaine."[12]

## II

What features have characterized the conceptual field of Revolution since 1789? This is a question concerning a few common attributes which emerge from the testimony of those contemporary with the inception of our modernity.

1. The first point that must be noted is the novel manner in which, since 1789, "revolution" has effectively been condensed to a *collective singular*; as is already apparent in Mercier's dictum, everything in this world is Revolution. As with the German concept of *Geschichte*, which in the form of "history pure and simple" contained within itself the possibilities of all individual histories, Revolution congealed into a collective singular which appeared to unite within itself the course of all individual revolutions. Hence, revolution became a *metahistorical concept*, completely separated, however, from its naturalistic origin and henceforth charged with ordering historically recurrent convulsive experiences. In other words, Revolution assumes a transcendental sig-

nificance; it becomes a regulative principle of knowledge, as well as of the actions of all those drawn into revolution. From this time on, the revolutionary process, and a consciousness which is both conditioned by it and reciprocally affects it, belong inseparably together. All further characteristics of the modern concept of revolution are sustained by this metahistorical background.

2. The experience of *acceleration* also cannot be overlooked. Behind Robespierre's vow to his fellow citizens to accelerate the French Revolution in order that freedom might be gained the sooner, it is possible to detect an unconscious secularization of eschatological expectation. From Laktanz to Luther and Bengel, temporal abbreviation was taken to be a sign of the approaching destruction of historical time in general. But since the onset of such acceleration, the tempo of historical time has constantly been changing, and today, thanks to the population explosion, development of technological powers, and the consequent frequent changes of regime, acceleration belongs to everyday experience. The uniform and natural horizon of history has since been left far behind; the accelerative experience drew forth new perspectives imbued with the concept of Revolution.

Chateaubriand, for example, in 1794 outlined a parallel of the old and the new Revolution, so that he could, in the usual fashion, draw conclusions for the future from the past. Nevertheless, he soon had to recognize that the French Revolution exceeded all comparison. And so, thirty years later, Chateaubriand revised his superseded essay through the addition of notes which ventured progressive constitutional prognoses no longer dependent upon parallelism, that is, upon the repeatability, of old revolutions.[13]

3. Characteristic of all prognoses made since 1789 is their incorporation of a coefficient of movement which is held to be "revolutionary," whatever the tendency out of which such prognoses issue. Even the state was swept into the grasp of "Revolution," so that it becomes quite understandable that the neologism *contrerévolutionnaire* was translated into German around 1800 as *Staatsfeind*, enemy of the state.[14] Whoever had respect for the state had to be "revolutionary," anticipating the definition of the Left-Hegelian position. It was not a question of whether the *Ständestaat* could further the revolution or prevent it. The alternative, rather, was transformation of the *Ständestaat* in a peaceful or a bloody fashion; or, as expressed by Struensee or Kant, revolution from above or below. Once the revolutionary trend

had been unleashed, the concept "reform" converged here and there with that of "revolution," a convergence which, while often severely strained by political polemic, was in essence contained within a general impulse to plan the social future.

4. The degree to which the prospect of the future continually altered accordingly changed the view of the past. Therefore, a new space of experience opened up whose perspective was aligned with respect to the various phases of the concluded Revolution of 1789. According to interest and situation, one could identify oneself with one or the other stages of the last revolution and in this way draw conclusions for the future. The Revolution was transformed for everyone into a historicophilosophical concept, based on a perspective which displayed a constant and steady direction. There might be arguments over "earlier" versus "later," or "retardation" versus "acceleration," but the actual direction appeared to have been established once and for all. The Revolution limps, scoffed Rivarol; rights move continually to the left, but the left never to the right.[15] This opens a space within which, since then, all political events could become estranged in terms of a historical philosophy. But behind such expressions, which moved from the spatial to the temporal, an undeniable experience registers itself. Historicophilosophical perspectives share with prognoses an implicit and irreversible trend covering all tendencies simultaneously. Thus, the repeated contamination of revolution and evolution since the nineteenth century does not only indicate linguistic carelessness or political accommodation; the extensive interchangeability of both concepts indicates structural dislocations in the entire social structure which provoke answers differentiated only on a political plane. Evolution and revolution become, as antitheses, partisan concepts; their similar usage denotes the general expansion of a movement for social emancipation driven by industrialization.

5. We are therefore dealing with the path or the *step from political to social revolution* which marks the modern concept of revolution. It is quite obvious that all political unrest involves social elements. But what is new is the idea that the objective of a political revolution should be the social emancipation of all men, transforming the social structure. In 1794, Wieland had carefully registered this new vocabulary of revolution, at that time still a linguistic borrowing: the intention of the Jacobins was, he wrote, "to make out of the French Revolution a Social Revolution, that is, an overturning of all currently existing

states."[16] The prevailing linguistic uncertainty does not conceal the actual state of affairs. Once the declaration of human rights had opened up the social space of expectation, every program strove for further realization in the name of freedom or equality or both.

It was Babeuf who first predicted that the French Revolution would not reach its conclusion until exploitation and slavery were abolished. In this way, an objective was established which, with the development of industrial labor, was bound to become an ever-stronger demand. From the 1830 revolution on, formulas proliferated according to which the trend leads from political to social revolution. One thinks, for example, of Lorenz von Stein, Radowitz, and Tocqueville. The young Marx coined the dualistic formula, "Every revolution dissolves the *old society*, and to that extent it is social. Every revolution overthrows the old power, and to that extent it is *political*."[17] Thus he formulated in general terms something that could only be conceived in the aftermath of 1789.

In 1832, Heine had more strongly differentiated the temporal coefficients of both concepts of revolution:

The writer who wishes to bring about a social revolution may nonetheless be a century ahead of his time; the tribune, however, which has in view a political revolution cannot remove itself too far from the masses [i.e., from the immediate life of the present].[18]

The degree to which political and social revolution coincide, and whether they are at all dependent on each other, remain central questions of modern history. While the political emancipation of former colonies may be nearly complete, political freedom only becomes a reality if emancipation is continued as a social process.

6. Here we touch on a sixth feature, which arises directly out of the step from political to social revolution. If the declarations of the American, French, and Russian revolutions are taken literally, there is no doubt that their "achievements" are intended to be to the advantage of all mankind. In other words, all modern expressions of "Revolution" spatially imply a *world revolution* and temporally imply that they be *permanent* until their objective is reached. Today we may already place the Chinese Revolution within this sequence. Whatever the prospects are for the realization of this program, its continuity is identical with that of its predecessors.

Robespierre observed in lofty tones: "La moité de la révolution du monde est déjà faite; l'autre moité doit s'accomplir."[19] He added the naturalistic metaphor according to which the reason of man is comparable to the globe on which he lives. One-half of the globe is plunged into darkness, while the other half sparkles in the light. Here he contradicts himself in a worn allusion to older, naturalistic comparisons. Half of the earth will always be wrapped in darkness, only the half will continually change. No matter how much politicians since the time of Napoleon have pursued the goal of "setting an end to revolution," the totalizing concept of world revolution has nevertheless established itself. Ever since the foundation of the various Internationales the concept of world revolution has entered programs of direct political action.

If earth is to be revolutionized in its entirety, it necessarily follows that the revolution must last until the time this goal is achieved. After the fall of Napoleon the supposition became rapidly established that the restoration was no end to revolution—as once had been the case— but rather signaled the entry into a new phase. In 1815, Koppe, councillor to the Prussian government, wrote that "Bonaparte is not, and never has been, anything other than the personification of the revolution in one of its stages. [His fall] might well end one stage of the revolution, but in no way the revolution itself."[20] Already this turn of phrase makes clear that the modern collective singular "the revolution" implies its enduring nature: the history of the future will be the history of the revolution.

Immediately following the July Revolution of 1830 the expression "revolution in permanence" appeared.[21] Proudhon made use of it in a social-revolutionary fashion, as Marx was to do in 1850 in a similar manner.[22] The defeat to which the 1848 Revolution had led was used at that time by Marx to draw the dialectical conclusion that the victory of a truly revolutionary party was approaching. In this defeat, he wrote, it was not revolution that was vanquished. It was, rather, the prerevolutionary and traditional remnants.[23]

Whatever the disappointment provoking this analysis, the (permanent) revolution that survived the (actual) revolution of 1848–50 was a historicophilosophical category. It served in this fashion for the development of proletarian consciousness, and in this way even Marx resorted to the older sense of revolution as repetition, for he could not completely escape its distant echoes. The creation of a united and powerful counterrevolution, he suggested, clarified the lines of battle so that the class enemy might be overthrown at the next, repeated, attempt.

What was novel about Marx, however, was his conception of the repetition represented by the actual revolutions of 1830 and 1848 as merely a caricature of the great French Revolution; on the other hand, he sought to effect this repetition in consciousness so that the past might be worked off. Marx sought to engender a learning process which would, through the acquisition of a new revolutionary language, found the singularity of the coming revolution.

Earlier revolutions required recollections of past world history in order to dull themselves to their own content. In order to arrive at its own content, the revolution of the nineteenth century must let the dead bury their dead.[24]

The social revolution must write off the past and create its substance out of the future. Socialism is the "revolution's declaration of permanence."[25] Within the declaration of the revolution's permanence lies the deliberate and conscious anticipation of the future, as well as the implicit premise that this revolution will never be fulfilled. Here, Marx went beyond Kant, who in 1798 concluded from the failure of the first attempt that victory approached for "Revolution or Reform"; the "lessons of recurring experience"[26] would at some time or other, with certainty, produce their lasting effect. Marx, who had diagnosed the process of upheaval as a social and industrial revolution, found a most concise formula to characterize its individuality and futurity: however, this Revolution became for him a personified agent of history disengaged from reality in such a manner that communism, as a domain of freedom, remains unrealizable.

7. Behind this paradox of a utopia that sees itself compelled to constantly reproduce is hidden for us a further phenomenon, which can be treated as the seventh feature. Hitherto, Revolution has been presented as a metahistorical category which served to define social and industrial occurrences in terms of a self-accelerating process. It is precisely this formulation that becomes the conscious claim to leadership for those who believe themselves to be initiated into the progressive laws of a Revolution understood in this fashion. The noun denoting action, *Revolutionierung*, and its associated verb, *revolutionieren*, emerge. Also, since 1789 the instances of the word *Revolutionär*, another of the numerous neologisms in our semantic field, mount. This is a

concept denoting the *duty* of activism, a meaning earlier inconceivable, but which directly heralds the professional revolutionary as a figure molded in the course of the nineteenth century and typified by Lenin. Intimately bound up with this is the conception that men could make revolutions, an idea that was previously unutterable.

This feasibility (*Machbarkeit*) of Revolution offers merely the internal aspect of that revolution whose future laws revolutionaries were believed to have recognized. The explanation of how one must create (*produire*) and direct (*diriger*) a Revolution for the benefit of liberty comes from Condorcet. "Une loi révolutionnaire est une loi, qui a pour objet de maintenir cette révolution, et d'en accélerer ou régler la marche."[27] The transpersonal structures of Revolution and its growing manipulability stemming from knowledge of it appear to have mutually sustained each other. In 1798 the young Schlegel perceptively noted why Napoleon was able to assume a dominant role in the French Revolution: "Revolutions can create, develop and annihilate themselves."[28] This, quite apart from its historical accuracy, defines prognostically a feature of the modern professional revolutionary. To the extent that he knows how to efface himself, he is capable of "putting together" (*bewerkstelligen*) revolutions, as was formulated by a later writer, Weitling.[29]

The amalgamation of a general historicophilosophical perspective with especial revolutionary commitment also makes clear why it was increasingly possible to openly discuss and announce a planned inauguration of a "revolution" in the form of an uprising, without at the same time affecting the chances of success, as in August 1792 in Paris, and in Palermo in 1848, and in Petersburg in October 1917. Behind this combination, according to which the self-governing revolution was organized and must be organized, there is a criterion that we will deal with last of all: that of the *legitimacy* of Revolution.

8. In 1848, Stahl coined the expression *absolute revolution*,[30] indicating that legal title for all actions were derivative of the revolutionary movement. The historical derivation of law from the past was in this way carried over into a "warranty in permanence" secured historically-philosophically. Whereas the legitimacy of a Restoration remained bound to past tradition, revolutionary legitimacy became a coefficient of movement, mobilizing history in terms of the prevailing prospect of the future. Ranke still thought in 1841 that it is the "misfortune of the Revolution never to be at the same time legitimate."[31] It was Metternich, however, who recognized the position more clearly when

he sarcastically remarked in 1830 that it was the Legitimists themselves who legitimated the Revolution.

The concept of a legitimate revolution necessarily became a partisan historicophilosophical concept, since its claim to generality rested on the existence of its contrary, "reaction" or "counterrevolution." While revolution was initially induced by its opponents as well as its proponents, once established in its legitimacy, it proceeded to continually reproduce its foe as a means through which it could remain permanent.

Here, the extent to which the concept of revolution has, since 1789, reassumed the logic of civil war becomes quite clear. For the modern professional revolutionary, the determined struggle by legal as well as illegal means belongs to the anticipated course of a revolution; the revolutionary feels free to use any means available because the revolution is, for him, legitimate. The elasticity and pliability of a historicophilosophical "reinsurance" depends on "the Revolution" providing a lasting title of legitimacy in the form of a metahistorical constant.[32]

In this way the historicophilosophical value of "civil war" is displaced. For instance, when Leninism declares and initiates civil war as the sole legitimate form of war (to abolish war altogether), the particular state and its social organization are not the only space of action and target of civil war. At stake is the abolition of domination in general: the fulfillment of the historical goal is thus posed as a global and infinite task.

Applied to our present international political situation, the question arises how the hypostasized legitimacy of civil war relates to the background legitimacy of permanent world revolution. Since the end of the Second World War, our planet has seen a raging succession of civil wars, burning on between the great power blocs. From Greece to Vietnam and Korea, from Hungary to Algeria to the Congo, from the Near East to Cuba and again to Vietnam—limited civil wars, whose awfulness is, however, boundless, stretch around the globe. We have to ask whether these numerous, regionally limited but globally conducted civil wars did not long ago consume and replace the concept of legitimate and permanent revolution. Has not the "world revolution" been reduced to an empty formula which can be appropriated pragmatically by the most diverse groups of countries and flogged to death?

The concept that contrasted with the civil wars of the past was that of the state. And the traditional doctrine of *Staatsräson* considered wars to be a vent preventing civil wars. According to this theory, war served the purpose of social relief and was often enough—viewed eurocentrically—discharged abroad. In the epoch of European imperialism, this period already belonged to the past. But since the time when the infinite geographical surface of our globe shrunk into a finite and interdependent space of action, all wars have been transformed into civil wars. In this situation it becomes increasingly uncertain which sphere the social, industrial, and emancipatory process of revolution might occupy. In any case, "world revolution" is subject to political constraints because of the civil wars, which are not contained in its historicophilosophical program, it appears to conduct. This is apparent in the contemporary nuclear stalemate.

Since 1945 we have lived between latent and open civil wars whose terribleness can still be outbid by a nuclear war, as if the civil wars that rage around the world are, reversing the traditional interpretation, our ultimate savior from total destruction. If this infernal inversion has become the unspoken law of present international politics, a further question arises. What kind of political title does a civil war possess which feeds off both the permanence of revolution and the fear of global catastrophe? The clarification of the reciprocal relation of these two positions can no longer be the business of a *Begriffsgeschichte* as presented here.

We wish to guard against the acceptance or misinterpretation of all previous definitions as the reality of our history. Nevertheless, *Begriffsgeschichte* reminds us—even when it becomes involved with ideologies—that in politics, words and their usage are more important than any other weapon.

# Historical Prognosis in Lorenz von Stein's Essay on the Prussian Constitution

## I

"It is possible to forecast the approaching future, but one would not wish to prophesy individual events."[1] The truth of this statement, formulated by Stein in 1850, finds confirmation in his most important work. In terms of intellectual history, one might perceive in this pronouncement a secularized version of Christian prophets of doom whose lasting certainty always exceeded the accuracy or inappropriateness of individual short-term expectations. Stein's declaration was, however, based on diligent sociohistorical and administrative studies and acquired its sense of immediacy from the historical circumstances in which it arose. Stein delivered prognoses because he had made the movement of modern history—and hence its futurity—his diagnostic theme. In retrospect, it can be seen that his predictions have endured the test of history, more indeed than in a merely historiographic sense. The power of events, those of the past as well as of our present, has proved the truth of his prognoses.

Stein's long-term forecasts are an integral moment of our history, like those of Tocqueville, Bruno Bauer, Friedrich List, or Donoso Cortes. In their form of reflection and their vision, they belong to the revolutionary era; they point to our century and have only the slightest attachment to a previous epoch. The art of soothsaying and foreknowledge is an old one, in whatever form. What is the historical space in which Stein was able to develop his art to profound mastery? What distinguishes Lorenz von Stein from other historical thinkers?

Until the eighteenth century it was an almost universally accepted doctrine that one could, from the history of the past, learn lessons for the future. Knowledge of what had been and foreknowledge of what was yet to come remained connected through a quasi-natural horizon of experience, within which nothing essentially new could occur. This was as true of a believing Christian awaiting the End as of a Machiavellian man of politics. History (*Historie*) comprised a collection of instructive alien experiences which could be appropriated by learning. Thus one held oneself to be equipped to repeat the successes of the past instead of committing old mistakes in the present. In the contained space of personal politics among the European upper strata, and still at the beginning of processual change brought about by technology and industrial capitalism, history provided and ensured juristic, moral, theological, and political constancy. No change was without its divine sense or naturally conditioned regularity. Surprises had their higher or lower meanings. The thesis of the iteratability and hence the instructiveness of historical experience was itself a moment of experience: *historia magistra vitae*. No prediction departed from the space of previous history, and this was true in the same way for astrological and theological prophecies which remained tied to planetary laws or old promises.

During the Enlightenment all this changed slowly and then, with the French Revolution, quite radically. The horizon of possible prognostication was at first broadened, then finally broken through. While the exemplary nature of the Ancients or the figures of biblical typology retained their control of the future until the eighteenth century, with the turbulence of the Revolution this was no longer possible. The decade from 1789 to 1799 was experienced by the participants as the start of a future that had never yet existed. Even those who invoked their knowledge of the past could not avoid confirming the incomparability of the Revolution. Its incomparability did not so much consist in the new circumstances, suggested Rupert Kornmann, as "in the extreme speed with which they arise or are introduced. . . . Our contemporary history is a repetition of the actions and events of thousands of years, all in the briefest of possible periods."[2] Even those who were not taken by surprise were overwhelmed by the accelerated tempo, which seemed to open up a new and different age.

Through its consciousness of a general renewal, which consigned previous history to a faded prehistory, the Revolution altered the space of experience. The new history became a long-term process which, while it could be directed, all the same unfolded itself above the heads of the participants. This being the case, conclusions drawn from the past about the future not only seem out of place but also appear impossible. The "ruse of reason" forbids one to learn from history; it subjects men. Apart from the accuracy of Hegel's dictum, it indicates a new experience. Hegel's experience does invoke "history," but history in its totality, which, in its rising consciousness of liberty, was drawn to the French Revolution. The processual course of this history is always unique.[3] *Historie* and prognosis henceforth alter their historical quality, losing their naive-pragmatic coherence and regaining it at a more reflective level. Lorenz von Stein will testify to this.

In fact, the Revolution liberated a new future, whether sensed as progressive or as catastrophic, and in the same fashion a new past; the increasingly alien quality of the latter rendered it a special object of historical-critical science. Progress and historism, apparently mutually contradictory, offer the face of Janus, that of the nineteenth century. Only a few citizens of this century were successful in observing this dual countenance without discontent. Lorenz von Stein was one of them. He managed to assimilate historical data and facts with immense learning without at the same time losing sight of the future as the more urgent prospect. On the contrary, this became the regulating principle of his knowledge.

"History in and for itself"—we find this expression from the last third of the eighteenth century on—and the "work of history," once established as a challenge, required more than a simple historical retrospect.[4] They gave rise to a philosophy of history and pointed toward a future both unknown and unimagined. Thus progress was not simply an ideological mode of viewing the future; it corresponded, rather, to a new everyday experience which was fed continually from a number of sources: technical development, the increase of population, the social unfolding of human rights, and the corresponding shifts in political systems. A "labyrinth of movement" developed, as Stein once characterized it,[5] and he made this the objective of his research. If, in the course of his historical analyses and social diagnoses, he makes acute prognoses which still have the capacity to surprise us today, then this is because he knew how, in the realm of progress, it was possible to develop historical doctrines.

But this alone is not sufficient to set Lorenz von Stein apart. The challenge of progress reacted everywhere upon *Historie*. Since the revolutionary break had dislocated the traditional space of experience, tearing past and future apart, *Historie*'s didactic role also altered its traditional quality. The Ciceronian topos gained a new dimension, a specifically temporal dimension which, in the perspective of a comparatively natural and static history, it could not yet have. A space of experience opened, for the most part consciously, whose perspective was traced in terms of the different phases of the completed Revolution. After the fall of Napoleon, the stages through which the French Revolution had run offered a new course of history in the form of a model, with which the coming generations believed it possible to read off the future course of their own history, depending on their political persuasion. In other words, even the progressive prospect of the future was oriented by its own historical experiential space—the French Revolution and the unfolding of its stages. On top of that, there followed, from West to East, the experience of industrialization, together with its previously unknown social consequences. What set Stein apart was his ability to place himself in a historical-critical relation to this labile, constantly shifting, experiential space of the present.

The movement of modernity was the dominating theme of his research. For historical-critical research in general, the posing of such an actual problem remained a gamble, and its greatest representatives increasingly restricted themselves to the preterit tense and renounced a direct applicability of their knowledge and teaching. Perthes had some difficulty finding contributors for his great publishing project on the history of European states, which dared to touch on contemporary matters: the present seemed to change from day to day and thus evade knowledge that was scientifically assured.[6]

Stein was among the few researchers in the past century who did not capitulate before this acceleration and flee into history. He submitted his research to the principle of a prognosis that should be adequate to the shifting temporalities.

The old conditions are overturned, new ones appear and are even themselves resisted by newer conditions; whole legislative apparatuses change, contradictory orders pass rapidly; it is as if historical writing is no longer in a position to keep up with history.

Although the young Stein in 1843 characterized the situation in this fashion, he continued:

Nevertheless, closer examination reveals quite the opposite. As all these various forms appear at a stroke, so they permit themselves to be comprehended at a glance. Here is the major difference between this and previous times: now a correct judgment depends more on the point of view, while previously it depended more on historical knowledge.[7]

This insight into the dependence of all historical knowledge on a positional quality was already recognized in the eighteenth century, just as the Enlighteners took pleasure in looking back on the pure erudition of past times. But Stein was not concerned with making the subjectivism of historical judgment conscious, nor with emphasizing the originality of his own work. Stein's wish to grab hold of history from one viewpoint—a wish that was registered in every question he posed—corresponded to the structure of movement in modern history. In terms of the history of ideas, one might want to place him on the margins of a historicophilosophical certainty sustained by the Spirit of the World, or on the approaches to an epistemological relativism which consumed all certainty. But the specific localization (*Standortsbezogenheit*) of the Steinian diagnosis does not permit of such miscalculation. It is this alone that provides the perspective in terms of which social and political movements can be arranged. If history is experienced as the movement of diverse streams whose mutual relations constantly undergo different degrees of intensification, petrification, or acceleration, then its general motion can only be apprehended from a consciously adopted point of view. Stein had attained such a viewpoint by uniting critical distance with progressive perspective. This is what distinguished him as much from professional historians as from utopian philosophers of history. He used the tools of the one to disclose the unilinear teleologies of the other as ideal constructions, just as he knew how to appraise, without prejudice, the interests, hopes, and plans of all parties as the historical potentialities of a common movement.

It would be wrong, therefore, to treat Stein's position as intermediate to an increasingly petrified historical idealism, on the one hand, and a rising empiricism, on the other. This would miss the point of his individuality. Stein did without both a totalizing design and a precisely additive chronology. Both aspects—the metahistorical and the chronological—are, however, taken up in his theory of history. He thereby stripped them of all utopian pretense and robbed them of the accidental quality of daily politics, opening up a prospect of the great movement of history.

Stein developed a theory of history.[8] He used it to open up all events: their enduring preconditions, on the one hand, and the forces lending them motion, on the other. Stein was a historical ontologist in the full and ambiguous sense of the word. Historical duration and historical contingency (*Zeitlichkeit*) were separated by Stein only theoretically and only to establish the uniqueness of given circumstances. This theoretical procedure has proved itself. He gained two mutually illuminating aspects without having to make either of them absolute.

Stein was able to assess the possible trends of the given social classes and declining *Stände* through the theoretical development of enduring structures without, however, crossing the boundary of utopianism. He ventured statements almost axiomatic in nature which referred to permanent conditions of the modern state of motion. Among them are statements on economic society, in which a struggle for political power unleashed by a new legal order remorselessly induced the imposition of class domination; and claims that pure democracy would remain unattainable; that the propertyless, as such, would have only a slim chance of achieving power, and if successful, would in any case not put an end to unfreedom; that the increasing preponderance of administration as constitutional questions diminished would not eliminate problems of rule, but would pose them anew and only occasionally alter them; and that all social order rested on the distribution of property, and consequently the state had a responsibility to regulate the distribution of property to prevent class society from degenerating into civil war. The list could be extended.

All these elements of history, which Stein subsumed under the then fashionable nomenclature "laws," had only a limited duration within his theory. They did cover the "whole" of history, but only to the extent that it could be experienced. "To whom has the future ever revealed itself?"[9] asked the same man who was able to venture predictions. Only in the bedrock of his structural declarations was Stein able to make clear the motion of the movement and to indicate its possible direction. Here is the other aspect of his theory, in which duration and time are harmonized in a historical ontology.

Stein's involvement with this modern movement (and hence also with the future) unavoidably raised, alongside the question of the existing (*Sein*), the question of what was and ought to be (*das Sollen und Wollen)*; but he did not confuse them in a utopian manner. Stein's capacity to project aspirations into the future is extraordinary. Instead of remaining wishes and hopes, these aspirations were used to sharpen a perception of the possible. He was a sociologist whose gaze was politically unclouded. While postulating the desirability of a republic of mutual interest by setting in relation *social democracy* and *social monarchy*, he simultaneously recognized that the administration of the future might well become task-oriented but that it would not be without a dominating power. One should not be misled by the contemporary cast of Stein's formulations; he tied his hopes to optimal possibilities, while at the same time knowing that in social conflicts, all "attempts at a solution through the use of weapons . . . [could not bring about] a final decision."[10] He knew that the problems of a transitional period, apparent since the time of emancipation, could not be resolved by posing an apparently given objective and the associated means for its realization, but only through knowledge of the paths and direction that had to be maintained.

Thus, Stein was no political fortune-teller, predicting this or that, estimating cameralistically, interpreting chimeras, or calculating politically. Stein addressed himself to what had become possible only since the French Revolution: the long-term conditions of the possibility of social movement. In so doing, he freely overused the claim of necessity. But it would be wrong to accuse him of historicophilosophical arrogance on account of this. Certainly, from the point of view of a strict historian, he oversteps the border of tautology, since the addition of the epithet "necessary" to a cited fact can never augment its substance. Consecration through necessity changes facticity not one jot. But it was different for Stein who, when considering the uniqueness of modern events as he proposed some forecast, had also to take into account the uniqueness of what would succeed them. He thus made use of the category of the necessary, limiting it, however, to his theoretical discourse. Applied to his research, the concept of the necessary coincided with the demonstration of long-term, irreversible tendencies. Only in the course of critical research—sociological and historical— was he able to establish the minimum of future necessity that made prediction possible with a maximum of probability. Here, he went further than the professional historians with whom he was contemporary. But he did not go as far as the naive progressive who confused their own optimism with far-sight.

Stein was therefore distinguished by his philosophy of history: it united enduring structures and forces of motion, but only so that they could be historically verified. The transposition of the course of advancement into foreknowledge was possible only through the medium of scientific proof. If Stein obtained empirical proof *hic et nunc*, then a historically immanent indicator of action to be taken was contained in it. This did not concern the today and tomorrow of a political prognosis that alters the situation as soon as it is made. Stein proposed rational, conditional prognoses which, within a specified course of necessity, opened up an extensive space of possibility. His predictions therefore contained lessons of history; but these were lessons that acted only indirectly on praxis, clarifying the inevitable so that freedom of action might be engendered. "It is possible to forecast the approaching future, but one would not wish to prophesy individual events."

An exemplary case of this art is to be found in the short essay on the Prussian constitutional question of 1852.

## II

Stein published his essay in Cotta's quarterly journal,[11] which was a rallying point for the bourgeois intelligentsia and the public which they constituted. This publication first appeared in 1838, in the *Vormärz*, continued through the Revolution of 1848, and finally ceased publication in 1869 between the wars of unification. This is the epoch that Stein took in at a glance, as one might say today. Summarized in one sentence, his basic thesis was that Prussia was not capable of constitutional rule (*verfassungsfähig*) in the Western sense, but that all the historical barriers to the creation of a Prussian constitution resulted in pressure toward the formation of a German constitution. Here, we have a structural prognosis whose rectitude was demonstrated in the years 1860 to 1871, despite the actual path taken in these years being unforeseeable—the path that Bismarck as Prussian prime minister felt constrained to follow during this decade, and which he therefore trod.

Stein's Prussian essay is an appendix to his great work *The History of the Social Movement in France*, which he had published two years earlier, in 1850. The intellectual connecting link is to be found in the final chapter of the theoretical introduction, in which Stein assessed the degree to which one could, by analogy, draw conclusions from

France's situation for Germany.[12] It was here that he formulated the decisive distinction between the two nations and their modes of motion. The simple doctrine of stages, according to which a direct line connected the society of orders, the Liberal and the Social movements, was held for the German case to be crossed with a national question that had in France long since been resolved. The paradoxical outcome of this, argued Stein, summarizing the German experience of the 1848 Revolution, was that both tendencies, Liberal and Social, mutually paralyzed each other. The rectitude of this idea has endured longer than Stein could have foreseen. The principles of a free society and those of the Social blocked each other and, in this way, both played into the hands of Reaction. The conclusion drawn by Stein in 1852 was that during the coming period, all social questions would be displaced by the nationalistic movement, only to rapidly gain ground once more with the achievement of unification. That is what in fact happened. It was within this prognostic horizon that Stein sought to deal specifically with the Prussian constitutional problem.

In considering national unity, Stein did not succumb to premature conclusions based on the analogies that offered themselves. This set him apart from the majority of national Liberals. His point of departure was neither one of patriotic hopes which interpreted the present in terms of some future condition nor, despite his recognition of its desirability, from a *rechtsstaatlich* objective. Instead, he preserved himself from "confusing that which is abstractly right with that which is practically possible."[13] Stein sought the concrete preconditions of a constitution, its conditions of possibility. "For constitutional law does not arise out of right established by laws, but rather out of right established by relations."[14] Viewed in this way, for Stein, the parliamentary model does not by itself adequately guarantee its construction. It would be wrong to attribute an illiberality to him on account of this, merely because he made unpleasant truths apparent, truths whose unpleasantness he himself keenly felt. Stein, however, thought historically, and not in a utopian fashion; he drew conclusions from a known present for the possibilities of tomorrow, moving from diagnosis to prognosis, and not vice versa. "But here is confirmed the familiar experience by which men would rather err while following established patterns of thinking than be proved right while following unaccustomed ideas."[15]

While the factors contained in the Steinian diagnosis will be outlined below, it is not desirable to break down the texture of his mode of proof, nor is it possible for historical description to surpass *ex post* Lorenz von Stein's theoretical achievement. His essay is as singular as the theme that he addresses.

It must be said at once that the military conflict which gave rise to the Prussian constitutional crisis, and which was resolved only with German unity, had not been predicted by Stein. He had, nevertheless, foreseen that "wherever constitution and government become involved in serious conflict it is always the government which overcomes the constitution."[16] Stein had dissected the intellectual contradictions of the constitutional system with an acuity that provoked alarm, without, however, denying the historical viability of this system. He subsumed the Prussian Constitution of 1850 under the category "sham constitutionalism." Here the opposition did not sit in parliament; more, the parliament was established in the opposition; here, the government formed parties, rather than parties forming the government. These were general statements on political structure which have been borne out by French history since 1815. The example of conflict in Prussia was defined as a "dispute without referee,"[17] in that popular representation would be worsted.

What were the reasons advanced by Stein that permitted him to make such an apodictic prognosis, a prognosis that broke apart the Liberal movement's horizon of expectation and that placed itself at right angles to the progressive succession of stages which quickened the hopes of the up-and-coming citizen?

Stein sought three preconditions for a robust parliamentary constitution founded within society: historical, economic, and social. He did not consider any of these three to be present in Prussia.

1. Prussia lacked entirely the historical precondition of a general political (*landständisch*) tradition of the sort which in the West had proved to be an integrating force on the road to nation-building. Prussia lacked territorial coherence, was bereft of the historical roots of popular representation, and instead owed its rise to the royal army and state administration. "It is thus the government which provides both the constructive and maintaining elements in Prussia."[18] In this formulation, Stein took up a commonplace of Prussian administration according to which the unity of the state since the great reforms had been underwritten by the unity of administration.[19] Not that Stein had

great sympathy for the "pullulating bureaucracy," but he did take account of its organization and self-confidence: any popular representation (not historically given) could be perceived by the Prussian administration only in terms of "participation" in the state, which was to be either promoted or regulated. A road that led to popular sovereignty via the administration was hardly accessible.

On the other hand, the old *ständisch* tradition, where it survived in East Elbia, led ultimately into a parliamentary path. Hardenberg was forced away from this course of constitutionalization, since every step along it strengthened the old *Stände* who, once established at the level of the state as a whole, would have blocked the very reforms necessary to found the economic preconditions of the constitution. Above all, the territorial *Stände* constituted where they were most heavily concentrated, at the local district level, a system of regional checks which regionally blocked the formation of a civil society (*staatsbürgerliche Gesellschaft*). Through the elections of the *Landräte*, they indirectly controlled the numerous self-governing towns, and in the rural East they dominated, more or less legally, nearly half of the population. Stein's diagnosis was, therefore, accurate in a dual sense: the old *ständisch* traditions not only made no contribution to the construction of a free society, they in fact stood in its way. The Revolution had proved this. Hardly a single owner of a *Rittergut* entered the National Assembly by means of a general election; but from the positions they retained in the army, they were able to organize the counterrevolution and reestablish the local pattern of rule.

2. The constitutional viability of Prussia was much less clearly subject to dispute when economic conditions were considered. In this sphere the Prussian administration had held fast, practically without hesitation and in spite of the reactionary nature of domestic politics, to the implementation of liberal economic objectives, not the least in their stubborn struggle against the old *ständisch* positions in town and country. The administration had given rise to free economic forms which reduced the contrast of East and West and which increasingly brought with them provisions of a generalized nature. The number of general laws increased steadily from the end of the thirties: the Railway Act (1838); the Law for the Limitation of Child Labor (1839); laws on domicile, begging, and poverty (1842, 1843); the Law of Limited Liability (1843); establishment of the Trade Ministry (1844); the general regulation of industrial occupations (1845); and the general establishment

of chambers of commerce, shortly before the Revolution. Without any doubt, the Prussian administration had created the economic conditions that inclined *homo oeconomicus* toward participation in the exercise of political power. "While historical justification is wanting, popular representation has an adequate foundation in the economic life (*Güterleben*) of the people," Stein wrote.[20]

Nevertheless, in 1852, Stein did not anticipate the eventual inevitability and necessity of the victory of popular representation over administration. Instead, he referred to the greatest achievement of Prussian administration, the *Zollverein*. At that time, it was undergoing a severe crisis. Stein thought it impossible for the administration to surrender its efforts precisely when it was a case of preventing domestic Prussian conflicts of interest spreading over into the endangered Pan-German economic unity. Stein was proved right here as well, for his structural prognosis was realized according to the limitations he had indicated: in 1868, the first meeting of the expected Pan-German representative assembly took place in the form of the *Zollparlament*, the preliminary to the *Reichstag*.[21] It was in the economic sphere that the comparatively less serious barriers had existed, and they were the first to be removed.

3. Stein saw the major obstacle to a flourishing popular representative body on Prussian soil as Prussia's social conditions. This leads to the third and most decisive point that he introduced. As is known, Lorenz von Stein unraveled the course of modern history, in which the older *societas civilis* slowly disintegrated, according to the contrast of State and Society. The actual nature of this conceptual couple—and this involved, if we might be allowed some slight exaggeration, a heuristic principle more than tangible factors—was demonstrated in its application to the Prussian constitutional problem. According to his theory, every leading class in a society had the tendency to transform its constitution into an instrument of domination over the lower classes. He regarded the conditionality of all public and social law on the social movement as a fundamental so significant that "the ultimate aim of all historical writing" consisted in its demonstration.[22]

The findings Stein came up with through the application of his theoretical premises to Prussian reality were astounding enough. He ascertained that "this state does not possess a social order peculiar to itself, and this is the real meaning of the oft-cited expression that there is no such thing as a Prussian people."[23]

The antinomy "State and Society" did not, therefore, fall into the then current sense which articulated it with respect to a given arrangement of parliament and government, the charged field between monarchic principle and popular sovereignty. The internal "duality on which Prussia is based" thus was not found by Stein in the usual contest between political state and bourgeois society, which, through their mutual dependency, fell into conflict. The duality of Prussia rested instead on the absence of the kind of homogeneous society which could have found adequate expression in a constitution. Seen in this light, the constitutional conflict was the outcome of a completely different conflict: how it might be possible to organize the State of a heterogeneous and shifting Society. This outcome sounds both alien and astonishing.

Now, it was taken for granted at that time that Prussia possessed neither territorial, confessional, legal, nor linguistic unity. Stein took account of all these factors, but his attention was primarily taken up by the question of social structure. Some kind of order capable of supporting a constitution must be detected here if the constitution was to prove anything more than a sham. For this reason, Stein queried the legal conditions that did in fact secure in Prussia de facto a free economic society. True to his historico-ontological theory, he sought the prevailing elements of economic order in the distribution of property; thus he saw a political people initially determined by the "special social order of the population,"[24] and not in terms of race, nationality, or language. Armed with these general structural questions, he traced the peculiar historical place of Prussia within the greater modern movement. The conclusion he reached was that the social articulation and diversity of Prussia displayed insufficient homogeneity for the creation and maintenance of a parliamentary constitution.

The fertility of Stein's theory was proved by the manner in which, transcending more simplistic conceptions of social order, it brought to light the peculiarity of the Prussian state. To use another phrase of Stein's, Prussia had an economic society but no *staatsbürgerlich* society. So that this might be properly appreciated, some remarks will be made on the Prussian *Bürgertum*, which was the presumptive bearer of the order within which constitutional law and social structure would have to coincide.

The social development of the nineteenth century had in fact resulted in the social fragmentation and political mediation of the Prussian bourgeoisie. At the higher level, a significant, financially powerful, and adventurous stratum entered the open *Stand* of *Rittergutsbesitzer*. Around the midpoint of the century, this stratum already possessed more than 40 percent of the estates previously held by the nobility. Once installed in the countryside, these *homines novi* were absorbed by the nobility within at most one generation. In other words, the noble had not lost priority over his privileges. The liberal agrarian reforms occurred at a time when the older *Stände* could strengthen themselves at the cost of the rising bourgeoisie. Another stratum, particularly the educated bourgeoisie, entered state employment. The variety of exemptions that bound both direct and indirect officials to the state was abolished in 1848, but to become a member of the administration still implied accession to quasi-*ständisch* powers and rights. The corps of officials represented the last *Stand* in which social and state functions still coincided; here also, a fusion took place between bourgeoisie and nobility at the expense of the former. Compared with the social prestige of the intelligentsia who, in 1848, made up about 60 percent of all representatives in Berlin, the individual *Bürger*, the entrepreneurs and merchants, were politically overshadowed, despite their important representatives and their economic power. In 1848, the Prussian bourgeoisie was homogeneous enough to begin a revolution but not sufficiently so to ensure its victory.[25]

However this picture might be corrected or elaborated, Stein's investigation of the distribution of property and the social organization appropriate to it proved successful as a strategy for assessing the constitutional maturity of a society. This heterogeneous society was in itself not yet capable of supporting a suitable constitution.

It now becomes apparent why Stein did not only define the State as one dominated by classes and interests, but also as one which was *sui generis* a historical entity. It was his dualistic appraisal that made it possible to describe the constitutional reality of the Prussian state and, more than this, to predict the course of the constitutional conflict and its outcome. This should suffice to protect Stein from accusations of methodological inconsistency on account of his idealistic and normatively colored conception of social monarchy. The historical cast of his thought is contained in his combining the statement of structural conditions with the analysis of unique factors.

The fact that the Prussian state, especially during the fifties, represented particular *ständisch* desires and rigorous class interests did not prevent it (considering the diversity of its fragmented social strata) from being more than a state founded on interest. Its modernity is marked out by the manner in which it drove forward, in the realm of economic policy, the transformation of a society of orders into a class society. In some respects it was even the non-*ständisch* proletariat that constituted from East to West by its social condition, if not its consciousness, the first homogeneous stratum of Prussian society. In this fashion, the state became *nolens volens* additionally responsible for the social question Stein had expected to become politically dominant only after the foundation of the *Reich*. From this time on, it was no longer a specifically Prussian problem but, rather, one of the new industrial society and a common German constitution. Stein's essay ends with both a prediction of and a demand for such a constitution.

Lorenz von Stein had theoretically anticipated the Prussian constitutional conflict and its resolution within a German *Reich*, not as the program of a German nationalist politics, but as the course of political probability determined by economic and social forces. His conditional prognosis was sufficiently elastic to describe the barriers and necessities, if not the timetable and constitutional form, that would arise in the future.

The rectitude of the Steinian analysis cannot and should not be evaluated in terms of a reality which subsequently emerged. In many respects this reality was also the outcome of contingency. Bismarck remains the unique individual without whose presence unification would not have happened in the way that it did. That Stein's prognosis was realized nevertheless indicates to us, rather, the historical clarity of his theory: it excludes the impossible and opens up the prospect of a historical reality in which "the given relations [always] mean something other and more than what they themselves are."[26]

# II

## Theory and Method in the Historical Determination of Time

# Begriffsgeschichte and Social History

According to a well-known saying of Epictetus, it is not deeds that shock humanity, but the words describing them.[1] Apart from the Stoic point that one should not allow oneself to be disturbed by words, the contrast between "pragmata" and "dogmata" has aspects other than those indicated by Epictetus's moral dictum. It draws our attention to the autonomous power of words without the use of which human actions and passions could hardly be experienced, and certainly not made intelligible to others. This epigram stands in a long tradition concerned with the relation of word and thing, of the spiritual and the lived, of consciousness and being, of language and the world. Whoever takes up the relation of *Begriffsgeschichte* to social history is subject to the reverberations of this tradition. The domain of theoretical principles is quickly broached, and it is these principles which will here be subjected to an investigation from the point of view of current research.[2]

The association of *Begriffsgeschichte* to social history appears at first sight to be loose, or at least difficult. For a *Begriffsgeschichte* concerns itself (primarily) with texts and words, while a social history employs texts merely as a means of deducing circumstances and movements that are not, in themselves, contained within the texts. Thus, for example, when social history investigates social formations or the construction of constitutional forms—the relations of groups, strata, and classes—it goes beyond the immediate context of action in seeking medium- or long-term structures and their change. Or it might introduce economic theorems for the purpose of scrutinizing individual events and the course of political action. Texts and their attributed conditions of emergence here possess only a referential nature. The methods of *Begriffsgeschichte*, in contrast, derive from the sphere of a philosophical history of terminology, historical philology, semasiology, and onomatology; the results of its work can be evaluated continually through the exegesis of texts, while at the same time, they are based on such exegesis.

This initial contrast is superficially quite striking. Once engaged methodologically, however, it becomes apparent that the relation of *Begriffsgeschichte* and social history is more complex than would be the case if the former discipline could in fact be reduced to the latter. This is immediately apparent when considering the domain of objects which the respective disciplines study. Without common concepts there is no society, and above all, no political field of action. Conversely, our concepts are founded in politicosocial systems that are far more complex than would be indicated by treating them simply as linguistic communities organized around specific key concepts. A "society" and its "concepts" exist in a relation of tension which is also characteristic of its academic historical disciplines.

An attempt will be made to clarify the relation of both disciplines at three levels:

1. To what extent *Begriffsgeschichte* follows a classical critical-historical method, but by virtue of its greater acuity, also contributes to the tangibility of sociohistorical themes. Here, the analysis of concepts is in a subsidiary relation to social history.
2. To what extent *Begriffsgeschichte* represents an independent discipline with its own method, whose content and range are to be defined parallel to social history, while both disciplines, at the same time, mutually overlap.
3. To what extent *Begriffsgeschichte* poses a genuine historical claim without whose solution an effective social history cannot be practiced.

There are two limitations on the following considerations: first, they do not deal with linguistic history, even as a part of social history, but rather with the sociopolitical terminology relevant to the current condition of social history. Second, within this terminology and its numerous expressions, emphasis will be placed on concepts whose semantic "carrying capacity" extends further than the "mere" words employed in the sociopolitical domain.[3]

## The Method of *Begriffsgeschichte* and Social History

So that the critical-historical implications of *Begriffsgeschichte* might here be demonstrated to be a necessary aid to social history, it is most convenient to begin with an example. It comes from the time of the French, and of the emergent industrial, revolutions; hence, from a zone that was to prove decisive for the development both of sociology and of sociohistorical questions.

Hardenberg, in his well-known September Memorandum of the year 1807, drew up guidelines for the reorganization of the Prussian state. The entire state was to be socially and economically restructured according to the experiences of the French Revolution. Hardenberg wrote:

A rational system of ranks, not favoring one *Stand* over another, but rather providing the citizens of all *Stände* with their places alongside each other according to specific classes, must belong to the true needs of a state, and not at all to its immaterial needs.[4]

In order to understand what is, for Hardenberg's future reform policy, a programmatic statement, an exegesis is required which, through a critique of the sources, can unlock the specific concepts which the policy contains. The transfer of the traditional differentiation between "true" and "immaterial" from the *Stände* to the state was a conception current for just half a century and will not be examined here. What is initially striking, however, is that Hardenberg opposes the vertical ranking of the *Stände* with a horizontal articulation of classes. The *Standesordnung* is evaluated pejoratively insofar as it implies the favoring of one *Stand* over another, while all members of these *Stände* are, at the same time, citizens and as such should be equal. In this statement they do, as citizens, remain members of a *Stand*; but their functions are defined "according to specific classes," and it is in this way that a rational system of ranks should arise.

Such a statement, liberally sprinkled as it is with politico-social expressions, involves, on the purely linguistic level, not inconsiderable difficulties, even if the political point, exactly on account of its semantic ambiguity, is clear. The established society of orders is to be replaced by a society of citizens (formally endowed with equal rights), whose membership in classes (yet to be defined politically and economically) should make possible a new, state-based system of ranks.

It is clear that the exact sense can be obtained only by reference to the complete Memorandum; but it is also necessary to take into account the situation of the author and the addressee. Due regard also must be paid to the political situation and the social condition of contemporary Prussia; just as, finally, the use of language by the author, his contemporaries, and the generation preceding him, with whom he shared a specific linguistic community, must be considered. All of these questions belong to the usual critical-historical, and in particular historical-philological, method, even if problems arise that are not soluble by this method alone. In particular, this concerns the social structure of contemporary Prussia, which cannot be adequately comprehended without an economic, political, or sociological framework for investigation.

Specific restriction of our investigation to the concepts actually employed in such a statement proves decisive in helping us pose and answer the sociohistorical questions that lie beyond the comprehension of such a statement. If we pass from the sense of the sentence itself to the historical arrangement of the concepts used, such as *Stand*, "class," or "citizen," the diversity of the levels of contemporary experience entering this statement soon becomes apparent.

When Hardenberg talks of citizens (*Staatsbürger*), he is using a technical term that had just been minted, that is not to be found in the Prussian Civil Code, and that registered a polemical engagement with the old society of orders. Thus, it is a concept that is consciously deployed as a weapon in the struggle against the legal inequalities of the *Stände*, at a time when a set of civil rights which could have endowed the Prussian citizen with political rights did not exist. The expression was novel, pregnant with the future; it referred to a constitutional model yet to be realized. At the same time, at the turn of the century, the concept of *Stand* had an endless number of shades of meaning— political, economic, legal, and social—such that no unambiguous association can be derived from the word itself. Insofar as Hardenberg thought of *Stand* and privilege as the same thing, he critically undermined the traditional rights of domination and rule of the upper *Stände*, while in this context, the counterconcept was "class." At this time, the concept "class" possessed a similar variety of meanings, which overlapped here and there with those of *Stand*. Nevertheless, it can be said for the language in use among the German, and especially the Prussian, bureaucracies, that a class at that time was defined more in terms of economic and legal-administrative criteria than in terms of political status or birth. In this connection, for instance, the physiocratic tradition must be taken into account, a tradition within which the old *Stände* were first redefined according to economic criteria: a design which Hardenberg shared in its liberal economic intention. The use of "class" demonstrates that here a social model which points to the future is set in play, while the concept of *Stand* is related to a centuries-old tradition: it was once again given legal expression in the Civil Code, but the Code's ambivalence was already increasingly apparent and in need of reform.

Surveying the space of meaning of each of the central concepts employed here exposes, therefore, a contemporary polemical thrust; intentions with respect to the future; and enduring elements of past social organization, whose specific arrangement discloses a statement's meaning. The activity of temporal semantic construal simultaneously establishes the historical force contained within a statement.

Within the practice of textual exegesis, specific study of the use of politicosocial concepts and the investigation of their meaning thus assumes a sociohistorical status. The moments of duration, change, and futurity contained in a concrete political situation are registered through their linguistic traces. Expressed more generally, social conditions and their transformation become in this fashion the objects of analysis.

A question equally relevant to *Begriffsgeschichte* and social history concerns the time from which concepts can be used as indicators of politico-social change and historical profundity as rigorously as is the case with our example. It can be shown for German-speaking areas from 1770 onward that both new meanings for old words and neologisms proliferate, altering with the linguistic arsenal of the entire political and social space of experience, and establishing new horizons of expectation. This is stimulating enough without posing the question of priority in this process of change between the "material" and the "conceptual." The struggle over the "correct" concepts becomes socially and politically explosive.

Our author, Hardenberg, likewise sets great store by conceptual distinctions, insisting on linguistic rules which have, since the French Revolution, belonged to the everyday business of politicians. Thus he addressed noble estate owners in assemblies, as well as in writing, as "estate owners" (*Gutsbesitzer*), while he did not forbear from receiving representatives of regional *Kreisstände* quite properly as *ständische* deputies. "By confusing the names, the concepts also fall into disorder," Hardenberg's opponent, Marwitz, stated irritably, "and as a result the old Brandenburg Constitution is placed in mortal danger." While correct in his conclusion, Marwitz deliberately overlooked the fact that Hardenberg was using new concepts and hence initiating a struggle over the naming of the new form of social organization, a struggle which drags on through the following years in all written communication between the old *Stände* and the bureaucracy. Marwitz certainly recognized that what was at stake in this naming of *ständisch* organization was the title of right that he sought to defend. He therefore disavowed a mission of his fellow *Stand* members to the chancellor because they had announced themselves as "inhabitants" of the *Mark* Brandenburg. They could do that, he suggested, as long as the question concerned "the economic. If the issue, on the other hand, concerns our rights, then this single word—inhabitant—destroys the point of the mission."[5] In this fashion, Marwitz refused to follow any further the course toward which, on economic grounds, other members of his *Stand* were then inclined. They sought to exchange their political privileges for economic advantage.[6]

The semantic struggle for the definition of political or social position, and defending or occupying these positions by means of such a definition, is conflict which belongs quite certainly to all times of crisis that we can register in written sources. Since the French Revolution, this struggle has become sharper and has altered structurally; concepts no longer merely serve to define given states of affairs, they reach into the future. Increasingly, concepts of the future were created; positions that were to be captured had first to be formulated linguistically before it was possible to even enter or permanently occupy them. The substance of many concepts was thus reduced in terms of actual experience and their aspirations to realization proportionally increased. Actual, substantial experience and the space of expectation coincide less and less. It is in this tendency that the coining of numerous "isms" belongs, serving as concepts for assembly and movement of newly ordered and mobilized masses, stripped of the organizational framework of the *Stände*. The breadth of usage of such expressions reached, as today, from slogan to scientifically defined concept. One needs only to think of "conservatism," "liberalism," or "socialism."

Ever since society has been swept into industrial movement, the political semantic of its related concepts has provided a means of comprehension in the absence of which, today, the phenomena of the past cannot be perceived. It is necessary only to think of the shifts in meaning and the function of the concept "revolution," which at first offered a model formula for the probable recurrence of events; was then reminted as a concept of historicophilosophical objective and political action; and is for us today an indicator of structural change. Here, *Begriffsgeschichte* becomes an integral part of social history.

From this, a methodologically minimal claim follows: namely, that social and political conflicts of the past must be interpreted and opened up via the medium of their contemporary conceptual limits and in terms of the mutually understood, past linguistic usage of the participating agents.

Thus the conceptual clarification of the terms introduced here by way of example, such as *Stand*, class, estate owner, owner, the economic, inhabitant, and citizen, serve as a prerequisite for interpreting the conflict between the Prussian reform group and the Prussian Junkers. The fact that the parties involved overlapped personally and socially makes it all the more necessary to semantically clarify the political and social fronts within this stratum, so that we are able to seize upon hidden interests and intentions.

*Begriffsgeschichte*, therefore, is initially a specialized method for source criticism, taking note as it does of the utilization of terminology relevant to social and political elements and directing itself in particular to the analysis of central expressions having social or political content. It goes without saying that historical clarification of past conceptual usage must refer not only to the history of language but also to sociohistorical data, for every semantic has, as such, an involvement with nonlinguistic contents. It is this that creates its precarious marginality for the linguistic sciences[7] and is, at the same time, the origin of its great advantages for the historical sciences. The condensation effected by the work of conceptual explanation renders past statements precise, bringing more clearly into view the contemporary intentional circumstances or relations in their form.

## The Discipline of *Begriffsgeschichte* and Social History

Up to this point the emphasis has been laid on source criticism in the specification of concepts as an aid in formulating sociohistorical questions: *Begriffsgeschichte* is, however, capable of doing more than this would indicate. More precisely, its methodology lays claim to an autonomous sphere which exists in a relation of mutually engendered tension with social history. From the historiographic point of view, specialization in *Begriffsgeschichte* had no little influence on the posing of questions within social history. First, it began as a critique of a careless transfer to the past of modern, context-determined expressions of constitutional argument,[8] and second, it directed itself to criticizing the practice in the history of ideas of treating ideas as constants, articulated in differing historical figures but of themselves fundamentally unchanging. Both elements prompted a greater precision in method, such that in the history of a concept it became possible to survey the contemporary space of experience and horizon of expectation, and to investigate the political and social functions of concepts, together with their specific modality of usage, such that (in brief) a synchronic analysis also took account of the situation and conjuncture.

Such a procedure is enjoined to translate words of the past and their meanings into our present understanding. Each history of word or concept leads from a determination of past meanings to a specification of these meanings for us. Insofar as this procedure is reflected in the method of *Begriffsgeschichte*, the synchronic analysis of the past is supplemented diachronically. It is a methodological precept of diachrony that it scientifically defines anew the registration of the past meanings of words.

Over time, this methodological perspective consistently and substantially transforms itself into a history of the particular concept in question. Insofar as concepts, during this second phase of investigation, are detached from their situational context, and their meanings ordered according to the sequence of time and then ordered with respect to each other, the individual historical analyses of concepts assemble themselves into a history of the concept. Only at this level is historical-philological method superseded, and only here does *Begriffsgeschichte* shed its subordinate relation to social history.

Nevertheless, the sociohistorical payoff is increased. Precisely because attention is directed in a rigorously diachronic manner to the persistence or change of a concept does the sociohistorical relevance of the results increase. To what extent has the intentional substance of one and the same word remained the same? Has it changed with the passage of time, a historical transformation having reconstructed the sense of the concept? The persistence and validity of a social or political concept and its corresponding structure can only be appreciated diachronically. Words that have remained in constant use are not in themselves a sufficient indication of the stability of their substantial meaning. Thus, the standard term *Bürger* is devoid of meaning without an investigation of the conceptual change undergone by the expression "Bürger": from (*Stadt-*)*Bürger* (burgher) around 1700 via (*Staats-*)*Bürger* (citizen) around 1800 to *Bürger* (bourgeois) as a nonproletarian around 1900, to cite as an example only a very crude framework.

*Stadtbürger* was a concept appropriate to the *Stände*, in which legal, political, economic, and social definitions were indifferently united— definitions which, with other contents, made up the remaining concepts of the *Stand*.

Toward the end of the eighteenth century, the *Stadtbürger* was no longer defined in the *Allgemeines Landrecht* (Prussian Civil Code) in terms of a listing of positive criteria (as in the draft), but negatively, as belonging neither to the peasant or noble *Stand*. In this fashion, a claim was registered in a negative manner for a higher generality, which was then conceptualized as *Staatsbürger*. The negation of the negation was accordingly achieved as, in 1848, the *Staatsbürger* assumed positively determined rights which had previously been enjoyed only by "inhabitants" and shareholders of a free economic society. Against the background of the formal legal equality of a liberal economic society underwritten by the state, it was then possible to assign this *Bürger*, in a purely economic fashion, to a class according to which political or social functions were only subsequently derived. This generalization is true both for systems of voting by class and for Marx's theory.

It is the diachronic disposition of elements which discloses long-term structural changes. This is, for instance, characteristic of the creeping transformation of the meaning of *societas civilis*, or politically constituted society, to *bürgerliche Gesellschaft sine imperio*, which can finally be conceived as an entity separate from the state; this is a piece of knowledge relevant to social history, which can only be gained at the level of the reflections engendered by *Begriffsgeschichte*.[9]

Hence, the diachronic principle constitutes *Begriffsgeschichte* as an autonomous domain of research, which methodologically, in its reflection on concepts and their change, must initially disregard their extralinguistic content—the specific sphere of social history. Persistence, change, or novelty in the meaning of words must first be grasped before they can be used as indices of this extralinguistic content, as indicators of social structures or situations of political conflict.

Considered from a temporal aspect, social and political concepts can be arranged into three groups. First are such traditional concepts as those of Aristotelian constitutional thought, whose meanings have persisted in part and which, even under modern conditions, retain an empirical validity. Second are concepts whose content has changed so radically that, despite the existence of the same word as a shell, the meanings are barely comparable and can be recovered only historically. The variety of meanings attached today to the term *Geschichte*, which appears to be simultaneously its own subject and object, comes to mind, in contrast with the *Geschichten* and *Historien*, which deal with concrete realms of objects and persons; one could also cite "class" as distinct from the Roman *classis*. Third are recurrently emerging neologisms reacting to specific social or political circumstances that attempt to register or even provoke the novelty of such circumstances. Here, "communism" and "fascism" can be invoked.

Within this temporal scheme there are, of course, endless transitions and superimpositions. The history of the concept "democracy" can, for example, be considered under all three aspects. First, ancient democracy as a constantly given, potential constitutional form of the Polis: here are definitions, procedures, and regularities that can still be found in democracies today. The concept was modernized in the eighteenth century to characterize new organizational forms typical of the large modern state and its social consequences. Invocation of the rule of law and the principle of equality took up and modified old meanings. With respect to the social transformations following the industrial revolution, however, the concept assumed new valencies: it became a concept characterizing a state of expectation which, within a historicophilosophical perspective—be it legislative or revolutionary— claimed to satisfy newly constituted needs so that its meaning might be validated. Finally, "democracy" became a general concept replacing "republic" (*politeia*), that consigned to illegality all other constitutional types as forms of rule. This global universality, usable for a variety of distinct political tendencies, made it necessary to refurbish the concept by adding qualifying expressions. It was only in this manner that it could retain any functional effectivity: hence arise representative, Christian, social, and people's democracies, and so forth.

Persistence, change, and novelty are thus conceived diachronically along the dimension of meanings and through the spoken form of one and the same word. Temporally testing a possible *Begriffsgeschichte* according to persistence, change, and novelty leads to the disposition of persisting, overlapping, discarded, and new meanings which can only become relevant for a social history if the history of the concept has been subject to a prior and separate analysis. As an independent discipline, therefore, *Begriffsgeschichte* delivers indicators for social history by pursuing its own methods.

This restriction of analysis to concepts has to be elaborated further, so that the autonomy of the method can be protected from a hasty identification with sociohistorical questions related to extralinguistic content. Naturally, a linguistic history can be outlined which can itself be conceived as social history. A *Begriffsgeschichte* is more rigorously bounded. The methodological limitation to the history of concepts expressed in words must have a basis that renders the expressions "concept" and "word" distinguishable. In whatever way the linguistic triad of word (signification)—meaning (concept)—object is employed in its different variants, a straightforward distinction—initially prag-matic—can be made in the sphere of historical science: sociopolitical terminology in the source language possesses a series of expressions that, on the basis of critical exegesis, stand out definitively as concepts. Each concept is associated with a word, but not every word is a social and political concept. Social and political concepts possess a substantial claim to generality and always have many meanings—in historical science, occasionally in modalities other than words.

Thus it is possible to articulate or linguistically create a group identity through the emphatic use of the word "we," while such a procedure only becomes conceptually intelligible when the "we" is associated with collective terms such as "nation," "class," "friendship," "church," and so on. The general utility of the term "we" is substantiated through these expressions but on a level of conceptual generality.

The stamping of a word as a concept might occur without noticeable disturbance, depending on the linguistic use of the sources. This is primarily because of the ambiguity of all words, a property shared by concepts as words. Their common historical quality is based on this. This ambiguity can be read in diverse ways, according to whether a word can be taken as a concept or not. Intellectual or material meanings are indeed bound to the word, but they feed off the intended content, the written or spoken context, and the historical situation. This is equally true for both word and concept. In use, however, a word can become unambiguous. In contrast, a concept must remain ambiguous in order to be a concept. The concept is bound to a word, but is at the same time more than a word: a word becomes a concept when the plenitude of a politicosocial context of meaning and experience in and for which a word is used can be condensed into one word.

Consider the variety of objects that enter the word "state" so that it may become a concept: domination, domain, bourgeoisie, legislation, jurisdiction, administration, taxation, and army, to invoke only present-day terms. A variety of circumstances with their own terminology (and conceptuality) are taken up by the word "state" and made into a common concept. Concepts are thus the concentrate of several substantial meanings. The signification of a word can be thought separately from that which is signified. Signifier and signified coincide in the concept insofar as the diversity of historical reality and historical experience enter a word such that they can only receive their meaning in this one word, or can only be grasped by this word. A word presents potentialities for meaning; a concept unites within itself a plenitude of meaning. Hence, a concept can possess clarity but must be ambiguous. "All concepts escape definition that summarize semiotically an entire process; only that which has no history is definable" (Nietzsche). A concept binds a variety of historical experience and a collection of theoretical and practical references into a relation that is, as such, only given and actually ascertainable through the concept.

It becomes plain here that, while concepts have political and social capacities, their semantic function and performance is not uniquely derivative of the social and political circumstances to which they relate. A concept is not simply indicative of the relations which it covers; it is also a factor within them. Each concept establishes a particular horizon for potential experience and conceivable theory, and in this way sets a limit. The history of concepts is therefore able to provide knowledge which is not obtainable from empirical study (*Sachanalyse*). The language of concepts is a consistent medium in which experiential capacity and theoretical stability can be assessed. This can, of course, be done sociohistorically, but sight must not be lost of the method of *Begriffsgeschichte*.

Naturally, the autonomy of the discipline must not be allowed to lead to a diminution of actual historical materiality simply because the latter is excluded for a specific section of the investigation. On the contrary, this materiality is itself given voice by withdrawing the analytical frame from the linguistic constitution of political situations or social structures. As a historical discipline, *Begriffsgeschichte* is always concerned with political or social events and circumstances, although indeed, only with those which have been conceptually constituted and articulated in the source language. In a restricted sense it interprets history through its prevailing concepts, even if the words are used today, while in turn treating these concepts historically, even if their earlier usage must be defined anew for us today. If we were to formulate this in a somewhat exaggerated fashion, we could say that *Begriffsgeschichte* deals with the convergence of concept and history. History would then simply be that which had already been conceptualized as such. Epistemologically, this would imply that nothing can occur historically that is not apprehended conceptually. But apart from this overvaluation of written sources, which is neither theoretically nor historically sustainable, there lurks behind this theory of convergence the danger of an ontological misunderstanding of *Begriffsgeschichte*. This would result in the sociohistorical dissipation of the critical impulse toward the revision of the history of ideas or of intellectual history, and along with this, the potential critique of ideologies that *Begriffsgeschichte* can initiate.

Moreover, the method of *Begriffsgeschichte* breaks out of the naive circular movement from word to thing and back. It would be a theoretically irredeemable short circuit if history were to be constructed out of its own concepts, establishing a kind of identity between linguistically articulated *Zeitgeist* and the conjunction of events. Rather, there exists between concept and materiality a tension which now is transcended, now breaks out afresh, now appears insoluble. Between linguistic usage and the social materialities upon which it encroaches or to which it targets itself, there can always be registered a certain hiatus. The transformation of the meaning of words and the transformation of things, the change of situation and the urge to rename, correspond diversely with each other.

Methodological complications follow from this. The investigation of a concept cannot be carried out purely semasiologically; it can never limit itself to the meanings of words and their changes. A *Begriffsgeschichte* must always keep in view the need for findings relevant to intellectual or material history. Above all, the semasiological approach must alternate with the onomasiological; i.e., *Begriffsgeschichte* must register the variety of names for (identical?) materialities in order to be able to show how concepts are formed. So, for instance, the phenomenon of *Säkularisation* cannot be investigated solely on the basis of the expression itself.[10] For the historical treatment of words, parallel expressions like *Verweltlichung* (secularization) and *Verzeitlichung* (temporalization) must be introduced; the domain of church and constitutional law must be taken into account historically; and in terms of intellectual history, the ideological currents which crystallized around the expression must be examined—all before the concept *Säkularisation* is sufficiently worked up as a factor in and indicator of the history to which it relates.

To take another phenomenon, the federal structure of the old *Reich* belongs to long-term political and legal facticities which have, from the late Middle Ages down to the Federal Republic of today, laid down a specific framework of political potential and political action. The history of the word *Bund* by itself, however, is not adequate to clarify federal structure in the historical process. We can sketch this very roughly here. Formed in the thirteenth century, the term *Bund* was a relatively late creation of German jurisprudence. *Bundesabmachungen* (*Einungen*), insofar as they could not be subsumed under such Latin expressions as *foedus*, *unio*, *liga*, and *societas*, initially could only be employed orally in this legal language. At first, it was the aggregation of completed and named *Verbündnisse* that brought about the condensation into the institutional expression *Bund*. Then, with the increasing experience of *Bünde*, linguistic generalization was possible, which then became available as the concept *Bund*. From then on, it was possible to reflect conceptually on the relation of a *Bund* to the *Reich* and on the constitution of the *Reich* in the form of a *Bund*. But this possibility was barely made use of in the final decades of the Middle Ages. The concept's center of gravity remained associated with estate rights; in particular, designating *Städtebünde* (town unions), as opposed to *fürstlichen Einungen* (unions constituted of the rulers of principalities) or *ritterschaftlichen Gesellschaften* (societies of knights). The religious loading of the concept *Bund* in the Reformation era resulted—in contrast with the Calvinist world—in its political corrosion. As far as Luther was concerned, only God was capable of creating a *Bund*, and it was for this reason that the Schmalkand *Vorstand* never characterized itself as a *Bund*. It only became referred to as such historiographically at a much later time. Simultaneous and emphatic use of the term, in a religious as well as a political sense, by Müntzer and peasants in 1525 led to discrimination against usage in the form of a taboo. It thus went into retreat as a technical term of constitutional law, and the confessional forces assembled themselves under expressions which were initially interchangeable and neutral, such as *Liga* and *Union*. In the bloody disputes that followed, these expressions hardened into religious battle cries which in turn became notorious in the course of the Thirty Years War. From 1648 on, French terms like *Allianz* permeated the constitutional law of the states in the empire. Penetrated by terminology drawn from the Law of Nations, it was covertly subject to alteration. It was only with the dissolution of the old imperial *Standesordnung* that the expression *Bund* reemerged, and this time it did so at the levels of society, state, and law, simultaneously. The social expression *bündisch* was coined (by Campe); the legal distinction of *Bündnis* and *Bund*—equivalent in meaning earlier—could now be articulated; and ultimately, with the end of the *Reich*, the term *Bundestaat* was discovered, which first brought the formerly insoluble constitutional aporia into a historical concept oriented to the future.[11]

This brief outline should suffice to indicate that a history of the meanings of the word *Bund* is not adequate as a history of the problems of federal structure "conceptualized" in the course of *Reich* history. Semantic fields must be surveyed and the relation of *Einung* to *Bund*, of *Bund* to *Bündnis*, and of these terms to *Union* and *Liga* or to *Allianz* likewise investigated. It is necessary to question the (shifting) concepts in apposition, clarifying in this fashion the political fronts and religious and social groupings that have formed within federal potentialities. New constructions must be interpreted; e.g., it must be explained why the expression *Föderalismus*, entering language in the latter eighteenth century, did not in the nineteenth become a central concept of German constitutional law. Without the invocation of parallel or opposed concepts, without ordering generalized and particular concepts, and without registering the overlapping of two expressions, it is not possible to deduce the structural value of a word as "concept" either for the social framework or for the disposition of political fronts. Through the alternation of semasiological and onomasiological questions, *Begriffsgeschichte* aims ultimately at *Sachgeschichte*.[12]

The variant valency of the expression *Bund* can be especially suggestive of those constitutional conditions only conceptually formulable (or not) in terms of it. Insight into constitutional history is thus provided by a retrospectively oriented clarification and modern definition of past usage. Discovering whether the expression *Bund* was used as a concept associated with *Stand* rights, whether it was a concept of religious expectation, or whether it was a concept of political organization or an intentional concept based on the Law of Nations (as in Kant's minting of *Völkerbund*): clarifying such things means discovering distinctions which also "materially" organize history.

Put in other terms, *Begriffsgeschichte* is not an end in itself, even if it follows its own method. Insofar as it delivers indices and components for social history, *Begriffsgeschichte* can be defined as a methodologically independent part of sociohistorical research. From this autonomy issues a distinct methodological advantage related to the joint theoretical premises of *Begriffsgeschichte* and social history.

## On the Theory of *Begriffsgeschichte* and of Social History

All examples introduced so far—the history of the concepts of *Bürger*, democracy, and *Bund*—have one thing formally in common: they (synchronically) treat circumstances and (along the dimension of diachrony) their transformation. In this way, they are organized in terms of what in the domain of social history might be called structures and their change. Not that one can be directly deduced from the other, but *Begriffsgeschichte* has the advantage of reflecting this connection beween concept and actuality. Thus there arises for social history a productive tension, pregnant with knowledge.

It is not necessary for persistence and change in the meanings of words to correspond with persistence and change in the structures they specify. Since words which persist are in themselves insufficient indicators of stable contents and because, vice versa, contents undergoing long-term change might be expressed in a number of very different ways, the method of *Begriffsgeschichte* is a *conditio sine qua non* of social historical questions.

One of the advantages of *Begriffsgeschichte* is that by shifting between synchronic and diachronic analysis, it can help to disclose the persistence of past experience and the viability of past theories. By changing perspective it is possible to make visible dislocations that exist between words whose meaning is related to a diminishing content and the new contents of the same word. Moribund meanings which no longer correspond to reality, or realities which emerge through concepts whose meaning remains unrecognized, can then be noted. This diachronic review can reveal layers which are concealed by the spontaneity of everyday language. Thus the religious sense of *Bund* was never completely abandoned once it became descriptive of social and political organization in the nineteenth century. This was acknowledged by Marx and Engels when they created the "Manifesto of the Communist Party" out of the "articles of faith" of the *Bund der Kommunisten.*

*Begriffsgeschichte* is therefore capable of clarifying the multiple stratification of meaning descending from chronologically separate periods. This means that it goes beyond a strict alternation of diachrony and synchrony and relates more to the contemporaneity of the noncontemporaneous (*Gleichzeitigkeit des Ungleichzeitigen*) that can be contained in a concept. Expressed differently, it deals with the theoretical premises of social history when it seeks to evaluate the short, medium, or long term, or to weigh events and structures against one another. The historical depth of a concept, which is not identical with the chronological succession of its meanings, in this fashion gains systematic import, which must be duly acknowledged by all sociohistorical research.

*Begriffsgeschichte* thus takes as a theoretical principle the idea that persistence and change must be weighed against each other, and measured in terms of each other. To the extent that this is conducted in the medium of language (both of the original source and of modern scientific discourse), it reflects the theoretical presuppositions with which even a social history concerned with "materiality" must come to terms.

It is a general property of language that each of the meanings of a word reach further than the singularity to which historical events can lay claim. Each word, even each name, displays a linguistic potentiality beyond the individual phenomenon that it characterizes or names at a given moment. This is equally true of historical concepts, even if they initially serve to conceptually assemble the singularity of complex structures of experience. Once "minted," a concept contains within itself, purely linguistically, the possibility of being employed in a generalized manner, of constructing types, or of disclosing comparative insights. The reference to a particular party, state, or army linguistically involves a plane which potentially includes parties, states, or armies. A history of related concepts leads to structural questions that social history has to answer.

Concepts do not only teach us the uniqueness of past meanings but also contain the structural possibilities, treat the concatenations of difference, which are not detectable in the historical flow of events. For the social historian prepared to think conceptually, seizing past facts, relations, and processes, these concepts become the formal categories which determine the conditions of possible history. It is only concepts which demonstrate persistence, repeatable applicability, and empirical validity—concepts with structural claims—which indicate that a once "real" history can today appear generally possible and be represented as such.

This becomes even clearer if the method of *Begriffsgeschichte* is applied to the relation of the language of original source and the language of analysis. All historiography operates on two levels: it either investigates circumstances already articulated at an earlier period in language, or it reconstructs circumstances which were not articulated into language earlier but which can be worked up with the help of specific methods and indices. In the first case, the received concepts serve as a heuristic means of access to the understanding of past reality. In the second case, history makes use of categories constructed and defined *ex post*, employed without being present in the source itself. This involves, for example, principles of theoretical economics being used to analyze early phases of capitalism in terms unknown at that time; or political theorems being developed and applied to past constitutional relations without having to invoke a history in the optative mood. In either case, *Begriffsgeschichte* makes plain the difference prevailing between past and present conceptualization, whether it translates the older usage and works up its definition for modern research, or whether the modern construction of scientific concepts is examined for its historical viability. *Begriffsgeschichte* covers that zone of convergence occupied by past and present concepts. A theory is therefore required to make understanding the modes of contact and separation in time possible.

It is clearly inadequate, to cite a known example, to move from the usage of the word *Staat* (*status*, *état*) to the modern state, as has been demonstrated in detail recently.[13] The question why, at a particular time, particular phenomena are brought into a common concept remains a suggestive one. Thus, for instance, it was only in 1848 that the Prussian states were legally established as a state by Prussian jurisprudence, in spite of the established existence of the army and bureaucracy, i.e., at a time when liberal economic society had relativized the distinctions associated with the *Stände* and engendered a proletariat which had penetrated every province. Jurisprudentially, it was in the form of a bourgeois constitutional state that the Prussian state was first baptized. Certainly, singular findings of this nature do not prevent historical discourse from scientifically defining established historical concepts and deploying them in different periods and domains. If an extension of the term is warranted by a *Begriffsgeschichte*, then it is possible to talk of a "state" in the High Middle Ages. Naturally, in this way, *Begriffsgeschichte* drags social history with it. The extension of later concepts to cover earlier periods, or the extension of earlier concepts to cover later phenomena (as is today customary in the use of "feudalism"), establishes a minimum of common ground, at least hypothetically, in their objective domains.

The live tension between actuality and concept reemerges, then, at the level of the source language and of the language of analysis. Social history, investigating long-term structures, cannot afford to neglect the theoretical principles of *Begriffsgeschichte*. In every social history dealing with trends, duration, and periods, the level of generality at which one operates is given only by reflection on the concepts in use, in this way theoretically assisting clarification of the temporal relation of event and structure, or the succession of persistence and transformation.

For example, *Legitimität* was first a category in jurisprudence and was subsequently politicized in terms of traditionalism and deployed in interparty strife. It then took on a historicotheoretical perspective and was colored propagandistically according to the politics of whoever happened to be using the expression. All such overlapping meanings existed at the time when the term was scientifically neutralized by Max Weber, making it possible to establish typologies of forms of domination. He thus extracted from the available reserve of possible meanings a scientific concept; this was both formal and general enough to describe constitutional potentialities both long-term and short-term, shifting and overlapping, which then disclosed historical "individualities" on the basis of their internal structures.

*Begriffsgeschichte* embodies theoretical principles that generate statements of a structural nature which social history cannot avoid confronting.

# History, Histories, and Formal Structures of Time

The dual ambiguity of the modern linguistic usage of *Geschichte* and *Historie*—both expressions denoting event and representation—raises questions that we wish to investigate further. These questions are both historical and systematic in nature. The peculiar meaning of history, such that it is at the same time knowledge of itself, can be understood as a general formulation of an anthropologically given arc linking and relating historical experience with knowledge of such experience. On the other hand, the convergence of both meanings is a historically specific occurrence which first took place in the eighteenth century. It can be shown that the formation of the collective singular *Geschichte* is a semantic event that discloses our modern experience. The concept "history pure and simple" laid the foundation for a historical philosophy within which the transcendental meaning of history as space of consciousness became contaminated with history as space of action.

It would be presumptuous to claim that, in the constitution of the concepts "history pure and simple" or "history in general" (underwritten specifically by German linguistic developments), all events prior to the eighteenth century must fade into a prehistory. One need only recall Augustine, who once stated that, while human institutions constituted the thematic of *historia, ipsa historia* was not a human construct.[1] History itself was claimed to derive from God and be nothing but the *ordo temporum* in which all events were established and according to which they were arranged. The metahistorical (and also temporal) meaning of *historia ipsa* is thus not merely a modern construction but had already been anticipated theologically. The interpretation according to which the experience of modernity is opened up only with the discovery of a history in itself, which is at once its own subject and object, does have strong semantic arguments in its favor. It was in this fashion that an experience was first articulated that could not have existed in a similar way before. But the semantically demonstrable process involving the emergence of modern historical philosophies should not itself be exaggerated in a historicophilosophical manner. We should, rather, be given cause to reflect on the historical premises of our own historical research by this once-formulated experience of history in and for itself, possessing both a transcendent and a transcendental character. Theoretical premises must be developed that are capable of comprehending not only our own experience, but also past and alien experience; only in this way is it possible to secure the unity of history as a science. Our sphere of investigation is not simply limited to that history which has, since the onset of modernity, become its own subject, but must also take account of the infinite histories that were once recounted. If we are to seek potential common features between these two forms, the unity of the latter under the rubric of *historia universalis* can only be compared with history pure and simple. I propose, therefore, to interrogate the *temporal structures* which may be characteristic of both history in the singular and histories in the plural.

Bound up in this question, naturally, is a methodological as well as a substantive intention, which has a dual aim. History as a science has, as it is known, no epistemological object proper to itself; rather, it shares this object with all social and human sciences. History as scientific discourse is specified only by its methods and through the rules by means of which it leads to verifiable results. The underlying consideration of temporal structure should make it possible to pose specific historical questions which direct themselves to historical phenomena treated by other disciplines only in terms of other systematic features. To this extent, the question of temporal structure serves to theoretically open the genuine domain of our investigation. It discloses a means of adequately examining the whole domain of historical investigation, without being limited by the existence, since around 1780, of a history pure and simple that presents a semantic threshold for our experience. Only temporal structures, that is, those internal to and demonstrable in related events, can articulate the material factors proper to this domain of inquiry. Such a procedure makes it possible to pose the more precise question of how far this "history pure and simple" does in fact distinguish itself from the manifold histories of an earlier time. In this way, access should be gained to the "otherness" of histories before the eighteenth century without, at the same time, suppressing their mutual similarity and their similarities to our own history.

Finally, the question of temporal structures is formal enough to be able to extract in their entirety the mythological or theological interpretations of possible courses of historical events and historical description. This will reveal that many spheres which we today treat as possessing innate historical character were earlier viewed in terms of other premises, which did not lead to the disclosure of "history" as an epistemological object. Up until the eighteenth century, there was an absence of a common concept for all those histories, *res gestae*, the *pragmata* and *vitae*, which have since that time been collected within the concept "history" and, for the most part, contrasted with Nature.

Before presenting some examples of "prehistorical" experience in their temporal dimensionality, three modes of temporal experience will be recalled in a schematic fashion:

1. The irreversibility of events, before and after, in their various processual contexts.

2. The repeatability of events, whether in the form of an imputed identity of events, the return of constellations, or a figurative or typological ordering of events.

3. The contemporaneity of the noncontemporaneous (*Gleichzeitigkeit der Ungleichzeitigen*). A differential classification of historical sequences is contained in the same naturalistic chronology. Within this temporal refraction is contained a diversity of temporal strata which are of varying duration, according to the agents or circumstances in question, and which are to be measured against each other. In the same way, varying extensions of time are contained in the concept *Gleichzeitigkeit der Ungleichzeitigen*. They refer to the prognostic structure of historical time, for each prognosis anticipates events which are certainly rooted in the present and in this respect are already existent, although they have not actually occurred.

From a combination of these three formal criteria it is possible to conceptually deduce progress, decadence, acceleration, or delay, the "not yet" and the "no longer," the "earlier" or "later than," the "too early" and the "too late," situation and duration—whatever differentiating conditions must enter so that concrete historical motion might be rendered visible. Such distinctions must be made for every historical statement that leads from theoretical premises to empirical investigation. The temporal determinations of historical occurrences, once encountered empirically, can be as numerous as all the individual "events" which one meets with *ex post*, in the execution of action or in anticipation of the future.

Here, we initially wish to articulate the difference between natural and historical categories of time. There are periods that last until, for example, a battle is decided, during which the "sun stood still"; i.e., periods associated with the course of intersubjective action during which natural time is, so to speak, suspended. Of course, events and conditions can still be related to a natural chronology, and in this chronology is contained a minimal precondition of its actual interpretation. Natural time and its sequence—however it might be experienced—belong to the conditions of historical temporalities, but the former never subsumes the latter. Historical temporalities follow a sequence different from the temporal rhythms given in nature.

On the other hand, there are "historical," minimal temporalities which render natural time calculable. It still has to be established what minimum planetary cycle has to be supposed and recognized before it is possible to transform the temporalities of the stars into an astronomically rationalized, long-term, natural chronology. Here, astronomical time attains a historical valency; it opens up spaces of experience which gave rise to plans which ultimately transcended the yearly cycle.

It seems obvious to us today that the political and social space of action has become severely denaturalized under the impulse of technology. Its periodicity is less strongly dictated by nature than previously. It need only be mentioned that in the industrialized countries, the agricultural sector of the population, whose daily life was completely determined by nature, has fallen from 90 percent to 10 percent, and that even this remaining 10 percent are far more independent from natural determinations than was earlier the case. Scientific and technical domination of nature has indeed shortened periods of decision and action in war and politics to the extent that these periods have been freed of influence from the changing and changeable natural forces. This does not mean that freedom of action has thereby been increased. On the contrary, such freedom of action in the political domain seems to shrink as it becomes increasingly dependent on technical factors, so that—paradoxical as it might seem—these could prove to represent a coefficient of delay for political calculation and action. Such reflections should serve only to remind us that a denaturalization of historical temporalities, insofar as it is demonstrable, might primarily be defined technically and industrially. It is technical progress, together with its consequences, that delivers the empirical basis of "history pure and simple." It distinguishes modernity from those civilizing processes that are historically registered in the developed cultures of the Mediterranean, Asia, and pre-Columbian America. The relations of time and space have been transformed, at first quite slowly, but in the nineteenth and twentieth centuries, quite decisively. The possibilities of transport and communication have given rise to completely new forms of organization.

No one could claim that the intersubjective conditions of action in twentieth-century politics can be deduced solely from technology and that it is only today that one knows a historical time produced by human action. It is the case, rather, that a variety of temporal determinations are circulating whose discovery, experience, and formulation in writing must be attributed to the Greeks or the Jews. One has only to think of the chains of motives or modes of conduct whose effects were formulated by Thucydides or Tacitus. One could also think of the sevenfold relations possible between master and servant that Plato outlined as basic elements of political order, whose contradictory quality simultaneously provided the motive power of historical movement. Temporal elements are established in the classical writings that are still heuristically relevant enough to examine and employ as a frame for historical knowledge. There are temporal structures contained in everyday life, in politics, and in social relations which have yet to be superseded by any other form of time. A few examples follow.

1. The Greeks, without having a concept of history, identified the temporal processes within events. From Herodotus comes the sophisticated disputation in which the question of the optimal constitution is discussed.[2] While the protagonists of aristocracy and democracy each sought to highlight their own constitutions by proving the injuriousness of the others, Darius proceeded differently: he showed the immanent process by which each democracy and aristocracy was eventually led by its own internal disorders to monarchy. From this,

he concluded that monarchy should be introduced immediately, since it not only was the best constitutional form but would prevail in any case in the course of time. Aside from all technical, constitutional argument, he lent in this way a kind of historical legitimacy to monarchy that set it apart from all other constitutions. Such a form of proof can be characterized for us as historical. Before and after, earlier and later assume here in the consideration of forms of rule a temporal cogency immanent to its process, a cogency that is meant to enter into political conduct. One should also remember Plato's third book of Laws.[3] Plato examined the historical emergence of the contemporary variety of constitutions. In his "historical" review he did make use of myths and poets, but the process of historical proof is contained for us in the question of the probable period within which the known constitutional forms could emerge. A minimum period of experience, or a loss of experience was required before it became possible for a patriarchal constitution to develop and give way to a monarchic and, in turn, a democratic constitution. Plato worked with temporal hypotheses (as we would say today) and sought to derive a historical periodization of constitutional history from this history itself. The review of this history is reflected in such a manner that Plato observed that one could only learn from past incidents what could have occurred for the better, but that it was not possible to anticipate experiences, which required the expiry of a definite interval before they could be gathered.[4] This again is an eminently historical thought oriented to temporal sequence and is no longer bound to a heroic prehistory in the sense of the logographers. Measured against these "hypothetical" considerations of Plato, the Polybian schema of decline, fulfilled within three generations, is less elastic and more difficult to discharge empirically.[5]

These three doctrines of constitutional process share the idea of a space of political experience limited by nature. There was only a definite number of constitutional forms, and the real business of politics consisted in evading a threatened natural decline through the construction of a just combination of forms. The skillful management of a mixed constitution was (if you like) a "historical" task which is reflected from Plato to Aristotle to Cicero. Without acknowledging, or indeed even formulating, a domain of history pure and simple, all these examples register (by contrast to myth, even if also by means of it) a finite number of given constitutions, which while repeatable, are determined in such a way that they are not freely exchangeable one for the other. They are subject to immanent material forces, as (for example) analyzed by Aristotle in his *Politics*, and overcoming these forces meant creating a "historical" space with its own temporality.

The formal, temporal categories noted above are contained in Greek figures of thought. Even if *Historie* as a body of knowledge and mode of exploration (*als Kunde und Erforschung*), to use Christian Meier's phrase, covers the whole human world and thus reaches beyond that domain which would later be called the Historical, it still shows what irreversible temporal processes and fateful intervals are. Implicitly, the ancients developed theorems regarding specific sequential spans, within which a constitutional transformation, given certain possibilities, is generally conceivable. This is a matter of historical temporalities which are indeed determined by nature and in this respect remain bound to it, but whose genuine structures enter into historical knowledge.

It was in this way that, within the Greek space of experience, diverse and historically variant constitutions coexist and are thereby comparable. The sequential course of the noncontemporaneous, which issued out of the diachronic approach, was thus demonstrable as the contemporaneity of the noncontemporaneous (*Gleichzeitigkeit des Ungleichzeitigen*). This was masterfully developed in Thucydides' *Proömium*.

Within this experience was contained the repeatability of histories, or at least of their constellations, from which their exemplary and instructive nature could be deduced. This entire complex persists, as it is known, into the eighteenth century. The investigation of this complex as a unity remains a task to be undertaken by our science, even if the theoretical preparatory work necessary to achieve comparability is stunted, thanks to the primacy of a chronological arrangement of epochs within our guild.

Finally, in considering the naturally derived "historically immanent" concept of time, reference might be made to the metaphor present in the *corpus* doctrine,[6] ultimately taken up and developed by natural law in the Baroque era, which aimed at a *societas perfecta*. The comparisons of constitutions with the human body, together with its functions and ailments, customary since Antiquity, naturally introduce given constants against which decline or approximation might be measured. Here we have natural constants which, for their part, make possible temporal determinations without, however, involving a purely natural chronology based on biology or astronomy. Instead, historical motion is first recognizable as such because its interpretation is bound up with natural, organic categories. It remains an open question whether a "history pure and simple," experienced historically or historically-philosophically, can escape this interpretive tendency stretching from Antiquity to the natural law of the eighteenth century. Probably not, for the naturalistic determinants that penetrate all histories—here more so, there less—are not, on their side, "historicizable" without remainder.

2. If we examine the Judeo-Christian tradition, another space of experience opens up. This tradition contains theological, temporal determinations which lay transverse to "empirical" findings. Without treating history directly, the Judeo-Christian interpretative approach introduces standards which exhibited historical structures of a kind not formulated previously. Seeing things from the point of view of the opponent—Herodotus's achievement and the methodological dictate of Lucian—was also possible for the Jews, if effected in a manner different from that of the Greeks. The Jews even gained a sense of their own history from the victories of their enemies. They could contritely accept defeat as a form of punishment, and this made their survival possible. Precisely because of their self-image as the chosen people, the Jews were able to integrate the great powers of the Orient into their own history. The absence of universal human history in the Old Testament does not mean that "humanity" had not entered into their own history.

As a further example of the enormous transformative power of theological experience and of the theological problematic, a power which serves knowledge, we turn to Augustine. Here we have a synthesis of both ancient and Judeo-Christian trains of thought. Whatever the apologetic motivation for Augustine might be, his doctrine of the two empires made it possible for him to develop an "enduring answer" to every historical situation. The historical declarations on temporality that Augustine made are not distinguished by their linear form and substantial determinations. Augustine theologically articulated an internal experience of temporality which made it possible for him to relativize the entire domain of earthly experience.[7] Whatever might happen on this earth was thereby structurally iterable and in itself unimportant, while being, with respect to the Hereafter and the Last Judgment, unique and of the greatest importance. Exactly because the meaning of history lies beyond history itself, Augustine gained a freedom of interpretation for the sphere of human action and suffering, providing him with the advantage of perceiving earthly events in an acute manner.

Augustine certainly made use of various doctrines concerning the age of the world—such as the doctrine of the three phases before, during, and after the Law (*Gesetz*), or the doctrine of *aetatis*. Such forms of periodization, reaching from mythology to modern historical philosophies, direct themselves fundamentally to ideas of origin and objective; the given situation is determined again and again by reference to implicit points of departure and termination. To this extent they represent transhistorical interpretive strategies. What was decisive in the case of Augustine—and this goes for all attempts to transform doctrines concerning the age of the world into forms of historical chronology—was his arrangement of the stages of the world's age in such a way that the period following the birth of Christ became the final epoch. Since the birth of Christ, therefore, nothing new could occur, and the Last Judgment was approaching. The sixth *aetas* is the final one and hence structurally uniform. Here, Augustine had gained a dual advantage. While he could no longer be surprised by anything empirical, theologically everything was novel once again. Augustine could define time, insofar as it was only the internal mode of experience of Augustine *qua* divine creation, specifically as a spiritual expectation of the future. This future, however, was theologically placed across the path of empirical histories, even if the latter were disclosed by the former as terminal histories. Thus, Augustine outlined a horizon for the *civitas terrena* within which he formulated a series of regularities which, in their formal structure, delineated the conditions of possible historical motion. He formulated enduring rules of an apparently atemporal nature, but which were, at the same time, necessary for the knowledge of historical movement: they present a framework within which comparability can be identified, and they offer constants that make prognoses possible. There is no such thing as a prognosis which projects itself into the absolute unknown; even possible transformations presuppose a minimal constancy within such changes.

Augustine therefore proposed the rule: "Non ergo ut, sit pax nolunt, sed ut ea sit quam volunt."[8] (Not that one shuns peace, but that each seeks his own peace.) The failure of peace in the earthly sphere was not due to a want of peaceful sentiment, but to the fact that at least two persons sought to attain peace and thereby generated a situation of conflict obstructing the attainment of peace. In this way historical time was similarly released. This conception was naturally deduced in a theological manner by Augustine from his doctrine of the just peace to be found only in the Hereafter. But with this, he established for *civitas terrena* an enduring motive for historical turbulence that finds in a just peace no guarantee for its maintenance, and even in striving for such a peace finds no guarantee of its fulfillment.

He deduced a similar rule from his doctrine of the just war: the justness of a war, formulated as a moral postulate, provided no certainty that it was in fact just. Here, too, Augustine developed, at first theologically, a factor of movement which perpetually made it possible to deduce the earthly course of events from the relativity and limitation of prevailing forms of justice.[9]

Augustine drew a further regularity from Roman imperial history, whose immanent meaning he stripped of theological significance. The greater an empire becomes, he argued, the more warlike its desire for security; the weaker the external enemy, the more endangered its internal peace. With an almost automatic inevitability, the danger of civil war grows with the size of an empire, which in this process increasingly stabilizes its foreign relations.[10]

Thanks to his theologically founded approach, Augustine is able, within this domain of uniformity, to formulate insights which, even in the absence of their theological basis, reveal temporal sequential tendencies. Expressed in a modern fashion, Augustine produces formal categories which are introduced as a conditional network of possible historical motion. He makes structural long-term forecasts whose substantial terms are always related to the finitude of historical constellations and hence to their temporality, but whose reproduction is held to be probable under comparable circumstances.

The final example of what is for us a genuinely historical form of knowledge cloaked by theology comes from Bossuet, whose *Discours de l'histoire universelle* stems from Augustine. Following the Augustinian theodicy, Bossuet formulates statements which contain a similar theoretical capacity without having to be read theologically, in the same way that Lübbe claims Hegel's historical philosophy can be read. The constantly given difference between human design and fulfillment, between conscious engagement and unwelcome effect, or between unconscious action and deliberate intention: these differences are deduced by Bossuet quite traditionally from the will of God, and are explained as such. The ancient theological idea concerning the gulf dividing divine providence and human design thus assumes historical validity. This arises in the transposition of the problematic of foresight and its workings into the continually surprising difference between plan and effect; out of the theological epiphenomena emerges a historical phenomenon. One gains an insight into the manner in which historical structures unfold over time. The heterogeneity of ends can be cited as a factor which is interpreted by Bossuet in a far more worldly manner than Augustine had ever done. Or again, Bossuet employs the ancient topos according to which cause and effect relate for centuries, but which can only be recognized *ex post* by historians through the assumption of providentiality. Such long-term sequences, which transcend the experience of any particular human community, no longer have any connection with mythical or theological epochal doctrines. They do stem from the doctrine of Providence, from whose predestined intention such long-term causal chains can be deduced. Should Providence as divine arrangement suffer an eclipse, it would be replaced not by human design but by that perspective which makes it possible for the observers of history (as with Fontenelle, for instance) to discover history in general, a history which gives rise to contexts of activity reaching over several human generations.

It is possible to regard men as the heirs of divine foresight. From this perspective, modern historical philosophy would indeed be a secularization or, to use Gilson's term, a metamorphosis of the Augustinian doctrine of the two empires.[12] But the question posed here concerning temporal structures and their presence within a historical experience of history is more productive. If one considers this, it might also be possible to discover a common standard for a possible critique of utopias. This would involve finding the temporal structures which could define as unreal the empirical content of both theological eschatology and historico-philosophical utopias. The point is not to deny the historical efficacy of such positions, but rather to indicate that the question of the extent to which they might be realized is easier to answer.

In this context it would also be appropriate to investigate the typological and figurative referential field which should be contained within a time prophetic in itself.[13] It remains an open question whether modern developmental doctrines, which conceive the sequential phases of the French Revolution typologically, represent a straightforward secularization or whether they represent a proper form of knowledge.

Certainly all the temporal declarations noted above arose in a pre-modern context which never organized itself in terms of "history in general" but which had developed against the grain of all potential individual histories. What we today call history was certainly discovered, but history was never explained in terms of history. The naturalistic attachment of historical process in the world of Greek cosmology or in the theological *ordo temporum* of the Judeo-Christian salvational doctrine involved historical knowledge which could be attained only by turning away from history as totality. This partly answers our question about the connection between the unitary history of modernity and the multitude of individual histories of the entire past. It might be discerned that historical structures and temporal experience had long been formulated before the point when the history of progress and historism, "history pure and simple," could be semantically appropriated.

In conclusion, we can once again pose the contrasting question: by means of which categories can the specificity of modern history be distinguished from the regularity of recurring sequences outlined above? To deal with this, it is necessary to introduce into our hypothesis coefficients of motion and acceleration which are no longer derivative of expectations of the Last Judgment (as was earlier the case), but which instead remain adequate to the empirical factors of a world increasingly technical in nature.

Our modern concept of history has initially proved itself for the specifically historical determinants of progress and regress, acceleration and delay. Through the concept "history in and for itself," the modern space of experience has in several respects been disclosed in its modernity: it is articulated as a *plurale tantum*, comprehending the interdependence of events and the intersubjectivity of actions. It indicates the convergence of *Historie* and *Geschichte*, involving the essence of both transcendental and historicophilosophical imperatives. Finally, it expresses the step from a universal history in the form of an aggregate to a world history as a system,[14] conceptually registering history's need for theory and relating it to the entire globe as its domain of action.

It has since been possible to grasp history as a process freed of immanent forces, no longer simply deducible from natural conditions, and hence no longer adequately explained in their terms. The dynamic of the modern is established as an element *sui generis*. This involves a process of production whose subject or subjects are only to be investigated through reflection on this process, without this reflection leading, however, to a final determination of this process. A previously divine teleology thus encounters the ambiguity of human design, as can be shown in the ambivalence of the concept of progress, which must continually prove itself both finite and infinite if it is to escape a relapse into the naturalistic and spatial sense it earlier embodied. Likewise, the modern concept of history draws its ambivalence from the necessity (even if only decreed aesthetically) of conceiving of history as a totality, but a totality that can never be complete, for, as we know, the future remains unknown.

# Representation, Event, and Structure

Epistemologically, the question of representation—arising from the narrative properties of historical description—involves a diversity of temporal extensions of historical movement.[1] The fact that a "history" exists as an extralinguistic entity does not only set limits to representational potential but also requires the historian to pay great attention to the nature of source material. This itself contains a variety of indices of temporal orders. Seen from the historian's point of view, therefore, the question can be reversed: we have here a variety of temporal layers, each of which necessitates a different methodological approach. But there is a preliminary decision contained in this for the historian. In the process of representation, distinct communicative forms emerge, for, as in Augustine's words, "narratio demonstrationi similis (est)."[2] To anticipate my thesis: in practice, it is not possible to maintain a boundary between narration and description; in the theory of historical temporalities there is no complete interrelation between the levels of different temporal extensions. For the sake of clarifying this thesis, I initially assume that "events" can only be narrated, while "structures" can only be described.

1. Events that can be separated *ex post* from the infinity of circumstances—or in relation to documents, from the quantity of affairs—can be experienced by contemporary participants as a coherent event, as a discernible unity which can be narrated. This explains, for instance, the priority of eyewitness accounts which were regarded, up until the eighteenth century, as a particularly reliable primary source of evidence. This explains the high source value placed on a traditional *Geschichte* that recounts a once-contemporary occurrence.

It is initially natural chronology that provides the framework within which a collection of incidents join into an event. Chronological accuracy in the arrangement of all elements contributing to an event is, therefore, a methodological postulate of historical narrative. Thus, for the meaning of historical sequence, there is a *threshold of fragmentation*[3] below which an event dissolves. A minimum of "before" and "after" constitutes the significant unity which makes an event out of incidents. The content of an event, its before and after, might be extended; its consistency, however, is rooted in temporal sequence. Even the intersubjectivity of an event must, insofar as it is performed by acting subjects, be secured to the frame of temporal sequence. One need only recall the histories of the outbreak of war in 1914 or 1939. What really happened in terms of the interdependence of what was done and what was neglected, was shown only in the hours that followed, in the next day.

The transposition of once-direct experience into historical knowledge—even if it is an unexpected meaning released as the fragmentation of a past horizon of expectation gains recognition—is dependent upon a chronologically measurable sequence. Retrospect or prospect as stylistic devices of representation (for instance, in the speeches of Thucydides) serve to clarify the critical or decisive point in the course of a narrative.

The before and after constitute the semantic dimensions of a narrative—"veni, vidi, vici"—but only because historical experience of what constitutes an event is always constrained by temporal sequence. Schiller's dictum that world history is the tribunal of the world can also be understood in this way. "What is left undone one minute / is restored by no eternity." Whoever hesitates to assume the consequence of Schiller's statement, and permit eschatology to enter into the processual course of history, must nevertheless make the sequence of historical time the guiding thread of representation, rendering "narratable" the irreversible course of event in politics, diplomacy, and civil or other wars.

Natural chronology is, of course, empty of sense with respect to history, which is why Kant demanded that chronology be arranged according to history and not history according to chronology.[4] The establishment of a historical chronology requires "structuration." This involves the unfamiliar form of a diachronic structure. There are diachronic structures which are internal to the course of events. Every history testifies to the fact that the acting subjects perceive a certain duration: of inauguration, high points, peripeteia, crises, and termination. It is possible to recognize internal determinants for successions of events — the distribution of possibilities, the number of adversaries, and, above all, the limitation or opening up of definite tempi — which all contribute to the structuring of diachrony. Consequently, it is possible to compare sequences of revolutions, wars, and political constitutions at a definite level of abstraction or typology. Besides such diachronic structures for events, there are also longer-term structures, which are more familiar today.

2. The dictates of a sociohistorical problematic have recently caused the word "structure" to penetrate history, in particular as "structural history."[5] "Structure," here, concerns the temporal aspects of relations which do not enter into the strict sequence of events that have been the subject of experience. Such structures illuminate long-term duration, stability, and change. The categories of "long term" and "medium term" formulate in a more demanding fashion what was in the past century treated in terms of "situations" (Zustände). The semantic trace of "layering" — a spatial conception tending toward the static — is summoned up metaphorically through an expansion of "structural history."

While before and after are for narratable events absolutely constitutive, the definition of chronological determinants is clearly less crucial to the possibility of describing situations or long-term factors. This is implied within the mode of experience for structural givens, for, while such experience enters into a momentary event, it is preexistent in a sense different from that contained in a chronological precedent. Such structures have names — constitutional forms, and modes of rule — which do not change from one day to the next and are the preconditions of political action. We can also take productive forces and relations of production which alter in the long term, perhaps by degrees, whereas nevertheless determining and shaping social life. And again, it is here that constellations of friend and foe definitive of peace or war belong, which can become entrenched without corresponding to the interests of either party. Here again, considerations of space and geography are related to their technical disposition, from which arise lasting possibilities for political action and economic and social behavior. We can also consider under this heading unconscious patterns of behavior which are either induced by specific institutions or characterize such institutions, but which in any case admit or limit the potentiality for experience and action. Further, there is the natural succession of generations, containing possibilities for the creation of conflict or the formation of tradition according to their domains of experience, quite apart from actions and their transpersonal results. Lastly, customs and systems of law regulating in the long or medium term the process of social or international life should be considered here.

Without weighing the relation of one such structure against another, it can be generally stated that the temporal constants of these structures transcend the chronologically ascertainable space of experience available to the specific subjects involved in an event. While events are caused or suffered by specific subjects, structures as such are supra-individual and intersubjective. They cannot be reduced to individual persons and seldom to exactly determinable groups. Methodologically, therefore, they demand functional determinants. Structures do not in this way become entities outside of time, but rather gain a processual character, which can then enter into everyday experience.

There are, for example, long-term elements which prevail whether they are promoted or opposed. Today, when considering the rapid industrial recovery after the 1848 Revolution, one can ask whether it occurred because of or in spite of the failure of revolution. Arguments exist both for and against; neither need be compelling, but both indicate the movement that swept across the stream of political forces of Revolution and Reaction. In this case, it is possible that the Reaction had a more revolutionary effect than the Revolution itself. If, then, Revolution and Reaction are both indices of the same movement, a movement which feeds from both political camps and is propelled onward by both, this dualism obviously implies a historical movement—the irreversible progress of long-term structural change—which transcends the political bipolarity of Revolution and Reaction.

What is today a methodological reflection of structural history can belong quite well to the everyday experience of once-living generations. Structures and their transformation are detectable empirically as long as their temporal span does not reach beyond the unity of the memory of the relevant generations.

There certainly are also structures which are so enduring that they remain in the domain of the unconscious or the unknown, or whose transformation is so slow that it escapes awareness. In these cases, only social science or history as a science of the past can provide information beyond the perceptible experience of given generations.

3. Events and structures thus have in the experiential space of historical movement diverse temporal extensions; these constitute the object of history as a science. Traditionally, the representation of structures is close to description (for example, the *Statistik* of enlightened absolutism), while that of events is closer to narration (the pragmatic *Historie* of the eighteenth century). Attributing *Geschichte* to either one or the other would be to express an unfounded preference. Both levels, event and structure, are related to each other without merging. Moreover, both levels shift their valency, the relation of their mutual arrangement, according to the problem that is posed.

Statistical time series thus live on concrete individual events which possess their own time, but which gain only structural expressiveness within the framework of long periods. Narration and description are interlocked, and the event becomes the presupposition of structural expression.

On the other hand, more or less enduring, or longer-term structures, are the conditions of possible events. That a battle can be executed in the simple rhythm "veni, vidi, vici" presupposes specific forms of domination, technical disposal over natural conditions, a comprehensible relation of friend and foe, etc.; that is, structures belonging to the event of this battle, which enter into it by determining it. The history of this one battle, therefore, has dimensions of different temporal extension contained in the narration or description long "before" the effect which lends "meaning" to the event of the battle is reflected. This is a matter of structures "in eventu," to use a phrase of H. R. Jauss's, notwithstanding the hermeneutical reassurance that they will only "post eventum" become semantically comprehensible. It is such structures that provide the general basis upon which Montesquieu can preserve the chance nature in the events of a battle which is, at the same time, decisive for a war.[6]

With respect to individual events, therefore, there are structural conditions which make possible the course of an event. Such structures may be described, but they can also be included in the context of a narrative, provided that they assist in clarifying events through their nonchronological, causal character.

Conversely, structures are only comprehensible in the medium of the events within which structures are articulated, and which are tangible as structures within them. A trial involving labor law, for instance, can be both a dramatic history in the sense of "event" and simultaneously an index of long-term social, economic, and legal elements. The valency of narrated history and the form of its reproduction shift according to the problematic: it is then, accordingly, differentially classified with respect to temporality. Either the dramatic before and after of the incident, the trial, and its outcome—together with its consequences—are treated, or the history is split down into its elements and provides indices of social conditions which the course of events makes visible. The description of such structures can be even "more dramatic" than the account of the trial itself. "The perspective relevance of a transcendent narrative statement" (Jauss)—even if a *conditio sine qua non* of historical knowledge—in this case cedes its privileged position to the perspective relevance of a transcending structural analysis.

The process of upgrading and regrading can be carried through from individual event to world history. The more rigid the systematic context, the more long-term the structural aspects, the less are they narratable within the terms of a strict before and after. Similarly, "duration" can historiographically become an event itself. Accordingly, as perspective alters, medium-range structures can be introduced as a sole complex of events within a greater context; we might take, as an example, the mercantile *Ständeordnung*. There they gain a specific and chronologically ascertainable valency so that, for instance, economic forms and relations of production can be separated into appropriate epochs. Structures once described and analyzed then become narratable as a factor within a greater context of events. The processual character of modern history cannot be comprehended other than through the reciprocal explanation of events through structures, and vice versa.

Nonetheless, there remains an indissoluble remainder, a methodological aporia, which does not allow the contamination of event and structure. There is a hiatus between both entities, for their temporal extension cannot be forced into congruence, neither in experience nor in scientific reflection. The interrelation of event and structure must not be permitted to lead to the suppression of their differences if they are to retain their epistemological object of disclosing the multiple strata of history.

The before and after of an event contains its own temporal quality which cannot be reduced to a whole within its longer-term conditions. Every event produces more and at the same time less than is contained in its pregiven elements: hence, its permanently surprising novelty.[7] The structural preconditions for the Battle of Leuthen are not sufficient to explain why Frederick the Great won this battle in the manner he did. Event and structure can certainly be related: the Frederician military organization, its system of recruitment, its involvement in the agrarian structure of East Elbia, the system of taxation and military finance built upon this, Frederick's military skill within the tradition of military history: all this made the victory of Leuthen possible, but 5 December 1757 remains unique within its immanent chronological sequence.

The course of the battle, its effects on war politics, and the relevance of the victory in relation to the Seven Years War, can only be recounted in a chronological manner to be made meaningful. But Leuthen became a symbol. The outcome of Leuthen can take on a structural significance. The event assumed a structural status. Leuthen in the traditional history of the Prussian conception of the state, its exemplary effect on the revaluation of military risk in the military designs of Prussia–Germany (Dehio): these became lasting, long-term factors that entered into structural constitutional preconditions which had, in their turn, made the Battle of Leuthen possible.

If one methodically relates the modes of representation to the temporal extensions ascribed to them in the "domain of objects" of history, three consequences follow: first, however much they condition each other, the temporal levels do not merge; second, an event can, according to the shift of the investigated level, gain structural significance; and third, even duration can become an event.

This leads us to the epistemological relation of both concepts, which has until now only been outlined in their mode of representation and their corresponding temporal levels.

4. It would be erroneous to attribute to "events" a greater reality than so-called structures, on the grounds that the concrete course of the event is bound up with an empirically demonstrable before and after in a naturalistic chronology. History would be limited if so restricted at the expense of structures which, while operating on a different temporal level, are not thereby any less effective.

Today it is usual in history to change the level of proof, deducing and explaining one thing from another and by another. This shift from event to structure and back does not, however, resolve the problem of derivability: everything can be argued for, but not everything by means of anything. Only theoretical anticipation can decide which argument could or should count. Which structures provide the framework of potential individual histories? Which incidents become an event, and which events combine in the course of past history?

It belongs to the historicity of our science that these various preliminary questions cannot be reduced to a common factor, and it is a methodological dictate to first clarify the question of temporal plane. For historical knowledge, event and structure are similarly "abstract" or "concrete," depending on the temporal plane on which they move. To be for or against the reality of the past is no alternative.

Two epistemological remarks can be made here: the facticity of events established *ex post* is never identical with a totality of past circumstances thought of as formerly real. Every event historically established and presented lives on the fiction of actuality; reality itself is past and gone. This does not mean, however, that a historical event can be arbitrarily set up. The sources provide control over what might not be stated. They do not, however, prescribe what may be said. Historians are negatively obliged to the witnesses of past reality. When interpretively extracting an event from its sources, an approach is made to the "literary narrator" (*Geschichtenerzähler*), who likewise pays homage to the fiction of actuality when seeking in this way to make *Geschichte* plausible.

The quality of reality of past events that are narrated is no greater epistemologically than the quality of reality contained in past structures, which perhaps reach far beyond the apprehended experience of past generations. Structures of great duration, especially when they escape the consciousness or knowledge of former participants, can even be (or have been) "more effective" the less they enter as a whole into a single, empirically ascertainable event. But this can only be the basis of hypothesis. The fictional nature of narrated events corresponds at the level of structures to the hypothetical character of their "reality." Such epistemological handicaps cannot, however, prevent the historian making use of fictionality and hypothesis so that past reality might be linguistically rendered as a condition of reality.

To do this, the historian employs historical concepts which take account both of the fullness of past events and of the need to be understood today by both historian and reader. No event can be narrated, no structure represented, no process described without the use of historical concepts which make the past "conceivable." But this conceptual quality goes further than the singularity of the past which it helps to conceptualize. Linguistically, the categories employed to recount the unique event cannot claim the same uniqueness as the event in question. At this stage, this is a triviality. But it must be recalled to make clear the structural claim which arises on the basis of the unavoidable use of historical concepts.

Historical semantology[8] shows that every concept entering into a narrative or representation (e.g., state, democracy, army, and party, to cite only general concepts) renders relations discernible by a refusal to take on their uniqueness. Concepts not only teach us of the singularity (for us) of past meanings, but also contain structural potential, dealing with the contemporaneous in the noncontemporary, which cannot be reduced to the pure temporal succession of history.

Concepts which comprehend past states, relations, and processes become for the historian who employs them formal categories which are the conditions of possible histories. Only concepts with a claim to durability, repeated applicability, and empirical realizability—concepts with a structural content—open the way today for a formerly "real" history to appear possible and be represented as such.

5. From the diverse ordering of event and structure, and out of the long-term shifts of semantic content in historical concepts it is now possible to deduce the changing valency of *Historia magistra vitae*. A final remark can be made here:

The temporal extensions of historical circumstances, themselves varying in their susceptibility to exposition, provoke in their turn distinct historical doctrines. *Fabula docet* was always an empty term which could be filled in different ways and, as every collection of proverbs shows, provided with current directives. That concerns its contents. With respect to formal, temporal structure it can, by contrast, be asked at what level *Historie* teaches, can teach, or should teach: at the level of short-term contexts of action, with the situational moral supplied to history by the experiential model, or at the level of medium-term processes from which trends can be extrapolated for the future. In the latter case, history outlines the conditions of a possible future without delivering prognostications, or it relates to the level of meta-historical duration, which consequently is not yet timeless. Perhaps here belongs Robert Michels's social-psychological analysis of Social Democratic parties which sought the regularities within the constitution of elites, as a precautionary tale for political conduct. It is also here that the proverb "pride goeth before destruction" comes, a dictum which simply formulates a historical possibility even if it arises only occasionally.

Where history indicates the possibility of repeatable events, it must be able to identify structural conditions sufficient for the creation of such an analogous event. Thucydides, Machiavelli, but also Montesquieu, Robert Michels, and to some extent, Guicciardini, have all, to use a modern expression, calculated in terms of such structural conditions.

If these conditions change—e.g., technology, economy, or the whole society together with its form of organization—then history must, as in modernity, be able to account for such changing structures. The structures themselves prove to be mutable, in any case more than was previously the case. For, where formerly long-term processes became abbreviated through altering or even accelerating speed, the spaces of experience were rejuvenated by the continual requirement to adapt. In this fashion, the singularity of history could simply become an axiom of all historical knowledge.

The singularity of events—the theoretical premise of both historism and of the doctrine of Progress—knows no iteratability and hence permits no direct instruction. To this extent, modern "history" has dethroned the older *Historia magistra vitae*. But the doctrine of individual singularity which marks out the modern concept of history, viewed structurally, relates less to the actual novelty of events that arise than to the singularity of modern transformations themselves. It proves itself in what is now called "structural change."

However, it does not yet follow from this that the future also escapes the application of historical teaching. Such teachings instead move on a temporal level organized in a different theoretical manner. Historical philosophy and the differential prognostics which followed from it both addressed themselves to the past so they could draw from it instruction for the future. Tocqueville, Lorenz von Stein, and Marx are all proof of this. If a step is taken out of the inherited space of experience into an unknown future, an initial effort is made to conceive this experience as a "new era." From this point on, the referential character of a "history" alters. Diagnosis and prognosis can continue to build upon enduring structures of a uniform natural kind, making possible conclusions for the future from a theoretically defined iterability. But this iteratability clearly does not cover the whole space of experience existent since the French and industrial revolutions. Long-term structural transformation and its ever-shorter periodicity give rise to forecasts which direct themselves to the conditions of a possible future, not to its concrete individual features. "It is possible to forecast the approaching future, but one would not wish to prophesy individual events."[9]

Individual history is thus no longer an exemplar of its potential iteratability, or for avoiding iterability. It assumes, rather, a valency, in terms of a structural statement, for processual occurrence. Even when the heterogeneity of ends is introduced as a constant factor of destabilization, structural-historical analysis retains its prognostic potential. No economic planning today is possible without reference to the scientifically digested experiences of the world economic crisis of about 1930, a crisis which was itself unique. Should historical science dispense with this role in favor of the axiom of singularity? History indicates the conditions of a possible future which cannot be derived solely from the sum of individual events. But in the events which it investigates there appear structures which condition and limit that scope of the future. History thus shows us the boundaries of the possible otherness of our future without having to do without the structural conditions of possible repetition. In other words, a justifiable critique of the voluntaristic self-assurance of utopian planners of the future can only be effected if history as a *magistra vitae* draws instruction not from histories (*Geschichten*), but rather from the "structure of movement" of our history.

# Chance as Motivational Trace
# in Historical Writing

Speaking about chance in terms of historiography is difficult, in that chance has its own history in the writing of history, but a history which has yet to be written. "Chance" can certainly be adequately clarified only when the complete conceptual structure of the historian making use of a "chance occurrence" is taken into account. For example, one could examine the counterconcept that the chance sets free, or the overall concept which is relativized. For instance, Raymond Aron begins his *Introduction to the Philosophy of History* with an antithesis taken from Cournot of "order" and "chance," and he concludes: "The historical fact is essentially irreducible to order: *chance is the foundation of history.*"[1] Measured against the model of a lawlike natural science, chance might constitute the essence of all history, but the influence of particular historical circumstances on such formulations is perfectly obvious. In the course of his investigation, Aron dissolves the crude antithesis, and accordingly the meaning of chance alters within his historical epistemology. An event can appear accidental or not according to the standpoint of the observer. This also does away historiographically with the idle antithesis of chance and necessity. Consideration of one set of circumstances can make an event appear accidental, but consideration of another set can make it appear unavoidable. This position is also adopted by Carr in his book on history; chance becomes a concept dependent upon perspective.[2] In this way, a level of reflection is achieved that treats chance systematically. However, this is not at all obvious, nor was it ever so.

Speaking temporally, chance is a pure category of the present. It is not derivative of the horizon of future expectation except as its sudden manifestation; neither is it possible to experience it as the outcome of past causes: if it were, then it would no longer be chance. Insofar as historical writing aims at illuminating the temporal course of relations, chance remains an ahistorical category. But the category is not, because of this, unhistorical. Rather, chance is more suited to depict the startling, the new, the unforeseen, and like experiences in history. A circumstance might therefore initially arise on the basis of chance, or a fragile situation might need a chance occurrence as a stopgap. Wherever chance is made use of historiographically, it indicates an inadequate consistency of given conditions and an incommensurability in their results. It is precisely here that we may find its historical nature.

Without any doubt, it is a property of modern historical methodology to avoid chance wherever possible. By contrast, up until the eighteenth century, it was quite usual to make use of chance, or luck in the form of fortune, in the interpretation of histories. This custom has a long and very changeable history, which can only be broadly outlined here.[3] Fortuna was one of the few heathen deities transposed into the Christian historical panorama. With the bitter logic characteristic of the Christian "Enlightenment," Augustine had ridiculed the contradictions a goddess of chance brought with her. "Ubi est definitio illa Fortunae? Ubi est quod a fortuitis etiam nomen accepit? Nihil enim prodest eam colere, si fortuna est."[4] His purpose was to deduce all chance as the singular work of God, and to this extent Fortuna disappeared from a rigorous Christian experience of history. When, for instance, Otto von Freising introduces chance, as he often does, it is only to explain it as God's work.[5] Precisely the initial incomprehensible character of such works indicated God's hidden decree. Fortuna was theologically mediated and in this manner superseded.

If Fortuna was, despite this, received into the Christianizing world—whether in popular belief or in succession to Boethius—it was definitely because her place in everyday life or within the frame of *Historien* could not simply be left unoccupied. The complete ambiguity offered by Fortuna, from chance via "grace" to good or ill fortune, was a structural element for the representation of individual *Historien*.[6] She indicated the permanence of change, a transpersonal pattern of events which escaped the control of men and women. However virtue and belief might relate to her—whether deduced from God or (as later) discharged by God—Fortuna, stronger than the plans realized by humans, remained indicative of the changing times, of changing constellations.[7]

So far, both Christians and humanists were at one on the nature of Fortuna as "daughter of foresight" or "mother of chance."[8] The metaphor of the circling wheel,[9] which Boethius introduced into Christian historical interpretation, pointed to the iteratability of all occurrence, which in spite of all ups and downs could not introduce anything which was, in principle, new to the world before the time of the Last Judgment. At the same time, Fortuna could be employed as a symbol of the incommensurable for the justification of God—likewise for Boethius. It was possible to do this with respect to both luck and misfortune, which broke into a human context exactly because they did not appear immanent to it, although they made its meaning intelligible. The two faces of Fortuna opened up a space for all possible histories; her endowments created space for "all centuries."[10] Her changeability secured the ever-constant preconditions for earthly events and their representability. Fortuna belonged, so to say, to the doctrine of *Geschichten*, to the historical, and not to histories themselves. Thanks to her help, *Historie* was able to elevate itself into exemplariness. Until then, Fortuna could only be rationalized in a theological or moral-philosophical fashion, but not historically: as soon as she was interpreted empirically or pragmatically, she became pure chance.

The problem of historical accident was first prompted methodologically when foresight was replaced by arguments which were no longer sufficient to account for miracles and, of course, chance occurrences. It also required a particular type of historically immanent reason (for instance, psychological or pragmatic *causae*), ruling out Fortuna and thus rendering chance a problem. The famous nose of Cleopatra which, according to Pascal, changed the face of the world,[11] reaches from one epoch to another: chance becomes an immanent cause from which significant consequences can be drawn. Precisely the inconsequentiality and superficiality of the chance element suited it as a *causa*. Thus, in his *Antimachiavelli*, Frederick II traced the Peace of Utrecht to a pair of gloves that the Duchess of Marlborough had hastily ordered.[12]

In the eighteenth century, an entire historical tendency developed around such forms of argument; from Richer's *Essay sur les grands évenemens par les petites causes* (1758), to the derivation of state affairs, to the intrigues of mistresses; as Voltaire argued, the devastation of

Europe in the Seven Years War was sparked by the *amour propre* of two or three persons.[13] Chance here is fully at the service of arguments delivered by the moralizing historian. Thus, for example, Duclos wrote of the politics of Louis XIV: "When one considers our misfortunes, it is obvious that they must be entirely laid at our door; for our salvation, on the other hand, we have only chance to thank."[14] Chance is indicative of the absence of moral and rational modes of conduct which should belong to a proper politics. Chance, which can equally well be transient, is only the stopgap of a rationalizable politics.

"La fortune et le hasard sont des mots vides de sens," stated the young Frederick;[15] they emanate from the heads of poets and owe their origin to the deep ignorance of a world which had given hazy names (*des noms vagues*) to the effects of unknown causes. The misfortune (*l'infortune*) of a Cato, for example, was due only to the unforeseeable nature of overlapping cause and effect which the adverse times (*contre-temps*) had ushered in and which he, therefore, was not able to forestall. Frederick directed his efforts to the development of a political system that would permit him to place all of the circumstances of the time at the service of his plans. He thereby departed from the Fortuna of Machiavelli without, however, being able to completely do without the name's semantic content. Its place was taken by concepts of time (*temps* and *contre-temps*), but its room for maneuver was limited by the questions of causes and intentions. The timely chance then revealed itself as a collection of causes, becoming a mere name without reality. Thus, it also became clear, added Frederick, why "fortune" and "chance" were the sole survivors of the heathen deities (a passage, however, that Voltaire struck out of the page proofs for him).[16]

The extent to which chance dissolved under the purview of an enlightened historian, and where it nevertheless reemerged, be it on account of the situation or of the demands of representation, will now be shown in more detail in the work of von Archenholtz.

# I

Von Archenholtz, formerly a captain in Royal Prussian service, was, in the second half of the eighteenth century, one of the most widely read historians and one of the authors of the "portrait of manners" (*Sittengemälde*), which can be seen as a forerunner of modern sociology. In his popular book on the Seven Years War, Archenholtz repeatedly addressed the question of chance. In doing so, as in our problematic, he had to risk being suspected of making forbidden forays into extra-historical concepts for the sake of the consistency of his historical material, so that he might chivalrously conceal gaps in the evidential support for his representation. Let us consider three of the chance occurrences that Archenholtz concerned himself with. At the beginning, in the description of the infamous coalition of the Catholic courts of Vienna and Versailles—a coalition which appeared to overturn the entire established European political system, the shock effects of which were not dissimilar to those of the Hitler–Stalin pact of 1939—Archenholtz wrote: "This union of Austria and France, which both astonished the world and was considered to be a political masterstroke, was nothing but a coincidence (*Zufall*)."[17] As Archenholtz explained, France had no intention of destroying the King of Prussia, however enraged it might be over the Prussian treaty with England and however much Kaunitz might have aroused resentment in Paris. The primary objective of France was "the conquest of the Duchy of Hanover so that more important ends might be achieved in America." Here he identified a motive that Frederick also regarded in his memoirs as decisive and which occupies a central place in the subsequent historiography, since it characterizes the global context of the Seven Years War and makes it possible to view this war as the first world war of our planet.

What was the chance or coincidence that Archenholtz brought into play? He saw clearly the worldwide interdependence in which the political aims of the coalition were realized. But what appeared to be the primary objective, viewed from Versailles, was for the Prussian reader a mere coincidence. The coalition directed itself primarily against England, as far as the French Ministry (not Madame Pompadour) was concerned, and the stake was transoceanic domination. What appeared to be absurd for the centuries-old European domestic policy of equilibrium made sense if viewed globally.

Thus, chance was for Archenholtz not just a stylistic device for intensifying the drama in his account, but served to outline a specific perspective: that of contemporaries. His history was composed while he was a contemporary of and protagonist in this war. For the central European reader, chance was introduced quite properly in its full force as the unexplained (*des Unmotivierbaren*), only then to be motivated through the superior viewpoint of the historian. This motivation, however, arose out of causal relations which were not available through experience to the presumptive reader. The coincidence introduced by Archenholtz proved to be chance, but was also shown to be susceptible to explanation. Scientific historians of the following century (Ranke, for instance) dispensed with such alterations of prospective; but, like few others, the historians of the Enlightenment were trained to regard history not only as a science but also—and precisely as a science conveying knowledge—rhetorically, as a form of representation. The rupture in the coherence of the experiential space for the German reader is thus made visible (hence, the "pure chance" of the coalition) and is bridged, since the historian writing around 1790 already looked for world-historical causes wherever he could.

What happens with the second instance that we will consider, in which Archenholtz seeks an explanation for the first decisive battle of the Seven Years War? "An extremely commonplace accident," he wrote, "a stroll taken by a clever monk during the first days of the siege saved Prague and the (Austrian) monarchy. This man Setzling, not unknown to literary history, noticed a pillar of dust which was approaching the northern part of the city."[18] There follows a detailed description, in which our monk suspects the Prussians, hurried to the observatory, confirmed his suspicions by using a telescope, and was able to report in good time to the City Commander and suggest that he occupy a tactically advantageous height before the enemy could do so.

Archenholtz, prompted by previous discussion among historians about Pyrrhonism to weigh questions of historical certainty and probability against each other, thereby preventing a slide into the domain of the fabulous, hurried to relativize his coincidence. He took it seriously, as a fact, but only to immediately measure it against the military scale of the Seven Years War. Archenholtz continued: "The overrunning of a city occupied by an army of 50,000 experienced soldiers, and moreover in broad daylight, has never been heard of in the annals of warfare and is inconceivable for every soldier; it was barely regarded as plausible by generations then living and has since come to be viewed as fabrication."

This chance occurrence, which was decisive for the course of the Battle of Prague and involved a completely unmilitary world reaching into the war, was transposed by Archenholtz into the domain of military possibilities. Measured in these terms, the quality of the chance altered:

it became an anecdote, which did, nevertheless, throw an ironic light on the contrast of Catholic and Protestant in the struggle for Bohemia. In terms of a rationally calculable military technology and the kinds of weapons then available, however, the concidence was ruled out as of no significance. Not explicable as the cause of Prague's salvation, unless Archenholtz took the Prague legend to be the work of God, which, as an enlightened Prussian, he hardly would have been prepared to do, the coincidence moved, through its outcome, into a more plausible context. From the point of view of its result, the determining nature of the battle following our monk's stroll is stripped of its accidental character. Inserted into the rationalizable bases and consequences of warfare at that time, this external factor is registered by Archenholtz but indirectly devalued as an interchangeable event. The author gives us to understand that if this event had not saved Prague from being overrun, then without doubt another would. That this event, in particular the stroll of a cleric, *was* the event is itself singular and accidental; but viewed strategically, it is irrelevant.

Archenholtz makes use of two chains of thought in locating chance in this way and eliminating its effect: first, reference to the military structure of possibilities, and second, consideration of the comparison of history and fantasy (*Dichtung*). The old Ciceronian contrast of *res factae* and *res fictae*, passed on from generation to generation of historians since Isidor,[19] is cited to distinguish what is militarily probable—not actual—against the background of what is militarily improbable and hence "fantastic."[20] The absent chance could have led into the domains of the possible and the conceivable, but likewise into the improbable. Prague could just as well have fallen absurdly. Only then would chance be complete, and would the improbable become an event.

That such experiences were not unknown to contemporaries of that time is shown by the commemorative coin minted for the town of Kolberg in 1760, after it was freed at the last moment from 23,000 Russian besiegers. The inscription on the coin was taken from Ovid: *res similis fictae*, or, as Archenholtz translated it, "an occurrence as if fabricated."[21] Measured against the example of Kolberg, it becomes clear once more what concerned Archenholtz in the case of Prague. The meditatively perambulating monk was mediated through military history. Chance was *ex post* stripped of its accidental character. Fortuna thus remained in play. But she was demoted to second place in the causal structure, however much she initially appeared to be the first and unique agent.

In his text on the magnificence and decline of the Romans, Montesquieu appeared to offer a simple and rational explanation of these features. All chance occurrences are subordinated to general causes,

and if the chance of a battle, that is to say, a particular cause, ruins a state, then there is a general cause which dictates that this state should perish in a solitary battle. In a word, the principal turning point carries with it all particular accidents.[22]

Whoever becomes involved with causes will never be short of a causal element. It would certainly be irresponsible to dismiss the historian's business in this manner. Archenholtz's skill as a historian consisted in his ability to allow incommensurable entities to exist side by side and nevertheless provide a historically adequate response. He later described the siege of Breslau during 1760 in this fashion. Before the walls of the city were encamped 50,000 Austrians under their most capable general, Laudon. Within were 9,000 Austrian prisoners of war, ripe for an uprising, with many Austrophile citizens. The defenders numbered only 3,000, of whom only 1,000 were active soldiers. Archenholtz called the successful defense an incident "which is guaranteed to provide the philosopher with a problem and which the astute historian (Geschichtsschreiber) hardly dares to introduce, on account of its improbability." He continued, "Such a miracle could only be effected by the power of Prussian military upbringing."[23] One can argue about the reasons for this miracle, introduce other causes, and strip the miracle of its miraculous character; but the trend is clear: miracles, accidents, and the like are only referred to so that the ordinary reader, who most readily expects them, might be reeducated.

The final example is drawn arbitrarily from the history of the Seven Years War. How does our author proceed in the case of the defeat at Kolin? "It was not bravery and military skill which decided the result of this memorable day, but accidents." At Leuthen, later contrasted to Kolin, the victory was decided solely by "bravery and military skill."[24] Here, Prussian national pride appears to run off with the old soldier, and it is perfectly clear that reference to accidental occurrences, in the case of Kolin, is introduced for apologetic reasons. In the course of his account, Archenholtz enumerates the individual accidents of the battle: as is known, the battle was lost tactically because Frederick's overextended battle line broke and he was unable, in the face of the Austrians' superiority, to throw reserves into the gaping holes. Exactly why this line of battle should break open is explained by Archenholtz in detail through the use of psychology. Against the orders of the king, troops who were being held in reserve attacked; soldiers were therefore scattered and absorbed along the line instead of moving up in sequence to support the attacking wings.

"Imprudence and belligerent hotheadedness" on the part of the subordinate commanders are made responsible for the accident. Here, our author has to ask himself whether these, too, are not martial qualities, whether faulty military skill and inappropriate bravery led to this defeat after all. "Alter Fritz" did not, in his later account, make use of chance as a way of glossing over his defeats. He identified specific mistakes which had undermined his plans, only occasionally suppressing his own errors. He attributed the defeat at Kolin to the tactical failure of his generals in going against his orders. The third example of chance that we have found in Archenholtz, when examined causally, thus fades to a greater degree than the previous examples, and does so in a way not unknown to the author, as is unconsciously acknowledged.

To summarize, in the first case, that of an alliance between France and Austria, chance involved a question of perspective. The continental European absurdity, the novelty and the unexpectedness of the Franco-Austrian alliance, was made comprehensible from a world-historical viewpoint. The second instance, that of the peripatetic monk, was derived from motivational spheres different from those of the course of the Battle of Prague. Viewed from different points, their coincidence was accidental; transposed to the level of strategic possibility, chance received a rationally calculable valency, and the accidental disappeared from general view. Not so with the third example. Here, chance was only a word patriotically inserted at the right time and designed to play down the superiority of the Austrians and the decisive attacks of the Saxons. The psychological categories that Archenholtz employed were substantially on the same level. To this extent, we have a dubious coincidence which is suited to the closing off of further explanation or self-reproach. As Gibbon said of the Greeks, "After their country had been reduced to a province, [they] imputed the triumphs of Rome not to the merit, but to the fortune, of the Republic."[25]

The advantage we have over Archenholtz in establishing that he construed two of his chance events properly, whereas in the third case he used chance simply as a means of concealing a misfortune which he felt personally, is attributable to and only conceivable since the theoretical destruction of chance in the eighteenth century. We have cited Montesquieu and Gibbon as primary witnesses; we can cite Frederick as well. Weighed down by the lost Battle of Kolin, in which he suspected he had experienced his Pultawa, he wrote to his friend Marshall Keith that "fortune" had deserted him. "Fortune on this day turned its back on me. I should have known that it was a woman, and I am not a chivalrous type. It declares itself for the women who wage war with me." In 1760 he wrote to the Marquis d'Argens that he was unable to direct fortune, and that he must increasingly allow for chance because he lacked the means to fulfill his plans by himself. This final, private statement does not depart from the system of political relations that he formulated in *Antimachiavelli* and which he, as in his missive to Keith, dismissed so ironically.

So far as I can tell, Frederick consistently dispenses in his military-historical memoirs with resort to a fortune which, one could say un-historically, finally did serve him well. The memoirs address themselves to a rational and consistent listing of the mistakes and successes of the given antagonists in terms of their supposed plans. The axis of this calculation thus takes the form of action and its result. The result, however, almost never coincides with the original plan of an agent. Frederick thus gained from the consistency of his rational approach the insight that history always produces more, or less, than is contained in the sum of its given preconditions. Here, Frederick exceeded the pure form of causal explanation in the direction of what in the nineteenth century was called the *verstehende* Historical School.

## II

Chance, or the accidental, was completely done away with by the Historical School during the nineteenth century, less through a systematic extension of the principle of causality than through theological, philosophical, and aesthetic implications contained within the modern concept of history. This will be demonstrated once more with reference to Archenholtz.

While it has previously been shown how far Archenholtz could rationalize chance into the concept of perspective employed for stylistic ends in creating space for causal relations, Fortuna enters the battlefield at a most prominent point, and in a historically matchless fashion, at that: the death of Czarina Elizabeth in 1762. This death is dramatically introduced as the work of fate. Frederick, in his history of the Seven Years War, merely noted that this death had upset all plans and agreements prepared by politicians; and Ranke later suggested that this death simply revealed the negligible "internal necessity" implicit within the previous "combination of circumstances."[26] Archenholtz, however, presented the death as the work of fate. He described the resulting turn of events as "Fortuna's greatest deed," saving Frederick and Prussia from defeat.[27] Archenholtz here made use of the older concept of Fortuna in such a way that the concept was not immanent to circumstances but superior to them. This is not a rationalistic, stylistic device, but rather denotes the penetration of natural possibilities into the course of a carefully planned war. Fortuna is here not a substitute for causality. Instead, the concept preexists all events. This conception ties Archenholtz to the older mode of experience which he shares with humanists and Christian historians: that *Historie* has a natural foundation, and that *Geschichten* are related via Fortuna to extrahistorical conditions.

The death of a ruler at that time was, of course, generally subject to probability calculations, but it could not be influenced by any rational design (apart from poison or the dagger); it eluded pragmatic *causae* even when possible consequences were calculated and planned, such as in the "Pragmatic Sanction" of 1713. War and diplomatic affairs usually acquired their justification from questions of succession among rulers, and the political horizon was bounded by the possible life span of given rulers.[28] Archenholtz's invocation of Fortuna in this natural historical space was no breach of style.

For all his modernity, Archenholtz lived in a continuum embracing all former *Geschichten*. His writings constantly referred to the events and deeds of antiquity, which he compared with those of the Seven Years War. The parallels he drew were not in furtherance of a historicophilosophical interpretation of all that had occurred, but rested, rather, on an implicit presupposition of the natural identity of all historical conditions. Hence, Fortuna remained a standard of comparison and judgment that permitted the treatment of Frederick, Hannibal, and Alexander as potential contemporaries, or the conception of Cannae and Leuthen as broadly similar.[29]

This ambivalence of Archenholtz's, whereby he rationally decomposes the accidental, on the one hand, while maintaining an allegiance to Fortuna, on the other, indicates the great distance separating him from the Historical School. Humboldt, who was the theoretical pioneer for this school, did not renounce the eighteenth-century conception according to which one could, as it were, causally assess "the entirety of world history of the past and future," but argued that the limits of such assessment lay only in the extent of our knowledge of effective causes. To this degree, chance was eliminated; but Humboldt suggested that it was precisely in this conception that one missed the specificity of history. History was distinguished by that which was eternally new and had never been experienced; such are the creative individualities and inner forces which, while they cohere in their superficial sequence, are never to "be deduced from their accompanying circumstances" in their given singularity and orientation.[30] The inner unity of history and its quality of uniqueness eluded causal deduction (the progressive aspect of the historical world view is embodied in this idea), and it is therefore open neither to Fortuna (who is symbolic of repetition) nor to chance, for the singularity of chance is absorbed by the singularity of "history in itself."

Humboldt lived within a new experience of history, and he conceptually formulated this in a manner which made possible the self-conception of historism. The singularity of history did away with the accidental. To express the same thing differently, if history in its singularity surpassed all *causae* that might be summoned up, then chance likewise lost its historical weight as an accidental cause.[31]

Leibniz, in defining two kinds of truth—that of reason tolerating no contradiction, and that of facts which, while adequately established, allowed the contrary to be conceived—defined with *verités de fait* that domain which was later to be named "history." The historical facts of the past, as well as those of the future, are possibilities that either have been or can be realized and which preclude compelling necessity. Facts remain contingent, however much they can be grounded; they arise in the space of human freedom. To this extent, the past and the coming future are always accidental; but for Leibniz, the chain of "coincidences" has a unique certainty in the course of the world, for it is laid down and preserved in the divine plan of the optimal world.

Subsumed by the dictates of theodicy, even contingent (historical) events show themselves to be necessary, not in the sense of geometric proof but "necessaire . . . ex hypothesi, pour ainsi dire par accident."[32]

Chance proves itself from a superior perspective, which can later be formulated to be historically necessary. Motivational remainder, since then, has not been covered by chance; rather, such motivational remainder is more or less excluded a priori from the new theory of history, on the basis of the slow developments of the eighteenth century. This is the theological principle of the singularity of all earthly affairs with respect to God, and the aesthetic category of the inner unity of history: both enter modern historical philosophy and make possible the modern concept of "history." Thus, in 1770, Wieland could talk of the "thousand unavoidable accidents" which forced mankind along the irreversible path of infinite fulfillment.[33] Likewise, Kant could outline the ruse of nature, which anticipates Hegel's "ruse of reason," through which all apparently chance occurrences gained their meaning.

Philosophical reflection has no other intention than the removal of the accidental. Chance is the same as external necessity, that is a necessity which relates to causes which are themselves merely superficial circumstances. We must seek a general purpose in history, the ultimate purpose of the world.

This passage from Hegel demonstrates the degree to which he had outstripped the rationalization of chance completed in the previous century, and how chance was excluded far more consistently by a teleological unity of world history than was ever possible for the Enlightenment. "We must bring to history the belief and conviction that the realm of the will is not at the mercy of contingency."[34]

It was not the theological heritage that excluded all chance within the idealist concept of history; apparently meaningless coincidence was excluded by the literary and aesthetic reflections which constituted, in terms of internal probability and hence a superior reality-content, the representational art of historiography. In 1799, Novalis summarized the current discussion: the heaping up of isolated dates and facts with which historians customarily busy themselves "allows the most important aspect to be forgotten, which is that which makes history into history, uniting the diversity of chance events into a pleasing and instructive whole. If I see aright, then it seems to me that a writer of history must necessarily also be a poet [Dichter]."[35]

The Historical School gained its impulse from both poetics and idealist philosophy, which combined the conception and scientific reflection of history as an immanently meaningful unity, anterior to all events. "Let them measure and estimate; our business is theodicy" (Droysen). If all events become unique, with "each epoch . . . directly [related] to God,"[36] then the miraculous is not eliminated, and the whole of history becomes a single miracle. "One learns to worship," as Droysen continued.[37] This robs chance of its freedom to be accidental.

It would be pointless to separate the theological, philosophical, or aesthetic implications that merge in the Historical School; it is sufficient here for us to establish that they all combined into a concept of history which did not permit the conditions of chance to emerge.

The aesthetic components of historism forestalled motivational remainder and chance far beyond their once-theological bases. Whether historical knowledge was thereby properly served, and done so better than in the period in which Fortuna played a part, is a question that must today be raised once more. Perhaps it could be shown that it was precisely the abolition of all chance that led to demands for consistency which were too high. Indeed, because of the abolition of the accidental, chance became absolute within the plane of historical uniqueness. The role Fortuna played in the space of a prehistoric conception of history has in modernity become that of ideology, impelled to ever more novel manipulation the more it assumes the guise of immovable lawfulness.

# Perspective and Temporality: A Contribution to the Historiographical Exposure of the Historical World

The historian's pledge to seek and recount only that which is true is an old one. This pledge is still valid today and meets in general with undivided agreement. On the other hand, the claim that it is only possible to discover the truth by adopting a definite position or even through partisanship is a product of modernity.

If it was said today that every historical statement is bound to a particular standpoint, this would hardly provoke any objection. Who would wish to deny that history is viewed from different perspectives, and that change in history is accompanied by alterations in historical statements about this history? The ancient trinity of place, time, and person clearly enters the work of a historical author. If place, time, and person should alter, then new works would emerge, even if they dealt with the same object, or appeared to do so.

Whoever tries to clarify epistemologically this current historiographical position—more exactly, this shift of position—gets into difficulties soon enough, being confronted with accusations of subjectivism, relativism, or even historism. Whatever else the worn-out catchword "historism" might mean, it certainly is concerned with this change of perspective forced upon anyone involved with the course of history. New experiences are gained, old ones are superseded, and new expectations are formed; in addition, new questions are posed to our past, questions which demand that history be reconsidered, reviewed, and reinvestigated.

Contemporary historical science is thus subject to two mutually exclusive demands: to make true statements, while at the same time to admit and take account of the relativity of these statements. In this dilemma, various arguments are deployed for defense. In the first place, the historian can point to the enormous success achieved by this science in its slow growth from early modernity, success that is owed to the methods used. In approximately two hundred years, we have come to know more about the past of mankind in general than mankind had in this past known about itself. There is much that we can no longer recover because of the state of the sources, but nevertheless we have learned much that escaped the knowledge of past contemporaries. In many respects, then, we know more than we once did, and such knowledge frequently is more soundly based than was earlier possible. A defense conducted by the historian in this way, invoking the empirical body of research presently existing, is in itself conclusive and is difficult to refute.

A second line of argument seeks to disarm accusations of subjectivism and relativism in a theoretical and methodological fashion. Historical science has also developed a methodology specific to itself which enables it to make objective statements. Source criticism is at any time communicable, verifiable, and subject to rational criteria. Here we have the doctrine of *Verstehen*, which gained entry into historical science through Schleiermacher and Dilthey. In the words of Dilthey:

*Das Verstehen* and interpretation is the method which realizes *Geisteswissenschaft*. All functions are united in this method. All truths characteristic of *Geisteswissenschaft* are contained within it. At every point, *Verstehen* opens up a world.[1]

Thus, if the essence of the historical world is its transformation, so the medium of *Verstehen* allows every unique situation to be understood. Even the alien and distant past is susceptible to understanding, transmission, and hence recognition through self-involvement and empathy.

Such a theory of the *Geisteswissenschaften* is ultimately founded on an implicit and stable human nature which comprehends an infinite possibility for the human being. Through *Verstehen*, texts that are fundamentally susceptible to transmission are disclosed; the failure or success of actions and plans of the past can be assessed and past sufferings made comprehensible. Admittedly, the historian, like every person, must have a particular standpoint: the whole of the historical world is opened up to the historian by virtue of his source criticism conducted in the medium of *Verstehen*. Through participation in the past or continuing objectification of historical persons, a historical individual of today can likewise objectify this form of history.

Thus we have an empirical and a theoretical argument which should disarm accusations that historism constantly supersedes itself. In both research and *Verstehen*, history is closed down, even if the historian experiences himself as and knows himself to be a changing part of this history.

We are, therefore, in a stalemate. All historical knowledge is locationally determined and hence relative. Aware of this, history allows itself to be assimilated critically-*verstehend*, leading in turn to true historical statements. To exaggerate somewhat, partisanship and objectivity are mutually exclusive, but in the course of historical work they relate to one another.

We will roll out this epistemological dilemma once more in hopes of showing, in the form of a historical exposition, how the emergence of historical relativism is identical with the discovery of the historical world. In concluding this essay, some theoretical remarks, which are perhaps capable of making this dilemma more bearable, if not altogether dispensable, will be attempted.

## The Premodern Imagery of Suprapartisanship

Since Antiquity, it has been a part of the topology of history as art and as science that accounts of human acts and omissions, deeds and sorrows should be truthfully recounted by the historian. The pledge to proceed in this way continually appears in works of historical writing. Since Lucian, or Cicero, two rules have belonged to the methodological self-assurance of all historians who do not wish to wander into the realm of the fabulist: one may not lie, and one should tell the complete truth.[2]

What is striking about this position is not the appeal to truth as such, but rather the related demand that the truth be permitted to appear, pure and unmediated. Only by disregarding one's own person, without passion and ardor (*sine ira et studio*);[3] that is, nonpartisan or suprapartisan, is it possible to bring truth to speak.

Notwithstanding the polemical thrust that such ideas might have against adversaries or professional colleagues, there lurks behind them a form of naive realism, if one is looking for epistemological names within epochs when such labels were foreign.

An unfailing index of this naive realism, which aims to render the truth of histories in their entirety, is provided by the metaphor of the mirror. The image provided by the historian should be like a mirror, providing reflections "in no way displaced, dimmed, or distorted."[4] This metaphor was passed down from Lucian until at least the eighteenth century; it can be found in Voss's 1623 definition of *Historie* as the *speculum vitae humanae*,[5] as in the emphasis by the Enlighteners on the older, moralistic application demanding of historical representation that it give to men an "impartial mirror" of their duties and obligations.[6]

A variant of epistemological nonchalance, just as frequently encountered, can be found in the form of the "naked truth"[7] that a historian is supposed to depict. One must not underestimate the persisting impulse expressed in this metaphor, namely, that one should permit the truth of a history to speak for itself if it is to be experienced and have any effect. Taken at its word, however, this demand forces the author to withhold any judgment, and in this way the metaphor of the mirror is only strengthened.

*Historie*, wrote Fénélon in 1714, has a *nudité si noble et si majestueuse*,[8] requiring no poetic adornment. "Saying the naked truth; that is, recounting events that have occurred without varnish"—this was the task of the writer of history, according to Gottsched.[9] Even the young Ranke, in 1824, invoked "naked truth without adornment," betraying "Guiccardini's false stories" by use of this "concept of history."[10] Blumenberg rightly argues here that this almost involves an Enlightenment anachronism,[11] even if it was the Enlightenment itself that had undermined the stability of this metaphor of the naked truth. The older Ranke still maintained this idea, though with reservation, as he formulated, in 1860, his oft-cited confession: "I would like to efface myself entirely and allow only things to talk, simply allow the mighty forces to appear. . . ."[12]

A third topos, stemming like the others from antiquity, leads us to the heart of our problematic. It was Lucian who introduced into the conceptual apparatus of history the term "apolis." A writer of history must be "in his work a stranger, having no country, autonomous, the subject of no ruler." One could only hold to the truth in a space free of domination; one could here "report what had occurred" unreservedly.[13] The step to Ranke does not seem very far, given the way the latter defined his historical approach: he sought neither to judge nor to teach; "he merely wishes to show how it really was" (*er will bloss zeigen, wie es eigentlich gewesen*).[14]

The scientific postulate of nonpartisanship, in the sense of non-adherence to party, abstinence, or neutrality, continues unbroken into the eighteenth century. Bayle, Gottfried Arnold, Voltaire, and Wieland committed themselves to this just as much as Niebuhr, who "sought the truth, without party and polemic."[15] Even a historian as politically involved as Gervinus assumed that belief, loyalty, and fatherland should not confuse the issue, if one was to be able to write in an "unrestrained and impartial" manner.[16] "Everything is related," wrote his distanced opponent Ranke, "critical study of the genuine sources, impartial outlook, objective presentation—the objective is the realization [*Vergegenwärtigung*] of the entire truth," even if it is not fully attainable.[17] According to Ranke, "The truth can only be one."[18]

So much for the topology, which could be illuminated further with countless examples. Notwithstanding the alterations of context, it remains an imperative for the course of research that suprapartisanship be aspired to, so that the contrary positions or views might be articulated. Whether it is to give them their due, or whether—and this is more modern—it is to relate all parties or forces in a historical process in such a way that the process itself is foregrounded. To the extent that this is done, the call to tolerate the dominance of no partisanship is today repeated with justice.

The historical world, however, was not constituted by a methodological research precept according to which suprapartisanship must be promoted. This was effected, rather, by the connection of history to its own conditions of action and knowledge, opening the way for modern history in the domains of the scientific and prescientific, the political and social. A new concept of "history" emerged.[19] Modern history is initially distinguished from earlier forms by its revelation of an objectless "history in and for itself" through the reflections of the Enlighteners. The conditions of historical processes and the conditions of action in this process (and knowledge of this process) have, since the Enlightenment, been related. But this relation is not to be had without a defined location vis-à-vis historical movement.

Naturally, earlier doctrines of historical artifice considered the influence of the narrating or writing subject on the form of presentation. The association of *Historie* with grammar, rhetoric, and ethics, increasingly followed by poetics and aesthetics, dictated that the productive performance of the author be discussed.

The historian as artist or as moral judge played a productive role which had to be continually measured against the demands of an effective delivery. Lucian himself had relativized his metaphor of the mirror by his direct comparison of the historiographer with the sculptor whose material lies ready, but who must, as with Phidias, work it up in a manner as true to reality as possible. As the saying goes, the listener must be able to clearly "see," with his own ears, the events reported to him. The comparison with the productive sculptor in this way remained within the domains of sight, display, and reflection.

All metaphors that ultimately refer to a naked, unadorned, unequivocally reproducible truth refer us to a state of reality which constituted historical representation until well into the eighteenth century. Such metaphors involving a naive realism draw primarily on eyewitnesses (less on "earwitnesses") whose presence guarantees the truth of a history.[20] The methodological point of departure was the historical writing of the present or recent past. Everywhere they were capable, as in Herodotus, of reaching back three generations so that, with the aid of surviving earwitnesses, past events could be recovered and made plausible. The precedence of contemporary historical writing, reinforced by the growing body of memoir-literature in the early modern period, remained unbroken. It was likewise to be found preserved wherever recourse in the past was made. The signs of authenticity were centered on the eyewitness; whenever possible, the acting or participating agent, be it for the history of revelation, or for the continuing history of church or worldly events.

Historical experience therefore related itself to the present, a present which in its forward movement collected the past without, however, being able to significantly change itself. *Nil novum sub sole*: this was true both for classical antiquity and for Christians awaiting the Last Judgment. Related as it was to a given contemporary view, the metaphor of the mirror, of reflection or of the naked truth, was founded on a present state of experience whose historiographic apprehension corresponded to the recourse to an eyewitness. To establish the true nature of circumstances or of states of affairs, the historian must first question living eyewitnesses, and second, surviving earwitnesses. There is no great leap from this manner of disclosing reality to the demand for impartiality in the reproduction of an event in all its aspects, or to the idea that judgment is to do justice to all participants. History as a continuing present exists through its eyewitnesses; the interrogation of such eyewitnesses requires distance and impartiality.

There is no doubt that this canon, whose metaphors imply a continuous and unbroken present space of experience, can still today lay claim to methodological validity. It has not, however, called a halt here.

## The Discovery of Positional Commitment as a Precondition of Historical Knowledge

It seems to be a linguistic irony that, in the domain of sight and eyewitness, mirror-based metaphors and the undistorted truth, it is precisely the question of position or location which can assume the role of furthering understanding without straining these metaphors and the experience which they embody. If the historian is supposed to question all witnesses for the purpose of selecting the best and demoting the rest, why should the position adopted by the historian not have an influence on his presentation? This question arises quite naturally, not least under the influence of the doctrine of perspective, which originated during the Renaissance. Thus, Comenius, in 1623, compared the activity of historians with the view provided by telescopes which, like trombones, reached back over their shoulders. This prospect of the past was used to gain instruction for one's own present and for the future. Surprising, however, were the warped perspectives which cast everything in a varying light. Thus one could in no way "depend on it, that a thing really behaved in the way that it appeared to the observer."[21] Everyone trusted only in his own view, and from this there followed nothing but argument and bickering.

Cartesian doubt and Pyrrhonistic skepticism contributed to the formation of a guilty conscience among historians, who doubted that they could offer any representation adequate to reality. Thus, Zedler, still oriented to the realistic ideal for knowledge and transmitting the metaphors of Lucian, stated, full of reservation, that it would be very difficult, in fact practically impossible, "to be a complete writer of history. Whoever aspired to such, if possible, should have no allegiance to order, party, country, or religion."[22] The demonstration that precisely this is an impossibility is owed to Chladenius.[23]

Chladenius (1710–1759), at that time completely under the influence of the idea that authenticity resides in the testimony of the eyewitness, developed the domain of objects of *Historie* in terms of the contemporary *Geschichten* of living generations and hence made a distinction between future *Geschichten* and "ancient *Geschichten*."[24] This division did not, however, arrange itself according to substantive or chronological givens, and it no longer involves epochs; it is, in fact, conceived epistemologically. "Author, originator, or spectator" are more reliable than "reporters [*Nachsager*]"; verbal tradition is superior to written. Ancient history thus begins at the point where no eyewitnesses exist and directly mediating earwitnesses can no longer be questioned. With the demise of generations, then, the boundary of ancient history is displaced, and it advances at the same rate that witnesses disappear. It is no longer a given temporal order—for instance, a God-given order—of all of history that arranges the material of history, but instead the history of the future and the history of the past ("ancient history") are determined by desires and plans, as well as the questions, which arise in the present. The experiential space of contemporaries is the epistemological kernel of all histories.

To this extent, the epistemology of premodern *Historie* was supplied by Chladenius and established in a fashion that is today still unsurpassed. At the same time, however, Chladenius is thereby rendered the harbinger of modernity. Since that time, the temporal arrangement of history depends on the position one occupies within history.

Chladenius assumed that history and conceptions about it usually coincide. The exposition and evaluation of a history required, however, a methodological separation: "History is one, but conceptions of it are various and many." A history as such is, in his view, conceivable without contradiction, but any account of such a conception involves a break in perspective. It quite simply is decisive whether a history is judged by an "interested" or an "alien party," by "friend" or "foe," "scholar" or "lay person," "courtier" or "*Bürger*" or "peasant," or, finally, "insurrectionary" or "loyal subject."[25]

Chladenius deduced two things from this: first, the relativity of all intuitive judgments and of all experience. Two contradictory accounts can exist, both of which have a claim to truth. For there is

a reason why we see the thing in this way and no other: this is the viewpoint of the same thing. . . . It follows from the concept of points of view that persons regarding one thing from different points of view must have different conceptions of the thing . . .; *quot capita, tot sensus.*[26]

Second, Chladenius deduces from his analysis of the eyewitness and of political and social attitudes the perspective of later investigation and representation. Certainly, through proper questioning of opposing witnesses and the preservation of evidence, one has to endeavor to recognize past history oneself—to this extent, even Chladenius renders homage to a moderately realistic epistemological ideal—but the coherence of past events is not reproducible in its entirety by any form of representation. The "archetype of history" is itself transformed during the creation of a narrative.[27] Restriction to a particular position not only limits the witnesses, it also affects the historian. A history, once it has passed, remains irrevocably the same; but the prospects enjoyed by historians are kaleidoscopic in their variety of standpoints. A good historian, in particular, wishing to recount "meaningful history," can do no more than reproduce it in "rejuvenated images."[28] He must select and condense, employ metaphors, and use general concepts; in this way, he inevitably gives rise to new ambiguities which require exposition in turn. For "a writer of history composing rejuvenated images always (has) something in mind,"[29] and readers must be able to deal with this if they are to evaluate the history at stake.

"History," from that which is experienced to that which is scientifically consumed and digested, is always realized within social and personal perspectives which both contain and create meaning. "Those who require that a writer of history assume the position of a person without religion, fatherland, or family are greatly in error; they have not considered the impossibility of that which they demand."[30] From the time of Chladenius on, historians have been more secure in their consideration of the probability of an individual, historical form of truth. Positional commitment since then has not been an objection, but rather a presupposition of historical knowledge.

To be sure, Chladenius draws a clear line against deliberate invention or falsification that does not adhere to the rationally verifiable canon of interrogation of witnesses and source exegesis. The inevitability of perspective does not lead to a "partisan account" in which events

against knowledge and conscience are intentionally contorted or obscured. . . . An impartial account cannot, therefore, mean relating a thing without any point of view, for this is not at all possible; and relating in a partisan fashion cannot amount to relating a thing and history according to its points of view, for then all accounts would be partisan.[31]

In this appreciation of the lack of identity between a perspectivist mode of forming judgments, on the one hand, and partisanship, on the other, Chladenius established a theoretical framework which today has still to be superseded. For the sources of past events display a resistance and retain a weight that is not susceptible to displacement *ex post* through a partisan evaluation, whether positive or negative. Differing prospects can certainly result in differing results being drawn from the same sources. This point will be returned to in the conclusion.

Chladenius's epistemology was like an act of liberation. The extension of the witness's perspective (previously an object of historical inter-rogation) to that of the historian won for the historian a freedom previously unimagined. In terms of the poetic criteria which could at that time be adopted, the historian could henceforth be in a position to "produce" history by weighing causes, examining long-term re-lations, reorganizing the beginning and end of a history. He was able to design systems which appeared more appropriate to the complexity of histories than the simple addition of knowledge. In Klopstock's words, out of polyhistory arose polytheory.[32] Mindful of the discipline provided by the sources, the historian could ultimately construct hy-pothetical histories which drew more attention to the prerequisites of all histories than to these histories themselves. In short, the historian could become a philosopher of history, which had not before been possible.

Fénélon had forecast this breakthrough when he proposed, in 1714, that the true completeness of history rested in its ordering. To arrive at a good order, the historian must encompass the whole of his history with one glance and must turn it from side to side until he has found the true point of view (*son vrai point de vue*). He could then outline history as a unity and trace the most important events to their causes.[33]

Chladenius had provided this approach with a theoretical foundation, but in so doing he had relativized the question of what is the appropriate, true point of view for the historian, or, if you like, historicized it. He stumbled upon a plurality of points of view which necessarily belonged to historical knowledge without at the same time surrendering what they shared in common, historical truth. He had simply shifted the emphasis from truth itself to the epistemological conditions of truth.

From then on, the historian, inspired by the example of Chladenius, gained the courage to openly and consciously assume a "position" if he wished to reflect a point of view. This breakthrough was effected in the second half of the eighteenth century.

## Temporalization of Historical Perspective

Chladenius's work had a dual impact. His epistemology drew on the precedence of the optical, evident in all his imagery and comparisons. The eyewitness as guarantor of the realization of an occurrence remained the primary witness of all history. The historical space of experience corresponding to this approach was a space of acting and suffering persons, a space of events whose verifiability increased with their adjacency to a given present, and decreased with their removal. Accordingly, his *Allgemeine Geschichtswissenschaft* dealt first with the conditions of historical knowledge of the present, and then, on the basis of this, with the sources of past histories and their exposition. Past histories external to the living community of memory were merely a supplement to contemporary historical experience. But future history also belonged to the organon of historical exposition, since, for Chladenius, plans, hopes, and wishes were just as constitutive of the coming histories as those of one's own recent past. The three temporal dimensions remained anthropologically founded and likewise related to each other in a static fashion. After Chladenius, this rapidly altered, not least under the influence of the other part of his theory, his modern doctrine of historical perspective.

Whereas, in terms of its metaphorical employment, it was related initially to the space of a given present, this perspective extended itself more and more into the temporal depths. It gained, in addition, a temporal significance which articulated an increasing difference between past histories, one's own history, and the history of the future. Indeed, modes of perception were themselves endowed with temporal coefficients of change corresponding to the rapidly spreading contemporary conception that history was accelerating. This can be briefly outlined through the medium of historiography.

The expressions "point of view," "position," and "standpoint" (*Sehepunkt, Standort,* and *Standpunkt,* respectively) rapidly gained acceptance. Schlözer, Wegelin, and Semler also made use of them, and to the degree that the perspectival approach was taken seriously, the status of a once-and-for-all past history also altered. It lost its character of necessarily remaining identical with itself in order for it to possess verity.

Thus, Thomas Abbt wrote his *Geschichte des menschlichen Geschlechts*, "soweit selbige in Europa bekannt worden," and deduced from his "position" that "the history of a people in Asia is different from that of one in Europe."[34] There certainly was here the impact of a growing experience of overseas conquest, in which countless histories awaited integration into the world of European Christianity. But the idea that perspective should be spatially determined (i.e., must remain bound to one position) and that this would result in diverse but equally valid texts on the same substantial matter was before this point not accepted.

Temporal relativity now joined the spatial relativity of historical statement. It had not occurred to Chladenius that the course of time could also alter the quality of a history *ex post*. He had distinguished quite rigorously between an established and thenceforth consistent past, and the variety of accounts to which it gave rise. Gatterer had doubts here: "The truth of history remains fundamentally the same: I at least assume this here, although I know well that one may not assume even this everywhere." And he sought in an *Abhandlung vom Standort und Gesichtspunct des Geschichtschreibers* to demonstrate that it was ultimately selection that constituted a history. Selection, however, did not depend only on social or political circumstances, or on the supposed addressee, but also on temporal distance. Thus, Gatterer developed criteria which a German Livy (for example, a Protestant professor living under a mixed constitution) would today need in order to rewrite and write anew the Roman history of the authentic Livy, and accordingly improve this history by means of viewpoints newly attained.[35]

Historical time acquired a quality of generating experience, which, retrospectively applied, permitted the past to be seen anew. Büsch said in 1775: "Hereby can newly arising occurrences render important to us a history which had previously interested us little or not at all,"[36] referring to the history of Hindustan, which had first been introduced into a world-historical context by the English twenty years earlier. The factual effects of a history and its historical reflections thus mutually constituted each other. Opined Schlözer nine years later: "A fact can today appear extremely insignificant, but in the long term or the short term become decisively important for history itself or for criticism."[37]

But it was not simply the alteration of contemporary experience that displaced the valency of past events and hence the historical quality of those events. The mutual relation of temporal dimensions was also shifted by methodological focus and proficiency. Slowly the practice of writing a continuous "current history" (*Zeitgeschichte*) lost its methodological dignity. Planck was one of the first to establish that the increase of temporal distance raised rather than reduced the prospects for knowledge. This led to the exclusion of the eyewitness from his privileged position, which had already been relativized by Chladenius. The past was henceforth no longer to be preserved in memory by an oral or a written tradition, but rather was to be reconstructed through the process of criticism. "Every great occurrence is, for the contemporaries upon which it directly acts, wrapped in a fog, and this fog clears away very gradually, often taking more than a few human generations." Once sufficient time has elapsed, the past can appear "in a completely different form," thanks to a "historical criticism" capable of making allowances for the polemical partiality of earlier contemporaries.[38]

The old space of experience which had covered at any one time three generations was methodologically opened up. It was no longer a former present which constituted the thematic of *Historie*, extrapolating and handing down *Geschichten*. Now the past was itself made an object of study and, in terms of a specificity which is only today apparent, "in a completely different form." From a narrative of former presents there develops a reflective re-presentation (*Vergegenwärtigung*) of the past. Historical science, mindful of its temporal location, becomes the study of the past. This temporalization of perspective was certainly advanced by the swift change of experience embodied in the French Revolution. The break in continuity appeared to uncouple a past whose growing foreignness could only be illuminated and recovered by means of historical investigation. But this in no way means that historical research would be *eo ipso* nostalgic or restorative. The statement that the later a past is expounded, the better, is rather a product of the prerevolutionary philosophy of progress.

This philosophy discovered in history that temporal quality distinguishing the Former from Today, and that Today needs to be regarded as basically distinct from Tomorrow. The thesis of the possible repetition of events is discarded. If the whole of history is now unique, then to be consistent, the past must be distinct from the present and the present from the future. In brief, the historicizing of history and its progressive exposition were at first two sides of the same coin. History and Progress shared a common factor in the experience of a genuinely historical temporality. To recognize this, a particular viewpoint was needed which, in turn, had to perceive itself as historically conditioned.

In Germany, this is particularly apparent in the writing of the history of the Protestant Church which, as enlightened *Historie*, covertly became historical theology and sustained the new historical philosophy.

The anticipation of a genuinely historical temporality was outlined especially early by Bengel,[39] whose exposition of the Apocalypse of St. John implied the irreversible singularity of historical events. In doing so, Bengel proceeded in both empirical and reflective modes. Former interpretations of the Apocalypse were viewed not only as a collection of errors but as a progressive history of revelation. Each earlier exegesis was conceived as an act of obscurity foreseen by God, whose successive illumination was the task of later interpreters. From the collective misinterpretations and their correction, there finally emerged the ultimate, true insight. So much for the reflective aspect which was based upon belief.

According to Bengel, the events which had been biblically forecast occurred to the degree that the interpretation of such events increasingly proved accurate. The clearing away of past errors was at the same time made possible by the course of history. And in this way, the phenomenology of spirit is outlined. The interpretation of historical experience becomes the inherent moment of a history which leads to true knowledge.

Bengel proposed a model of progress, as was later demonstrated. Revelation disclosed itself in the forward movement of history or, more precisely, in the progressive coincidence of empirical events and salvational interpretation. Event and interpretation progressively converged, but only in the medium of a genuine historical temporality. The mode of interpretation remained the same, while its content altered.

This is apparent, for instance, in Semler, in the context of his rational historiography. The accent shifted from the divine economy of salvation to a historical economy of time, which permitted a progressive interpretation not only of what was foretold biblically, but of all historical events.

From the epistemological point of view, Semler based himself entirely on Chladenius's doctrine, except that he consistently temporalized historical perspective. He did further separate "real history" from its reproduction, but the history of historical reproduction became for him a moment of real history. Historians did not merely report, they "created" histories.

The influence of the will, intention, or objective, if it has just emerged and is not present in ancient times, gives the narrative a real direction which was not formerly present in the occurrence itself.

This retrospective structuration of the past was not traced by Semler to "evil or partisan intention," which occurred often enough. Instead, he said, "this distinction is quite unavoidable."[40] In the course of time, the conditions and circumstances according to which history is practiced are continually changing: "It is precisely this distinction of successive periods which brings about the fact that repeatedly new histories can and must arise."[41]

Semler concluded from this temporalized perspective that historical writing was only possible through the critical review of previous historiography. Stated more generally, historical knowledge always is simultaneously the history of historical science. The presuppositions according to which reports are made and processed must themselves be considered and critically reviewed. "I believe that one has previously paid too little attention to this former history composed by all previous historians." Here, Semler formulated a methodological principle which has since then been indispensable.

The doctrine of the temporal change of perspective was now preserved in a theology of progress which lent meaning to this change. God had intended it "for the further and ever new moral education of men." Because of his temporal approach, Semler was already forced into the position of a historical relativist for whom all histories were more of less partisan. He was only able to contain this dilemma by sketching in his own location in the course of a progressing knowledge and a rising morality. "The real stages of an ever unequal culture"[42] became for him the stages of growing knowledge which enabled those born later to see through and disclose the partisan interests of earlier generations and their historians. Semler intended to do exactly this with the three early Christian centuries. It was, he wrote, a blessing of Providence that "our life and epoch is placed so far beyond those Christian centuries." For it was only now possible to undertake a "free revision" which disclosed "for us, with regard to us, the really true history of [the Church] of that time."[43] Truth and temporal perspective are no longer separable. Whoever today claimed in his account the "unchangeability of the church system" was the slave of prejudice and served hierarchical ruling interests. He obstructed the moral development of Christian religion, "and no greater sin against all historical truth can exist."[44]

After being plunged into the temporal perspective of its historical development, a superior truth emerged out of historically relative truth. The theoretical condition of this superior position was the perspectival and (following from this) actual otherness of the past when compared with one's experience of today and expectation of the morrow. Goethe, soon afterwards, wrote:

There remains no doubt these days that world history has from time to time to be rewritten. This requirement does not arise, however, because many occurrences are rediscovered, but because new views emerge; because the contemporary of a progressive age is led to standpoints which provide new prospects of the past and permit it to be evaluated in a new manner.[45]

Goethe here articulates a historical experience which had slowly formed and whose theoretical construction in Germany has been followed in the above from Chladenius on: that relation to a particular location is constitutive for historical knowledge. This corresponded to a state of reality which increasingly allowed the dimensions of past, present, and future to break away from one another in the progress of time. The temporalization of this history endowed with an interrupted perspective made it necessary to consider one's position, for this altered with and in the historical movement. This modern experience, formerly more a revelation of theory, was now substantiated by the unrolling events of the French Revolution. This in particular provided a concrete constraint forcing the adoption of a partisan standpoint.

## The Partisan Constraint and Its Historiographic Constitution

Whereas the concept of party within German historiography to the eighteenth century was based upon confessional division and the fronts constituted around this, the concept assumed new force through the socially motivated constitutional conflict that broke out after the collapse of the system of estates in France and which soon afterward involved the whole of Europe. As Gentz noted in 1793, since the collapse,

> every democratic and antidemocratic party, in Germany as everywhere else, has split up into a great number of smaller parties [*Unterparteien*]. . . . Thus there exist today democrats until 5 October 1789, democrats until the formation of the Second Legislature, democrats until 10 August 1792, democrats until the murder of Louis XVI, and democrats until the expulsion of the Brissot faction in the month of June this year.[46]

Within this temporal perspective, still before the fall of Robespierre, Gentz quite concisely described the process of radicalization, hidden until then by the Revolution, which had generated the division of parties. The formation of political parties, while it may be a structural element of all history, in any case belongs since that time to the everyday experience of European modernity.

A sign of their modernity was that these parties did not simply mutually distinguish themselves socially or politically through substantial programs; these distinguishing features themselves involved a temporal factor of change. One placed oneself within the sequence of a continually changing history: toward the front (progressive), in the middle or toward the back (conserving). All titles to legitimacy are bound to a temporal scale if they seek any effect. As Rivarol noted, making metaphorical use of the parliamentary seating arrangements: "The Revolution limps. Rights move continually to the Left, but the Left never to the Right." Progress into an open future involved party perspectives, plans, and programs which dissolved in the absence of temporal criteria of movement or direction.

How, then, did *Historie* react to this new substantial reality? A few answers can be given. Gentz himself considered the temporal self-identification of the parties an error of perspective. "A writer who teaches the consideration of the Revolution as a whole" would come across the internal principles of movement compared with which the formation of parties is a superficial matter. Here he had discovered a response which ultimately implied a theory of revolution. Such theories, which seek to consider at once the plurality of all parties, developed in the succeeding period in great number and entered, for example, into the systems of German Idealism.

This led certainly only to a shift of the current demand to assume a party standpoint. This was openly expressed by Friedrich Schlegel, who had himself, in the course of time, decidedly changed camps. It was an illusion if one hoped "to find pure historical truth solely and alone in the so-called nonpartisan or neutral writers."[47] The formation of parties is a factor in history itself, and if parties, as, for example, in England, continuously reach into the present, one cannot avoid adopting a particular position. He thus demanded as a methodological principle that the historian openly state "views and opinions, without which no history can be written, at least no descriptive history." One could no longer complain of the "partisanship" of such a historian, even when one did not share his opinions.[48]

For Schlegel, the methodological condition for relief from partisanship lay in the separation of facts established independently of party positions from the formation of judgments on such facts. In this fashion, "factual exactness is itself not seldom promoted by dispute, since every party has the criticism of all others to fear, and thus they watch over each other and themselves."[49] Here, Schlegel has described—empirically, quite accurately—the reaction of political positions upon the practice of investigation, a practice which primarily seeks to preserve the separation of knowledge of the facts from the formation of judgment. This is the attempt to save objectivity without having to dispense with a partisan standpoint.

But even Schlegel found this approach inadequate. For it is impossible to answer in this way "which the right party" might be. As an investigator of empirical history, he found himself referred back to a theory of history in that he endeavored to raise himself to the "great standpoint of history," to use his words. Without "the general development of human fates and of human nature in view," the historian found himself caught up in mere political scribbling (*Schriftstellerei*).[50] Or, as he later stated in a more subdued fashion in the *Signatur des Zeitalters*: one could not "permit the party to count just as a party. . . . We should indeed be partisans of the food and the Divine . . . but we should never be partisan or even create a partisan position."[51]

Notwithstanding the religious position which Schlegel seeks to mediate through the historical movement, there is behind his ambivalent thoughts a historicotheoretical claim: history does not exhaust itself in the process of parties, for there plainly are long-term trends which, while promoted by disputes between parties, nevertheless do extend through their positions. Such long-term "tendencies," "ideas," or "forces," as one then said, became central to the interpretive apparatus of the Historical School, making it possible to arrange the entire course of history into epochs. The validity or plausibility of such factors cannot be assessed by means of empirical statements bound to specific sources; here, the field of theory alone is decisive. For this reason, the Historical School remained, part consciously, part unconsciously, under the influence of idealist philosophy.

Hegel, in separating his philosophical world history from the subjectivity of the know-all, defined its "spiritual [*geistiges*] principle as the "sum total of all possible perspectives."[52] Therefore, the demand for impartiality was justifiable. It alone saw to it that "that which existed [facticity] prevail" against an interested one-sidedness. In this way, Hegel gave due recognition to the inherited canon of historical investigation. Theoretically, however, he demanded partisanship. To stretch impartiality so far that it forced the historian into the role of "spectator," recounting everything without purpose, would rob impartiality of purpose:

Without judgment, history loses interest. Proper historical writing must, however, know the essential; it is a partisan of that which is essential and holds fast to that which has relation to it.[53]

It was plain to Hegel what the criterion of "the essential" (*das Wesentliche*) was: historical reason. But Hegel might here, without coincidence, have coined an empty formula, for it needs to be ever occupied anew within the temporal passage of history. Impartiality, indispensable in the methical course of investigation, cannot, however, relieve the historian of the necessity of identifying the criteria for the essential. Since the French Revolution, however, this is no longer possible without possessing, consciously or not, a theory of historical time.

In conclusion, this will be demonstrated by two examples.

It was generally accepted around 1800 that an epochal turning point had arrived. After the fall of Napoleon, Perthes wrote:

All comparisons of our time with turning points in the histories of individual peoples and individual centuries are far too petty; one will only be able to sense the immeasurable significance of these years if one recognizes that the whole of our part of the world is in a period of transition, a transition in which the conflicts of a passing and of an approaching half-millennium collide."[54]

Earlier developments could have produced a change of direction only for several centuries, but today the relations of old and new were shifting with "unbelievable speed." By way of compensation, interest in history was increasing. Perthes, therefore, sought to launch his *Europäische Staatengeschichte* in what was clearly a favorable state of the market. But he had difficulties, stemming from the new historical experience of acceleration. This caused professional historians to hesitate to write modern histories, especially those which, as had previously been customary, led as far as "contemporary history."

The three dimensions of time seemed to have fallen apart. The present was too fast and provisional. Rist wrote Perthes that

We have no kind of secure, established viewpoint from which we can observe, judge, and trace phenomena in their course toward us; [one lives] in a time of decline that has just begun.

This was confirmed by Poel:

Is not the condition everywhere—in bourgeois, political, religious, and financial life—a provisional one? But the aim of history is not that which is emerging, but that which has emerged. [Thus the planned *Staatengeschichte* has] a twin defect in seeking to relate to the transitory and to that which is imperfectly understood.

The future is likewise not knowable: where is the man who can see it even dawning? If he sought to write a history, he would have to

anticipate the birth of a functioning time together with its hopes and conjectures. His history would, as would everything which emerges with spirit from stirring times, increase the ferment, arouse passions, create conflict, and be an eloquent monument to the present, but not a history of the past. Such a history must not be written, and a different history cannot be written.

The past might now still be recognized, for "it should outline earlier history in relation to its present condition"; but this was impossible in the current "process of transformation." In a sentence, "From a history that is to be written now, nothing lasting, no real history, can be expected."[55]

Both of the academics who were approached thus based their refusal on a historicotheoretical argument. In other words, the acceleration of history obstructed the historian in his profession. Confronted with this, Perthes asked, "When will the time come when history comes to a halt?" As a result of this, there emerged that tendency dedicated to the reconstruction of a lost past in a methodologically rigorous investigation. This is the historical tendency about which Hegel had already made some ironical remarks; of which Dahlmann sarcastically said it was "a history far too respectable to approach the present day";[56] and which Nietzsche finally described as "antiquarian."

Pure investigation of the past was not, however, the sole response that was found for the acceleration of history. In this second camp, which, like the first, permits of no clear-cut political classification, Lorenz von Stein can be found. In 1843, Stein had clearly formulated the idea that temporal perspective was involved in a continually changing and accelerating movement and was itself driven by this movement. For fifty years, life had been accelerating in pace.[57] "It is as if the writing of history is no longer capable of keeping up with history." Thus was established the importance of the position from which one could apprehend the singularity of the modern movement in a single glance and which permitted one to form a judgment.

Perhaps without knowing it, Stein seized on arguments of Enlightenment theory. These gained ground steadily for those wishing to become involved with "contemporary history," for, if the periodic rhythm of history was undergoing change, an appropriate perspective was needed. Therefore, Stein searched for the laws of motion of modern history so that he could deduce from them a future that he wished at the same time to influence. The more he had before his eyes the advancing course of the French and English examples, out of which he endeavored to derive directions for political conduct in Germany, the more he was able to risk a prognosis on the basis of his diagnosis. A prerequisite of this was a history whose long-term effective factors remained susceptible to influence, but which initially were constant conditions of continual change. In this fashion, the historical perspective shifted completely from a pure condition of knowledge into a temporal determinant of all experience and expectation that derived from "history itself." In Feuerbach's words, "History has only that which is itself the principle of its changes."[58]

Both responses outlined here repeatedly appear in various guises. They react to a history which, in its change, demands that the relation of past and future be defined anew. Neither position is radically reducible to an alternative: here partisanship, there objectivity. The scale is a sliding one, as can be seen from what separates and what is shared by Ranke and Gervinus. Thus, Gervinus, as the propagator of a liberal politics, also entered a plea for a methodologically required impartiality: [The historian] must be a partisan of fate, a natural proponent of progress," for the representation of the cause of freedom is indispensable.[59] Opposing this move toward partisanship, Ranke deliberately assumed the contrary position, that of the timeless nature of historical research produced through the proper method. Writing an obituary, Ranke noted:

Gervinus frequently repeated the view that science must intervene in life. Very true, but to be effective it must above all be science; for it is not possible for one to adopt a position in life and transfer this into science: then life affects science, and not science life. . . . We can then only exercise a real influence on the present if we first disregard it, and fix our thoughts on a free objective science.

He strictly rejected any view "which considers all that has occurred from the standpoint of the present day, especially since the latter changes itself continually."[60] For Ranke, historical specificity remained an objection against historical knowledge. Not that Ranke could have done without the effectivity (even party-political) of historical knowledge. Rather, he wished to mediate it through a science distanced from the everyday so that past history might itself be initially recognized. He scented behind questions guided by interest the danger that they would obstruct precisely the historical knowledge that might today be needed.

Thus we stand in the middle of the previous century before the same dilemma that still dominates our discussion today. The historical doctrine of perspective has indeed helped us disclose the historicity of the modern world, but in the dispute between objectivists and representatives of partisanships the camps are divided. They have separated, notwithstanding the great historiographical attainments that have issued from both camps.

## Theoretical Prospect

The foregoing historical outline lays no claim to establish in a hard-and-fast way the chronological succession of the positions presented. Rather, these were ordered with respect to a systematic viewpoint which may need to be altered or supplemented in the light of material from different countries and periods. Nevertheless, the problem of a modern historical relativism and its scientific assimilation will not substantially alter. It is, therefore, possible to draw some conclusions here from the arguments which, in Germany, first posed the questions of locational determination and formulated the various responses to these questions.

Since the ancient doctrines of historical artifice, there has been a dispute about the degree to which an interpreter can himself present a history, or whether history can be brought to life only in a rhetorical performance. Chladenius drew a distinction between true histories that were in themselves unchanging and exposition that was determined by a particular position. The temporalization of perspective made the issue more complex, since henceforth the history of influence and of reception of past events became part of the experiential substance of "history in general," entering into the individual histories. Likewise, the new positions gave past "facts" a continuing validity independent of the judgments made upon them later. The separation of fact and judgment was even accepted by Hegel, to the extent that he associated the methodological establishment of facts with impartiality, demanding partisanship only for the formation of historical judgment—partisanship of reason, hence partisanship for the suprapartisan.

Past facts and contemporary judgment are, within the practice of investigation, the terminological poles which correspond to objectivity and partiality in epistemology. From the viewpoint of investigative practice, however, the problem becomes less critical. There is probably only an apparent problem concealed behind the epistemological antithesis. In the historiographic context, facts are also conditioned by judgment. In Gentz's words, whether Louis XVI was murdered, executed, or even punished is a historical question; but the "fact" that a guillotine of a given weight separated his head from his body is not.

Methodologically, so-called pure establishment of the facts is indispensable, but it involves the principles of general verifiability. Historical method has its own rationality. Questions regarding original source authenticity, document dating, statistical figures, reading methods, and text variations and derivations can all be answered with an exactitude similar to that of the natural sciences, such that results are universally communicable and verifiable independent of the position of a historian. This canon of methodical accuracy, developed through the centuries, offers a solid barrier against arbitrary claims made by those convinced by their own certainty. But the real dispute over the "objectivity" of the "facts" to be established from remnants does not primarily take place within the domain of scientific technique. There are degrees of correctness for historical observations that can be definitively determined. The dispute over "objectivity" becomes explosive when a "fact" moves into the context of the formation of historical judgment. Thus the suggestion being made here is to shift the problematic.

The real tension, indeed a productive tension, which a historian should see himself confronting, is that between a theory of history and the given sources. Here, we are falling back on experience and results assembled before the establishment of historism, drawing on knowledge developed by Enlightenment and Idealism thinkers that has been outlined here.

There is always more at stake in historical knowlege than what is contained in the sources. A source can exist or be discovered, but it can also be missing. This, then, makes it necessary here to take the risk of making statements which are perhaps not completely founded. But it is not only the patchiness of all sources — or their excess, in the case of recent history — which hinders the historian in establishing, on the basis of sources alone, either past or contemporary history. Every source — more exactly, every remnant that we transform into a source through our questions — refers us to a history which is either more, less, or in any case something other than the remnant itself. History is never identical with the source that provides evidence for this history. If this were so, then every cleanly flowing source would be the history we sought.

This might be true for the history of art, whose sources are, at the same time, its objects. This might be true for biblical exegesis, in which the statements of the Bible are the object. It might also work for the analysis of laws, to the extent that they claim a normative validity. Historical science is, however, required from the first to interrogate sources in order to encounter patterns of events that lie beyond these sources. This requirement also contains the boundary of any doctrine of *Verstehen*, which remains primarily oriented to persons, and their testimony or works, and which forms the objects for interpretation. Even explanatory models employed, for instance, in the interpretation of long-term economic change, escape the method of *Verstehen*, which functions only at the level of the source. As historians, then, we have to go a step further when we consciously make history or wish to recall a past.

The step beyond immanent exegesis of the sources is made all the more necessary when a historian turns away from the so-called history of events and directs his gaze at long-term processes and structures. In written records, events might still lie directly to hand; but processes, enduring structures, do not. And if a historian has to assume that the conditions of possible events are just as interesting as the events themselves, then it becomes necessary to transcend the unique testimony of the past. Every testimonial, whether in writing or as an image, is bound to a particular situation, and the surplus information that it can contain is never sufficient to grasp the historical reality that flows through and across all testimony of the past.

Thus we need a theory: a theory of possible history. Such a theory is implicit in all the works of historiography; it is only a matter of making it explicit. There is a wide variety of statements on history in its entirety or individual histories which cannot be directly related to the sources, at least in the second phase of study.

On the basis of everyday experience, it cannot be denied that an economic crisis or the outbreak of war is perceived by those affected as divine punishment. Theological science can essay an interpretation, in the form, for instance, of a theodicy that lends meaning to affliction. Whether this kind of explanation will be accepted by historians, or whether they would rather find other reasons (for instance, the catastrophe as the outcome of erroneous calculations of power) or look for psychological, economic, or other kinds of explanations, cannot be decided at the level of the sources. The sources certainly might provide an impulse toward a religious interpretation. The decision of which factors count and which do not rests primarily at the level of theory, and this establishes the conditions of possible history. The question of whether a history should be read economically or theologically is initially one that has nothing to do with the state of the sources, but is a theoretical decision that has to be settled in advance. Once this decision is made, the sources begin to speak for themselves. On the other hand, they can remain silent because, for instance, there is no evidence suited to a question formulated economically, and the question is not thereby a false one. Therefore, the primacy of theory brings with it the compulsion of having the courage to form hypotheses. Historical work cannot do without this. This does not mean that research is given a free hand. Source criticism retains its irreplaceable function. The function of the sources, their criticism, and their exposition must be defined more closely than was previously customary under the doctrine of *Verstehen*.

In principle, a source can never tell us what we ought to say. It does prevent us from making statements that we should not make. The sources have the power of veto. They forbid us to venture or admit interpretations that can be shown on the basis of a source to be false or unreliable. False data, false statistics, false explanation of motives, false analyses of consciousness: all this and much more can be revealed by source criticism. Sources protect us from error, but they never tell us what we should say.

That which makes a history into the historical cannot be derived from the sources alone: a theory of possible history is required so that the sources might be brought to speak at all.

Partisanship and objectivity cross one another in a new fashion within the force field between theory formation and source exegesis. One without the other is worthless for research.[61]

# III

## Semantic Remarks on the Mutation of Historical Experience

# The Historical-Political
# Semantics of Asymmetric
# Counterconcepts

Pugnant ergo inter se mali et mali; item pugnant inter se mali et boni;
boni vero et boni, si perfecti sunt, inter se pugnare non pussunt.
Augustine, *De Civ. Dei* XV, 5

Names for oneself and for one's family belong to the everyday life
of men and women. They articulate the identity of a person and of
that person's relation to others. In this process there might be agreement
on the use of such expressions, or each might use for his opposite a
term different from that employed by the latter. It makes a difference
whether mutually recognized names are spoken (e.g., Hans and Liese),
or whether these are replaced by abusive nicknames. So, for instance,
among relatives there is a difference between the use of "mother"
and "son," and "old bag" and "layabout." In the same way, it makes
a difference if certain functions are defined as "employer" and "em-
ployee" or as "exploiter" and "human material."

   In the one case, one's names for oneself and names others call one
coincide, whereas, in the other, they diverge. The first case implies a
mutual linguistic recognition, while, in the second, the characterization
takes on a disparaging meaning such that the subjects, while feeling
themselves addressed, do not feel properly recognized. These conflicting
classifications, employed only in one direction and in an unequal fashion, are what will here be called "asymmetric" classifications.

   The efficacy of mutual classifications is historically intensified as
soon as they are applied to groups. The simple use of "we" and "you"
establishes a boundary and is in this respect a condition of possibility

determining a capacity to act. But a "we" group can become a politically effective and active unity only through concepts which are more than just simple names or typifications. A political or social agency is first constituted through concepts by means of which it circumscribes itself and hence excludes others; and therefore, by means of which it defines itself. A group may empirically develop on the basis of command or consent, of contract or propaganda, of necessity or kinship, and so forth; but however constituted, concepts are needed within which the group can recognize and define itself, if it wishes to present itself as a functioning agency. In the sense used here, a concept does not merely denote such an agency, it marks and creates the unity. The concept is not merely a sign for, but also a factor in, political or social groupings.

There are innumerable concepts of this kind which, while being concretely applied, have a general utility. An acting agency might, therefore, define itself as a polis, people, party, *Stand*, society, church, or state without preventing those excluded from the agency from conceiving of themselves in turn as a polis, people, and so on. Such general and concrete concepts can be used on an equal basis and can be founded upon mutuality. They are transferable.

It is certainly true, however, that historical agencies tend to establish their singularity by means of general concepts, claiming them as their own. For a Catholic, "the Church" might be only that to which he belongs; similarly, "the Party" for a Communist, and "the Nation" for the French Revolutionary. The use of the definite article here serves the purpose of political and social singularization.

In such cases, a given group makes an exclusive claim to generality, applying a linguistically universal concept to itself alone and rejecting all comparison. This kind of self-definition provokes counterconcepts which discriminate against those who have been defined as the "other." The non-Catholic becomes heathen or traitor; to leave the Communist party does not mean to change party allegiance, but is rather "like leaving life, leaving mankind" (J. Kuczynski); not to mention the negative terms that European nations have used for each other in times of conflict and which were transferred from one nation to another according to the changing balance of power.

Thus there are a great number of concepts recorded which function to deny the reciprocity of mutual recognition. From the concept of the one party follows the definition of the alien other, which definition can appear to the latter as a linguistic deprivation, in actuality verging on theft. This involves asymmetrically opposed concepts. The opposite is not equally antithetical. The linguistic usage of politics, like that of everyday life, is permanently based on this fundamental figure of asymmetric opposition. This will be examined in the course of the following discussion.

There is one qualification, however: we will deal here only with pairs of concepts that are characterized by their claim to cover the whole of humanity. Thus we are dealing with binary concepts with claims to universality. The totality of humanity can, of course, also be comprehended without remainder by classificatory couples involving a mutual recognition of the parties involved (for instance, men and women, parents and children, juveniles and adults, the sick and the healthy). These terms comprehend humanity as a whole by introducing their natural structure. Notwithstanding the susceptibility to political accentuation and explosiveness which all these terms once had or will have, it is not possible to directly transfer such naturalistic expressions into political language.

The historical world, by contrast, operates for the most part with asymmetrical concepts that are unequally antithetical. Three will be examined: the contrast of Hellene and Barbarian, Christian and Heathen, and finally, the contrast that emerges within the conceptual field of humanity between human and nonhuman, superhuman and subhuman.

Before we begin to more closely analyze these counterconcepts and the various ways in which their negation is expressed, it is desirable to make three additional methodological points which will enable us to more exactly specify our problematic. The first concerns the relation between concept and history; the second, the historical aspect; and the third, the structural aspect of counterconcepts.

1. Historical movement always takes place within zones mutually delimited by functioning agents, and it is in terms of these zones that the agents simultaneously effect their conceptual articulation. But neither social nor political history is ever identical with its conceptual self-expression. History can only be written if the correspondence between material that was once comprehended conceptually and the actual material (methodologically derived from the first) is made the subject of investigation. This correspondence is infinitely variable and must not be mistaken as an identity; otherwise, every source that was

conceptually unambiguous would already be the history that was sought within it. In general, language and politico-social content coincide in a manner different from that available or comprehensible to the speaking agents themselves.

It is a quality of political language that its concepts, while being related to agencies (institutions, groups, and so forth) and their movement, are not assimilated by them. In the same way, history is not the sum of all articulated namings and characterizations in political language, nor of political dialogue and discussion. Similarly, history is not assimilated by the concepts through which it is comprehended. What is at stake here is the avoidance of a short circuit between conceptual language and political history. This difference between history and its "conceptualization" will be charted with the methods of historicopolitical semantics.

2. Especial care is called for in investigating what are not simply individual concepts but pairs of concepts whose world-historical effectiveness cannot be doubted. One can certainly assume that rigorous dualisms—above all, those which divide all of humanity into two groups with opposing modalities—were politically efficacious and will always be so. On the other hand, the historical record does show that all these global dualisms formerly in use were overtaken by historical experience and to this extent refuted. The suggestively autonomous force of political counterconcepts should not tempt one to regard relations of reciprocity implicit within such couples (and often created by them) as if they continued ever onward in the form of this once-established dualism. Past antitheses have tended to be too crude to serve as categories of historical knowledge. Above all, no historical movement can be adequately evaluated in terms of the self-same counterconcepts used by the participants of such a movement as a means of experiencing or comprehending it. Ultimately, that would mean the perpetuation of a victor's history by his seeking to make permanent a temporary dominance through the negation of the defeated.

Concepts employable in a particularly antithetical manner have a marked tendency to reshape the various relations and distinctions among groups, to some degree violating those concerned, and in proportion to this violation rendering them capable of political action. The recognition of such a dynamic requires that former linguistic usage must itself be placed in question. A distinction will therefore be made here between past historical usage of antithetical concepts and the semantic structures they are invested with.

3. The following reflections will not be concerned with historical process or the emergence and articulation of dualistic counterconcepts, their change, and the history of their likely effects. It is obvious that historical investigation cannot dispense with the posing and consideration of such questions. The methodological intention of the following is, however, on a different level: the structure of argument within once historically extant, dualistic, linguistic figures will be examined for the manner in which the given counterpositions were negated.

It must be admitted that the structural aspect implies the historical, and vice versa. In this way, the sources can be read in two ways at once: as the historical utterance of agencies, and as the linguistic articulation of specific semantic structures.

It is characteristic of counterconcepts that are unequally antithetical that one's own position is readily defined by criteria which make it possible for the resulting counterposition to be only negated. This is what makes up the counterconcepts' political efficacy but at the same time renders them unsuitable for scientific knowledge. In Kant's words, ". . . dividing things in half leads to the placing together of heterogeneous objects and not at all to a specific concept."[1] The recognition of historical bisections in their linguistically asymmetric forms requires the examination of common and distinguishable structures.

Once they had emerged historically, the conceptual pairs Hellene-Barbarian, Christian-Heathen, Human-Nonhuman indicated particular modes of experience and expectational possibilities whose given arrangement could turn up under different labels and in different historical situations. Each of the antitheses to be examined here has its own structures, but it also has structures in common with the others. These structures are continually evident in political language, even if the words or names alter with time. The structure of the counterconcepts does not depend solely on the words from which the conceptual pairs are composed. The words are replaceable, whereas the asymmetric structure of the argument survives.

Considered from the viewpoint of their structure, conceptual pairs can be separated from their original conditions of emergence and their former concrete context: they are historically transferable. This makes possible a history of the effects of concepts, and on this transferability is based the structural property that certain experiential frameworks are repeatedly applicable and open the way for analogies.

Of course, specific pairs of concepts change their nature and consequences in the course of time. Experiential spaces shift their ground and new horizons of expectation open up. Linguistic possibilities develop or lapse into disuse, old meanings fade or are enriched, such that temporal sequence is just as irreversible in the usage of pairs of concepts, driving onward their unmistakable singularity.

The methodological antinomy that prevails between the linguistic figures of historical singularity and structural iterability is merely a consequence of what was established above: history is never identical with its linguistic registration and formulated experience, whether this is expressed orally or in writing, but at the same time, that it is not independent of these linguistic articulations. Our counterconcepts then prove the iteratability, as well as the novelty, of the situations they refer to. But these situations are themselves at once the same and something other than what their linguistic self-registration can make known.

The following three sections thus are subject to a methodological limitation. The vast quantity of material that is structured and stylized by counterconcepts cannot be exposed here. Instead, the semantic structure of a few politically employed and asymmetrically applicable counterconcepts will be outlined in the course of their emergence. This will make clear how the structure of the first pair, Hellene and Barbarian, continuously reappears; that particular features of the second pair, Christian and Heathen, were contained in the first; and finally the counterconcepts that emerge in the semantic field of Humanity in general contain both Greek and Christian elements without, however, being reducible to them.

The accumulation of temporalities finally makes it possible for the structure of all these counterconcepts to appear together. Today we have both antithetical linguistic figures appearing alongside each other, and the contemporaneity of the noncontemporaneous which is contained within a single pair of concepts, thanks to the historical diversity of the zones of experience that this pair comprehends.

Very roughly, the three pairs can be distinguished in the following way: in the case of the Hellene and the Barbarian, we have, in the first place, mutually exclusive concepts, the groups to which they refer (also in the realm of reality) being spatially separable. The alien other is negatively marked off but (and this represented a historical achievement) also recognized as being so. The concepts impute naturalistic constants to the relevant groups, and these constants do not appear to be freely disposable. This quickly changes, however. The territorialization of the concepts is followed by their spiritualization, and this was to be continually and variously repeated in the succeeding history.

Second, the counterconcepts are related. That which the Greeks only suggest becomes central for the couple Christian-Heathen. The relation of reciprocity is subject to a temporal loading, which determines a future displacement that can go as far as abolishing the Other. The temporalization of the counterconcepts leads to a shift in the relation of experiential space and the horizon of expectation. From this arises a dynamic which negates the existing Other, a dynamic hardly known to non-Christian Antiquity.

Third, the invocation of humanity involves a claim to generality which is so total that no human being appears to be excluded. If counterconcepts that intend to annihilate the Other emerge nevertheless, they can be characterized by an ideological fungibility which, by definition, departs from earlier concepts. The capacity for differentiating the inner and the outer, which is a property of the first conceptual couple, appears to vanish within the horizon of a unitary mankind. This capacity does, however, creep into the new formation and leads to consequences that we live with today.

**Hellenes and Barbarians**

"Barbarian" has until the present generally been usable in a neutral scientific language, as well as in a more charged political language. On the other hand, the expression "Hellene," which had originally defined "Barbarian" negatively, survives only as a historical or specific name for a people.[2] The classical conceptual couple thus belongs to history, though it displays model-like features which recur throughout the course of history.

The words existed as independent terms before being arranged as polarities. All non-Greeks were treated as Barbarians before the Greeks collectively dubbed themselves Hellenes.[3] From the sixth to the fourth centuries B.C. the conceptual couple of Hellene and Barbarian became a universal figure of speech which included all of humanity through assignation to one of two spatially separated groups. This figure was asymmetrical. Contempt for aliens, stammerers, and the incoherent was expressed by a series of negative epithets degrading the whole of humanity beyond Hellas. The Barbarians not only were formally non-Greek, or aliens, but also, as aliens, were defined negatively. They were cowardly, unskillful, gluttonous, brutish, and so on. For every definition there was empirical evidence: contact with overseas traders, the mass of foreign slaves, devastation of the homeland by invading Persians, and similar experiences could easily be generalized without seeming to need revision.

The Greek intelligentsia was certainly clear-sighted enough to notice deviations from this pattern. For example, Herodotus came to realize the relativity of the concept "Barbarian,"[4] and Plato criticized the lack of equilibrium in the conceptual couple arising from the divergence of typification and the criterion of division.[5] The name of one people— the Hellenes—became the counterconcept for all the rest, who were assembled under a collective name which was simply the negative of Hellene. Asymmetry was thus semantically based on this conscious contrast of a specific name with a generic classification.

It was certainly possible for the Greeks to point to features that they had in common and which the aliens lacked: the creation of the *polis* as a civil constitution opposed to oriental monarchy, their physical and intellectual education, their language and art, their oracles and cult festivals—these united the Hellenic peoples but also excluded the Barbarians. Thus there was evidence that appeared to confirm the positive image of the Hellenes as mild, educated, free citizens. The "barbaric" fashion in which Hellenes actually treated themselves and where their self-image was correct, where it was not, and where it was wishful thinking, were described soberly and sympathetically by Jacob Burckhardt.[6]

Aside from the relevance or irrelevance of this dualistic evaluation, the conceptual couple assumed a semantic structure which made political experience and expectation possible while at the same time restricting it. This is apparent in the arguments that were used to justify the differentiation of the two concepts. Plato, with typical seriousness, but certainly with an intention to provoke, reduced the contrast to one of nature. *Physei* the Hellenes are a distinct species that degenerates with increasing intermingling with Barbarians.[7] From this naturalistic definition he draws the political conclusion that any dispute among Greeks is an argument among brothers (*stasis*), a civil war, and therefore pathological. A war with Barbarians—*polemos*—on the other hand, is justified by nature. Conflicts among Greeks should be conducted in a mild manner and with minimal force, while wars against Barbarians should aim at annihilation.[8] This asymmetrical dualism, then, contributes to the creation of a political interior which is shielded from the entirety of the outside world.

This maxim was given greater edge when Aristotle designated the Barbarians as natural slaves and described the Greeks by contrast as optimally combining strength and intelligence and who, if they were to form a single *politeia*, would be able to rule over all Barbarians.[9] In support of his view that the Barbarians are natural servants, he cited Euripedes' verse, according to which the Greeks are destined to rule over the Barbarians, and not vice versa. This verse could be taken in many ways: as challenging Alexander to subjugate the Persians, but also as being of use internally. The separation of interior and exterior which had initially characterized the spatial contrast of Hellenes and Barbarians was used by Aristotle to give added support to the interior structure of rule. The counterconcepts also serve to illuminate a differentiation of domination from top to bottom. Barbarians reduced to their animal-like natural properties were suited within a *polis* to the work of Perioecians, or slaves.[10] The very same barbarian characteristics that led in the East to the development of tyranny served within the community of citizens to make possible the self-rule of free Hellenes.[11] Hellenes and Barbarians had been so widely separated by nature that the distinction assisted in the foundation of both an internal constitution and external politics. Whereas Plato wished to deflect civil war from Hellas to the East, Aristotle restricted the title of legitimation: the asymmetry of the counterconcepts secured the preeminence of the Greek citizen both internally and externally.

The reduction of the contrast to *physis*, dividing humanity into two parts of unequal size and value could itself not be taken too far as a Hellenic argument. Derivations of this nature can be interpreted as claims to self-protection. This ideological-critical view can be found confirmed in the texts of Plato[12] and Aristotle[13] to the degree that both authors also perceived the Barbarians in a more differentiated fashion. It was not possible to subsume all Barbarians under this dualistic concept. Aristotle had some difficulty in rebutting the sophistic argument[14] according to which Hellenes, Barbarians, and slaves all were naturally equal and distinguished only by law and activity. The given physical or spiritual properties supposedly characteristic of a free man or a slave by no means always coincided with their actual properties or with the positions they occupied,[15] forming the basis for the expressions "noble heathen" or "northern soul in an eastern body."

The naturalistic counterpoint of Hellene and Barbarian was probably tempered by archaic and diffuse ethnocentric features which were then taken up by a Greece that was becoming increasingly conscious of itself, used to typify its singularity, and thereby were generalized. This involved a degree of wishful thinking. Nevertheless, contained within this reduction of mankind into two mutually opposed but naturally associated human types is a semantic function of some political effect. The aliens remained recognized as such, even if it was with animadversion; and this is not self-evident. Within the interior of the *polis*, master and slave were related to each other and were, as humans, capable of friendship.[16] Externally, the Barbarians were bound by a constitution which was determined by nature and climate, resulting in the formation of a different sort of people. This form of substantial association between political concepts and natural properties could not be easily displaced or dislodged by the conceptual couple. The constancy of concepts and of the human world, both of which only they made comprehensible, provided the foundation and limit of what could be politically experienced.

The whole of the following history is characterized in this way by the recurrence of simplified, dualistic forms encoding ethnic, *ständisch*, popular, or state agencies. These agencies, while recognizing the quasi-natural otherness of the aliens or subjects, might also despise them, but nevertheless accepted them as aliens, or claimed them as subjects. More recently, one can point to Boulainvilliers or Gobineau, whose doctrines of superimposition related to static natural entities;[17] the consequences of the seemingly biological doctrine of race which the National Socialists adopted go far beyond this. Or one might recall Harold Nicolson's remark concerning a French Secretary of State who, "despite his marked francophile tendencies . . . was at heart an internationalist. He recognised that other countries, notwithstanding their barbarity, did nonetheless exist."[18]

The Greeks were aware of an argument that ran counter to the naturalistic reduction and which had the affect of historically relativizing the natural duality. While it served to account for Greek superiority, it remained subsidiary, for it was not provided with theoretical foundation. In Thucydides, Plato, and Aristotle we find repeated comparisons of the cultural difference prevailing between Greeks and Barbarians with that of an earlier time, when the names had not yet been placed in opposition to one another.[19] Then the Greeks had shared the crudity and simplicity of barbaric customs; for instance, they appeared in contests clothed, carried weapons in times of "peace" and practiced piracy, bought women, wrote in a poor style, privileged the accuser in a trial, voluntarily elected rulers with unlimited powers, practiced exchanges in kind—all forms of behavior that are superseded with the advance of civilization and division of labor. "Many other examples could be given of the way in which ancient Hellenes lived according to the same customs that prevail among the Barbarians today."[20]

The dualism thus assumed a historical perspective, as we say today. The present contemporaneousness of Hellene and Barbarian is perceived in terms of the noncontemporaneousness of their cultural levels. Customs that changed over time were endowed with an argumentative force attributable to this elapsed time. The politicocultural comparison was not, then, simply a contractual antithesis; it was, in addition, historically mediated. The attachment of this difference, itself constituted according to origin or *physis* and not to an open future that could be projected in a progressive modality, provided the Greeks with a substantial argumentative element which later was to be quite freely adopted.[21] Above all, it was the temporal comparison with the past that made a lasting impression.

For Jacob Burckhardt, the "real feature which significantly distinguished barbarism from culture" was contained in the question: "Where in the past and in the present does life, i.e., the distinctive comparison, begin? At what point does the merely ahistorical present cease?"[22] Not that Burckhardt could have substantially adopted Greek criteria and applied them, for example, to the Egyptians, a people that he "placed in the vanguard" by virtue of their historical consciousness. Burckhardt instead assumed the Greek potential for the construction of argument. The Greek method of historical comparison was viewed by him as a lasting criterion of distinction with respect to barbarism. In a similar manner, Ernst Troeltsch was able to define the turning away from culture into barbarism as a relapse into ahistoricity.[23] While speaking at a higher level of generality—of culture and barbarism, not of Hellenes and Barbarians—both authors made use of a perception

whose historical perspective had already been opened up by the reflections of the Greeks. The alternative to barbarism was derived not
only from physical and spatial properties but also from the past, without
ceasing, however, to be an asymmetrical and universal alternative.

In the course of a rapidly passing Greek history, the actual polarities
of the conceptual couple—attributable as they were to *physis*—did
become less sharp. The Hellenic antithesis was negated by Diogenes
when he privately described himself as *apolis, aoikos,* or *patridos hester-
amenos* without, however, becoming a non-Hellenic Barbarian. He
coined the universalistic concept "cosmopolite" with the object of
transcending the usual dualism.[24] The antithesis became appreciably
less evident following Alexander's forcible fusion of Greek and Barbarian. Mankind and its political organization appeared to approximately coincide, first under Alexander and later within the Roman
imperium.

Within this new unity and its intellectual apprehension, as *homonoia*
(or later as *concordia*) of all humanity, the older dualism was nonetheless
preserved; it was simply recast, without relinquishing the continued
division of all humanity into Hellenes and Barbarians under identical
terms.[25] The distinction that had formerly been made spatially came
to be deployed horizontally as a universal criterion of differentiation:
"Hellene" was a person with sufficient education, whether Greek or
non-Greek, who merely had to be able to speak proper Greek; the
remainder were Barbarian. Thus, this new antithesis, which was organized around education, no longer derived from natural qualities;
to this extent, the counterconcepts were denaturalized and stripped
of all spatial connection. Linguistic usage became functionally mobile.
The criterion of education was transferable, and the term "Hellene"
was applicable to ever more human groups. The directly political
function of the dualism—defining and promoting a condition of domination—was lost, and from that point on, the duality instead served
as an indirect protection for the role of social leadership of the Hellenic
educated stratum, which persisted through the political upheavals of
the Diadochi period and Roman occupation.

The striking antithesis of educated Hellene and crude Barbarian
could also be employed in reverse, forming an underlying and continually reemerging tradition which was cultivated in particular by the
Cynics.[26] "Barbarian" here served as a positive contrast to a cultivated
existence and its consequences. Features charged with utopianism

were twined around these simple, genuine beings who were close to nature and removed from civilization: the antithesis was turned on its side, its terms were changed, and it was put back into use. The characteristic asymmetry was thus maintained within the same experiential space, except that the counterconcept now performed the function of critique and self-criticism.

The linguistic figure was in this sense, through the exchange of terminology, historically recallable. It is not possible to investigate the analogies here, but one could cite the "noble heathen" honored (not exclusively) by the Christian knights during the Crusades,[27] or the *bon sauvage* with which Jesuit and Enlightener placed in question their own society of orders.[28] As long as there existed functioning political agencies that typified their consciousness in a movement from internality to externality, or vice versa, this asymmetric linguistic figure survived, and along with it the constantly recast and also positive concept of the Barbarian.

Even the Stoics, who never tired of criticizing the Aristotelian contrast of Hellene and Barbarian as unnatural, and who drew a parallel between cosmic order and the unity of a humanity in a civil community directed by a single ruler, did not renounce the antithesis by means of which they had secured their position with respect to the rest of mankind. Thus, Plutarch rejected even custom and language as criteria of demarcation on the grounds that they were accidental (only, however, to define virtue as a Hellenic quality and depravity as Barbarian).[29] The use of terminology in such a moralistic fashion removes its autonomous, systematic force.

In this respect, there appear in the Stoics other dualistic formulations that illuminate their doctrine. These must be mentioned here because of their temporal propinquity to Christianity as well as to a universalistic doctrine of mankind. Disregarding the manner in which their rigorous moral dualism[30] led to asymmetric concepts that approached the Hellenistic usage, which equated the educated with the Greeks and the uneducated with the Barbarians[31] (as, for example, when Chrysippus confronted the *spoudaioi* with the *phauloi*[32]), the Stoics did employ a form of doctrine of the two realms, except that the realms were not related to each other by negation.

The Stoics considered the cosmos, governed by *logos*, as their home in which all humankind—freeman and slave, Hellene and Oriental, just as much as the gods and the stars—had a part. Political agencies were built into this cosmopolis, although the Stoics could never have identified the supervening with the empirical order.[33] The assignation of the earthly realm to megalopolis, to cosmopolis, was conceived as an apparent equality or as mimesis[34] which, while diminishing the difference of logos from experience, did not, however, entirely seek to do away with such difference. The cosmic law which guided the Stoics and which provided the basis for a life ruled by reason, when properly understood, also guided the external laws of human society. Even outbreaks of unrest, civil wars, and the sufferings they brought were integrated in a higher order which would, for some time to come, intervene repeatedly. Mediating the tension between cosmic reason and situations of political conflict was, for the Stoics, a constant challenge in their practice of philosophical reasoning. In contrast to the later Augustinian doctrine of the two realms,[35] a universal realm was implicit within the possible thought and experience of the cosmologically oriented Hellenes and the Hellenistic Romans. The series *familia* to *urbs* to *orbis* could be arranged as continuous steps determined by its *logos*.[36]

Within this experiential space, the drastic dual formulations of the Stoics, however much they comprehended the entire human world, performed a function different from that of the contrast of "Hellene" and "Barbarian," or "Christian" and "Heathen." A human being could at the same time be a citizen, but a Christian could not simultaneously be Heathen, or a Hellene, Barbarian. "Duas res publicas animo complectamur, alteram magnam et vere publicam, qua dii atque homines continentur ... alteram cui nos adscripsit conditio nascendi."[37] According to Seneca, the first fatherland was the cosmos, and the second, that to which one was by chance born. "Quidam eodem tempore utrique rei publicae dant operam, majori minorique, quidam tantum minori quidam tantum majori. Huic majori rei publicae et in otio deservire possumus, immo vero nescio an in otio melius. ..."

We do not here have mutually exclusive concepts but rather supplementary concepts of varying magnitude, which are intended to mediate between the political tasks of the day and the general philosophical apprehension of the world. The stylistic dualism does not depend upon negation.

This is likewise the case for Marcus Aurelius,[38] who as Antonius had Rome as a fatherland, and as a human being had the cosmos, without having been able to attempt a union of the two orders (for instance, by conferring civil rights on all subjects). As a citizen, Epictetus also was conscious of two *polis*—one a member of the cosmos to which gods and humans belonged, and the other a member of the political community, which he conceived of as an image of the cosmic polis.[39] Metaphorically, each refers to the other, even if the superordinate *polis* embodied those laws of reason that provided a more important precedent for life than did the immaterial things of the city. The emperor might see to the securing of external peace, but one's own peace was to be found within.[40]

This and similar dualisms stemming from the later Stoics, who had a more distanced relation to politics, have resonances that affected the antithesis of Christian and Heathen.[41] No epochal experience, no common signature of Stoic and Christian language can, however, conceal the fact that different conceptual couples are involved here. The Stoics did not consider the cosmically ordained order as polar to the political world; dualistically formulated concepts served solely to render their tension discernible and bearable and ultimately reveal it as irrelevant. No matter how much a Christianity adapted to an inner world took up such arguments to justify its God, the Paulinian-Augustinian conception of the world led to series of negations which placed in question everything the Stoics had previously sought to mediate.

Long before this, the contrast of Hellene and Barbarian had grown dim. It was relativized with the entry, after the Romans and the Christians, of a *tertium genus*[42] into the domain of action represented by the Mediterranean. Cicero had emphasized that the distinction of *graeci* from *barbari* was either purely nominal and hence devoid of meaning, or that it related to customs, in which case Romans and Greeks were equal.[43] The triad of Roman, Hellene, and Barbarian became widely used.[44] Barbarians once again retreated beyond the borders of the Empire that supposedly coincided with the known *oikumene*. There then emerged Germans and alien soldiers, described as *barbari* and proud of the name.

Since then, the chain can be extended: to the Middle Ages with its "barbaric" Saracens, Avars, Hungarians, Slavs, and Turks and farther to modern times with their imperial ideologies. The linguistic figure was preserved to the degree that there was a pole opposite Barbarian which was open to occupation, and which thereby shielded or extended one's given position through negation.

## Christians and Heathens

The entry of the Christians into Mediterranean world history rendered the former characterizations inaccurate. Even when their sects were regarded as "barbaric," Christians could not be comprehended by the dualism Hellene-Barbarian. They recruited from both camps. Not only was the meaning of this traditional antithesis superseded by the new religion, but also the semantic structure of the counterconcepts coined by the Christians was novel.

Within the immediate expectations of the apostolic communities there was at first no concept for "Christians," who regarded themselves as incomparable with Romans, Hellenes, or Jews (the name was given to them by others [Acts 11.26]); neither did the name "Heathen" initially exist as a collective term for non-Christians. At first, use of available dualities or counterconcepts continued, although they were related in a different manner. The linguistic usage of the Pauline mission no longer included concepts of division and distinction, but rather collective concepts for "all men" to whom the Gospel was directed (1 Tim. 2.4; Rom. 5.18).

Thus, as far as the Jews were concerned, Paul divided men according to whether they were circumcised or uncircumcised, but to all of whom he appealed impartially (Gal. 2.7). From a Hellenic point of view, he distinguished between Greeks and Barbarians (which Luther translated as *Ungriechen*, non-Greek), or between the wise and the unwise, to whom he was equally indebted (Rom. 1.14). He used another formulation in gathering together humanity as Hellenes and Jews, in which, rather than referring to Hellenes, he used the term *ethnai*, those coexisting with the Jewish people (*laos*). It was humanity in general that was continually the subject of address; human differences were erased so that the way could be opened from "Jewish Christians" to "Heathen Christians."[45] Jews and Hellenes are different addressees of the mission, but they are not divided by the alternative that Christianity offers them.

The real antitheses derive from true belief, for instance, when Paul, initially considering internal divisions, distinguishes between believers and unbelievers in a heretical community (1 Cor. 14.22) and when he goes a step further and introduces the separation as a criterion of true belief: "For there must be also heresies among you, that they which are approved may be made manifest among you" (1 Cor. 11.19).

Proper receptivity to the Gospel of Christ constituted the basis upon which a negative series could be built and which ultimately characterizes all unbelievers negatively: they are *asbeia*, rooted in *adikia* (Rom. 1.18), or Hellenes and Jews "all under sin" (Rom. 3.9). In the words of Karl Barth, "Whoever says mankind, says unredeemed mankind."[46]

Hence, mediation is possible between the contrasting figures drawn from belief and traditional terminology. Paul went further, however, in the use of counterconcepts which proved to be of assistance in the foundation of his mission through their comprehension of all humanity. He developed from them linguistic paradoxes which were enriched by apocalyptic imagery. These paradoxes provided the outline for the claim of exclusivity which later had an influence on the empirically founded antithesis of Christian and Heathen.

Paul consciously confronted the noncomparable so that the implausibly apparent might come into being through negation of the empirical world. In Col. 3.11 and Gal. 3.28, there is a general denial of the usual dualities, of all the counterconcepts which signify the totality of humanity: through belief in Christ, one is neither Hellene nor Barbarian, circumcised nor uncircumcised, Barbarian nor Scythian, freeman nor servant, man nor woman.[47] All positions and negations of humanity, people, order, race, and religion are transcended for those redeemed by Christ. The Pauline negation is more radical than previously appeared possible. The linguistic antithesis of Christian and all humanity is no longer asymmetric; the denial of asymmetry accompanies it so that the certainty of salvation might be assured. The contrast between all of humanity and the baptized is not any more quantifiable, after the fashion of former categorical names; what happens instead is that the reference group is doubled. Every person should become a Christian if he wishes to evade eternal damnation.

The Pauline dualism—here, all of humanity; there, those saved by Christ—permits of only one solution if the paradox is not to remain in place. The Christian, or more precisely, he who lives in Christ, is the new man who has done away with the old (Col. 3.9, Eph. 4.24). In this way it is possible to negatively confront the totality of previous humanity with the (potential) generality of Christian humanity. "For the love of Christ constraineth us; because we thus judge, that if one died for all, then were all dead. . . . Therefore if any man be in Christ, he is a new creature: old things are passed away; behold, all things are become new." (2 Cor. 5.14, 17)

The Pauline negation is no longer organized spatially, but is predominantly temporal.[48] By contrast with the Greek perspective on the past, which merely deduced the ruling contrast of Hellene and Barbarian historically, temporal tension structures the Pauline antithesis itself. All the existing peoples—Hellenes, *ethnai*, *gentes*, and so forth—who became defined in a Christian perspective as "Heathens," *gentiles*, or *pagani*, belong as such to the past. By virtue of the death of Christ, the future belongs to Christians. The future bears the new world.

It is this temporal implication that differentiates the Pauline dualism from those considered previously. The parties involved were, in principle, not reducible to territory, as was initially the case with Hellene and Barbarian. The contrast was just as little interpretable as a comparison, as was suggested by the antithesis of educated and uneducated and as was implied by the later form of Hellene and Barbarian. The Pauline dualism likewise is not susceptible to elaboration as a universal and as a concrete, specific meaning, as was the Stoic opposition of man and citizen.

The history that was approaching shows that it was these three other predetermined, experiential frameworks, manifested in the form of linguistic antitheses, which continually resurfaced. Antitheses coined using the concept of the (Pauline) Christian were also impregnated by them. In proportion to the degree to which the church institutionalized itself, its doctrine became morally based, and its believers disciplined; it became more difficult to redeem the Pauline paradox. Alternative positions were adopted from which new negations could be developed by resurrecting older linguistic possibilities.

In this way the counterpoints of Christian and Heathen could be territorialized as soon as the spiritual concept of the Christians was established in the form of a visible church. This is as true of the Constantinian theology of the imperial church as of the period of the Crusades. Alternatively, the relation of the Christians to the (still existing) world was spiritualized to such an extent that the Stoic pattern of inner and outer worlds became usable once more.[49] One could remain a Christian without ceasing to be Hellene or Barbarian, Frank or Roman, king or peasant, freeman or slave, man or woman. The territorial or spiritual reformation of the Pauline paradox contained the basis of its chance of survival.

Characteristic of this rising, repeatedly rethought and rearranged bilaterality, is the ambivalence of the concept of *christianitas*. This signified both the functioning unity of the believers ("Christendom") and the extent and nature of the actual belief ("Christianity") that was not susceptible to firm territorial or institutional association.[50]

Nevertheless, the temporal implication of all conceptual couples derivative of Christianity was preserved, and this has been decisive for subsequent history. With respect to a future containing the Last Judgment, a judgment which would enact the last division of all, every counterconcept originating from "Christian" contained a lasting principle of distinction and distribution.

Beyond this, it was inherent temporal tension that made it possible for the antithesis of humanity and Christianity to continually transform itself. The chronological range between "old world" and "new world," despite and because of the impossibility of realizing it on earth, rendered the Pauline mode of expression particularly usable and transformable. It could be adapted to all situations without having to sacrifice any of its effectiveness. This will next be shown for a few linguistic expressions which subsequently emerged.

The Christian people—in Tertullian's words, *gens totius orbis*—for all their expectation and indeed certainty of salvation, occupied the very same world that was ruled by unbelievers, even if they thought the world due to be transformed. Consequently, the occupants of this earth necessarily had to be organized into two mutually exclusive categories. It is a measure of the slow pervasion of the Christian view that the previous counterconcepts were, as a whole, reversed in their polarity. Thus the polytheistic Hellene became simply a Heathen. "Hellene," already a name for a people and an index of education, was (in spite of the continued use of these semantic elements) ultimately theologized into a counterconcept for "Christian," the way being prepared by Paul. "Hellene" became synonymous with *apistos, paganus,* and *gentilis; hellenismos* then meant "paganism," and *hellenizein,* "to be paganistically disposed."[51] Following this reclassification of the word, the Hellenes of Constantinople, once they were Christianized, had to rename themselves: they became *rhomaioi,* despite having resisted this name for centuries. Only in this way were they able, as Christian citizens, to combine the title of legitimacy of the Roman Empire with the salvational claim of the general Church. The success of the new antithesis is demonstrated by the fact that, in the fourth century, even "Hellene" and "Barbarian" could converge. The fact that former "Hellenes" and "Barbarians" were followers of many gods place them in the same category within and beyond the frontier.

Because the continued existence of the two human groups had been distinguished only along theological lines, geographical difference was transformed into chronological difference. The groups' spatial contrast had to be chronologically arranged in such a way that the victory of Christianity could be secured in advance. This is shown in the henceforth customary trinity (Christian–Jew–Heathen) by means of which the whole of mankind was comprehended until the Late Middle Ages.[52] Ultimately, this is a matter of a duality which is differentiated only along a temporal dimension. By believing in God the creator and sharing the Old Testament, Jews and Christians move together; theologically, however, they are so joined only to the point of Christ's appearance. Up to this point, Jews had the same advantage as the Heathens, but the challenge of the Gospel and their refusal of it places them in the same camp as the Heathens. The valency of the concepts alters according to historical situation: *sub specie Dei* Jews and Heathens are confronted with the same alternative: be converted or perish.

The polemic conducted by Origines against Celsus demonstrates the extent to which it was precisely this eschatological dimension that proved capable of illuminating anew the hypostasized but unrealized unity of the world at peace.[53] Celsus considered it desirable that all peoples—Hellenes and Barbarians, Europeans, Asians, and Libyans—might live united under a single law. Confronted with the impossibility of fulfilling this hope, he gave it up. Origines declared that this state of peace, described, for instance, in Zeph. 3.8–9, could be achieved for all men possessing reason, but only subsequent to the great turning point marked by the future Judgment, however temporary such a turn might be considered. In this way, Origines, in his diagnosis of the disputed reality, moved very close to Celsus; a unity of the world is not possible, he said, but added, "not yet." Prophecy went beyond this. In the state of things to come, all would be peaceably united.

The emergent difficulties apparent in spiritual, territorial, and eschatological interpretation of the contrast of Christ and the world were solved by Augustine. This was effected by his doctrine of the two *civitates*, providing a surprising, relatively coherent, and thus lasting solution. He was primarily responding to a specific situation.

The singularity of the situation—the invasion of the principal world city by the Goths—imposed a similarly unique problem upon the

Christians, who had for the past century concerned themselves with inwardly adapting to the Roman Empire. This sudden flood of historical events rendered the Christians apparently responsible for the catastrophe: Paganism had made Rome great, whereas Christianity had brought it down. An exonerating response was as hard to find as this *post hoc ergo propter hoc* explanation was self-evident. The Church had assimilated itself to pagan myths and, following the sound ideas of a Eusebius or a Prudentius, had attached the rule of Christ to the persistence of Rome. This situation not only robbed Christians of an easy answer, but the capture of Rome by Barbarians seemed to confirm the accusation. Even Christians saw their Church placed in question, because eschatological speculation had focused on the end of Rome; and with the actual end of Rome the Last Judgment failed to materialize.

Augustine developed his historical theology in opposition to both fronts, and in this way he was able to transcend all previously formulated solutions. So that it might be possible to free Christianity from the charge of responsibility for the fall of Rome, the situational challenge demanded that the rule of Christ and that of an earthly entity, such as the Roman Empire, be not in any way identified. His response to this problem was to attempt to demonstrate that peace on earth and the peace of God could not in any way be identical.

Thus, Augustine developed his doctrine of the two *civitates*, which comprised both Church and worldly organization and which was neither reducible to nor assimilated by them. The empire of God holds sway over the world and is present in the Church, but the inner community of believers is constantly on a pilgrimage; their empire is merely built upon hope.[54] The worldly empire, by contrast, is based on property: "Cain, quod interpretabitur possessio, terrenae conditor civitatis ... indicat istam civitatem et initium et finum habere terrenum, ubi nihil speratur amplius, quam in hoc saeculo cerni potest."[55]

The empires relate asymmetrically to each other. They are not empires founded upon a Manichaean opposition but rather constitute—both of them still being entwined within the hierarchical laws of a created cosmic order[56]—a processual occurrence whose certain but chronologically indeterminate demise will lead to the triumph of the *civitas Dei*. In this way, all worldly occurrences remained relativized, without, however, losing their singularity before the Final Judgment. Within the space of the earthly world, exposed to sin, every event assumed, in view of the final verdict, the status of a preliminary adjudication. This amounted to a temporalization of the asymmetrical structure. Not every malefactor becomes good, but no one can become good who has not first been bad.[57]

In concrete terms, this meant that the Roman Empire was transcended by the mystic unity of *civitas terrena*; it is only one, if a particularly splendid and outstanding, articulation of the sin that rules on earth. The fall of this empire is thus indicative of an unsurpassable meaning: that of the salvation one can find in *civitas Dei* and for which the believer has good cause to hope, precisely in the moment of catastrophe. The real answer Augustine gave to the decline of the universal Roman Empire did not play down earthly affliction or involve a flight to the realms of eternity, but rather was an eschatological conception of two realms that were unequally contrary. The deterritorialization or dislocation of both *civitates* and their consequent spiritualization were never taken so far that their irreversible course toward the Last Judgment, a course that was registered historically, could not be maintained. The chronological course and its irreversibility were both constitutive of the process that was to present worldly affairs to the coming Judgment, without Augustine having to concern himself with a genuine world history, which, in any case, was completely removed from his perspective. Augustine's eschatology thus became a persisting response to all worldly, historical situations that retained their singularity only in view of the ultimate division of the two realms.

Within this chronological perspective, even antitheses that are empirically perceptible assume their own valency. Augustine outlined a hierarchy of counterconcepts. Evil struggled against evil, and good against evil; only the good, to the degree that it is complete, knows no dispute. The existential order of good and evil laid down in Antiquity can also be found within this sequence, between the *civitates*. The hope of a secure existence for mankind is an illusion of Original Sin which reproduces itself. All the units of rule that Augustine had taken from the Stoics—*domus*, *urbs*, and *orbis*—are marked by the fact that no lasting conclusion to mistrust and betrayal can be found in them at a stage higher than war and, at the level of universality, civil war. Even in the highest sphere, where the believer might hope to find peace with the angels, he is not exempted from covert temptations of the Devil.[58] Despite the hierarchic arrangement of stages, therefore, the cosmos is fundamentally fissured. That universalism dissolves into the process of the two realms, within which process men are indeterminately entangled. Men live in a *civitas permixta*, and while their disengagement is preserved within God's decree, it is not realizable *hic et nunc*. The non-Christian also is tied to a godly order, just as, by contrast, the Christian is not absolutely certain of being saved. While the persecution of Christians by Heathens is unjust, the persecution of Heathens by Christians is, on the other hand, just.[59] The judgments handed down by God do, however, ultimately remain unknown; in secret they are just, and justifiably they are secret.[60] Quite obviously, suffering is the same for all in the world; only the sufferers are differentiated.[61] To this extent, Augustine can say that whoever does not belong to the *civitas Dei* is consigned *e contrario* to eternal damnation. But this contrast remained concealed to the last.

In this fashion, Augustine created for himself a flexible potential for argument that could judge all misery at once and also be able to explain it as justified by God. The asymmetry of the contrary positions made it possible to present as just the success of evil or the misery of the good, and, of course, the reward for the good and punishment for the evil.[62] This was possible only because the final date was not known, as was the Judgment which would separate the truly elect from the damned. The doctrine of the two realms was thus sufficiently formal to permit every concrete experience a dualistic interpretation, without renouncing the tension of a future salvation in which the true separation would be made.

Transferred into the language of politics, the Augustinian argument lent itself to a variety of uses.[63] The course of development of a European Church led to a change in meaning for the doctrine of the two realms, which was being applied (within) to spiritual and temporal force as well as being used (without) in a geographically more comprehensible sense as an indicator of the opposition of Christian and Heathen. The asymmetrical structure of the counterconcepts remained temporally structured: the course followed by the struggles of the two powers was not reversible.[64] "Christianity does not seek belief in Jewry; rather, Jews should seek belief in Christianity," as it was put by Ignatius of Antioch, who coined the term *christianismos*.[65] The relation of Christian to Heathen was also chronologically irreversible. "And this gospel of the kingdom shall be preached in all the world for a witness unto all nations; and then shall the end come" (Mat. 24.14).

As Guibert of Nogent described the Crusades after 1100, "Ubi nunc paganismus est, christianitas fiat,"[66] in which spatial expansion was thought to be temporally irreversible. It was precisely this ambivalence in a concept of Christianity apprehended in both temporal-spatial and spiritual domains which, confined within the sequence of time, lent it a particularly acute force. William of Malmesbury commented in these terms on Urban II's call for a crusade against the *inimicos Dei*. In so doing, he transformed a Stoic dual formula in a Christian fashion, encouraging the Crusaders to spare no heathens: "Nullum natalis soli caritas tricet, quia diversis respectibus Christiano totus est mundus exilium et totus mundus patria; ita exilium patria, et patria exilium."[67]

One should not be overly concerned with life, but rather direct efforts toward the liberation of Jerusalem. Aside from this contemporary point, the conceptual couple in which this world was related to the next reveals the manner in which claim was laid to the whole world, to the degree that one was able to rise above it as a Christian existing in exile. The counterconcepts as alternatives were so narrowly defined that no legitimate place remained for the Heathens. By contrast with the Stoic idea of dissolving all external ties so that one might be inwardly free and at home throughout the world, this universal, dual formulation assumes here an activistic, expansive sense of exclusivity directed toward the future.

Everyone was a potential Christian, as an addressee of the mission; but once one became a Christian, it was impossible to revert to being a Heathen; the backslider became, rather, a heretic. For this reason, it was necessary, according to Aquinas, to proceed more severely with heretics than with Jews and Heathens who were still at the beginning of the path to God.[68] Expressed temporally, the Heathen was "not yet" a Christian, whereas the heretic was "no longer" a Christian: as such, they had different qualities. Thus the eschatological horizon contained a processual moment in the arrangement of the counterconcepts which was capable of unleashing a greater dynamic than that inhering in the ancient counterconcepts. The Spanish Inquisition can be viewed as an extreme form of this processualization, which did not permit Jews to survive even as converts (*conversos*). This clearly can be attributed to the appearance, in the Court of Heresy, of an argumentation based on physique and race that differed from the terms of the formerly prevailing and historically transcendent eschatology.[69]

Notwithstanding the temporal interpretive framework, which lent the contrast of Christian and Heathen its force and direction, the concepts were at the same time subject to an increasing territorialization, which had as an apparently surprising consequence the concept that the Heathen could be revalued. At the beginning of the Crusades, in the eleventh century, we still find in the *Song of Roland* the formulation which presupposes unilateral exclusiveness: Christians are in the right, and Heathens are not. (*Paien unt tort e chretiens unt dreit*).[70] This simplified but nonetheless eschatologically interpretable contrast was at the same time susceptible to spatial calculation. First came the pressure of the Arabs, and then, following the counterstrokes which the occidental Christians delivered with the Crusades, the concept of Christianity consolidated its territorial association. Gregory VII could therefore refer concretely to *fines christianitatis*, and Innocent III could speak of *terrae christianorum*[71] which, according to Augustine, would have meant a referral to the domain of Cain, based on *possessio*.

Similarly, pre-Christian linguistic models emerge which qualify the contrast in terms of regionality in the same way that Aristotle drew the distinction between Hellene and Barbarian. The inhabitants of Europe are described as noble and brave and who, because they live in a mild climate, are destined (following the division of the earth between Noah's children) for superiority over the sons of Ham in Africa and of Sem in Asia.[72] Even the Barbarians reemerge, existing as non-Christians without the *christianitas*.

The opponents were indeed discriminated against in the literature of theological dispute by a long series of negative judgments: they are *infideles, impii, increduli, perfedi, inimici Dei*, enriched by the sorcery of the Devil, and moreover have black skin. To kill such Heathens as one would a dog is to do God a favor.[73] A growing and changing experience leads, however, to a shift in the valency of these Heathens. At first they are thought of not only in terms of theological topoi but also of ancient Barbarism: they are, as in the early knightly epics, cowardly, treasonous, monstrous, and the like. The actual designation of the enemy, however, makes lesser use of the general theological concept of the Heathen: Franks are opposed by Saracens, and one fights with Persians and Turks, but above all with persons, or with heroes, which the leading enemies eventually become.

If the opponent was initially bad because he was a Heathen, he could later become good despite being a Heathen, and in the end be noble because he was a Heathen.[74] Whether this was because one's reputation is increased if one fights with an equal foe; because a certain common honor arose which covered both fronts; or because of the need for treaties with the superior forces of the Mohammedans: for whatever reason, recognition developed in the course of the Crusades. This was apparent in interconfessional marriages or interconfessional enfeoffment, both of which belonged to the stirring themes of courtly epic. If, in the *Song of Roland*, the corpses of the enemy were separated out, so in Wolfram the enemy bury their dead in common.[75] Praise for the noble Heathen at last became fashionable.

Not only by virtue of their territorialization, but also because of their spiritualization, the counterconcepts (as regarded by the "Christians") took on other valencies. This can be illuminated by a comparison with the Stoic couple of man and citizen. The paradoxical claim of exclusivity which initially prevailed between the Christian and worldly realms did not fundamentally disappear here. It could be actualized at any time.

Thus it was Augustinian usage to employ "spiritual" and "worldly" together so that a Christian standard might be brought to bear on *ständisch* tasks and duties. It was then possible to confront a peasant, citizen, knight, cleric, or prince engaged in worldly doings with their Christian task. In 384, Ambrosius taught Valentinian that a ruler did not belong to the Church only in a private capacity but was by virtue of office a soldier of God [*advocatus ecclesiae*], as it was later known. His politics were to be arranged according to divine instruction, as mediated by the Church.[76] Involved here is an asymmetrical usage of the conceptual couple Christian and Ruler similar to that of the two-person doctrine of Man and Citizen associated with the Stoics: the concepts which are applicable to the same person are limited in such a way that an external state is defined in accordance with an inner judgment (on the part of philosopher or cleric).

In his definition of worldly opponents, Gregory VII went further when he developed the claim to exclusivity implicit in the couple of Christian and worldly men, for purposes of polemic. In 1081, he directed the doctrine of two persons against Henry IV, not only with regard to a bilateral elaboration, but also antithetically. Furthermore, he pushed the antithesis to the point at which the opposing position disappeared. He opined that it was in fact more fitting to speak of good Christians than bad rulers as kings.[77] The former—that is, the kingly Christians—rule themselves through their search for the glory of God. The latter are against this and, pursuing their own pleasure, are their own enemies and are tyrannical toward others. The former belong to Christ, the latter to the Devil. *Hi veri regis Christi, illi vero diaboli corpus sunt.*

Instead of subordinating the external function—that of the ruler—to a Christian judgment, so that the king might be qualified or disqualified as Christian, Gregory reserves the title of king for the true Christian so the worldly function of his opponent might be placed in question. This usurpation of the counterconcept may be attributed to his situational political rhetoric, but it was possible only because Christians were called to assimilate and renew the entire world. The established and institutionalized contrast of spiritual and worldly forces is distorted in this linguistic figure to such a degree that those who are of the world are no longer allowed their own space. Though still bound to a specific meaning of "Christian," this represents an anticipation of the future opposition of man to king, which was to be the general characteristic of Enlightenment polemic against the monarchy.

As a final example of dualistic Christian usage that not only negates the opposing position but seeks to exclude and abolish it, we can turn to the Puritans. Richard Hooker investigated the divergent linguistic techniques by means of which the Puritans sought to establish their position.

This hath bred high terms of separation between such and the rest of the world; whereby the one sort are named The brethren, The godly, and so forth; the other, worldlings, time-servers, pleasers of men not of God, with such like. . . . But be they women or be they men, if once they have tasted of that cup, let any man of contrary opinion open his mouth to persuade them, they close up their ears, his reasons they weigh not, all is answered with rehearsal of the words of John, "We are of God; he that knoweth God heareth us:" as for the rest, ye are of the world.[78]

Hooker develops out of biblical exegesis an analysis of the behavior of those who employ biblical texts to deduce a sense of rectitude transcendent of this world, but which at once obliges and enables them to act in this world.

This linguistic model deciphered by Hooker in terms of a critique of ideology survives unbroken, with a change of antitheses, to this day. It testifies to an experiential framework, shot through with Christianity, simultaneously negating and laying claim to this world. In this way, dualities arose whose paradoxes should disperse *sub specie futuri.* The way this would happen was altered early on, according to the power-position of the Church, which came under the influence of sect, order, and heresy, which in turn provided new impulses. The antitheses did, however, draw their overwhelming force from anticipation of the future; since this was not susceptible to refutation through contrary experience, it was constantly open to repetition. That which today is ruled out by negation will be regarded in the future as superseded. A dualism temporalized in this manner sorts out possible experiences and opens up a horizon of expectation that is quite elastic. Out of this emerges impulses for historical movement unlike those emitted by the counterconcepts of Antiquity. Without having to introduce a thesis of general secularization, we have in the temporally arranged counterconcepts a form of experience which, once articulated linguistically, has outlasted by far original impulse and point of departure.

### Mensch and Unmensch, Übermensch and Untermensch

It will not be possible in what follows to trace the history of the concept of *Menschheit* and its equivalents. Instead, a few dualistic linguistic figures will be introduced as emergent from the constitution, or rather experience, of *Menschheit* as a politically intended unity. *Mensch* and *Unmensch*, and *Übermensch* and *Untermensch*[79] are such conceptual couples, disclosing and articulating new political possibilities with their linguistic potential for argument. The asymmetrical nature of these counterconcepts, deeply polemical in form, is characterized by a semantic structure different from those outlined up to now, even though it can be shown that elements of the figures "Hellene and Barbarian" or "Christian and Heathen" enter into them or affect them.

The dualistic criteria of distribution between Greek and Barbarian, and between Christian and Heathen, were always related, whether implicitly or explicitly, to *Menschheit* as a totality. To this extent, *Menschheit*, *genus humanum*, was a presupposition of all dualities that organized *Menschheit* physically, spatially, spiritually, theologically, or temporally. It will now appear that *Menschheit*, up to this point a condition immanent in all dualities, assumes a different quality as soon as it enters into argument as a political reference. The semantic function of distributional concepts alters as soon as a totalizing concept—for this is what is involved with *Menschheit*—is brought into political language, which, in spite of its totalizing claim, generates polarities.

Among the Stoics, where *genus humanum* can be addressed most honestly as a political entity, the adjective *inhumanum* already appears as a means of defining the boundary at which a person ceases to be a member of universal human society. Cicero had refined all the transitional routes from the family to universal society to such an extent that, placed as they were under the one *lex naturae*, all distinction between an internal and an external morality escaped him. *Qui autem civium rationem dicunt habendam, externorum negant, ii dirimunt communem humani generis societatem.* Any tensions that might arise between the claims of different agencies would be easily solved. He who placed his own self-interest before the interest of others behaved inhumanly, against the law of nature. Whoever consigned his action to the scales of common interest was permitted to kill tyrants, with whom no community could exist. "Hoc omne genus pestiferum atque impium ex hominum communitate exterminandum est . . . sic ista in figura hominis feritas et immanitas beluae a communi tamquam humanitate corporis segreganda est." A tyrant, an animal in human form, is not only an enemy of the commonality, but also of the human species in general.[80]

To the extent that *Menschheit* is introduced into language as a political reference it requires an additional qualification: for example, the *Mensch* as citizen, which itself is not derivable from the linguistic usage of *Mensch*. Who was Christian or Heathen, Hellene or Barbarian, could be deduced from the prevailing positivity of a concept, and even the negative counterconcepts had an intelligible and immanent meaning. He who appeals to *Menschheit* is placed under a linguistic drive toward occupation, for anyone who wishes may appeal to *Menschheit*. It is, therefore, necessary to define exactly who and what *Menschheit* might be so that the concept can be qualified in political fashion. Whoever fails to do this falls under the suspicion of promoting ideology. As a consequence of the ambivalent possibilities arising out of the claim of universality, linguistic usage rapidly degenerates into uncertainty: it can be directed to all *Menschen*, excluding no one—or it can gain a certain quality (for instance, that of *humanitas* [humanness, *Menschlichkeit*]), such that exclusions which do not yet inhere in the word become possible.

The ambivalence of the concept of Christianity, whereby it is at once both qualitatively and quantitatively readable, becomes critical in the use of the concept of *Menschheit*. It is possible for substantial and numerical determinations to converge (for example, in Bentham's proposal for the greatest happiness of the greatest number), but it also implies that a calculable minority are excluded from the identified human objective.

Before we proceed to the dualities which can be attributed to the concept of *Menschheit* (or which can be deduced from the concept itself), three long-term, world-historical factors will be identified which permit the concept of *Menschheit* to advance to a central position. The revival of the Stoic doctrine of *societas humana* in early modernity also takes a place within this context of effects, realizing *Menschheit* as a political concept.

First, it seemed that with the discovery of America, and thereby the discovery of the globality of the earth, the Christian Gospel finally achieved *usque ad terminos terrae*.[83] The annexation of space and temporal fulfillment could now converge, in the same manner in which Columbus thought of his voyage as a way of accelerating the promised end of the world. The challenge turned out surprisingly different, consisting instead in the need to integrate within experience a number of alien peoples not foreseen by the account of the Creation. It was the growing apprehension of planetary finitude which, in the course of succeeding centuries, drew attention to *Menschheit* as referent, indeed, increasingly as the intended acting subject of its own history. In Kant's words, it is the "global form" of the earth upon which men "are not able to infinitely disperse themselves, but must eventually tolerate one another." In this fashion, an intersubjective and closed space of action emerged that was sufficiently small that "an infringement of right in one place on the earth is sensed everywhere."[84] However *Menschheit* might be interpreted, it has since then been linguistically available as an empirical substratum.

Second, parallel to this process, it became ever more difficult to divide the totality of *Menschheit* into Christian and Heathen, for the concept of Christian itself became disputed. The annexation of lands overseas, which had as a consequence the empirical gathering of *Menschheit*, came about as a struggle between Christian voyagers. One was Catholic, Calvinist, Lutheran, or whatever: judgments concerning heresy, civil war, and warfare between states were unable to produce a new unity among the Christians. The concept of *Menschheit* grew in proportion into a negative counterconcept which provided a minimal definition comprehending the Christians who were themselves divided.

Thanks to its generalization in terms of natural law, it was likewise directed at the overseas peoples.

Third, the figure of God the creator, previously apprehended theologically as a counter to sinful humanity, slowly moved out of the domain of argument constructed around political theory. Henceforth, the "earthly gods" could become the presumptive acting subjects of a history which was no longer the history of God with his humanity, but rather the history of "*Menschheit* itself." Characteristic of this insidious shift in the meaning of *Menschheit* is the recession of the previously theological meaning of the concept. Until the Enlightenment the expression possessed, above all, a religious quality (in German usage)[85] that implied the humanity of Christ, the Son of God, whose incarnation in human form was a pledge of salvation. The fading of this meaning before a quantitative and before a qualitative meaning (the latter freighted with neo-humanist or revolutionary significance) is an index of the claim to autonomy which has, since the eighteenth century, been implicit in the concept of humanity. Addressee and subject of itself, *Menschheit* became a political concept whose new opposing figures will be outlined in the following.

In the era of Enlightenment, the appeal to men or to humanity had a critical, even a negating function with respect to the counterposition. This was aimed in three directions: against the various churches and religions, against the *ständisch* degrees of rights, and against the personal rule of princes. Within this social and political context the valency of the expression *man* or *humanity* altered itself. That which literally is a general name comprehending all humans—*Menschheit*—became within political usage a negating counterconcept. The negation contained the title of legitimation suitable to fundamentally question ruling institutions, religions, or persons. Whoever concerned himself with *Menschheit* could thus lend to himself the greatest degree of generality contained *eo ipso* in the concept *Menschheit*. He who confronted men with the king, or religions with *Menschheit*, made use of two heterogeneous entities to play off against each other, without the concepts being initially susceptible to relation on the same level. Here lies the effectiveness of the Enlightenment technique of negation, but at the same time its ideological restriction. The appeal to *Menschen* contained a claim which no one could evade, for who wished to deny being human? It was precisely this initially unpolitical meaning of the word *Menschheit* which facilitated the claim to that greatest possible universality which, as justification of political critique and political action, could no longer be outbid. The numerical aggregate of all men—*Menschheit*—switched, without a change of word, into political self-legitimation, which did not, however, have to be identified as such. To this extent, the political usage of the expression *Mensch* or *Menschheit*—as long as it was not qualified in terms of constitutional law—delivered an ideological surplus which was not contained in the more concrete concepts of Greek and Barbarian or Christian and Heathen.

Accordingly, the moral weekly *Der Mensch*, in 1755, carried the following statement, still embellished in a Christian manner: "All *Menschen* remain *Menschen*, they may believe or think as they wish. . . . in Jews, Turks and Heathens I see *Menschen*: he is my neighbor; I wish to love him and through my love to shame him."[86] In 1769, Herder nonetheless composed a series of comprehensive negations: "What a wonderful topic—to show that to be what one should be, one might neither be Jew, nor Arab, nor Greek, nor savage, nor martyr, nor pilgrim."[87] Or, as Kotzebue caused to be proclaimed from a stage in 1787, "The Christian forgot the Turks, the Turk forgot the Christians, and both loved *Menschen*."[88]

What becomes quite apparent in these counterconcepts is the analogy with the Pauline paradox, according to which the totality of all people is negated through its difference, to the advantage of those who had found salvation in Christ. But while this analogy has a meaning shaped in terms of the history of its transmission, to the extent that we have here a transformation of the Christian claim to generality, this is not made necessary by the actual nature of the linguistic figure: the general concept of *Menschheit* becomes the counterconcept of particular concepts that are implicit within it, a situation which did not arise in the opposition of Christian and Heathen. The polarization is now sustained by rhetorical polemic. The illogical asymmetry prevailing between *Mensch* and specific religious adherents was set in play provocatively; it can no longer be derived theologically, as was the conceptual couple of Christian and Heathen. If one fails to hear the polemical, negative thrust, a proposition such as that by Freemason Blumauer becomes an empty tautology: "that the greatest dignity of a *Mensch* is—to be a *Mensch*."[89] Within the negation of previously dominant religions is contained a negation of the component of *Menschen* creative of meaning. It was only with the qualification of *Menschen* as rational or virtuous beings—however inadequate this might be—that a position could be defined.

This was also true for the critical remarks addressed by the Enlighteners to society and the *Stände*—for example, when Salzmann criticized in 1787 "factories" (*Fabriken*) as places where men were forced "to behave as *Nichtmenschen*, as machines."[90] Here, the concept of *Menschen* is itself negated so that the guilt can be attached to an economic institution that stands in the way of *Menschen*—to be allowed at minimum to be *Menschen*. Thus, Moritz, in 1786, referred to "*Menschheit* oppressed by bourgeois relations" because of the way that differences of *Stand* led to inequality between those who "labored" and those who "paid."[91] *Menschheit* is on the side of the oppressed, not on the side of the oppressor. It is always the negative force of the general concept of *Menschheit* that expresses the critical function.

The same holds in a more confined political domain. "The prince is *Mensch*, the slave is free, the golden epoch is approaching,"[92] runs the student rhyme that joins two concepts which are contraries along diverging dimensions. As liberty is by definition the opposite of slavery, so the prince moves suggestively in the counterposition to *Mensch*. Rousseau expressed this more clearly in confronting King with *Mensch*: if a king were to renounce the throne he would rise to the status of a *Mensch* ("il monte à l'état d'homme").[93] The antithesis of Man and King, continually varied by the Enlighteners, makes it especially clear that this is a matter of an asymmetrical linguistic figure whose references are quite heterogeneous. More or less consciously incomparable entities are confronted with each other so that the ruler, measured against *Menschen*, can be declared to be an *Unmensch*. This is certainly an extreme case of Enlightenment polemic, but it does demonstrate the semantic structure of a conceptual couple which had not previously been available in this form.

Whereas the Stoic approach to *Mensch* and citizen served to further mutual illumination, *Mensch* and prince are in this case introduced as mutually exclusive entities in which the invocation of *Mensch* renders the prince superfluous. While the critical usage of Christian and prince is based on a two-person doctrine present in the world order which has only to be properly followed for a ruling function to be substantively qualified, the conceptual couple employed by the Enlighteners dissolves this connection. The critical function of their conceptual couple is no longer, as with Christian and Ruler, immanent in a *Stand*, but directs itself to the rule of *Stände* in general.

For colloquial purposes and in general usage, a king remained a *Mensch* however bad a king he might be. As Frederick the Great remarked ironically of Louis XV: "He was a good, but weak, *Mensch*; his only mistake was to be king."[94] By contrast, the Enlighteners made use of the undifferentiable, general concept of man for the purpose of discriminating against a political office. The asymmetry of an antithesis which, from one concept to the other, changed its plane of reference was linguistically structured so that it became functionally accessible for one's own political intention.

This form of polemic is certainly open to historical explanation. The analogy of God and King, overlaid as it was by absolutism, placed *Menschheit* in the potential position of a counterconcept. It is thus no surprise when Harrington, following the death of Charles Stuart, effected a transfer and characterized the new sovereign as "King People."[95] In the succeeding century, Adam Smith was to observe that the treatment of monarchs as in all respects men—for instance, to engage in discussion with them—required a decisiveness of which few men were capable.[96] His contemporary, Johnson, familiar with the Court, dispensed with this;[97] and Blackstone, in his *Commentaries*, drew the following skeptical balance: "The mass of mankind will be apt to grow insolent and refractory, if thought to consider their princes as a man of no greater perfection than themselves."[98]

A polemical reversal of this position arises with Jefferson's definition (borrowing from Cicero) of a "class of lions, tigers, and mammoths in human form" called kings.[99] Enough of these examples from the English language; as long as divine attributes were claimed for monarchs, it was not difficult to constitute *Menschheit* as a counterconcept to King. As Schubart somewhat drastically formulated in 1776: "Despotism has choked *Menschheit* for so long, that its tongue will soon hang out and it will want to cry out: I want to be an animal."[100]

The situating of man in a relation of tension between animal and God had been since Antiquity a topological fact. What is peculiar to the eighteenth-century opposition of Man and King is the lack of alternative it left to the Prince. It is neither possible to place him, as had once been possible, "above," nor (seen from the standpoint of men) "below." Rather, he becomes, in the name of a simple moral exclusiveness of *Menschen*, an enemy who has to be destroyed. Louis

XVI was to learn this when he sought in his defense to argue that he also was only a man: "Je dis l'homme quel qu'il soit; car Louis XVI n'est plus en effet qu'un homme, et un homme accusé."[101] But I, retorted Saint-Just: "et moi, je dis que le roi doit être jugé en ennemi, que nous avons moins à le juger qu'à le combattre."[102]

This fractured even the appearance of the asymmetrical conceptual figure of Man and King. The concrete identification of an enemy that had remained veiled in the previous linguistic technique of the Enlightenment became quite open. The King, considered as a *Mensch* to be an *Unmensch*, had to be removed. There certainly existed enlightened and republican legal doctrines that traced the office of king to a politically definable characterization of man as citizen. In this context, however, we are interested in demonstrating that, with the linguistic figure of Man and King, a new structural element entered into political counterconcepts which can be distinguished from all previous forms: it was from the beginning a linguistic means functionally deployed by various, distinct interests; likewise, it was from the beginning under a compulsion to politically consolidate in order not to be disclosed as ideology. It was valid as an ideological means of struggle, while at the same time becoming an element in ideology. The reason for this was contained in its property of confronting heterogeneous categories in a way that made it possible, through the negation of the apparent counterconcept, to effect the annihilation of the given opponent. The totalizing concept of *Menschheit*, once applied politically, gave rise to totalitarian consequences.

The negating force in the usage of *Menschheit* certainly diminished as the successes of the French Revolution removed, at least in part, the objects of address. As soon as confessional disputes among Christians shifted from the center of politics, and as soon as the legal differences of the *Stände* were equalized, the polemical valency of *Menschheit* was altered: since then, further political use of the expression was meant to employ an empty category which constantly required filling with concrete meaning. It should, therefore, give rise to no surprise that new criteria of differentiation were sought in the domain of a *Menschheit* once held to be absolute and autonomous. *Übermensch* and *Untermensch* were provided with political qualities.

The expressions are themselves prerevolutionary.[103] Linguistically, they can be placed in the series of modes of life that stretches from animal to angel or demon, between which man is settled as a being charged with tension.[104] Thus the *Übermensch* appears in the ancient heroic cult, and as a characterization of the true reborn Christian it assumed a (disputed) religious significance. The expression was readily used, above all, in Gnostic, spiritualist, and mystic traditions; but it was also used to lend color to texts devoted to consolidating papal claims of rulership.[105] Luther turned the expression against the monks, and his own followers were scornfully described in the same way: "They walk alone in spirit and are *Übermenschen*."[106] Here, for the first time in German, the current adjective *übermenschlich* is turned into a substantive. Along the plane of a temporal perspective within which older men can be overtaken by the new, the term appears in a positive form within the pietistic tradition: "Among the new men you are a true man, an *Übermensch*, a man of God and Christ."[107]

To the extent that Christians claimed for themselves the title of true *Menschen*, the consequence was that non-Christians, the heretics and Heathens, were classified as *Nichtmenschen*. The *Unmensch* reaches back to usage of the judgments on heresy. Luther was dismissed in this way in 1521, as "this solitary, not a *Mensch*, but an evil enemy in the shape of a *Mensch*." In the formulation used by Cochlaeus, "Unicus iste, non homo: sed malus inimicus, sub specie homnis."[108] Even in the eighteenth century the theological adversary as *Unmenschen* could be applied to the Heathen: "I . . . do not live naturally, like Turks and other *Unmenschen*, but rather spiritually."[109]

Such evidence testifies to the manner in which dualistic figures of negation from the most diverse sources can overlap in the course of history. The *Übermensch* and the *Unmensch* were employed by Christians in variously accepted forms as a means of demonstrating their religious claims to truth and of securing their inner world. From the eighteenth century on, the valency of the old expressions altered. On the plane of "*Menschheit* itself," they became pure concepts of political struggle. Above all, *Übermensch* underwent, within the same generation, revaluation, devaluation, and reevaluation, as the polemical target required. Ruling members of the *Stände* who colloquially addressed their subjects as *Mensch* were critically described as *Übermensch*. "A time came when the word *Mensch* . . . assumed a completely different meaning; it meant a person bound to duties, a subject, a vassal, a servant . . . and those to whom the serving persons belonged were called *Übermenschen*."[110] Taking this colloquial form of address at face value gave it a republican aspect: a lord was defined as an *Übermensch* that he might be brought down to the same level as the "men" who were so addressed.

Parallel to and simultaneous with this negative freighting of *Übermenschen* emerged compensatory terms which were supposed to summon forth a new type from the now autonomous position of *Menschen*. The generally successful man became a genius, a god on earth, a man of power, a "more than man," a lad, a higher being, and so forth, in the same way that such terms sprang up out of the republicanizing *Sturm und Drang* movement.[111] In the same situation in which the Prince was negated as *Übermensch* or *Unmensch*, the new *Übermensch* emerged, belonging to no class and no hierarchy, since he did, in a quite complete sense, realize *Menschen*. Within this new linguistic figure the cult of Napoleon took up position, no longer stylizing the ruler in a royal manner but rather as leader and as incarnation of the *Menschen* that he led being rendered as an *Übermensch*.[112]

On the whole, the German neo-humanist maintained an especially critical attitude toward this linguistic usage. For instance, Herder stated that "all their questions concerning the progress of our species . . . are answered by . . . a single word: humanity (*Menschheit*). If the question were whether *Mensch* could or should become more than *Mensch*, an *Über-*, an *Aussermensch*, so would every line be superfluous."[113] Goethe also cautiously used the term: saying of Zacharias Werner that he (Goethe) would be an enemy of all those who vainly used the couplet of *Über-* and *Untermensch* and in so doing divided humanity in two.[114] "Hardly are you master of the first childish wishes that you think of yourself as *Übermensch* enough / to evade fulfillment of the duty of a man!"[115] With that, he placed the expression of the *Übermenschlich* in the only apparently polar semantic zone of the *Unmenschen*. Both were "devoid of God and the world."

Marx used the categories *Übermensch* and *Unmensch* in an ideological critique to destroy the doctrine of the two worlds, which maintained the religious reflection of *Menschen* in the image of heavenly *Übermenschen* and by means of which the *Menschen* degraded themselves to the status of *Unmenschen*.[116] In its place would in the future appear "the total *Mensch*," not only a personally successful prototype, but a type made socially possible in a world free of domination. We could place alongside him Dostoevski's "universal man"—the social fulfillment of "the general human association" through which Russian Christians would be able to abolish all contradictions.[117]

The expression became politically virulent only with the reception of Nietzsche. For him, the *Übermensch* is the man of the future, transcending the contemporary democratic man of the herd, "a higher type, a stronger form" compared with the "average man. My concept, my image for this type is, as is known, the word *Übermensch*." Man shall be transcended and will become the object of ridicule for the coming supermen. "Not *Menschheit*, but *Übermensch* is the goal!"[118]

At the moment that this expression was to be politically realized, the polar opposite was clearly no longer man as a backward creature, but rather the *Untermensch*, who was to be exterminated. Into this conceptual couple that was part of National Socialist language entered— considered in terms of conceptual reception—several components: at the apparently scientific level this conceptual couple concerned a physically calculable substantialization, which was then politicized by the concepts of race and type. To this was added the temporal tension of the once-Christian expectational horizon, which had the effect of securing domination in the future. But such derivations are not sufficient to decipher this totalitarian figure of speech.

The nature of the linguistic manipulation involved becomes clearer by analyzing the pair of opposites which was not simply used propagandistically, as were *Übermensch* and *Untermensch*, but which also entered into legislation: the contrast of Aryan and non-Aryan. The Aryan, first a term drawn from linguistics that implied nobility, was politically undefined, and in fact was a concept that was hardly definable politically. "Officials whose heredity is not Aryan are to be retired." Or with a double negative: "Editors may only be those of Aryan descent who are not married to a person of non-Aryan descent."[119]

The term "Aryan" was constituted as a political term by the conceptual field which it negated and to which any opponent could be consigned at will.[120] The non-Aryan is merely the negation of one's own position, and that is that. Who might be Aryan cannot be deduced from the concept of the Aryan, nor from that of the non-Aryan. This then defined an elastic figure of negation whose actual arrangement was at the disposal of whoever had the power to fill linguistic vacancies or empty concepts. The concept itself did not indicate that the Jews were specifically identified, but they found, by falling under the category of non-Aryan, that they were destined for potential nonexistence. The conclusion was drawn as soon as the Aryan as *Übermensch* felt himself legitimated in the removal of the non-Aryan as *Untermensch*. According to the capacity to ideologically freight negations which are themselves not confronted with a politically determinable position, we have here a case of structural application of the conceptual couple *Mensch* and *Unmensch*. The expression "non-Aryan" could be determined neither from the side of the Aryan nor from that of the non-Aryan in such a way that a clear position could be established. From the very first, the linguistic couple was accessible for functional employment by those with the power to affect the regulation of language.

*Mensch*, from whom the *Unmensch*, the *Übermensch*, and the *Untermensch* were derived, confirmed only an ideological arbitrariness which failed to appreciate what historically follows from the concept of *Menschheit*: that man is an ambivalent creature whose delimitation remains a political risk.

It is only within the horizon of expectation of a *Menschheit* left to its own devices that the formula "friend and foe" can be understood, a formula which is still today ideologically overused. Following upon the substantive emptying of this universalistic and at the same time dualistic conceptual couple in the twentieth century, it was the scientific achievement of Carl Schmitt, to formalize the contrast of classes and peoples and deploy them both functionally and ideologically in their various substantive formulations in such a manner that only the basic structure of possible contrasts became visible.[121] The conceptual couple Friend and Foe is characterized by its political formalism, delivering a frame for possible antitheses without identifying them. In the first place, because of its formal negation, this concerns purely symmetrical counterconcepts, for, in the case of Friend and Foe, there exists a definition of oneself or of one's Foe that is open to simultaneous use by both sides. These are epistemological categories whose substantial content (determined through historical experience) can serve to asymmetrically load both linguistic fields. However Schmitt might have concretized this contrast from his own position, he has coined a formula which cannot be outstripped as a condition of possible politics. This is a concept of the political, not of politics.

Whoever places peace as a concept overlaying Friend and Foe has to presuppose that, for peace, at least two parties exist who are willing and able to arrive at a settlement. *Non ergo ut sit pax nolent sed ut ea sit quam volunt*.[122] Not that one shies from peace, but that each seeks his own peace. As long as human agencies exclude and include, there will be asymmetric counterconcepts and techniques of negation, which will penetrate conflicts until such time as new conflicts arise.

# On the Disposability of History

Before dealing with the problem at hand, a story (*Geschichte*) must be told. In the year 1802, a morally zealous Briton, the Reverend John Chatwode Eustace, travelled through Italy. He sought, together with an aristocratic companion, to deepen his classical education at firsthand. Ten years later he published the results of his travels.

The Reverend Mr. Eustace had found Italy to be a victim of the French Revolution and was unsparing of learned quotations that should provide his readers with a historical attitude. To this end he offered them long-term perspectives. He cited Scipio who, seated on the ruins of Carthage, foresaw the coming fall of Rome. Naturally enough, he also declaimed Homer's lines from the *Iliad*: $\epsilon\sigma\sigma\epsilon\tau\alpha\iota$ $\eta\mu\alpha\rho$, the day that would come when Holy Troy itself collapsed. Drawing directly on an old topos, he argued that the "Empire" had since moved toward the West. Whoever might today consider the "dominions" of Great Britain and their great extent might claim without presumption that the imperium had now fallen to Great Britain. But, added the Reverend, the imperium was moving on; whether back toward the East or onward into transatlantic regions he did not know. No matter; the days of Britannia's glory were also numbered, and their end approached inevitably. This was the view of our witness in the year 1813, when Great Britain was about to rise to the peak of its maritime power. In days to come, the inhabitants of the British Isles, just as the sons of Greece or Italy, would lie at the feet of victorious enemies for whose sympathy they would beg in recognition of the greatness of their predecessors.

With such thoughts in his head, our traveller brought his sympathy to the inhabitants of Italy, a sympathy which did not, however, extend to their notions of hygiene. All the same, the Italians were descendants of those masters of the earth, those "Lords of humankind," the Romans, in the course of whose fame they were in actuality the predecessors of the Britons: *Terrae dominantis alumni.*[1]

If we had posed to our classically educated Reverend the question of whether fate still existed, he would have scarcely understood the question. He might have rejected it as a hybrid. History as "to and fro," as "up and down" in the unfolding of power: this was fate for him, whether conceived classically and fatalistically or in the spirit of Christian providentialism. If we had further asked him if it was possible for history to be made, he might perhaps have referred, as he in fact unfailingly did, to the chaos that the French had in his view just created in Italy. This is our story from 1802 and the report of it made in 1813.

We have already broached the issue to be discussed. It will be dealt with in two sections. First, it will be demonstrated when and in what manner the idea arises that one can make history. Here the discussion will be confined to sources in the German language. Second, we will seek to identify the boundaries which are set to such "makeability" by a properly conceived history.

Allow me to add a word here to those of our English witness from a contemporary who was younger than the Reverend at that time and who certainly cannot be suspected of being a partisan of modernity or even of revolution. Freiherr von Eichendorff once said in passing: "The one makes history, the other writes it down."[2] This formula appears to be clear and unambiguous. There is the actor, the doer, the perpetrator; and there is the other one, the writer, the historian. If you like, this involves a kind of division of labor that Eichendorff has outlined, in which it clearly is a matter of the same history which is made on the one side and written down on the other. History seems to be disposable in a dual fashion: for the agent who disposes of the history that he makes, and for the historian who disposes of it by writing it up. Viewed in this way, both seem to have an unlimited freedom of decision. The scope for the disposition of history is determined by men.

We are far from hanging such a significant conclusion on Eichendorff's casual wordplay. It is nevertheless important in studying our problem to know that Eichendorff was able to speak in terms of one being able to make history. We use the expression readily enough today in the constantly repeated semiquotation from Treitschke, according to which it is supposedly men who make history.[3] Under the influence of Napoleon it appeared quite evident that there was someone who had made history. Nonetheless, to say that someone "makes" history is a modern usage which could not have been formulated before Napoleon or in any case before the French Revolution. While for over two thousand years it was a property of Mediterranean and occidental culture that *Geschichten* were recounted, as well as investigated and written up, only since around 1780 was it conceivable that *Geschichte* could be made. This formulation indicates a modern experience and even more, a modern expectation: that one is increasingly capable of planning and also executing history.

Before history could be grasped as something that was disposable and constructible, the conceptual field of history itself underwent a far-reaching semantic change. I would like to outline this linguistic shift.[4]

Our contemporary concept of history, together with its numerous zones of meaning, which in part are mutually exclusive, was first constituted towards the end of the eighteenth century. It is an outcome of the lengthy theoretical reflections of the Enlightenment. Formerly there had existed, for instance, the history that God had set in motion with humanity. But there was no history for which humanity might have been the subject or which could be thought of as its own subject. Previously, histories had existed in the plural—all sorts of histories which had occurred and which might be used as exempla in teachings on ethics and religion, and in law and philosophy. Indeed, history (*die Geschichte*) as an expression was plural. In 1748 it was stated, "History is a mirror for vices and virtues in which one can learn through alien experience what one should do and what should be left undone."[5] Through repeated use of such reflections, this plural form was modified into an objectless singular. One of the conceptual achievements of the philosophy of the Enlightenment was enhancing history into a general concept which became the condition of possible experience and possible expectation. Only from around 1780 can one talk of "history in general," "history in and for itself," and "history pure and simple," and as all elaborations on this theme indicate, there was an emphasis on the departure of this new, self-referring concept from the traditional histories in plural.

If anyone had said before 1780 that he studied history, he would have at once been asked by his interlocutor: Which history? History of what? Imperial history, or the history of theological doctrine, or perhaps the history of France? As said earlier, history could only be conceived together with an associated subject that underwent change or upon which change occurred. The new expression, "history in general," was thus initally suspected as being modish, and the degree to which it was considered dubious is illustrated by the fact that Lessing, in his historicophilosophical outline of the eduction of the human species, avoided the expression *die Geschichte*, not to speak of the use of "history in general" without an article. The surprises that the new concept, soon a slogan, could give rise to are illuminated by a scene at the court in Berlin.[6] Biester once replied thus to Frederick the Great's inquiring after what he was doing: he occupied himself "famously with history" (*vorzüglich mit der Geschichte*). The king stopped short at that and asked whether that meant the same as *Historie*—because, Biester supposed, the king was unfamiliar with the expression *die Geschichte*. Of course Frederick knew the word *Geschichte*, but not the new concept: history as a collective singular without reference to an associated subject or, alternatively, an object determined by narration.

One may ask the meaning of such semantic analyses that are presented here in such a schematic and abbreviated fashion. It might be recalled that historical events and their linguistic constitution are folded into each other. The course of historical occurrences, the manner in which they are made possible linguistically, and the way in which they can then be worked over do not coincide in a simple fashion, such that, for example, an event only enters into its own linguistic registration. Rather, a tension prevails between these two poles that undergoes continual historical change. It is thus all the more important that we investigate the peculiarities of the way in which a given set of past events were articulated or anticipated. Stated another way: what is actually at stake when one talks of "history" that can, for instance, be "made"?

My first, historical thesis is that history first appeared to be generally at the disposition of men; that is, conceived as makeable, following the emergence of history as an independent and singular key concept. The step from a plurality of specific histories to a general and singular history is a semantic indicator of a new space of experience and a new horizon of expectation.

The following criteria serve to characterize the new concept:

1. "History pure and simple" was a collective singular that collected together the sum of all individual histories. "History" thereby gained an enhanced degree of abstraction, allowing it to indicate a greater complexity, which capability has since made it necessary for reality to be generally elaborated in a historical manner.

2. The by-now familiar Latin expression *Historie*; that is, the concept designating knowledge and the science of things and affairs was at the same time absorbed by the new concept of history (*Geschichte*). Put another way, history as reality and the reflection upon this history were brought together in a common concept, as history in general. The process of events and of their apprehension in consciousness converged henceforth in one and the same concept. To this extent one could characterize this new expression as a kind of transcendental category: the conditions of possible historical experience and of their possible knowledge were subsumed under the same concept.

3. Within this convergence, which initially was purely semantic, there was an implied renunciation of an extrahistorical level. The experience or apprehension of history in general no longer required recourse to God or nature. In other words, the history which was experienced as novel was, from the beginning, synonymous with the concept of world history itself. It was no longer a case of a history which merely took place through and with the humanity of the earth. In Schelling's words of 1798: man has history "not because he participates in it, but because he produces it."[7]

We will not continue here with further definitions of the new concept. We have already reached a position from which history can be conceived as disposable.

History that is history only to the extent that it is recognized is naturally bound more strongly to men than a history that overtakes men in the form of a fate that takes place. It is the conception of reflexiveness that first opens up a space for action within which men feel compelled to foresee history; to plan it; in Schelling's words, to "produce" it and ultimately to make it. Henceforth, history no longer means a simple concatenation of past events and the account of such events. The narrative meaning instead was diminished, and since the end of the eighteenth century, the expression has opened up social and political planes for planful activity that point to the future. In the decade before the French Revolution history, then promoted by the revolutionary upheavals, became a concept of action, even if not exclusively so.

It is certainly possible to regard the sequence of foresight, planning, and making as a basic anthropological determinant of human action. What is novel in what confronts us is the reference of this determination of action to the newly conceived "history in general." This seems to place on the agenda no more and no less than the future of world history, and even to make it available.

To elaborate, an outcome of so-called modernity (*Neuzeit*) was that at the end of the eighteenth century the idea of a "new time" was constituted. The concept of progress, which at that time was largely coincident with "history," encapsulated a form of historical time which was subject to constant renewal. The common achievement of both concepts was that they renewed and extended the horizon of future expectation.

Roughly speaking, until the mid-seventeenth century, expectation of the future was bounded by the approach of the Last Judgment, within which earthly injustice would find its transhistorical settlement. Fate was to this degree both unjust and merciful, and it was taken for granted that even then men had to exercise foresight and behave accordingly. The art of political prognosis in particular was developed from the sixteenth century on and became a part of the business of all men of state. Such practice did not, however, fundamentally transcend the horizon of a Christian eschatology. Precisely because nothing fundamentally new would arise, it was quite possible to draw conclusions from the past for the future. The inference from previous experience to anticipated future made use of factors whose structure was quite stable.

This changed for the first time during the eighteenth century, as the impact of science and technology appeared to open up an unlimited space of new possibilities. "Reason," said Kant in 1784, "knows no bounds for its designs."[8] Here Kant points to the shift whose theoretical definition concerns us, notwithstanding the numerous empirical factors this shift produced in the West somewhat earlier and in Germany somewhat later.

In his *Anthropology*, Kant spoke of the "capacity of foresight" as being of greater interest than other capacities: "for it is the condition of all possible practice and the goal to which man directs the use of his powers."[9] But a prediction that basically anticipated similitude—

and here he distinguishes himself from his predecessors—was for him no prognosis. Inference from past experience to expectations about the future would at most lead to "immobility" (*Tatlosigkeit*) and cripple all impulse toward action.[10] Above all, however, this conclusion contradicted Kant's expectation that the future would be better because it ought to be better.

All of Kant's efforts as a philosopher of history were directed toward translating the latent natural plan, which seemed set to force humanity onto the course of unlimited progress, into a conscious plan of the rationally endowed man. "How is a history possible a priori?" Kant asked, and answered: "when the soothsayer himself makes and organizes the occurrences which he announces in advance."[11] Semantically we can see at once that Kant does not simply state that history can be made; rather, he speaks of occurrences that a soothsayer himself brings about. In fact, Kant wrote this passage, today freely cited with agreement and praise, in an ironic and provocative spirit. It was directed against the prophets of decline who themselves created and promoted the predicted Fall, as well as against those supposedly realistic politicians who, shy of the public realm, fomented unrest through their fear of the Fall. Nevertheless, with his question concerning a priori history, Kant established the model of its makeability.

With the imperative of his practical reason, Kant sought to realize the optative mood of a progressive future that broke with the conditions of all previous history. As can be detected in a coded form of his Job allegory of 1791, it is "practical reason in possession of power . . . as it is proffered without further cause in legislation" that is capable of delivering an "authentic theodicy."[12] The meaning of creation is likewise taken up and transposed into the work of man as soon as practical reason assumes power, without being able thereby to lose its moral integrity.

The dark "foreboding" of a "fate which might be hung over us" thus becomes, in Kant's words, "a chimera."[13] Fate gives way to the autonomy of a ruling practical reason.

It is certain that the model presented here does not exhaust Kant's historical philosophy, which is replete with reservation serving to prevent an overflow into a utopia dispensing with all previous experience. But without a doubt the impulse derived from ethics, that conceives the design of the future as the task of a moral imperative, conceiving history as a temporalized house of correction for morality, deeply impressed itself on the coming century. A criticized and a vulgarized Kant initially had a greater influence than had Kant as a critical philosopher.

This can be seen, for example, in Adam Weishaupt, not unknown as the leader of the Illuminati in Bavaria.[14] Weishaupt crossed the threshold on the path to the constructibility of history, for he was the first to attempt to transfer the capacity of foresight, the ability to make long-term prognoses, into maxims for political action that derive their legitimation from a general history. According to Weishaupt, the most important vocation that existed (but which unfortunately had yet to become established) was that of philosophers and historians; that is, of the planful historical philosopher.

The straightforward transposition of goodwill into action had never been sufficient to justify a desired future, even less so to attain it. Thus, Weishaupt supplied (and here, he was advanced but not alone) a voluntaristic historical philosophy. It took the form of a reassurance. Weishaupt's political intention to undermine the state and render it redundant was imputed to nothing other than the work of a history which would sooner or later have its effect. Insofar as the future that was to be brought about was announced as the imperative of objective history, one's own intentions assume an impulsive force which is all the greater by virtue of its simultaneous supply of the guarantee of one's innocence. Future history whose outcome is foreseen serves in this way as a relief—one's will becomes the executor of transpersonal events—and as a legitimation which enables one to act in good conscience. In precise terms, history constructed in this way becomes a means of strengthening the will to hurry the advent of the planned future.

It is quite clear that it is only possible to outline such a history after the consolidation of "history" into a concept of reflection and action that renders fate manipulable; or, put another way, that also appears to make the distant consequences of one's action predictable.[16] The voluntaristic association of history with one's planning obscures the potential for the surplus and surprise characteristic of all history. As it is known, Weishaupt foundered upon the reaction of the Bavarian princes. His theoretical naïveté was a contributory factor and ended his plan before it had a chance to be realized. Subsequent events, however, teach us that theoretical naïveté is no protection against success.

The structure of argument that we can demonstrate in the case of Weishaupt has formally survived, notwithstanding the social, political, and economic diagnoses introduced into their prognoses on the part of Liberals, Democrats, Socialists, and Communists. Wherever the "makeability" of history might be implied, it was lent redoubled emphasis as soon as the actor invoked a history which, at the same time, objectively indicated the path he should take. This process of reassurance conceals the fact that such a design is not and cannot be anything more than the product of situationally and chronologically determined insight which goes no further than these limitations. Makeability thus for the most part remained only an aspect of a history whose course continually escaped the intentions of its agents, as is confirmed by experience. For this reason, the idea that history could be made did not become common property but rather was initially used within distinct social groupings and was associated with the decay of the society of orders.

Considered socially-historically, those who invoked the idea that history could be made were, for the most part, groups of activists who wished to establish something new. To be part of a history moving under its own momentum, where one only aided this forward motion, served both as personal vindication and as an ideological amplifier which reached out to others and caught them up.

History, which in the German language continued to be pervaded with a sense of divine Providence, was not transposed into the domain of makeability without a struggle. Perthes, born in 1772, hesitated as a politically active publisher even in 1822 to use the verb: he wished to publish for practical men, "for businessmen, for it is they and not the scholars who intervene in things and, so to say, make history."[17] He did, however, soon afterward make a plea for a self-conscious middle class that would agitate for participation in power; and that would, through an orientation toward achievement, dispense with the doctrines of the past, the old *historia magistra vitae*: "If every party were by turns to govern and oversee institutions, then all parties would through history wish that they had made themselves become fairer and wiser. Seldom do political equity and wisdom result from history made by others, no matter how much it might be written and studied; this is taught by experience."[18] The expression "making history" was employed here as a challenge and functioned as an appeal.

The expression "making history" therefore also entered into so-ciopolitical common language without the historicophilosophical re-assurance noted above; for example, it was used by Gagern in the 1848 Frankfurt Parliament to define the great tasks laid before it. Alternatively, we can cite a *Vormärz* democrat, Wilhelm Schulz, who was one of the most influential politicians and has been unjustly forgotten:

Peoples are just beginning to achieve a sense of their meaning. They thus still have little sense of their history and will not have such sense until they themselves make history, until they are more than dead material out of which [the history] of a few privileged classes is made.[19]

Such liberal-democratic linguistic usage had the character of an appeal, serving to raise the consciousness of rising strata and everywhere testifying to the certainty of a linear course of progress.

Here Marx and Engels, as spokesmen of classes which were pressing forward, were in this respect at once more cautious and more certain of themselves. The oft-cited 1878 dictum of Engels on the "leap of mankind from the realm of necessity into the realm of freedom" transferred the phase of sovereign disposability to the future of socialist self-organization. Only then would

the objective, alien powers which had until then dominated his-tory . . . [come under] . . . the control of men themselves. Only from that time on will men make their history themselves in all consciousness; only from that time on will the social causes that they have set in motion begin to assume to an increasing degree the effects that they wish to bring about.[20]

Paraphrased according to Kant, only then will a priori history be realized. Or expressed post-theologically, only then will the distinction of foresight, plan, and execution fall away, and man will become "God on earth."

With this we come to the second part. Where lie the boundaries that deny to a properly conceived history its makeability? If Engels were correct—that in the future, foresight, plan, and execution would coincide seamlessly—it would need only be added that in fact the end of all history had been reached. History is characterized (here is our second thesis) by the manner in which human foresight, human plans, and their execution always diverge in the course of time. By saying that, we are chancing a structural pronouncement or formulating a view that is older than the eighteenth century. But permit the addition of a statement that is an outcome of the Enlightenment: "history in and of itself" always occurs in the anticipation of incompleteness and therefore possesses an open future. That is, in any case, a lesson of all previous history, and whoever wishes to argue the opposite will have to prove his case.

I wish nonetheless to prove my thesis, indeed, through the use of historical examples which appear to lend support to the opposing view; namely, that history can be made. I will call upon four men to whom no one in the normal course of events would deny a role in the making of history: Marx, Bismarck, Hitler, and Roosevelt.

1. Wherever he could, Marx sought to dissolve substantially conceived concepts of history and attempted to reveal such concepts as "metaphysical subjects" in the language of his opponents.[21] It is not possible to reduce his historicophilosophical achievement solely to utopian goals that may have provided a worldwide echo for him. His historical analyses are fed, rather, by a fundamental determination of the difference that distinguishes human action from what actually occurs in the long term. This distinction provides the foundation for his analysis of capital as well as for his critique of ideology (for example, the critique of "ideologues" whom he derided as "manufacturers of history."[22] In the place where he appeared as a historian of the present after his failure of 1848, Marx outlined in an unsurpassed fashion the boundaries to the making of history: "Men make their own history, but they do not do so freely, not under conditions of their own choosing, but rather under circumstances which directly confront them, and which are historically given and transmitted."[23] Marx made use of his clear insight to derive practical directives for action. It was, rather, the "makeability" of politics and not its socioeconomic conditions that he had under theoretical consideration here. It could be supposed that the practical-political influence that Marx has rests upon such formulations—on historical insights that are capable of shifting the utopian horizon of expectation ever further into the distance.[24] This can be proved by the route which is traversed from Bebel, Lenin, Stalin, to Tito, or Mao.

2. No one will wish to deny that Bismarck was a unique individual in the absence of whose diplomatic skill the lesser German Empire never would have emerged in the way that it actually did. It is for

this reason that even today he is burdened with indisputable consequences, even by those who deny the role of men who make history
or at least theoretically exclude it from consideration. With this exclusion they certainly find agreement with Bismarck's own view. Bismarck always protested against the idea of making history. "An
arbitrary intervention in the development of history that is made only
for subjective reasons has always ended with the harvesting of unripe
fruit," Bismarck wrote in an 1869 decree to the Prussian envoy in
Munich, Von Werthern. "We can put the clocks forward but the time
does not therefore pass any the quicker."[25] Bismarck certainly used
his dictum against the idea of making history so that he could make
politics; he wished to calm Bavarian fears of Prussia's expansionary
desires so that he might conduct his own policy of unification all the
more successfully. For this reason, Bismarck repeated the expression
shortly afterward in a speech before the North German Imperial Assembly, for the purpose of holding back a premature constitutional
change. "My influence over the events in which I have been involved
is indeed substantially overestimated, but certainly no one should
expect of me that I make history."[26] He still found confirmation for
this view in his old age: "It is generally not possible for one to make
history, but one can learn from it the manner in which the political
life of a great people, its development, and its historical conditions
are to be properly conducted."[27]

The renunciation of the susceptibility of historical processes to planning emphasize the differential that must be drawn between political
action and long-term given tendencies. However divergent were the
political goals of Bismarck and Marx, and however much their diagnoses
or expectations differed, at the level of their historicotheoretical statements on the boundaries of "makeability," they are found to be as-
tonishingly close.

3. Hitler and his followers reveled in the use of the word "history,"
which was complained about as fate at the same time that it was held
to be available for "making." But even the inconsistency of the expressions that were constructed upon closer examination reveals their
ideological content. Hitler wrote in his second book in 1928: "Only
under the hammer of world history do the eternal values of a people
become the steel and iron with which one then makes history."[28] A
turn of phrase from the Lippe electoral campaign before 30 January
1933 shows that even futuristic obsessions had a secret prognostic

meaning: "It is ultimately a matter of indifference what percentage of the German people make history. The only thing that matters is that it is we who are the last to make history in Germany."[29] It would not be possible to formulate more clearly the self-ultimata according to which Hitler made his politics and thus believed himself to be making history. He did make history, but differently from the way he thought he had.

We need no reminder that the more Hitler placed himself under the ultimatum of having to make history himself, the more he miscalculated in assessing his opponents and the time that remained to him. The periods Hitler held to treaties he had concluded or promises he had made became ever shorter during the course of his rule, while the temporal objectives he drew up grew ever more distant. His politics was made under the compulsion of an acceleration which stood in an inverse relation to the spaces of time and to the eternity in whose name he claimed to act. Hitler thought his will greater than the circumstances: he had a solipsistic relation to historical time. Ultimately, however, for every history there exist at least two, and it is characteristic of historical time that it throws up factors that escape manipulation. Bismarck knew that and was successful; Hitler, who did not wish to believe it, had none.

4. On 11 April 1945, Roosevelt, the great adversary of Hitler, formulated his testament to the American people. "The only limit to our realization of tomorrow will be our doubts of today." The work which he sought to carry out on the morrow was "peace. More than an end of this war—an end to the beginnings of all wars."[30] Roosevelt was not able to make public this testament. He died the following day. He was right with his testament, but in a sense reversed from what he had intended. The end of all beginnings to war is one of the first formulations of cold war. The last war has not been terminated by a peace treaty, nor has war been declared since then. Instead, the wars which have since that time encircled our globe with misery, terror, and fear are no longer wars, but rather interventions, punitive actions, and above all civil wars whose initiation seems to occur under the pretense of avoiding nuclear war and whose end thus cannot be foreseen.

It could be that the doubt which Roosevelt sought to throw on the work of the following day was a presentiment of the fact that, in history, things tend to turn out differently from the way they were originally planned. But it could equally well be that a simple projection of one's own hopes into the future obstructed the fulfillment of such hopes, and continues to do so. Roosevelt probably did not think of that. *Non ut si pax nolunt, sed ut ea sit quam volunt.*[31] Not that one avoided peace, but that each seeks his own. Peace requires two participants, at least.

We are approaching the conclusion. We should guard against completely rejecting the modern turn of phrase concerning the makeability of history. Men are responsible for the histories they are involved in, whether or not they are guilty of the consequences of their action. Men have to be accountable for the incommensurability of intention and outcome, and this lends a background of real meaning to the dictum concerning the making of history.

The decline of the British Empire, which our first witness deduced as the unavoidable outcome of the course of all previous history, has taken place in the meantime. This long-term process was only accelerated by the British victory over Germany in 1945. Who would dare attribute this to the acts and deeds of individuals? What happens among men has not been the making of individual men for a long time. In Ireland, a remnant of earlier expansion, the English confront a hangover from their past which they appear incapable of removing, no matter how hard they might try. They become responsible for situations they would not create today, even if they were able to. The costs of economic exploitation, political slavery, and religious oppression cannot voluntaristically be wound up.

Many generations, through their action or suffering, have contributed to the rise of what has been the greatest world empire; up to now there have been few able to prevent the demise of Pax Britannica on our globe. Technical and economic conditions have changed in such a manner that today it is no longer possible to steer the fates of continents from a small island, or even exercise to any effective influence. The British—with their politics, political ethics, and achievements in science and technology—have themselves taken a leading role in this change. But they did not "make" the history which has resulted, and to which we are the witnesses today. It has—contrary to all intentions and deeds, but certainly not without intentions and actions—happened.

There always occurs in history more or less than that contained in the given conditions. Behind this "more or less" are to be found men, whether they wish it or not. These conditions do not change for a long time; and when they do, they change so slowly and over such a long period that they escape disposition, or makeability.

# Terror and Dream:
# Methodological Remarks on the
# Experience of Time during the
# Third Reich

## Res factae and res fictae

*Si fingat, peccat in historiam; so non fingat, peccat in poesin.* He who invents violates the writing of history; he who does not, violates poetic art. With this seventeenth-century statement Alsted formulated a simple opposition that had been a topos for two thousand years.[1] The business of *Historie* was to address itself to actions and events, to *res gestae*, whereas poetry lived upon fiction. The criteria distinguishing history from poetics involved the modes of representation, which (if we might exaggerate somewhat) were intended to articulate either being or appearance. The intertwined manner in which the rhetorical relation of history and poetry is defined cannot, of course, be reduced to such a handy couplet. Even the common concept *res* is ambiguous, for the reality of events and deeds cannot be the same as the reality of simulated actions.[2] Also, appearance can extend from the illusion of probability to the reflection of the true.[3] Until the seventeenth century, however, it is possible to derive from these extremities (notwithstanding numerous intermediate positions) two models which assign the higher rank to poetry and history, respectively.

Thus one considered the truth content of history higher than that of poetry, for whoever surrendered himself to *res gestae*, to *res factae*, had to demonstrate naked reality itself, whereas *res fictae* led to lies. It was primarily historians who used this argument, favorable as it was to their own position.

The opposing position invoked Aristotle's denigration of history at the expense of poetry. Poetry concerned itself with the possible and the general and it approached philosophy, while history was concerned only with the sequence of time in which many things occurred in a variety of ways.[4] It was therefore open to Lessing, the Aristotelian of the Enlightenment, to argue that, by contrast with the writer of history, who often had to make use of dubious or even improbable facts, the poet was "master of history; and he is able to cluster incidents as closely as he wishes."[5] The poet gained his credibility through the inner probability with which he connected the events and deeds represented, or rather produced, by him.

It was precisely this Aristotelian postulate which, from the Enlightenment, was taken up as a challenge by historians. One of the properties of the eighteenth-century experiential shift, in which history was formulated in terms of a new reflexive concept, was that the line dividing the camps of historians and creative writers became osmotically porous. It was demanded of the writer, especially the writer of novels, that he articulate historical reality if he wished to be convincing and have influence. On the contrary, the historian was asked to render plausible the possibility of his history through the use of theories, hypotheses, and reasoning. Like the writer, he was to distill from his history its meaningful unity.

It might be mentioned in passing that following this boundary shift the theological heritage of a Providence creative of meaning was opened up. The authenticity of biblical texts was indeed subordinated to worldly criticism, but the Enlightenment was also marked by the old doctrine of multiple meaning. Without the ability to read past events and texts at several levels, that is, to separate them from their original context and progressively reorder them, an advanced interpretation of confusing historical reality would not have been possible.

In this way the rhetorical opposition of inventive writing to the narration of history was neutralized. As soon as the historian was required to construct his history on an artful, moral, and rational basis, he was thrown upon the means of fiction. This in turn rendered more pressing the question of how historical reality, to which one had to relate, might be recognized scientifically. The rhetorical problem of the art of representation was modified epistemologically in the eighteenth century. It turned out, however, that even with this shift of attention to epistemological conditions, the old couplet *res factae* and *res gestae* took up position within the same perspective.

The demonstration that a reality once passed could be no longer recaptured by any representation was an achievement of Chladenius. Reality was instead reproducible in abbreviated statements. It was this knowledge of historical perspective which forced historians to become aware of the devices of fiction—of "rejuvenated images," in the language of Chladenius—if they wished to pass on meaningful histories. The historian was confronted with the demand, both in terms of techniques of representation and epistemologically, that he offer not a past reality, but the fiction of its facticity.[6] Hardly had this demand been taken seriously, however, before the historian found himself placed under an enhanced pressure for proof. He now had to engage in a critique of sources to avoid being thought restricted to recounting past events and adding novelties to them.

This led the Enlightenment in all consistency to the postulate that the complexity of history could only be recognized if the historian allowed himself to be guided by a theory. The historian should, to use an expression coined in Göttingen, translate history from an aggregate into a system that would enable him to arrange and question his sources and then allow them to speak. Even after this productive advantaging of historical consciousness, there was an unassimilated remainder that served to separate the status of historical representation from pure fiction. It is not possible to deny the difference that must prevail among accounts which report what has actually taken place, those which report what could have happened, those which propose that something might have happened, and those which dispense with any form of reality-signal. The difficulty in distinguishing these consists only in the fact that the linguistic status of a historical narrative or representation does not itself unambiguously announce whether it is rendering a reality or presenting mere fiction.

An author can assume the garb of a historian such that his text does not itself admit of a boundary, and in any case he might seek to undermine this boundary. The author may employ genuine or simulated sources, and the outcome might be an inner probability (he could here invoke Aristotle) that is more informative about historical problems or conflicts than would be possible in a historical account.

By contrast, the modern historian, like Ranke, had to ascend from particular to general statements or, as today, describe structures and trends without requiring in the process that individual events and occurrences, *res factae*, be directly articulated. The fictitious speeches of Thucydides, which do not reproduce addresses that were actually delivered but which serve to reveal a truth implicit in events, find their systematic counterpart in observations of the modern historian who reflects *ex post* on conditions and processes, ideas and epochs, and crises and catastrophes. Such interpretive frameworks or models deduced from so-called reality have, in pre-Enlightenment language, the status of *res fictae*. All the same they serve the knowledge of historical reality.

The Enlightenment thus forced *res fictae* and *res factae* out of their pure relation of opposition. In this process, the so-called process of aestheticization also took place, which was later to color historism. But there is more to this than aestheticization and the rising awareness of theory which has, since then, supposedly structured history. Behind this rearrangement of *res fictae* and *res factae* there is above all a modern experience of a genuine historical time which makes it necessary to blend fiction and facticity together.

"In the same town one will hear in the evening an account of a significant event different from that heard in the morning."[7] In his usual offhand manner, Goethe had in this way made a penetrating observation which says more than the older insight according to which men are inclined to account for the same thing diversely and contradictorily. Goethe is here indicating the nature of historical time, whose perspectivist compulsion is conceived in terms of the epistemology of the historical Enlightenment. As an authentic eyewitness to an incident was increasingly displaced from his favored and event-related role, so unobserved time gained a function creative of knowledge that comprehended the whole of history. Witnesses could be examined after additional time had elapsed and the status of a history altered by consequence. What "really" happened already lies in the past, and what is reported no longer coincides with it. A history is absorbed by its effect. At the same time, however, it consists in more than the given impact which it has in specific situations. For these effects change themselves without the past history ceasing to assist in the promotion of these effects. Each retrospective interpretation feeds off the pastness of an occurrence and seeks to articulate it anew in the present. A history thus enters a complexly fractured temporal succession and is continually rearticulated, whether consciously or unconsciously handed down.

For this reason Goethe concluded from his observation that his autobiography was "a kind of fiction," or "writing," which alone re-capitulated the truth of his life's path. He did not appeal to fiction because he wished that illusion or invention would enter his account: rather, it was the temporal aspect which bound the working over of past facticity to fiction. Because of this epistemologically irresistible need for chronological distance to re-create the past (and not because of a romantic flirtation with poetry), later historians also appealed to the proximity of historical and creative writing.

Reflected chronological distance compels the historian to simulate historical reality, and not just by using "it was" as a form of speech. The historian rather is fundamentally impelled to make use of the linguistic means of a fiction to render available a reality whose actuality has vanished.

The remarks made up to this point should suffice to make two things plain: first, that our classic couplet of res factae and res fictae continues to present an epistemomlogical challenge to the contemporary historian, practiced in theory and conscious of hypothesis; second, that it is in particular the modern discovery of a specific historical time which impels the historian toward the perspectivistic fiction of the factual if he wishes to restore a once-vanished past. No sworn or cited source is sufficient to eliminate the risk involved in the statement of historical reality.[8]

In the following, the relation of fiction and facticity will be considered from a more restricted point of view. Instead of questioning historical representation and its reproduction of reality, a methodological field will be delineated within which res factae and res fictae are mingled in an extraordinarily dramatic fashion. I have in mind the realm of dreams, a realm which is part of the daily and nightly world of acting and suffering mankind.

Dreams, while they cannot be produced, nevertheless belong to the sphere of human fictions to the extent that, as dreams, they offer no real representation of reality. This does not, however, prevent them from belonging to life's reality, and it is for this reason that from Herodotus to early modern times they were thought to be worthy of historical account. Apart from this, a divinatory power has, since ancient times, either been attributed to them or derived from them; they therefore possess a particular relation to the future. But we will not consider this as yet unwritten history of dreams in the following.[9]

Dreams will instead be introduced as sources which testify to a past reality in a manner which perhaps could not be surpassed by any other source. Dreams do occupy a place at the extremity of a conceivable scale of susceptibility to historical rationalization. Considered rigorously, however, dreams testify to an irresistible facticity of the fictive, and for this reason the historian should not do without them. To demonstrate this, we will begin with two accounts of dreams.

## Dreams of Terror—Dreams in Terror

Both accounts are brief. The first comes from a doctor in 1934. "While I am peacefully lying on the sofa after surgery, around nine in the evening, reading a book on Mathias Grünewald, suddenly the walls of my room and apartment disappear. Appalled, I look around: all apartments, as far as the eye can see, no longer have any walls. I hear a loudspeaker bellowing: 'in accordance with the decree of the seventeenth of the month on the abolition of walls.' "

The other account also comes from the thirties and is given by a Jewish lawyer: "Two benches stand in the Tiergarten, a green one and a yellow one (at that time Jews were only allowed to sit on benches painted yellow), and between the two a litter basket. I sat down on the basket and placed a sign around my neck in the fashion of blind beggars, but also as the authorities do with "racial offenders": the sign said, "if necessary I will give my place up to the litter!"

Both accounts are taken from a collection of dreams during the Third Reich edited by Charlotte Beradt.[10] The dreams are anonymous but authentic. Both dreams involve a narrative; they contain action with a beginning and an end, action which, however, never took place in the way that it was recounted. They are dreams about terror, or more precisely, dreams of terror itself. Terror is not simply dreamed; the dreams are themselves components of the terror. Both recount a vivid inner truth which was not only realized, but was immeasurably outbid by the later reality of the Third Reich. Consequently these dreamed stories do not only testify to terror and its victims, but they had at that time a prognostic content, as we might say today.[11]

If we recall our original alternative of fiction or historical reality, then both accounts clearly belong to the domain of fictional texts. It is possible to read them thus. Their dense and pregnant quality approaches the stories of Kleist, Hebbel, and even more so of Kafka. No one would deny their literary quality. In this, they approach the kind of writing which, expressed in Aristotelian fashion, does not report what has happened but rather what could happen. Both dreams contain a probability that exceeds what appeared to be empirically feasible at the time they were dreamed. They anticipate the empirical improbabilities that later, in the catastrophe of collapse, would take place.

Beradt collected the dreams of approximately three hundred people and preserved them during the emigration. In them are refracted experiential forms of disturbing force. Reference is occasionally made to the social standing of the dreamer; frequently social standing can be judged through indices of reality. Conventional behavior becomes evident which, confronted with the terror, is transposed into an oppressive response within the dream. Fiction still aims at facticity. Thus the perspective of the dream fully opens up all three temporal dimensions. The dimensions of contemporaries of the period—marked by the heritage of Wilhelmine Germany and disposed toward Weimar, and by the shock of the present and the disturbing prospect of a threatening future—all these are captured in the dream images. Insidious adaptation to the new regime, subjection to a bad conscience, the spiral of anxiety, the crippling of resistance, the interplay of hangman and victim—all this is realized in the images, which are sometimes a little estranged, but often realistic. The findings are oppressive.

These are the dreams of the persecuted, but also of those who accommodated or who wished to accommodate but were not permitted to. We do not know the dreams of the enthusiasts, the victors—they dreamed as well, but hardly anyone knows how the content of their dreams related to the visions of those that were crushed by these temporary victors.

For the historian involved in the history of the Third Reich, the documentation of these dreams offers a source of the highest quality. Levels are disclosed that are not touched even by diary entries. The dreams which have been collected are exemplary of the recesses of daily life into which the waves of terror penetrate. They testify to an initially open, then later insidious, terror, and anticipate its violent intensification.

Dreams are not part of the armory of sources from which historical science normally draws, be it on account of a methodically inspired caution, or be it on the plausible grounds of deficient accessibility. But no one can prevent a historian from elevating every piece of evidence into a source through its methodical interrogation. For this reason, these dreamed and then recounted stories make possible the tracing of inferences for historical reality after 1933. Used in this fashion the dreams have, as has been stated, the status of fictional texts, a literary quality, which opens up the prospect of a reality which is to be constructed from the emergent Third Reich. It is possible to more or less indirectly introduce each fictional textual unit, as evidence of facticity at any rate. But our problem can be made even more precise.

The two dreams described above are more than fictional testimony of terror and about terror. They are, though perceptible only in the form of recounted text, actually prelinguistic stories which have taken place by means of and within the persons concerned. They are physical manifestations of terror but without the witnesses having fallen victim to physical violence. In other words, it is precisely as fiction that they are elements of historical reality. The dreams do not only refer to the conditions which such dreams, as fiction, have made possible. Even as apparitions, the dreams are instrumentalisations of terror itself.

Thus the dreams reveal an anthropological dimension which goes beyond their status as written sources, and without this dimension it is not possible to understand terror and its effectivity. They are not simply dreams of terror; they are, above all, dreams in terror, terror which pursues mankind even into sleep.

Now both the dreams from the doctor and the Jewish lawyer, assuming that the biographical genesis is known, can certainly be interpreted in terms of individual psychological analysis. In our case, however, a political interpretation is possible independent of this. It is apparent that in the dreams Beradt presents, the latent and manifest contents of the dreams virtually coincide. The political meaning of the dreams, even if socially conditioned and concealing a private fate, remains directly evident. Political experiences and menace has—to retain the psychoanalytical metaphor—flooded over the gatekeeper and flowed unhindered into the so-called unconscious. Here, they have allowed imagistic stories to emerge whose political point directly illuminated consciousness.

The abolition of walls according to decree strips private space of protection. In the dream, the loudspeaker allows no doubt: the house is opened up to the benefit of a control which in the name of community can be exercised by each over all. The oppressive compulsion of the Jewish lawyer to make way even for litter, voluntarily even, needs no interpretive translation for anyone who has experienced this history. In the form of an automatic paralysis, the improbable became occurrence. He who was persecuted surrendered himself to an existential and banal absurdity before this persecution took place. There obviously is a reason belonging to the body that goes further than fear permits the dreamer while awake. That did not have to be so. George Grosz had a similar dream which, if we can believe his recollections, promptly compelled him to emigrate to America.[12]

Dreams—like all affairs that have an impact on someone, like all occurrences—are initially singular and related to individuals. All the same, groups of dreams have a supra-individual history. In the great number of dreams recorded by Beradt we find expressed a world of experience, organized in terms of specific social strata, which comes from the generational unity then existing. Its common signature is a lucidly registered, menacing proximity to reality in which the disposition of personal background and a dreamlike capacity for reaction come together in the everyday and release prognostic potential. However oppressive the content of the dream, the perception of the dreamers remained intact. The temporal dimensions of the world of experience were still ordered to such an extent that a conceivable space of action was available.[13]

This changes completely if we look at the reported dreams that come to us from the concentration camps, in which not a few of the strata we have been discussing met their end.

We are in a position to follow the dreams collected by Beradt with accounts of dreams given by Jean Cayrol, which originate in the concentration camp.[14] The dream figures have changed decisively in comparison with those present in the domain of freedom outside the camps. Cayrol's reports have been confirmed by other witnesses who, like Bruno Bettelheim, Viktor E. Frankl, and Margarete Buber-Neumann, have themselves recounted camp dreams.[15]

Representations of dreams from concentration camps reveal to us a domain in which human understanding appears to give way, where language is struck dumb. The dreams from the camps are characterized by a rapid loss of reality, while daydreams increase proportionally. This leads us into a sphere in which the written sources obviously are inadequate for forming any general conception of the situation. We are forced to rely on the metaphor of dreams so that we might learn what really happened.

Political and social occurrences are generally illuminated through texts which refer directly to the actions that compose such occurrences. Even the leaders of the SS, in the course of their official communications, speeches, and memoirs, made use of a language which is as open as a text to rational examination or ideological-critical revelation. Actions and their linguistic articulation here remain open to methodological scrutiny. What happened in concentration camps is barely comprehensible in written form, is scarcely tangible in descriptive or imaginative language. A relapse into a dumb condition is a sign of the totalitarian state. Even from 1933 Beradt recounts the dream of a cleaning woman in which dumbness was indicated to be a vehicle of survival: "I dreamt that as a precaution I spoke Russian (which I cannot do, and anyway I don't talk in my sleep) *so that I might not understand myself*, and so that no one might understand me in case I said something about the state, since that is of course forbidden and has to be reported."[16] A striking counterpart to this comes to us from the "Führer." Hitler at one time distinguished three levels of secrecy: that which he entrusted only to his immediate circle, that which he kept to himself, and that which he himself did not dare to completely think through.[17] This last zone takes us into the domain of the unutterable, which Cayrol, as former inmate of a camp, sought to decipher by means of the imagistic world of dreams. Here his analyses of dreams coincide entirely with those of other reports of camp dreams, even when their authors differ greatly in character, attitude and disposition.

In contrast with the dreams from the beginnings of the Third Reich that are characterized by a clear political perception, the dreams of concentration camp inmates lose all direct relation to reality. The dreams of 1933 and following years lived on a proximity to a reality which made it possible for the dreamers to work up the terror in biographical terms. Again, the images shift between background and approaching possibility in a consistent empirical sense. Clearly, the witnesses still had available to them an intact movement which allowed them to make prognostic observations. After their arrival in the camps this changed quickly and fundamentally. The inmates were paralyzed by the diabolic terror of the system of control which forced them into such a restricted space and robbed them, with few exceptions, of all spontaneous and direct perception. Pure fear blocked their view, changing at least their line of sight to such an extent that the world of dreams also had to change itself in accordance with their distorted behavior.

It is a characteristic common to all camp dreams that the actual terror could no longer be dreamed. Phantasy of horror was here surpassed by actuality. For this reason, the camp dreams can no longer be read in the usual way as fictional texts indicating a certain reality. If they nevertheless do so, then it is only in terms of a completely altered sign that indicates to us the changed anthropological dimension. This will now be elaborated.

Like our other witnesses, Cayrol distinguishes between dreams from the period of custody before internment, which substantially coincide with those dreams charged with a sense of reality collected by Beradt, and dreams from the concentration camp period, in which the relation to the past becomes loosened, family ties dissolve, and musical scenes or natural or architectonic landscapes extend themselves. Cayrol then finally separates off salvational or future-oriented dreams (while not covering in this framework dreams originating in the post-camp period). The salvational and future-oriented dreams possess for Cayrol a mutually exclusive function. This observation is confirmed by many inmates and by our other witnesses. The dreams of the future move in the temporal dimension of past life, fed by memory, and out of which all wishes and hopes are deduced. To a great extent, these wishes and hopes correspond to the daytime phantasies of the inmates. They subsist on a life from which the inmate is absolutely and irrevocably cut off. This is the matter of utopian camp dreams. They disclose a moving image of home beyond the electric fence, a home which the inmate seeks and recalls but which no longer exists for the inmate. The pure facticity of the camp is blanked out, and the past transferred into wishes for the future. Such dreams were the harbingers of death. Frankl tells of a fellow inmate who dreamed of the date of his release; it was the day of his death in the camp.[18] The same security of home life that appeared to offer some hope became the indicator of doom.

Dreams devoid of images and action, which Cayrol experienced and understood as salvational dreams, appear to be completely different. They correspond, while dispensing with all temporal dimensions, to the experience of the camp. That which in life usually heralds schizophrenia—the egocentric destruction of the intersubjectively experienced world terminating in pure anachronism[19]—assumes in the inverted constraints of concentration camp confinement a surprising and adaptive significance. In the camp, conditions prevailed that made a mockery of all previous experience; conditions that appeared unreal, but were real all the same. The compulsion to de-realize oneself in order to become paralyzed at the final stage of existence led also to an inversion of temporal experience. Past, present, and future ceased to be a framework for orienting behavior. This perversion, penetrating one's body, had to be savored to free oneself of it. The salvational dreams testify to this. They no longer craved to anchor the person of the dreamer in reality and thus became, apparently paradoxically, the sign of a chance for survival.

The vanishing point at which one endured one's own death offered grounds for hope. Because of this, the inmate, with his nearly ruined body, for the first time gained a minimal but decisive impulse to live on. The timelessness to which the inmates were condemned assumed in the salvational dreams a redeeming significance, more precisely, a redeeming power. Estrangement from the empirical self became a silent weapon against the system of terror that ran through both inmates and overseers in the concentration camp. The diabolic inversion, that death appeared to be a better life and life a worse death, was what had to be confronted. Only in salvational dreams did the inferno find its fictive termination "outside" of time and at the same time offer the inmate a grasp of reality.

Such salvational dreams, saturated with light and color but empty of action, resist any further sociohistorical examination. In individual cases they might be interpretable in terms of individual psychology, social disposition, or religious belief, as with some of our witnesses. Methodologically, however, the inferential path from individual salvational dreams to general behavior specific to one social stratum is blocked, for they contain no signals of reality that are politically or socially legible. If you like, the whole point of such dreams is to be apolitical. One could even go so far as to see in them covert enactments of a disposition to resistance. But even this anthropological finding can no longer be socially generalized. Thus the salvational dreams in the sense identified by Cayrol tell us nothing about other motives for the power of endurance, which might have been characteristic of, for instance, the communist leaders in the inmate hierarchy, or the homogenous sects engaged in biblical study. We have to leave it at that.

This or that biography or social genesis for various reasons resulted in dispositions that enhanced or diminished chances of survival.[20] It is sufficient for our problem concerning dreams in terror to see that even the dumb interior world possessed its own secret history within which deliverance or destruction was contained. This world secretes an eloquent testimony to the silent body and provides a testimony whose deciphering involves lifting a corner of the covering underneath which past horror has collected. The dreams are not simply witnesses to terror but are witnesses of terror itself. Thus we have here experiences that are not directly communicable, or as Cayrol says, "lazarene" experiences which escape the usual historical methodology, bound as they are to language.

To return to the methods that we have inherited: it is precisely against the background of Cayrol's dream indices that the calculable mortality statistics of the concentration camps assume a greater significance. Notwithstanding the disposition toward survival that we encounter in the salvational dreams, the inmates were killed, destroyed, exterminated, gassed: to speak of killing or murder sounds bland and conventional. Within the camp system it was courage and perseverance—that is, visible signs of powers of survival (one thinks of Bonhoeffer)—that could lead to destruction. On the ramp of Auschwitz only animalistic criteria prevailed. The inner evidence of the chance of survival evident in the spontaneous behavior of the inmate and in his dreams is not commensurable with the statistical frequency with which gassing took place. In this way, those destroyed were deprived of a final meaning, that of being a sacrifice; absurdity became event.

## Concluding Methodological Remarks on Diachrony and Synchrony

The dreams outlined above have been interpreted as testimony of terror, but with a slight change of perspective they are, in addition, forms of the realization of terror itself. Because of this, they have constantly been interpreted situationally, without considering more closely the timeless symbolism another approach might allow them. But even the dreams of survival that Cayrol reports subsist on a symbolism which comparatively is removed from reality, extrahistorical, unpolitical, and enduring, and for evidence of whose coincidence with a promise of life we must here rely on the authenticity of witnesses.

A historian is only able to read such sources in a rigorous fashion if he learns to anthropologically interpret the imagistic testimony of a dumb language. Beradt consciously rejected the idea of providing her dream collection with a psychoanalytic interpretation. Frankl and Bettelheim are as professional analysts also cautious, for the Freudian categorical framework is no longer adequate to this exceptional situation, with its logic of inversion.

Nevertheless, a fundamental advantage in the approach adopted here must be emphasized. The dreams witness to a state of experience *in eventu*. They indicate synchronous connections between persecutor and persecuted in the execution of terror. In this respect they resemble psychic "X-ray" images, contrasting with the countless images we have on film depicting the external aspect of this horror. The dreams illuminate the condition of those pursued by terror, in a manner which is certainly much clearer than that provided by any external image. To this extent, dreams have an advantage over diaries and memoirs, which are composed under various circumstances and in any case *ex post*. While the store of dreams is accessible only with difficulty, it should not be rejected in principle on this account, no matter how hard it is to interpret them with an established anthropological theory.

To indicate the boundaries which face an investigation of anthropologically legible texts, two historical procedures can be confronted with each other. They will be identified as synchrony and diachrony. Each procedure has advantages and disadvantages that relate in a complementary fashion. Ordinarily a historian would use both approaches, favoring synchrony when he describes, and diachrony when he narrates. Thus a historian works diachronically when attempting to explain an event or its context in a causal-genetic manner—in our case, National Socialism and its specific system of terror. Causal inference raises the question of the reason for this or that occurring in one way or another. Every diachronic explanation in this way permits additional, more extensive explanations. A few such explanations will be recalled here.

Thus unemployment is identified as the cause of National Socialism; more generally, the world economic crisis, even more generally, the capitalist economic system. Alternatively, behaviors typical of specific social strata could be identified and their traditional strands traced back into German social history: here, the petty bourgeoisie are favored since no one identifies with them. One could also raise the question of nationalism, which cannot be understood in the absence of international political developments; or one could talk of the experience at the front in wartime, the Versailles complex with the dogmatic compulsion that derives from it ("We'll show the supposed victors of 1918 that we can be the barbarians they made us in their propaganda"). From this one can deduce a pressure toward *völkisch* homogenization; and to this, anti-Semitism belongs as a preliminary to terror. Internal political affairs could be evoked: the irreversible days before 30 January, the authoritarian phase of chancellorship, the party system, the entire Weimar constitution, and finally, German constitutional history in general. If one were more inclined toward intellectual history, one could offer models of a secularization process from which lines of decline could be drawn using the works of Luther, Frederick the Great, Bismarck, Hindenburg, and Hitler; reorganizing in a negative manner a line of descent that had once been conceived positively. The causal genetic explanatory model in this way remains the same.

All series of explanations and causation can be more or less plausible. A few such attempts will gain in evidential status, especially when supported with appropriate proofs from the sources. What, then, do such genetic modes of proof have in common?

To begin with, they formally share an arrangement of diachronic series within short, medium, or long-term sequences. Events, trends, and structures can be introduced whereby the historian dispenses with monocausal explanation, making possible different sequences of proof which can be weighed with each other, thus rendering visible the pattern of dependencies. This interplay will emphasize a more or less articulated theoretical anticipation and source exegesis.

An additional common property of these procedures is that causal chains are extracted from the infinity of past data and a given event or set of events is interpreted as a resultant. It is always a question of an *ex post* causal procedure, a rationalization of a retrospective, or, in Lessing's words, a *logificatio post festum*.[21]

There are specific defects that are associated with this procedure, a procedure which ultimately derives from a pragmatic form of historical writing. One introduces for the understanding of a particular occurrence *causae* which are not contained by this occurrence. Such a form of proof can be infinitely extended. There is no rational and unambiguously demonstrable boundary of possible origination beyond which causes are no longer valid. In the same way, without theoretical clarification, there is no rational foundation to the question of which causes are permitted to count. Every explanatory structure is potentially as multifarious as the sum of all possible events and their relations in the past. Whoever becomes involved with causality naturally enough cannot explain everything by means of everything, but it is possible to advance as many causes for each event as one wishes.

At this point a second difficulty appears. A proof of causality cannot show which cause is more important than others, nor can it demonstrate which causes are necessary, compelling, or even adequate to the emergence of this or that. The elevation of causality to necessity ultimately leads to historically tautological statements. Showing an event to be necessary is nothing more than making a redoubled statement on the same event. Something does not happen because it must happen. *Post hoc ergo propter hoc* is possible but not compelling. There lurks behind this awkwardness a third difficulty which is not causally soluble. Ever since Humboldt's critique of pragmatic Enlightenment history, a structural feature of all history has become apparent: in every historical constellation, both more and less than was embedded in the given occurrence is contained. Here is founded history's surprising singularity, transformability, and its changeability. Without this, contemporary concepts flanking the modern concept of history, such as progress, regress, development, and fate, would be completely devoid of meaning.

This axiom of uniqueness should not contribute to the revival of the form of history or to its individuality, for all history contains formal structures of possible recurrence and repetition, long-term conditions which assist in the construction of similar constellations, among which, as we know, is terror. But that which is novel in every history is not accessible to causal explanation. Every causal explanation presupposes that one can deduce one phenomenon from another, even from dissimilar phenomena. In this way, a relation is set up that does not have to be contained by the phenomenon to be explained. Thus if one wishes to comprehend the singularity of a historical event, one can only use causal inferences in a subsidiary role.

To exaggerate slightly, and to remain at the level of our example: the unemployed man who was enlisting in 1932 is not the same as the SA man who became a reserve policeman after 30 January and had perhaps belonged to a gang. A veteran of the Freikorps of 1920 did not become the commander of a concentration camp first because he was in the Freikorps, next because he was unemployed, and then because of a few other things. In no case is it possible to grasp a particular history adequately by filling out the sequence of time into a causal chain of explanation.

For this reason, it is necessary to proceed in a synchronic as well as a diachronic fashion; not only to explain *post eventum* but also to show *in eventu* how something happened the way that it did. It can then be supposed that singularity or uniqueness will become especially apparent, which is not to say, however, that the factors defining an event are themselves unique. A corresponding attempt is at hand if, for example, the successes and consequences of Hitler are interpreted in terms of the supposed sociopsychic disposition of the German people in 1933. The dreams described above have already been used to show where it is possible to generalize anthropologically or sociohistorically in individual cases, and where such generalization is ruled out. Certainly further research on this is needed.

It is impossible to transfer the psychoanalytic apparatus from individual therapy to social diagnosis or even into historical analysis, for the subject of therapy is not identifiable as an individual and, moreover, already belongs to the past.[22] Similarly, metaphoric usage can take us further. Thus, for instance, the fixation of the German people on the Führer is described as a mechanism of projection; apparent relief in the transfer of responsibility is analyzed; and the fear and blindness unleashed by an irreversible process is uncovered.

One advantage of such interpretations is that one can attempt to explain a set of events on the basis of their occurrence. The anthropological composition of the agencies may become apparent; and it can be shown how specific behaviors on the part of groups, organizations, parties, social strata, and individual persons active within them, enter a reciprocal relation by means of which the events turned out in one way and no other.

Despite impressive attempts in this vein (for example, by Bruno Bettelheim), such procedures are bound up with disadvantages which behave in a manner complementary to diachronic analysis. Resort to the psychosomatic aspect of a set of events methodologically permits no controlling instance (as is the case with causal explanation) with whose help one could promote a counterproof. The plausibility of an interpretation stands or falls with the theoretical premise, which must simply be accepted, that external affairs must be reduced to the inner disposition of participants. In this way, proceedings are certainly described as they were, to the extent that they are interpreted using scientific categories which do not claim to exceed the bounds of the described phenomenon. The consequence is that we have to impute a compelling force to particular modes of behavior and are then unable to revoke this imputation methodologically. Once we discover that Frederick the Great had a despotic father who forced him into a military corset against his will, and that after the death of his father in 1740 Frederick had initiated the Silesian War, it is easy to claim that a father complex plays a determining role here, such that the young Fritz found himself compelled to demonstrate his worthiness to his father postmortem, so that he could free himself of him. The weight of such interpretations should not be underestimated, but all the same, we have here a mode of proof that is irrefutable. To explain external manifestations and occurrences through inner motivations imputes an inner compelling necessity to past facticity.

We have here described two models of explanation and understanding which were consciously represented as the antithetical extremes of diachrony and synchrony. In each case, the process of rationalization on the part of the historian takes place in a different way. If, for the first type, causal-genetic explanation *ex eventu* is never sufficient, other causes can be introduced without ever completely explaining a historical phenomenon, so this form of explanation and causation proves to be an unrecognized form of chance.

If the second form of causation—*in eventu*—appears adequate on account of its involvement with the phenomenon that it explains, it nevertheless falls under suspicion for constituting a dull necessity that is never able to demonstrate why something happened in one way and not in another.

Bettelheim vehemently opted for a processual anthropology—if one can describe his procedure in this way—so he could reject causal explanation of the past as a form of academic game. Nevertheless, a few sentences later, he makes use of precisely this explanatory form to interpret in a historicogenetic fashion the psychosomatic constellation in 1933 Germany and beyond.[23] This lapse reveals the need for proof into which all who one-sidedly emphasize the synchronic or diachronic approach fall. It remains necessary to use both procedures, for they are mutually complementary.[24]

# "Neuzeit": Remarks on the Semantics of the Modern Concepts of Movement

The emergence of new words in the language, their growing frequency of use, and the shifting meaning stamped upon them by prevailing opinion—all that which one can call the currently ruling linguistic fashion—is a not inconsequential hand on time's clock for all those able to judge changes in life's substance from minor phenomena.
—Wilhelm Schulz, 1841[1]

In the absence of linguistic activity, historical events are not possible; the experience gained from these events cannot be passed on without language. However, neither events nor experiences are exhausted by their linguistic articulation. There are numerous extralinguistic factors that enter into every event, and there are levels of experience which escape linguistic ascertainment. The majority of extralinguistic conditions for all occurrences (natural and material givens, institutions, and modes of conduct) remain dependent upon linguistic communication for their effectiveness. They are not, however, assimilated by it. The prelinguistic structure of action and the linguistic communication by means of which events take place run into one another without ever coinciding.

We find a similar tension if we turn our gaze from what is currently taking place toward past histories. There are different levels of experience and of that which can be experienced, of memory and of that which can be remembered, ultimately of that which has been forgotten or never passed down; according to the questions of the day these may be recalled or reworked. The nature of the prevailing linguistic or nonlinguistic factors decides the form and reproduction of past history. It is this preliminary selectivity which makes it impossible for an account of a past incident to register comprehensively what once was, or what once occurred. Stated more generally, language and history depend on each other but never coincide.

A dual difference thus prevails: between a history in motion and its linguistic possibility and between a past history and its linguistic reproduction. The determination of these differences is itself a linguistic activity, and it is the business of historians.

We thus find ourselves in a methodologically irresoluble dilemma: that every history, while in process and as occurrence, is something other than what its linguistic articulation can establish; but that this "other" in turn can only be made visible through the medium of language. Reflection upon historical language, upon the speech acts which assist in the constitution of events or constitute a historical narrative, is thus able to claim no material priority with respect to the histories to whose realization it contributes. Nonetheless, linguistic reflection assumes a theoretical and methodological priority with respect to all occurrences and history. The extralinguistic conditions and factors which enter into history can only be grasped linguistically.

It might be objected that such thoughts are trivial, that it is not worth discussing them. Such comments are nevertheless necessary to clarify the valency of the historical concepts to be dealt with below. Concepts within which experiences collect and in which expectations are bound up are, as linguistic performances, no mere epiphenomena of so-called real history. Historical concepts, especially political and social concepts, are minted for the registration and embodiment of the elements and forces of history. This is what marks them out within a language. They do, however, possess, by virtue of the difference that has been indicated, their own mode of existence within the language. It is on this basis that they affect or react to particular situations and occurrences.

If we direct our attention to past concepts embodied in words that might still be ours, the reader gains entry to the hopes and wishes, fears and suffering of onetime contemporaries. Moreover, in this way the extent and boundary of the expressive force of earlier linguistic constructions is revealed. The space of previous experience and expectation is surveyed and measured, to the degree that it could be conceptually registered with the past linguistic arsenal and is in actuality articulated within the source language.

The following thoughts on the semantics of the modern concepts of movement will be presented in three stages. First, we will consider whether the concept *Neuzeuit* does anything more than formally separate one historical period from its predecessor. Does it indicate anything like a new era? Second, we will direct attention to expressions which, as neologisms or through added meaning, conceptualize some form of historical movement or the temporalization of history. Third, we will move the problematic from general concepts of movement to those relating to concrete political and social domains of action, leading to the identification of some semantic and pragmatic criteria which are especially characteristic of *Neuzeit* around 1800. In general, this study limits itself to the German world of language and experience.

### *Neue Zeit* and *Neuzeit* in Historical Theory and Historical Writing

From the eighteenth century on, historiography increasingly speaks of a *neue Zeit*. The composite concept *Neuzeit*, according to Grimm, is to be found only since 1870, when it was first used by Freiligrath.[2] Whatever earlier use might be discovered (Ranke clearly avoided the term, as far as he is supposed to have known it),[3] the concise concept *Neuzeit* became established about four centuries after the beginning of the period it was to typify as a unity. It penetrated the lexica only during the last quarter of the previous century.[4] While this might be surprising when one considers the assurance with which even today investigations into the history of language use the sixteenth-century expression, it is not astonishing. Only after a certain amount of time has elapsed can a period be summarized into a diachronic denominator, as a concept which binds together common structures.

But there is something special about the concept *Neuzeit*. Why a specific period of time should be characterized by the term *neue Zeit* or even *Neuzeit* remains linguistically unclear, even if one reads it in terms of highlighting provided by the so-called end of *Neuzeit*. The expression itself refers only to time, characterizing it as new, without, however, providing any indication of the historical content of this time or even its nature as a period. The form of this expression takes on meaning only in contrast with the preceding "old" time, or inasmuch as it is used to conceptualize an epoch, by contrast with the condition of preceding epochs.

The vast majority of epochal doctrines do not, however, draw on temporal determinants, but rather assume their specificity as given epochs on the basis of substantial, material, or personal determinants. For instance, the sequence of mythical epochs is characterized through a metaphor involving different kinds of metal. The various doctrines of *aetates* within the Christian tradition rest on the application of the days of Creation to history, the ordering of periods to commandments or grace, or the exegesis of the four world monarchies in Daniel. The criteria according to which dynasties are structured are based on the life of a lineage or on the length of a ruler's reign. Other forms of division (to be found initially in Varro and more typically since the period of humanism) are based on the diverse quality of sources and the manner in which they have been preserved. Finally, there are growing attempts to arrange epochs according to intellectual, political, social, or economic structures, and this itself is a sign of *Neuzeit*.

No one today would use the still customary trinity Antiquity–Middle Ages–Modernity (*Neuzeit*) without building in substantial conditions which in their different ways mark out the epochs. Taken by itself, however, this trinity represents a relatively high level of abstraction. It does without substantial qualities, and its prime characteristic is a simple chronology lending it form and elasticity for various modes of dating and exposition. This is demonstrated by the numerous attempts to structure this formula and the manner in which they differ by many centuries.

In addition, it is apparent that in the German, *Zeit* only appears as a formal determination of generality in the compound *Neuzeit*, the terms for the preceding periods dispensing with this: *Mittelalter, Altertum*. This might well be an ingenious accident of language, since the previous expressions for *Mittelalter* (*media aetas*, middle age, *moyen age*) likewise qualify time or temporalities in general: as *mittlere Zeiten*, middle times, *moyen temps*; or earlier as *medium tempus, media tempestas, media tempora*. But as soon as the *mittlere Zeiten* were treated as a closed period, a designation became attached which, in the collective singular, referred to an age (*aevum, aetas*) and no longer to time in general.[5] In the periodization customary today, "time" (*Zeit*) is reserved primarily for combinations which serve to characterize the current epoch: *Neuzeit*, modern times, or *temps modernes*; and in addition to this, *Zeitgeschichte*, contemporary history, or *histoire contemporaine*.[6]

While this discovery should not be overrated as a systematic phenomenon, it raises the questions of what function the expression *neue Zeit* was supposed to fulfill when it came into use, and what role it had in fact played once it achieved a kind of temporal monopoly in he definition of epochs.

The expression *neue Zeit*, or a new history, carries a heritage that arises from the form in which the concept of the Middle Ages was established. The *mittlere Zeiten*—a term which was still current with Herder—demanded linguistically that a younger or also an older, a later or in fact a *neue Zeit* develop, but this did not mean that a new or even common concept was formed immediately.

Recourse on the part of the humanists to the model of Antiquity ruled out the intervening "barbarian" period as one which existed for itself and introduced (as can be seen in Petrarch[7]) the first usage of the term *medium tempus*, at once historical and no longer eschatological. This was meant, above all, to determine one's own epochal position, and later became accepted in scholarly circles concerned with the history of literature, philosophy, arts, and sciences, but in particular among scholars involved with historical geography. After Petrarch, however, it took another three hundred years until the Latin terms or their national equivalents were used as a comprehensive form of periodization. It seems no accident that it was in a textbook that Cellarius in 1685 demanded that universal history be divided "in Antiquam et medii Aevi ac novum"[8] on the grounds that the terms developed by the humanists remained formal enough in character to provide a generalized structural schema. The concept of the Middle Ages became generally accepted in the eighteenth century, retaining for the most part a pejorative sense; in the nineteenth century it became a definite topos of historical periodization.

In his lectures on world history, the young Ranke objected to the customary fashion in which everything was divided among three large pigeonholes, comprising ancient, middle, and new history. "This method has no inherent reason and is of no advantage," he added,[9] but all the same he never did without them.

The genesis of the concept *neue Zeit* or *neue Geschichte* is not recognizable without some examination of those two terms which circumscribe the junction connecting *mittlere* and *neue Zeit*.

Both of the concepts current today in linking up to the *mittlere Zeiten*—Renaissance and Reformation—initially were expressions related to specific phenomena and only slowly assumed a position within a diachronic schemata. Within this long-term process, the unfolding of the concept *neue Zeit* is contained and hidden.

The doctrine of rebirth, of "Renaissance," which was consciously opposed to the *mittlere Zeiten*, took much longer than the term *Mittelalter* to become condensed into a general concept of periodization. While humanists favored verbs and adjectival expressions for the renewal of return, awakening, or blooming, or for the description of return, the term "Renaissance" first appeared as late as the mid-sixteenth century and then only in an isolated fashion [*renascitá*, (Vasari, 1550), and *renaissance* (Belon, 1553)].[10] As a term primarily characteristic of epochs in the history of art and literature, "Renaissance" first entered regular use during the Enlightenment. It was stylized as a general concept of periodization by Michelet and Burckhardt in the nineteenth century. The term "Renaissance" therefore did not appear together with that of "Middle Ages" as a counterconcept, but rather established itself in a delayed manner as a form of historical-chronological determination after the establishment of *Mittelalter*.

Within the Protestant camp, the related term "Reformation" was more readily accepted,[11] initially as a concept of a new threshold, of a new epoch, and then later as the concept definitive of a period. Alongside this it retained, for a long time, its nonchronological and general meaning which could relate it to religious life, to the Church, or to traditional rights.[12] Thomas Müntzer saw before him "a supreme and insurmountable future reformation,"[13] while Luther and Melanchthon had used the expression hesitatingly and with caution.[14] Later Protestant writing on the history of the Church singularized the term to denote an exceptional period which signified Luther's reforms and those of his fellows. In this sense the term thus substantively referred to the Holy Gospel, which was held to have been restored to its purity without making necessary the beginning of a "new history." The onset of the Reformation as an epoch opened the final Christian period everywhere, such that even in Zedler the final concept of *Zeit* was defined as running "from the reformation of Luther to our time and that following"—before, that is, the end of the world.[15] Even Cellarius in 1696 made *historia nova* in a general sense begin with the onset of the reform of the Church.

From the second half of the seventeenth century, however, it was possible to regard the Reformation as a completed period. William

Cave, for instance, spoke of "saeculum reformationis."[16] The history of the influence of the Reformation then become increasingly important as the actual event became more distant: both in a religious sense, that the imperative of the Reformation should be further fulfilled (Spener) or that this fulfillment was taking place salvationally; and through the deduction of worldly, social, and political consequences from the unique event of past Reformation, as can be found in Mosheim, Semler, Schröckh, and Heeren. In this way the threshold became *neue Geschichte*.

Pütter coined (still in the plural) the canonical expression "Counter-Reformation," which first was singularized by Eichhorn and Ranke and then added on to the Reformation as an autonomous period.[17] This completes the historicization of the expression into a specific periodic concept. Ranke's *Deutscher Geschichte im Zeitalter der Reformation* (1839–47) consolidated its world-historical status.

The requirement that emerged, through constitution of the concept "Middle Ages," of identifying the succeeding period as a *neue Zeit*, was thus not initially met by the expressions "Renaissance" and "Reformation." It was only in the eighteenth and nineteenth centuries that the steady clarification of *renaissance* from a metaphor of rebirth to a form of periodization was completed. In the sixteenth century, the concept of the Reformation as the dawn of a new age in the sense of a revival of an original Christian era was current; but the period begun in this way was, from the standpoint of the seventeenth century, regarded as completed, such that in the succeeding period the concept was capable of denoting an epoch, as well as (diachronically) a universal-historical phase.

Where, then, does the *neue Zeit* fit into this unequal couple of Middle Ages–Renaissance/Reformation?

The thinkers and artists of the Renaissance, as well as the believers of the Reformation, did consider the question of whether a *mittlere Zeit* would by negation produce a *neue Zeit*, but none of them actually formulated this as a theoreticohistorical concept.[18] The exposure of a *neue Zeit* is a long-term process which takes place during the course of the following centuries, and whose outline becomes evident in the succcessive permeation first of "Middle Ages," then of "Reformation," and finally of "Renaissance" as periodic concepts.

It is necessary to refer to a semantic distinction embedded within the expression *neue Zeit* in order to disclose the experience of a modernity. This term can signify in a simple fashion that the contemporary *Zeit* is, by contrast with one previous, "new," whatever the mode of graduation. It is in this sense that the term *modernus* was coined, which has not, since then, lost the meaning "of today."[19]

Alternatively, the notion of a *neue Zeit* can register a qualitative claim—that of being new in the sense of completely other, even better than what has gone before. In this case, *neue Zeit* is indicative of new experiences never before had in such a fashion; it assumes an emphasis that attributes to the new an epochal, temporal character.

Finally, *neue Zeit*, on the basis of the first two semantic possibilities, can also retrospectively signify a period which, by contrast with the Middle Ages, is conceived to be new.

The first two possibilities are contained within prescientific linguistic usage, and it can be shown (roughly speaking) that initially it is the first meaning, not epoch-specific, that prevails; while the second meaning, aware of itself as an epoch, develops during the Enlightenment, without displacing the first meaning.

The introduction of a *neue Zeit* as a means of characterizing a period is contained within both forms of usage; whether, for example, a series of given "here and nows" are, after an interlude, aggregated into a *neue Zeit*, or whether this aggregation emphatically signifies something quite new that has hitherto not existed. This will now be outlined.

It is an everyday experience that (external) time always "flows on"; or that, subjectively speaking, tomorrow is constantly transformed into yesterday by the presence of today. Given eventualities were established and perpetuated by the writings of annalists and chroniclers who were caught up within such a notion of time. A property of both ancient and medieval historical writing is that it was composed according to a temporal sequence initiated by a given beginning: of the world, of a town, monastery, war, or lineage. A given history of the present had the methodological advantage and precedence arising from its capacity to resort to witnesses, or at best, agents.[20] The statements of active politicians enjoyed a methodological privilege (while not undoubted), whereas the witnesses of occasions of revelation possessed undisputed authority. Beyond all philosophical, theological (for instance, figurative or typological), or moral premises which lent histories their peculiarities, this kind of perpetuated history of the present belonged to the minimal preconditions of all history. The internal and substantial periodization of this experiential space, moving forward from event to event, was produced almost automatically, insofar as from day to day, from *saeculum* to *saeculum*, new events worthy of recounting and increasingly requiring placement in order occurred.

The characterization of one's own time thus *eo ipso* included the New, without assigning to it any kind of epochal character. This could be because histories repeated themselves structurally, or because nothing fundamentally new could occur before the End of the World.

Thus medieval historians saw themselves, as Melville has shown, as *successores* and demanded of their successors *ea superaddere que per temporum succesiones nova evenerint usque in finem mundi.*[21] As Landulph de Columna resolved, in 1320, *hystorias a creatione primi hominis usque ad moderna tempora abreviare.*[22] The "modern," the new within one's own time, entered into the characterization of the given actuality without providing additional qualifications to the present. . . . A history could be written *usque ad tempus scriptoris* (up to the time of the writer) just as well in the eleventh as in the seventeenth century, when Alsted arranged the times of all events *usque ad aetatem ejus qui scribit* (up to the age of the man who is writing). Within the framework of such an additive mode of historical writing, the novelty of the period in which one wrote was not accentuated as such. Accordingly, Alsted divided the histories of the homogeneous substantive domains of the four faculties into specific and autonomous *aetates* which, while distinct from each other, all debouched into the present. The last Church period, for instance, went from 1519 (Charles V) *ad nostram aetatem* (until our own time). General history, as *historia heterogenea*, was, by contrast, divided into the usual six parts, the last one beginning with Caesar and likewise extending *ad nostram usque aetatem.*[23]

Time as the formal and generalized condition for possible events remained quite neutral with respect to epochal episodes and historiographic periods. "Historia omnis Chronica est, quoniam in tempore fit" (history is a chronicle of everything that happens in the course of time), as Alsted said. Even Bacon, who distinguished ancient from modern history, dealt with *Historia temporum* according to method, type, and domain, but not according to temporal criteria of modernity or of archaism,[24] which would have been close to his new science and his dictum of "veritas filia temporis." It was Bodin who came up with perhaps the most pithy formulation for the constant projection of historical events into time: while empires age, history remains eternally young.[25]

The additive mode of historical writing corresponds to a uniform and static experience of time, registering ever-present novelty from event to event. Exemplariness empty of time, attributed since Humanism to all histories, contributed in particular to a tendency to look elsewhere than one's own time for what was specifically new, and rework it. "The world remains the world; therefore all action remains the same in the world, though people die," as Melanchthon, invoking Thucydides, stated in his best Lutheran tones.[26] The great historians of their own time (for instance, Thou, Clarendon, and Frederick the Great), aimed at preserving the memory of the most recent occurrences and, as much as possible, working them up for the coming generations. Such a view presupposes, however, that all histories resemble each other or are structurally similar: only on this condition is it possible to learn from them in the future.

The hermeneutical model for a form of historical writing which, with the passing of time, was continually "written on," was sketched out by Chladenius in the mid-eighteenth century.[27] He was still dominated by the notions of authenticity based on eyewitness, notions to which then-current knowledge of the present assigned a methodological priority. The histories of generations living together constituted given specific spaces of experience, out of which the histories of the future, and the distant or "ancient histories" could be revealed. Ancient histories therefore begin at that point where no eyewitness survives or when no direct earwitness can be found. The demise of each generation consequently shifts the boundary of ancient history, which advances in the same measure as witnesses disappear. This distribution, which formally remains the same, of a never-ending history into three eras continually moving forward in time encapsulates the temporal conditions of historical knowledge. Within this, Chladenius thinks in a "modern" fashion, for his arrangement no longer directs itself to substantive *aetates* which might, for example, be God-given, but rather addresses itself only to the formal determination of historical knowledge. At the same time, however, Chladenius provides an epistemological model that can accommodate the long tradition of a seamlessly advancing historical record without disruption. In this respect, Chladenius stands at the end of that history which allows a methodological precedence to event and witness, that is, the given present and its annalistic frame.

A method for determining the time from which the history of one's own time was sensed to be emphatically new is to ask when *nostrum sevum* was renamed *nova aetas*; that is, when one's contemporary time (which continually emerges in book titles) was renamed *neue Zeit*. This process, implicit in the conception of a Renaissance or a Reformation, first appears in outline during the seventeenth century and establishes itself very gradually.

When Petrarch spoke "de historiis . . . novis [et] antiquis,"[28] his interest was without doubt directed toward ancient history, not toward the new history laid out between himself and the Christianization of Rome. The expression of the New was still defined negatively—certainly no longer in the sense of biblical tradition, but measured against the evocative model of Antiquity.

In addition, a further linguistic usage then commonly encountered was directed backward: the term *Historia recentior* later gave rise to *neuere Geschichte*. This comparative term related not to new[29] but to middle or ancient history (for example, as in the praise directed in 1469 to Nicolaus von Cues from Andrea dei Bussi: "Historias idem omnes non priscas modo, sed medie tempestatis tum veteres tum recentiores usque ad nostra tempora retinebat").[30] In this, the opposition to the Middle Ages is played down and the comparative of *recentior* is a mere relational definition distinguishing only between "earlier" and "later" in the past. This relational meaning was just as widespread in current usage as when it was retained in the later expression *neuere Geschichte*.

So that it might be possible to decisively define the contrast with respect to preceding and thereby ancient history, not only a differentiating disposition toward the past was required, but even more so toward the future. As long as one believed oneself to live in the final epoch, the only new aspect of contemporaneity could be doomsday, putting an end to all previous time. "Et ob hoc sancti saepe hoc tempus novissimum et finem saeculorum nominant."[31]

It was only when Christian eschatology shed its constant expectation of the imminent arrival of doomsday that a temporality could be revealed that would be open for the new and without limit. Until then, it had been a question of whether the End of the World would occur earlier than anticipated; now, calculations concerning the timing of doomsday shifted gradually into a receding distance, to a point where it was no longer a matter of controversy. This orientation toward the future occurred following the destruction of Christian expectations through religious civil wars which, with the decline of the Church, had at first appeared to herald the End of the World. The advance of the sciences, which promised to discover and bring to light even more in the future, coupled with the discovery of the New World and its peoples, had a slow influence at first but helped create a consciousness of a general history which led into an altogether *neue Zeit*.[32]

If we consider the problem from the point of view of semantic history, it is apparent that the emphasis shifts: first *Historie*, then *Geschichte*, and finally *Zeit* itself is the bearer of the New as epithet. This is an indication of an increasingly reflected experiential change. In 1601, for instance, Lipsius spoke in a still unspecific fashion of *historia nova*[33] — the final epoch of Roman history in antiquity. Hornius in 1666 used *historia nova* and *recentior* by turns and dated them, as did Petrarch, from the fall of Rome. Voetius in 1517 began with a *nova aetas*, but only in the sense of a bibliographic division and not in a world-historical sense. The final emergence in Cellarius of a form of periodization with retrospective effect was as casual as it was successful. After that, *historia nova* was ever more frequently begun around 1500 together with the changes and discoveries of that time.[34]

The lack of emphasis given to the emergent construction *Neue Geschichte* is nonetheless demonstrated by the 1691 translation of Stieler, contemporary with Cellarius: "exemplum recens, nostri temporis, aevi, hujus seculi, cognitio rerum praesentium" — the usual manner in which a history of one's own time, constantly in forward motion, was described.[35]

Even Zedler, in whom we can usually detect the registration of the *neue Zeit*, remains within the limits of this traditional interpretation: "*Zeit, (neue)* [Latin] *tempus novum*, or *modernum*, if by this is meant current or present time."[36]

Remaining among the dictionaries for a moment, we can turn to Adelung, who notes no connection of *Zeit* with *neue* or *neuere*.[37] It is in 1811 that we re-encounter in Campe "*Die neue Zeit*, the present, that which is close to us. *Alte Zeit* and *neue Zeit*," that is, in a historical sense but without the construction of epochs.[38]

The degree to which Campe was searching for an emphatic concept of modernity as *Neuzeit* is testified by the recently coined terms which are directed toward this end and which he registers: "The New World, [and this does not mean just America, but] also contemporary living men as a whole," is such that one speaks of the "industry of the New World,"[39] or the "world of today" in contrast with the "previous world"[40] or, to characterize the *neue Zeit* in opposition to antiquity: *Das Neuerthum . . .* better, *das Neuthum*," since one knows oneself to be at the highest level of development yet attained.[41] The concept of *Neuzeit* is taking shape, but was as yet not minted, while *neue Zeit* remained established within historiographic tradition.

This lexical survey shows, at the least, that around 1800 the term *neue Zeit* had not assumed any special position within the everyday language of scholars, and that the linguistic transfer of a given present and current time into *neue Zeit* did not necessarily involve an increase in meaning. Above all, the usual terms comparative to *neuere Geschichte* or *neuere Zeiten* were primarily relational determinations oriented to the past. *Neue Zeit* as a historical concept embodying a particular experiential pattern, in which it was the future that was the bearer of growing expectations, is not one that is widespread in the historical writing and historical theory of the eighteenth century.

It would, however, be accurate to say that in the eighteenth century, *neue Zeit* played a role as a concept of periodization in opposition to the "Middle Ages." In this way it was taken for granted, as in Cellarius, that the time around 1500 represented the threshold of an epoch, lending to the succeeding *neue Zeit* a relative unity. For Gatterer, who divided universal history into four eras, it was indisputable that the final era, "*die neue Zeit* [extended] from the discovery of America in 1492 up to our present."[42] It was therefore less one's own time that was defined as specifically new, than the three hundred years or so of an era which assumed a collective designation. The triad Antiquity-Middle Ages-Modernity had met with no generalized acceptance in the eighteenth century, not even by Gatterer. It was only the idea of a threshold around 1500 that had become generally accepted and that repeatedly appears. Johannes von Müller entitled two of his "24 books of general histories" *The Manner in which the Transition from the mittlere Zeiten to the New Arrangement of Things was Gradually Prepared (1273 to 1453)*; and *On those Revolutions which have been Specifically Caused by the New Order of Things (1453 to 1517).*[43] Köster in 1787 declared that "since that time [1500], almost the whole of Europe assumed an entirely different form . . . and there appeared in this part of the world a practically new species of mankind."[44]

In the eighteenth century, therefore, the idea prevailed that for the last three hundred years, one had been living in a *neue Zeit* which was, emphatically, a specific period distinct from that which had preceded it.

A test case for historical consciousness is the introduction of the expression *neueste Geschichte*, which presupposes the existence of the new. Thus, for example, Büsch divided history in 1775 (i.e., before the French Revolution) "according to time": into ancient, middle, and "the new, up to our times, within which period we can even distinguish the newest (neueste) and by which the time of the last generation, or this century, might be understood."[45] *Neue Geschichte* no longer solely related itself to middle or ancient history, but gained a temporal autonomy which in turn demanded further differentiation.

A *neueste Zeit* beginning from a *neue Zeit* could certainly be read in terms of an annalistic addition. In this case, the given "last generation" or century would be the community represented by coexisting generations, as outlined by Chladenius in his historical hermeneutics. *Neueste Zeit*, in contrast with *neue Zeit*, was immediately adopted, however, as its emphatic actuality testifies.

The demands of the later Enlightenment and the events of the French Revolution led to the accumulation of experience which lent political and social force to the expression *neueste Zeit*. In comparison with the response to *neue Zeit*, it was adopted far more rapidly. The degree to which it was understood in an epochal sense shortly after its introduction is shown by the charge leveled at Heeren that he had not explicitly begun *neueste Zeit* with the French Revolution. Heeren, who had learned to think of the long term, defended himself through analogy, referring to the length of time *die neue Zeit* had taken before it was generally accepted:

It seemed to him [Heeren is referring to himself here] that the wish to separate *neueste Zeit* from *neue Zeit* was premature; perhaps the historical writers of the twentieth century will make such a distinction; but not those in the first quarter of the nineteenth; it would have been just as unacceptable to have begun the *neue Zeit* during the Reformation.[46]

Heeren's consideration of the future influence of the term is a modern feature of his argument, but the fact that *neueste Geschichte* required a minimum period before being conceptualized as such signified a renunciation of epochal emphasis. *Neueste Geschichte* should only come into effect as a long-term concept for periodization, analogous to *mittlere* or *neue Geschichte*.

The historical objection raised by Heeren was not accepted. For as long as he taught, Ranke lectured on the *Geschichte der neuesten Zeit* or *Neueste Geschichte* which he began, according to his lecture, with the older Frederick, starting with the American or French Revolution. Only when discussing his contemporary history did he switch to traditional usage and refer to it as *Geschichte unserer Zeit*.[47]

*Neueste Zeit* thus was characterized by the way in which it rapidly came to designate the epochal threshold which, in the minds of the participants, had been passed by the time of the French Revolution. The chronologically additive meaning which initially could have been taken by *neueste Zeit* (in the form of a simple historical extrapolation) was repressed. What could not be achieved in the concept of *neue Zeit* was effected by *neueste Zeit*. It became a concept for the contemporary epoch opening up a new period and did not simply retrospectively register a past period.

It was very slowly, over a long period, that *neue Zeit* had become established after the adoption of *historia nova*, and it only was so historiographically, as an *ex post* definition. On the other hand, the *neue Zeit* that in turn generated *neueste Zeit* now assumed historical qualities which led beyond the traditional linguistic schema of annalistic addition.

The differentiation of *neue* from *neueste Zeit* became the object of increasing reflection on the nature of historical time. Here the rapid manner in which the concept became accepted is an indicator of an acceleration in the rate of change of historical experience and the enhancement of a conscious working-over of the nature of time. There were numerous other terms available that might have lent emphasis to one's experience as genuinely novel, and in the decades around 1800 these had become accepted or given a new meaning: Revolution, Progress, Development, Crisis, and *Zeitgeist* all contained temporal indications that had never before been used in the same way.

The historiographic use of *neue Zeit* is valid only in a limited fashion, as lending emphasis to a characterization of a specifically new experience of time. For this reason, we will turn in a second section to other concepts and the temporal reflections that have entered into them. *Neue Zeit* can be heard in many contexts and places.

## Historical Criteria of Temporalization

From the second half of the eighteenth century on, there is a growing frequency of indices denoting the concept *neue Zeit* in a full sense. Time is no longer simply the medium in which all histories take place; it gains a historical quality. Consequently, history no longer occurs in, but through, time. Time becomes a dynamic and historical force in its own right. Presupposed by this formulation of experience is a concept of history which is likewise new: the collective singular form of *Geschichte*, which since around 1780 can be conceived as history in and for itself in the absence of an associated subject or object.[48]

In this connection it is important to note the way in which Campe defines *Zeitgeschichte*. No longer is it reserved for historical subsidiary disciplines, to *Chronologica*, as with Stieler; its prime meaning now is "history in general." Only secondarily does it mean "The history of a specific time; in particular, our time, *neueste Zeit*."[49] *Zeitgeschichte* today is used in a somewhat unsatisfactory, theoretical fashion. As soon as history was understood to be a genuine entity, its necessary relation to historical time was brought into a common concept. The idea that all history is *Zeitgeschichte* implies, in a quite specifiable manner, its temporalization. Certain criteria for this will be outlined in the following.

When Kant objected to the manner in which, until then, history had arranged itself according to chronology, he was criticizing the theological conception of time as a providential plan to which all histories had to adhere. It would be far more appropriate, argued Kant, if chronology followed history.[50] Kant raised a demand for historically immanent temporal criteria, and once introduced, these criteria became ever clearer in the historical and theoretical discussions of the later phases of the Enlightenment.

In the first place, the *saecula*, or *Jahrhunderte*, as one could say in German after the seventeenth century, take on a historical meaning peculiar to themselves. They become the pacemakers of temporal reflection. While the *saecula* at first were means of division, still marked in a chronological and additive manner and (as with Flacius Illyrus, for instance) deployed in the diachronic organization of a multitude of simultaneous domains, from the seventeenth century on they increasingly assumed a historically independent claim on existence. They were regarded as composed unities and were endowed with meaning.

The "Century of Enlightenment" was thought of as such even by its contemporaries and it knew how to distinguish itself from the century of Louis XIV, as did Voltaire. The concept of *genius saeculi* is a forerunner of *Zeitgeist*.[51] In this way, centuries became the chronological markers of historical experience, their unmistakable identity and their singularity providing the foundation for their conception in terms of processual unity.[52]

"Practically every century contains occurrences unique to it," as Köster said.[53] While initially the axiom of the singularity of unrepeatability was established first (in opposition to exemplary *Historie*), it was closely followed by the separation of the concept "centenary" from the simple means of division that it provided for additive computation in terms of centuries. Schröckh emphasized in 1768:

With a new century, the world does not at once assume a new form: many undertakings are only fully developed later in the century, while having been initiated long before in the century that has passed.[54]

The "new form of the world" is here interpreted in a centennial manner, although its genesis separates it from the schematic method of counting in centuries. Historical processes are construed reflexively; they "develop" (as one now says) to the point at which the concept of development itself was constituted.[55] In this way they gain their own temporal structure. "In actuality, every changing thing has the measure of its own time within itself," as Herder wrote in his *Metakritik* of Kant: "No two worldly things have the same measure of time. . . . There are therefore (one can state it properly and boldly) at any one time in the universe innumerably many times."[56] From that time on it was possible to investigate historical events and sequences for their own internal time: the unique point of time, for a specific temporal period, or for periods of different duration.

Second, the extent to which the internal time of individual histories structured the whole of history is shown by the theorem, born of much experience, of the noncontemporaneousness of diverse, but in the chronological sense, simultaneous histories.[57] The geographical opening up of the globe brought to light various but coexisting cultural levels which were, through the process of synchronous comparison, then ordered diachronically. Looking from civilized Europe to a barbaric America was a glance backward. This demonstrated to Bacon that man is a God for mankind: "non solum propter auxilium et beneficium, sed etiam per status comparationis."[58] Comparisons promoted the emergence in experience of a world history, which was increasingly interpreted in terms of progress. A constant impulse leading to progressive comparison was drawn from the fact that individual peoples or states, parts of the earth, sciences, *Stände*, or classes were found to be in advance of the others. From the eighteenth century on, therefore, it was possible to formulate the postulate of acceleration; or conversely, from the point of view of those left behind, the postulate of drawing level or overtaking. This fundamental experience of progress, embodied in a singular concept around 1800, is rooted in the knowledge of noncontemporaneities which exist at a chronologically uniform time. From the seventeenth century on, historical experience was increasingly ordered by the hierarchy produced through a consideration of the best existing constitution or the state of scientific, technical, or economic development.

From this point on, the whole of history gained its own temporal structure. Petrarch had uttered the wish to be born in a different epoch: "Nam fuit et fortassis erit felicius evum."[59] In the course of early modernity, such wishes gradually became statements of historical substance which immanently graduated the course of time. "Not everyone has discovered a time in their century which they would have wished to experience," wrote Zedler in Protestant North Germany in 1749. "It was an act of providence that Martin Luther was a man of his time; Johannes Hus, on the other hand, was not, and deserved a better century."[60]

D'Alembert and Diderot constructed the whole of history according to the spectrum of their immanent temporal rhythms. They looked for the unique conditions of historical phenomena, in particular of the sciences and possible intellectual constructions. Men who were ahead of their times were emphasized so that the subsequent fulfillment of their designs could be registered; the posteriority of the as yet unenlightened masses became a subject for their education, the project of the *Encyclopédie* being conceived in the consciousness of a unique historical situation. The two men saw themselves as pressed for time; preparation of all technical potentialities and all knowledge had to be made in time for future action, even in the event of catastrophe.[61] In this way, history constituted itself according to immanent, anthropologically based criteria of the "before and after," criteria which were for the past no longer susceptible to change. This historical reflection also evoked a "too early" or a "too late" as a means of influencing the future through accelerated enlightenment. The Encyclopedists operated this with a highly sensitized historical consciousness which developed for the moment of time, duration, and time period a common frame: the frame of progress, according to which the whole of history could be interpreted universally.

Within the plane of progress, the contemporaneity of the noncontemporaneous became a fundamental datum of all history—an axiom that was enriched in the course of the nineteenth century by social and political changes which led to the absorption of the phrase by everyday language. "If I deny German conditions of 1843 then, by French chronological standards, I barely stand in 1789, and even less at the focus of the present."[62] Here, Marx simply states emphatically that which since the French Revolution had required the interpretation of history to be effected according to temporal criteria organized by the alternatives of progress or conservation (*Bewahren*), catching up or delay.

Third—and this is connected to the experience of progress—the doctrine of subjective historical perspective, the localization of historical statement, gained a secure place in the canon of historical epistemology.[63] In Germany, Chladenius was a pathbreaker in this respect. There is hardly a historian of the Enlightenment who has not implicitly or explicitly drawn on his work. They shared his view that all historical representations depended on the author's selection, one which he has to effect since he moves within given social, political, and religious limits. For Thomas Abbt it was thus quite acceptable for one set of events to give rise to various accounts, all of which were equally valid.[64] But it did not stop at this.

This perspective was not simply a spatial entity, but it also assumed a temporal dimension. Gatterer, for instance, supposed that the truth of history was not everywhere the same.[65] Historical time took on a quality creative of experience, and this showed how the past could retrospectively be seen anew. In 1775, Büsch stated, "In this, newly arising incidents can render important to us a history which had previously been of no or little interest."[66] Pragmatic history did not only look for causes and effects and learn to weigh them. It made especial use of the topos of Tacitus that minor causes could have major consequences. This idea was however taken further. Now the course of influence attained the status of a history, converging in the idea "history in general."

In other words, events lost their historically secured character to the extent that they had previously been established and carried forward in an annalistic mode of writing. It became possible, even required, that the same occurrences would be reported and judged in a divergent manner in the course of time.

Such a procedure had been practiced for long enough, especially by polemical writings on Church history. What was new here was that the relativity of historical judgment was no longer treated as an epistemological defect, but rather as testimony to a superior truth itself determined by the passing course of history. It was subsequently possible for an event to change its identity according to its shifting status in the advance of total history. Perspectivistic judgment and the registration of a changing influence both assumed a retrospective force.

History was temporalized in the sense that, thanks to the passing of time, it altered according to the given present, and with growing distance the nature of the past also altered. Stated more exactly, history stood revealed in its current truth. *Neuzeit* lent the whole of the past a world-historical quality. With this, the novelty of a history in emergence, reflected as new, assumed a progressively growing claim to the whole of history. It became regarded as self-evident that history as world history had to be continually rewritten. "That world history has to be rewritten from time to time is no longer doubted by anyone these days," as Goethe soon afterward summed up this change in viewpoint. He explained this compulsion to continually write history anew not by referring to the discovery of new sources, which might have approached a kind of research strategy, but by tracing it to the historical conception of time, "because the contemporary of an advancing time is led into positions from which the past can be surveyed and judged in a new fashion."[67]

If in one's own history it was possible to register new experiences, those which supposedly no one had ever before had, it was also possible to conceive the past as something that was fundamentally "other." This in turn led to the fact that it was precisely along the plane of progress that the specificity of the epoch had to be expressed. Hence, diagnosis of the *neue Zeit* and analysis of the past eras corresponded to each other.

This association of historical reflection with the consciousness of forward movement allowed one's own modernity to be marked out only by reference to a previous period. In the words of Humboldt, "The eighteenth century occupies the most favorable place for the examination and appreciation of its own character in the history of all time." For it was only through reflection upon the effects and influence of antiquity and the Middle Ages that their specificity and difference could be marked off from that of the present, and in part this difference was then summarized as the entire *Vorzeit*.

In our standpoint we therefore enjoy the great advantage of completely and entirely overseeing both previous periods, whose actual consequences and purposeful combination makes possible consideration of the third.[68]

But with the advance of time, it was not only the developing prospect of the past which raised the challenge of discovering an ever-new knowledge of entire history. The *neue Zeit* of history was also impregnated with the difference which was torn open between one's own time and that of the future, between previous experience and the expectation of that which was to come.

Fourth, a characteristic of the new epochal consciousness emergent in the late eighteenth century was that one's own time was not only experienced as a beginning or an end, but also as a period of transition. Clearly there is a difference here between the initial reception of the French Revolution in Germany and the experience of those directly participating, a difference which at first emphasized the absolutely new beginning. However, by the time of the failed Restoration of 1815, at the latest, the consciousness of a transitional period had become the common property of the peoples of Europe, increasingly induced from the social changes resulting from the Industrial Revolution. In the personalized language of a Conservative:

Everything has begun to move, or has been set in motion, and with the intention or under the pretense of fulfilling and completing everything, everything is placed in question, doubted, and approaches a general transformation. The love of movement in itself, without purpose and without specific end, has emerged and developed out of the movement of the time. In it, and in it alone, one seeks and sets real life.[69]

Two specific temporal determinants characterize the new experience of transition: the expected otherness of the future and, associated with it, the alteration in the rhythm of temporal experience: acceleration, by means of which one's own time is distinguished from what went before. In his analysis of the eighteenth century, Humboldt had expressly emphasized this, and in this he was not alone: "Our epoch appears to lead out of one period, which is passing, into another, which is no less different." The criterion of this shift was based upon a historical time which generated ever-shorter intervals of time. For

whoever compares even superficially the present state of affairs with those of fifteen to twenty years ago will not deny that there prevails within this period greater dissimilarity than that which ruled within a period twice as long at the beginning of this century.[70]

The abbreviation of the periods which allow for a homogeneity of experience—stated differently, the acceleration of a change which consumes experience—has since then belonged to the topoi characteristic of the prevailing *neueste Geschichte*. As Gervinus wrote in 1853, the movements of the nineteenth century "succeed each other in almost geometrical progression." Fifty years later, Henry Adams developed a dynamic theory of history which applied the "law of acceleration" to all previously experienced history.[71] The historical axiom of the singularity of all that occurred was in this respect merely the temporal abstraction of modern everyday experience.

"That which then went at a steady pace is now at the gallop," as Arndt wrote in 1807 as he looked back over the previous twenty years.

Time is in flight; those who are clever have known this for a long time. Monstrous things have happened: the world has suffered great transformations silently and noisily, in the quiet pace of the day and in the storms and eruptions of revolution; monstrosities will occur, greater things will be transformed.[72]

With this the orientation toward the future necessarily changed, for in any case it would appear different from what was taught by all previous history—whether hoped for in a progressive spirit or feared in a conservative, it was all the same. The following appeared in 1793 in the *Schleswigsche Journal*:

In an epoch whose occurrences are completely different from the occurrences of all others; where words whose reverberation previously

had an indescribable force but which have now lost all significance . . . there only a fool or a zealot can imagine himself able to
determine with any certainty what lies hidden behind the future; all
human knowledge fails at that point, all comparison is impossible, for
no epoch exists which can be placed alongside the present one.[73]

Within the horizon of this conception of constant surprise, at that time
increasingly accepted, time altered layer by layer its everyday sense
of flowing and the natural circulation within which histories took place.
Time itself could now be interpreted as something new, since the
future brought with it something else, sooner than had ever before
seemed possible. Friedrich Schlegel in 1829 stated: "No time has ever
been so strongly, so closely, so exclusively, and so generally bound
up with the future than that of our present."[74]

The temporal dimensions of past, present, and future were now
folded into each other in qualitatively varying ways such that the
epochal renewal of the given *neueste Geschichte* could be initiated in
ever-advancing phases. "Epoch and contemporaries are properly one,"
claimed Arndt.[75] "Epoch" and "period," threshold and duration of
the *neue Zeit* coincide within the horizon of movement which continually
exceeded itself.[76] By virtue of this temporalization, providential anticipation and the exemplarity of ancient histories fade away. Progress
and historical consciousness reciprocally temporalize all histories into
the singularity of the world-historical process. Without resort to a
Hereafter, world history becomes the tribunal of the world, with Schiller's phrase being immediately taken up and continually cited as evidence of the change. The consciousness of epochal uniqueness likewise
entered the long term as a criterion of the later, so-called *Neuzeit*.

Fifth, it seems to be a paradox that within the perspective of an
accelerating period of transition, the usual forms of historical writing
on the present increasingly ran into difficulties, in some cases even
falling into discredit with professional historians. As a growing temporal
distance increased the prospects of knowledge of the past, so a history
written up on the basis of day-to-day events lost its methodological
dignity. The superior authenticity previously attributed to participating
eyewitnesses was placed in question by, for example, Planck in 1781,
on the grounds that "real" history emerged only after a certain amount
of time had elapsed, and thanks to historical criticism it then appeared
"in an entirely different form" from that which seemed visible to the
given contemporaries.[77]

As the methodological emphasis of historical research shifted to an ever greater degree toward the revelation of a more distant and more alien past, this was, in sociohistorical terms, an outcome of the upheaval in the final decades of the eighteenth century, when tradition and convention broke up.[78] At the same time, however, the difficulty of apprehending one's own time grew, since the course that it would follow could no longer be derived from previous history. The future became a challenge, a puzzle. "No mortal lives who might be granted the ability to assess the progress of coming centuries in invention and social circumstances."[79] It was this fact, that the course of past time was obviously different from that of the present and the future, which robbed the annalistic "onward-writing" of present incidents of its previous certainty. One could no longer rely on the conviction of an eyewitness to establish which events would matter, or which would have an impact.

The mode in which temporalization constantly reordered the three dimensions of past, present, and future with respect to one another led to a complete dislocation of their historical burden. Up until the middle of the eighteenth century, the history of one's own time enjoyed an undisputed precedence, not only on political and didactic grounds, but also for methodological reasons. The image of the past faded with the passing of time, as Bacon said; or in the words of La Popelinière, "Pource que la longueur des vieux temps, faict perdre la cognoissance de la Verité à ceux qui viennent long temps après."[80] This premise, arising as it did from everyday experience, still held for Pufendorf, Gundling, and Lessing.

The writing of contemporary history certainly had its snags. But one was all the sooner clear about the risks arising from political or moral pressures when one devoted oneself to the history of one's own time. "Whosoever in writing a modern history shall follow truth too near the heels, it may happily strike out his teeth," as Raleigh admitted in prison.[81] Objections to a history of one's own time made toward the end of the eighteenth century were made less and less on the basis of the political situation of the writer or of censorship; rather, they emerged from an altered perception of historical reality, that is, its temporal structuration. "The constitution of Europe has changed too much in the last three centuries" for it to still be possible to reproduce *neuere Geschichte* according to events in the individual states and the actions of particular persons, wrote Büsch in 1775. All "world affairs" of any significance transcended the states, economic involvements reached out overseas, so that events could really only be grasped in their world-historical context.[82] The growing call since the midpoint of the century for a new world history testifies to the depth of the experiential shift that can be traced to global interdependence. This is especially clear in the case of the Seven Years War. The only problem was that the influential factors within the course of affairs escaped the direct experience of those who were individually affected. The overall concatenation of events could no longer be dealt with in an annalistic manner; a higher degree of abstraction was demanded of historians to compensate for the disappearance of direct experience. It was for this reason that the Göttingen School proposed that history be written as a "system," and no longer as an "aggregate." Consequently, theories and philosophies of history current at that time blossomed everywhere, presenting the categories suitable for relating limited everyday experience to its universal context.

Following the French Revolution, temporal components were joined to the spatial ones, which, as an outcome of the experience of acceleration, made it ever harder to register the history of one's own time. Objections to this accumulated. For example, Krug in 1796 distinguished "*neuere Geschichte* from the *neueste*, that is, the history of the day" and found its distinguishing characteristic in the fact that "uncertainty often had in retrospect a great similarity to the mythic." Impartial enlightenment is delivered first by the future.[83] As in individual cases, so in the whole: Simon Erhardt in 1818 considered "world history," as was common by that time, as "the developmental history of mankind"; but it did not seem to him "possible for those individuals trapped within a particular time and space" to determine "in which epoch they actually existed."[84] Periodizations related to world history were held to be epistemologically unreliable. The question could no longer be answered unambiguously since, with the passing of time, the actual phases altered perspective. This was as true for the incomplete totality of history as it was for the history of the present, which could never be adequately established.

Diesterweg attested to the limits of his powers to diagnose the present for the "creature of time, man." It is certainly no easy matter to completely comprehend one's time, that is, the time in which one exists, if this time is a time of movement."[85] Perthes had his own difficulties in recruiting professional historians to complete, up to the present day, his planned history of the European states. One specialist responded by arguing that in the current process of transformation, in which everything was provisional, Perthes could not expect him to write history up to the present; moreover, the unknown future obstructed true knowledge of the past. For this reason the planned history had the "dual error of seeking to relate itself to the transitory and to that which was incompletely known."[86]

Enough of such evidence. The writings of daily history, which was of course carried on, descended into a lower class and was henceforth entrusted to journalists.[87] It was also pursued by those historians and philosophers who on normative or political impulse had the courage to prognosticate. History, once it had been systematically temporalized, could no longer be recognized as *Zeitgeschichte* if the potential future was not brought into consideration.[88] Only Droysen, von Stein, and Marx can be named as those whose historical writing on a coexisting time drew its impulse from a future they sought to influence on the basis of their historical diagnosis. Even Ranke's lectures on contemporary history, while mediated historically, possess this didactic aspect.

It is certainly inexact, or at least it calls for caution, to speak of the temporalization of history, since all histories, wherever they are to be found, are always concerned with time. Nevertheless, use of the expression as a scientific term seems appropriate and justified since, as it has been demonstrated, the *neuzeitliche* experience of history led to theoretically enriched concepts of time which demanded that the whole of history be read in terms of a temporal structure.

Individualization and the axiom of uniqueness penetrated a naturalistic chronology that was indifferent to the content of individual histories with temporal intervals and sequential rhythms associated with the process of historical reception. Toward the end of the eighteenth century the expression "development" incorporated many, though not all, of these theorems into a common concept.

The contemporaneity of the noncontemporaneous, initially a result of overseas expansion, became a basic framework for the progressive construction of the growing unity of world history. Toward the end of the century, the collective singular "progress" was coined in the German language, opening up all domains of life with the questions of "earlier than" or "later than," not just "before" and "after."

The doctrine of historical perspective legitimated the change in historical knowledge, ascribing to temporal sequence a function creative of knowledge. Historical truths, by virtue of their temporalization, became superior truths.

Finally, the divide between previous experience and coming expectation opened up, and the difference between past and present increased, so that lived time was experienced as a rupture, as a period of transition in which the new and the unexpected continually happened. Novelty accrued for the range of meanings embodied in "time" even before the technicizing of transport and information made acceleration a temporally specific datum point. Following this, in the sphere of the political and the social, even delay became a key historical principle, used both by conservatives to hold back movement and by progressives who wished to speed it up: both positions, however, are founded upon a history whose new dynamism demanded temporal categories of movement.

Concepts of historical enlightenment and science, which were initially inferred theoretically, entered the arsenals of legitimation possessed by all social and political groups. This process begins at the close of the eighteenth century, the time at which meaning was given to the concepts or when the terms themselves were coined. We will list the most significant: "history in general," which had to be created or before which one felt responsible; "development," which one had to follow, or "progress," which one sought to promote or to brake; the obligation, indeed the necessity of a "position" (*Standort*) or party membership to be able to act politically; and, ultimately deriving from these, the task, prescribed within the spectrum of potential futures, of promoting or superseding other positions, groups, *Stände*, classes, nations, sciences, and knowledges.

Theoretically formed basic concepts moved into the reservoir of catchwords which created opinion and legitimated party. This was the same for all parties. Proof of this is to be found in the excessive use of the term *Zeit*, beginning around 1800, to gain insight or power or both within the turmoil of social and political movement.

For the time between 1770 and 1830, the epochal threshold initially known as *neueste Zeit*, Grimm's dictionary contains over one hundred neologisms, compounds which qualified *Zeit* in a positive historical fashion.[89] *Zeit* was related to the following terms (to name only a few): "section," "regard," "view," "task," "expense," "predicament," "movement," "formation," "character," "duration," "development," "epoch," "event," "requirement," "fulfillment," "appearance," "abundance," "course," "feeling," and "spirit." This register can be conveniently broken off with *Zeitgeist*, certainly the most widespread compound and the most often invoked. These neologisms, which might be traced to a particularly linguistically creative generation from *Sturm and Drang* via classicism and Romanticism to young Germany: these are indicative of an experiential change of great depth. The expressions seek to qualify time, so that the social and political movement which had caught up within itself all strata of society might be diagnosed and directed.

Naturally, idioms and proverbs which capture the experience of time have a long and humanly venerable tradition. But a connection to history in the modern sense had not previously existed. The stars, nature, or living conditions, and calling, fate, or chance were more usually the source from which insight into time was gained or by means of which time was captured. Zedler, living during the period of the baroque society of orders, refers to the countless legal meanings implicit within the temporal compounds of his day—intervals, periods, and durations—without appreciating their historical possibilities. The other emphasis of traditional usage consisted in the moral-theological inexhaustibility of all doctrines invoking time as the "quintessence of past conditions and decaying uncertainty."[90]

Not that such doctrines were later abandoned—their further application or metaphorical reoccupation in the era of industry and technology is still in need of investigation—but they did retreat in comparison with the process of historical crystallization which around 1800 permitted the accretion of numerous points and semantic layers of the most diverse kind.

All shared the basic experience of movement, of change in the perspective of an open future; disagreement prevailed only on the question of the tempo and the direction which had to be taken. This dispute, initially one which took place only among those with the power to make political decisions, spread with the reordering of social strata and finally, by virtue of the development of parties, challenged everyone to make a choice. From that time on, historical time exercised a compulsion that no one could escape. It was up to us, wrote Baader in 1834, "to either become masters of time, or revolutionize it against ourselves by neglect of the evolution that it promotes or the reformation which overtakes this."[91]

Against the background of such a general temporalization we will, in conclusion, outline the depth to which time, as a mutable entity in itself, has entered into the terminology of social and political life.

## The Pragmatic Dimension of the Concepts of Movement

The evidence advanced so far demonstrates the rapidity with which basic temporal concepts entered into the everyday and the public domain. "Time" was one of those terms Clausewitz referred to as "for the most part, misused in the world."[92] Hardly anyone was able to evade the concept of time and the purposes it was supposed to fulfill. "Time" affected the entire linguistic stock and, from the period of the French Revolution at the latest, colored the entire political and social vocabulary. Since then, there has hardly been a central concept of political theory or social programs which does not contain a coefficient of temporal change, in the absence of which nothing can be recognized, nothing thought or argued, without the loss of conceptual force. Time itself becomes a title of legitimation open to occupation from all sides. Without a temporal perspective, specific concepts of legitimation would no longer be possible.

First, the long series of "isms" can be cited that projected historical movement into the "future perspective" and thereby sought their vindication. Kant was certainly the first to associate the concept of his objective, the ethically derived ideal republican constitution, with "republicanism" as a concept of movement. Even monarchial states (for instance, the Prussia of Frederick II), could through enlightened policy participate in republicanism. Kant excluded from the existing constitution desires bound up with the future and indicated the course along which a constitution based on the separation of powers had to work if monarchial or democratic despotism was to be made superfluous.[93] Soon afterward, the young Friedrich Schlegel replaced "republicanism" with "democratism" while admitting that the objective of true democracy, in bringing an end to all subordination and domination, could only "really be effected by means of an infinitely progressive approximation."[94] In this way, constitutional concepts like "republic" and "democracy," traditional and descriptive in form, were modified by a historical philosophy into concepts of movement which made obligatory intervention into everyday political affairs.

Soon "liberalism" joined the spectrum of temporal alternatives which divided up the entirety of political and social life according to orientation to past or future.

The liberal party is that which determines the political character of the *neuere Zeit*, while the so-called servile party behaves for the most part in the character of the Middle Ages. Liberalism thus advances at the same pace as time itself, or is inhibited to the degree that the past survives into the present.[95]

"Socialism" and "communism" followed and for their part claimed the future for their own:

Communism is for us not a *state of affairs* which is to be established, an *ideal* to which reality [will] have to adjust itself. We call communism the *real* movement which abolishes the present state of things. The conditions of this movement result from the premises now in existence.[96]

Temporalization, therefore, did not simply transform older constitutional concepts, but aided in the development of new ones that found their common temporal denominator in the suffix "ism." They share in common the facts that they only partially rest upon accumulated experience, and that the expectation of the coming time is proportionally greater the lesser such experience becomes. This then is a matter involving temporal "compensatory concepts." The transitional period between past and future thus is kaleidoscopically, with every freshly minted concept, projected anew.

The counterconcepts which accompany this (for example, "aristocracy," "monarchy," "conservatism," and "servility") surrender to the past the conduct or constitutional elements thereby implied, together with their representing agents in the conjuncture envisaged. The *Konservateure* were late in bowing to this pressure, hesitantly assuming in the mid-nineteenth century the alien term *Konservatismus*. For decades they had avoided the "ism" construction as a way of evading the pressure toward movement produced by the obsession with temporality.[97]

Alongside the neologisms are numerous concepts which, despite the formal identity of the words, have altered their temporal implications. Even when they had earlier contained quite definite temporal indicators, they were now swept away in the flood of temporalization. The concept "revolution" lost its older zones of meaning involving either regular recurrence in the sequence of constitutions or epochal points of upheaval. The temporal spectrum had changed following the ever-renewing waves originating in the French Revolution, and also from the time that industrialization and the social sphere had been subordinated to the concept of revolution. "Revolution" was completely temporalized, such that Jacob Burkhardt could define the French Revolution as "the first period of our current revolutionary world epoch." Like "crisis," "revolution," since the beginning of the nineteenth century, had increasingly registered the prevailing process of constant change, which was lent additional impulse by civil war.[98]

In the same way, "emancipation" lost its older, generally conditioned, but exact meaning as the ceremony proclaiming emancipation. The legal institute is absorbed by the temporal design of irreversible proceedings which, by virtue of history, should lead to an ever-extending self-determination of all mankind:

This extension is in no way accidental or arbitrary, but is founded by necessity in the nature of mankind; in the course of its development, emancipation has nearly become the most important of all concepts, central to all questions of state in the present, or our time.[99]

The corresponding concept "dictatorship," which was also taken from Roman legal language, follows a similar pattern of assimilation to the historical process. Since the time of Napoleon, its meaning has no longer been associated with the legal establishment of a time limit within which a dictatorship has to reconstruct the older order. Instead, it is now the enactment of historical transformation which is demanded of dictatorship, whether it be through the "dictatorship of the proletariat," or whether it be through the form of dictatorship which is implied by the Caesarism or Bonapartist conceptions of movement. This form of dictatorship, as, for instance, with Napoleon III, was no longer regarded by Konstantin Frantz as exceptional, as in other republics; here it became "principal," since it corresponded to a situation which had never before existed.[100] From the previously existent "dictator of limited duration" there developed the "sovereign dictator" who legitimated himself in terms of historical time.[101]

The singularity of the new situation is also shown by the manner in which the concept "dictator"—as with "revolution" and "emancipation"—was extended from a limited politico-legal sphere into that of society. As von Stein said of Napoleon I, this was a question of "social dictatorship," since it was a reaction to changes within civil society at once turbulent and long-term. Regarding the situation in 1848, he added that this dictatorship "is no institute, but a historical consequence. When it was established, it was no dictatorship; it had to create itself."[102]

In this way, "dictatorship" moved into the reflexive definition of time which had by this time caught up many other concepts, from the active "time itself" and "history in general" to "development" via "progress." Dictatorship which created itself provided its own historical legitimation. It is in the mode of expression that the politico-pragmatic dimension of the concept is contained. "Dictatorship" shares this with the various "isms" outlined above, as well as with "revolution" or "emancipation." The concepts are oriented in terms of an irreversible temporal process, loading its agents with responsibility while simultaneously relieving them of it, for the process of self-creation is included within the properties of the prospective future. It is from this that such concepts take their diachronic force, a force which sustains both speaker and addressee.

All the concepts of movement cited here, a series which could be extended without difficulty, embody temporal coefficients of change. For this reason, they can be arranged according to the manner in which they might correspond to the intended phenomenon, or might call the phenomenon in question into life, or might be a reaction to phenomena which already exist. To express it differently: the three temporal dimensions can be quite variously weighted more toward the present, future, or past as they actually enter into concepts. Like the historical circumstances they are to register, concepts themselves have an internal temporal structure.

Finally, the internal temporal structure of our concepts indicates two closely related conditions, which are characteristic of our modernity in a special sense. These will be considered by way of conclusion. Political and social concepts become *instruments for the direction* of historical movement. They are not simply indicators, but factors in all those changes which have overtaken civil society since the eighteenth century. It was only within the horizon of temporalization that it first became possible for political rivals to color each other in ideological terms. This led to the alteration of the functioning mode of sociopolitical language. Since that time, the *ideologization* of one's opponent has been a part of the mechanism controlling political language.

1. The linguistic space of premodern times was organized in terms of the "strata" of the *Stände*. In particular, until the middle of the eighteenth century, political language was a monopoly enjoyed by the nobility, lawyers, and scholars. The experiential space of social agencies was defined in terms of the *Stände* and was thus relatively closed; the spaces were mutually complementary, while the actual porosity of *ständisch* distinctions did not mean that such distinctions did not exist. In this fashion, the world of the *Stände* was one in which there existed complementary linguistic strata. This changed, however, with the unraveling of this system of social stratification. Adelung talked of a more rapid change in the language of the "wider world," of the arts and sciences, than in the "idiom of the common man," which has existed for "thousands of years without perceptible change."[103] Independently of the correctness of this judgment, Adelung here uses the new temporal coefficient of change to characterize the marking off of the *ständisch* linguistic zones. But these boundaries were soon to change.

The circles which learned to make use of political terminology, above all its catchwords, widened appreciably.[104] The space of linguistic communication occupied by the nobility and scholars was extended to include the educated bourgeoisie, and in the course of the *Vormärz*, elements of the lower strata, themselves the objects of political language, learned to manipulate this language. This sparked a struggle over concepts, as had occurred in revolutionary France; control over language became more urgent as the number of men whom it comprehended increased. This challenge of linguistic control and consequently power over the direction of consciousness and behavior altered the internal temporal structure of concepts.

While earlier concepts are distinguished by the manner in which they bring into one expression experience assembled over a period of time, the relation of concept to that conceived is now reversed. Modern political terminology is typified by its containment of numerous concepts (*Begriffe*) that are more exactly anticipations (*Vorgriffe*). These concepts are based on the experience of the loss of experience, and so they have to preserve or awaken new expectations. Moreover, for moral, economic, technical, and political reasons they call for objectives that assimilate more desires than previous history was able to fulfill.

This semantically demonstrable state of affairs corresponds to the influence of the French and the Industrial revolutions. If a society shorn of its *ständisch* structure is to be re-formed into communes, enterprises, associations, unions, parties, and organizations, then it has need of predictions of the future. The social and political significance of such predictions is shown by the manner in which they have to exceed what is empirically possible and by the extent to which this is done. The imperative of reorganization (the word "organization" here is a concept which derives from this new situation) stimulates the construction of concepts for the purposes of control and guidance that, in the absence of a temporal perspective of the future, would not have been formulable. The process of temporalization which, as has been shown, began to develop first in historical theory, now entered deep into daily life.

2. It was only in this situation that the art of ideological criticism could be specifically developed. Theories, concepts, and attitudes, programs and forms of behavior, which are graduated ideologically in this *Neuzeit*, are clearly distinct from utterances that can be called errors, lies, or prejudices. Lies can be seen through, errors corrected, and prejudices removed. The refutation of an adversary is effected in terms of criteria whose reasonableness is assumed by the other party and which can therefore be expected of him. Even the psychosocial reduction of modes of conduct, thought, and speech effected by prominent moralists stands on this same unsteady ground, upon which the exposer cannot distance himself from he who is exposed. He shares the insight into wretchedness.

Ideological criticism proceeds in a different fashion. It distances itself from the wretchedness it seeks to expose. It assumes in a modernistic way that concepts advance in their degree of generality and that it is only by virtue of this that modern experience can be assimilated. Daily life is increasingly distinguished by the loss of classifications capable of retaining their force and of the social or political substantiality first evoked by modern historical writing. It is in particular the technological and industrial conditions of everyday experience which evade just this experience. For this reason, the degree of abstraction rises for many concepts, since it is only in this way that the growing complexity of economic, technological, social, and political structures can be grasped. This has semantic consequences for linguistic praxis.

The more general the concepts, the greater the number of parties that can make use of them. The concepts become catchwords. Freedom as a privilege can only be called for by whoever possesses it; but everyone can call for freedom in general. In this way, a competitive struggle develops over the proper interpretation and usage of concepts. "Democracy" has become a universal constitutional concept, all camps claiming it for themselves in different ways.

The same concepts thus become available for perspectivic possession. As general concepts they invite occupation, no matter what concrete experience or expectations enter into them. In this way, dispute arises over the correct political interpretation; that is, the means of excluding one's opponent from using the same words to say and wish that which might differ from one's own conception.

In this situation, temporalization shows its reverse, bringing in evasiveness as a form of assistance. Ideological criticism as a linguistic weapon comes from the arsenal of historism. It is based on a kind of short-circuited historicization which even dissects the present with the aid of concepts of movement. Ideological criticism distributes the validation of political discourse among the succession of historical periods. It is precisely on the basis of the categories "earlier than" or "later than," and especially on that of "too early" or "too late," that attitudes can be "ideologically" deciphered in a way distinct from that followed with other modes of examination. Someone might argue in a rational and consistent manner, but all the same have a certified false consciousness of the matter he treats or attests to. Subjectively he may not be lying nor committing any error; he might even be able to recognize his prejudices. All the same, his attitudes or concepts will be relativized through their temporal grading and in this way ideologized. Ideological criticism which proceeds in this manner argues with concepts of movement whose burden of proof can only be summoned up in the future. The adversary thus is trapped in an argumentative dilemma. The historical chronological scale according to which he is measured is a mobile one.

For one thing, his present position will be held to be historically determined; he can neither escape nor transcend it. On the other hand, the same position can be relocated into the future in such a utopistic manner that it is unattainable, or into the present past so that it is, in truth, already superseded, backward, and therefore obsolete. This involves ciphers within a temporal dimension that can be lent any shape desired. And as soon as judgment is permeated by criteria of what might be desirable in the future, it ceases to be possible to empirically refute such ideological classification. A future first revealed by *Neuzeit* is pointed to, but since then it has never been attained.

The definition of *Neuzeit* as a transitional period thus has lost nothing of its epochal sense since its discovery. Unmistakable criteria of *Neuzeit* are its concepts of movement as indices of social and political change and as linguistic factors in the formation of consciousness, ideological criticism, and the control and management of behavior.

# "Space of Experience" and "Horizon of Expectation": Two Historical Categories

## Methodological Preamble

"Since it is so common to argue against hypothesis, one should some-time try to approach history without the aid of hypothesis. It is not possible to state that something is, without saying what it is. By just thinking of them one relates facts to concepts, and it is by no means a matter of indifference which concepts these might be."[1] In these few sentences Friedrich Schlegel summarized, on the basis of the past century's theoretical reflections, the nature of history, how it was to be recognized, and how it should be written. At the termination of this historical process of enlightenment stands the discovery of "history in and for itself," which is provoked by a history apprehended in terms of progress. Stated concisely, this discovery involves a transcendental category which joins the conditions of possible history with the conditions of its cognition.[2] Since Schlegel's summary, it has not been thought proper, even if it is quite usual, to deal with history scientifically without clearly establishing the nature of the categories by means of which it is articulated.

The historian reaching into the past—beyond his own experiences and memories, guided by questions and desires, hopes and troubles—is initially confronted by so-called residues which are still available to some degree. If the historian transforms these residues into sources providing testimony on the history he seeks knowledge of, then he is operating on two levels. He either investigates circumstances that have at one time been articulated in language; or he reconstructs circumstances which were not previously articulated in language but which, with the assistance of hypotheses and methods, he is able to extract from the relics. In the first case, the concepts lending the source-language its shape serve as a means of heuristic entry into a comprehension of past reality. In the second case, the historian makes use of concepts constructed and defined *ex post*, scientific categories applied to the sources without being present within them.

We are therefore dealing, on the one hand, with concepts embodied in the sources and, on the other, with scientific cognitive categories. These must be distinguished, although they are sometimes, but not always, related. It is often possible to use the same word for past historical concept and historical category, in which case it is important to make the difference in their uses quite clear. The measurement and investigation of differences among or convergence of old concepts and modern cognitive categories is performed by *Begriffsgeschichte*. To this extent, *Begriffsgeschichte*—however varied its own methods and apart from its actual empirical yield—is a kind of propaedeutic for a historical epistemology: it leads to a theory of history.

While "space of experience" and "horizon of expectation" as historical categories will be discussed in the following, it must be made clear that both terms will not themselves be investigated as concepts embodied in the source-language. Indeed, no conscious attempt will be made to historically deduce the background of these terms, an approach different from what one might usually expect from a professional historian of concepts. But there are research situations in which disregard of historicogenetic questions can sharpen the view of history. In any case, the systematic claim raised by the following remains clearer as a result of doing away with an initial historicization of one's own position.

It is apparent from everyday usage that, as expressions, "experience" and "expectation" do not initially convey any historical reality in the way that historical designations and appellations do. It is obvious that names such as "the Potsdam Agreement," "the ancient slave economy," or "the Reformation" indicate historical events, conditions, or processes. In this respect, "experience" and "expectation" are merely formal categories, for what is experienced and what is expected at any one time cannot be deduced from the categories themselves. The formal prospect of deciphering history in its generality by means of this polarity can only intend the outlining and establishment of the conditions of possible histories, and not this history itself. This then is a matter of epistemological categories which assist in the foundation of the possibility of a history. Put differently, there is no history which could be constituted independently of the experiences and expectations of active human agents. With this, however, nothing is yet said about a given concrete past, present, or future history.

This formalistic property is shared by our concepts with numerous other terms in historical science. "Master and servant," "friend and foe," "war and peace," and "forces of production and relations of production" come to mind; one might also think of the categories of social labor, political generations, constitutional forms, social and political agencies, or of limit, of space and time.

This property always involves categories which tell us nothing of a particular limit, a particular constitution, and so on. But that this limit, this constitution, or this experience and that expectation are questioned and brought to our attention presupposes the categorical use of the expressions.

A characteristic of practically all of the formal categories named here is that they all are, or were, historical; that is, economic, political or social concepts that come from the lived world. Here they perhaps share the advantage of theoretical concepts which in Aristotle convey meaning even on the basis of the form of the word itself, the everyday world of politics being preserved in its reflection. But it becomes clear when we consider the prescientific world with its social and political concepts that the list of formal categories deducible from it can be differentiated and graded. Who would deny that terms like "democracy," "war or peace," or "domination and servitude" are richer, more concrete, more perceptible, and more visible than our two categories "experience" and "expectation"?

Evidently, the categories "experience" and "expectation" claim a higher, or perhaps the highest, degree of generality, but they also claim an indispensable application. Here they resemble, as historical categories, those of time and space.

This can be explained semantically: concepts drenched with reality (cited above) presuppose, as categories, alternatives; meanings that they exclude. They thereby constitute more closely defined and concrete semantic fields, even if these remain related to one another. The category of labor thus refers to necessity, war to peace and vice versa, a frontier to an interior and an exterior space, a political generation to another or to its biological correlate, productive forces to production relations, democracy to monarchy, and so forth. The conceptual couple "experience" and "expectation" is clearly of a different nature. The couple is redoubled upon itself; it presupposes no alternatives; the one is not to be had without the other. No expectation without experience, no experience without expectation.

Without fruitlessly ranking them, it can be said that all of the conditional categories of possible histories named above are open to use in isolation, but none of them are conceivable without also being constituted in terms of experience and expectation. Accordingly, these two categories are indicative of a general human condition; one could say that they indicate an anthropological condition without which history is neither possible nor conceivable.

Novalis, another witness from the time when historical theory became fully fledged and before it was consolidated within idealistic systems, formulated this in *Heinrich von Ofterdingen*. The real sense of the histories of men developed quite late, he opined, alluding to the discovery of history in the eighteenth century. It was only when one was in a position to survey a long series and able to be discriminating, not maliciously confusing—only then did one "observe the covert inter-linking of the before and after, and learn how to compose history from hope and memory."[3]

*Geschichte* did not then primarily mean the past, as it did later; rather it indicated that covert connection of the bygone with the future whose relationship can only be perceived when one has learned to construct history from the modalities of memory and hope.

Notwithstanding the Christian background of this view, there is here an authentic case of that transcendental definition of history referred to at the beginning of this essay. The conditions of possibility of real history are, at the same time, conditions of its cognition. Hope and memory, or expressed more generally, expectation and experience— for expectation comprehends more than hope, and experience goes deeper than memory—simultaneously constitute history and its cognition. They do so by demonstrating and producing the inner relation between past and future earlier, today, or tomorrow.

This brings us to the thesis: experience and expectation are two categories appropriate for the treatment of historical time because of the way that they embody past and future. The categories are also suitable for detecting historical time in the domain of empirical research since, when substantially augmented, they provide guidance to concrete agencies in the course of social or political movement.

Take as a simple example the experience of the execution of Charles I, which revealed, over a century later, the horizon of expectation of Turgot as he urged upon Louis XVI reforms which should preserve him from the same fate. Turgot's warnings were in vain. Nonetheless, between the past English and the approaching French Revolution, there was a temporal relation that was ascertainable and revealed a relation that went beyond mere chronology. Concrete history was produced within the medium of particular experiences and particular expectations.

But our two concepts are not only contained within the concrete process of history and help its forward movement. They belong at the same time to those categories which are the formal determinants required to disclose this process to add it to our historical knowledge. They are indicative of the mortality (*Zeitlichkeit*) of men and thus, metahistorically if you wish, of the mortality of history.

An attempt will be made to elaborate this thesis in two stages. First, we will outline the metahistorical dimension: the degree to which experience and expectation are, as anthropological givens, the condition of possible histories.

Second, we will try to historically demonstrate that the classification of experience and expectation has been displaced and changed during the course of history. If the proof is a success, it will have been shown that historical time is not simply an empty definition, but rather an entity which alters along with history and from whose changing structure it is possible to deduce the shifting classification of experience and expectation.

## Space of Experience and Horizon of Expectation as Metahistorical Categories

If we begin with an outline of the metahistorical and thus anthropological meanings of our categories, it is hoped that the reader will forgive the brevity of this sketch, dictated by a desire to maintain some proportion in the arrangement of the text. Without metahistorical definitions directed toward the temporality of history we would, in using our terms in the course of empirical research, get caught up by the vortex of its historicization.

For this reason, some definitions can be offered: experience is present past, whose events have been incorporated and can be remembered. Within experience a rational reworking is included, together with unconscious modes of conduct which do not have to be present in awareness. There is also an element of alien experience contained and preserved in experience conveyed by generations or institutions. It was in this sense that *Historie*, since time immemorial, was understood as knowledge of alien experience.

Similarly with expectation: at once person-specific and interpersonal, expectation also takes place in the today; it is the future made present; it directs itself to the not-yet, to the nonexperienced, to that which is to be revealed. Hope and fear, wishes and desires, cares and rational analysis, receptive display and curiosity: all enter into expectation and constitute it.

Despite their respective present-centeredness, these are not symmetrical complementary concepts which might, for instance, as in a mirror image, mutually relate past and future.[4] Experience and expectation, rather, are of different orders. This is illuminated by a remark of Graf Reinhard, who wrote to Goethe in 1820 after the surprising renewal of revolution in Spain: "You are quite right, my friend, in what you say about experience. For individuals it is always too late, while it is never available to governments and peoples." The French diplomat had seized upon an expression of Goethe's which had at that time become widely used (for instance in Hegel), an expression which testifies to the end of the direct applicability of historical teachings. To explain why, I would like to draw attention to the following passage, notwithstanding the historical situation within which this statement was first conceived:

This is because completed experience is united into a focus, while that which has yet to be made is spread over minutes, hours, days, years, and centuries; consequently, that which is similar never appears to be so, since in the one case one sees only the whole while in the other only the individual parts are visible.[5]

Past and future never coincide, or just as little as an expectation in its entirety can be deduced from experience. Experience once made is as complete as its occasions are past; that which is to be done in the future, which is anticipated in terms of an expectation, is scattered among an infinity of temporal extensions.

This condition, which was observed by Reinhard, corresponds to our metaphorical description. Time, as it is known, can only be expressed in spatial metaphors, but all the same, it is more illuminating to speak of "space of experience" and "horizon of expectation" than of "horizon of experience" and "space of expectation," although there is still some meaning in these expressions. What is at stake here is the demonstration that the presence of the past is distinct to the presence of the future.

It makes sense to say that experience based on the past is spatial since it is assembled into a totality, within which many layers of earlier times are simultaneously present, without, however, providing any indication of the before and after. There is no experience that might be chronologically calibrated—though datable by occasion, of course, since at any one time it is composed of what can be recalled by one's memory and by the knowledge of others' lives. Chronologically, all experience leaps over time; experience does not create continuity in the sense of an additive preparation of the past. To borrow an image from Christian Meier, it is like the glass front of a washing machine, behind which various bits of the wash appear now and then, but are all contained within the drum.

By contrast, it is more precise to make use of the metaphor of an expectational horizon instead of a space of expectation. The horizon is that line behind which a new space of experience will open, but which cannot yet be seen. The legibility of the future, despite possible prognoses, confronts an absolute limit, for it cannot be experienced.

A recent political joke throws light on this:

"Communism is already visible on the horizon," declared Khrushchev in a speech.
Question from the floor: "Comrade Khrushchev, what is a 'horizon'?"
"Look it up in a dictionary," replied Nikita Sergeevich.
At home the inquisitive questioner found the following explanation in a reference work: "Horizon, an apparent line separating the sky from the earth which moves away when one approaches it."[6]

Notwithstanding the political point, it is possible to see that what is expected of the future is evidently limited in a manner different from that which has been experienced in the past. Cultivated expectations can be revised; experiences one has had are collected.

Today it can be expected of experiences that they will repeat and confirm themselves in the future. On the other hand, one cannot experience an expectation in the same way today. The prospect of the future, raising hopes or anxieties, making one precautionary or planful, is certainly reflected within consciousness. In this respect, even expectation can be experienced. But the intended conditions, situations, or consequences of expectation are not themselves experiential entities. Experience is specified by the fact that it has processed past occurrence, that it can make it present, that it is drenched with reality, and that it binds together fulfilled or missed possibilities within one's own behavior.

This, then, is a question not of simple counterconcepts; rather, it indicates dissimilar modes of existence, from whose tension something like historical time can be inferred.

This will be elaborated with a familiar example, the heterogeneity of ends: The unexpected undermines the expected ("erstens kommt es anders, zweitens als man denkt"—Wilhelm Büsch). This historical specification of temporal sequence is based upon the given difference of experience and expectation. The one cannot be transferred into the other without interruption. Even if one could formulate this as an irrefutable experiential statement, no precise expectations could be deduced from it.

Whoever believes himself capable of deducing his expectations in their entirety from his experience is in error. If something happens in a way different from what was expected, one learns from it. On the other hand, whoever fails to base his expectation on experience is likewise in error. He should have known better. There is clearly an aporia here that is resolved in the course of time. The difference indicated by both categories shows us a structured feature of history. In history, what happens is always more or less than what is contained by the given conditions.

This finding by itself is not really astonishing. Things can always turn out differently from what was expected: this is only a subjective formulation of an objective state of affairs in which the historical future is not the straightforward product of the historical past.

But, and this must be said, it could also have been different from what was experienced. An experience might contain faulty memories, or new experiences might open other perspectives. Time brings with it counsel; new experiences are collected. Thus, experiences had once in the past can change in the course of time. The events of 1933 have occurred once and for all, but the experiences which are based upon them can change over time. Experiences overlap and mutually impregnate one another. In addition, new hopes or disappointments, or new expectations, enter them with retrospective effect. Thus, experiences alter themselves as well, despite, once having occurred, remaining the same. This is the temporal structure of experience and without retroactive expectation it cannot be accumulated.

It is different with the temporal structure of expectation which, in the absence of experience, is not to be had. When they are fulfilled, expectations that are founded upon experience may no longer involve any degree of surprise. Only the unexpected has the power to surprise, and this surprise involves a new experience. The penetration of the horizon of expectation, therefore, is creative of new experience. The gain in experience exceeds the limitation of the possible future presupposed by previous experience. The manner in which expectations are temporally exceeded thus reorders our two dimensions with respect to one another.

In brief: it is the tension between experience and expectation which, in ever-changing patterns, brings about new resolutions and through this generates historical time. To introduce a final example, this can be seen very clearly in the structure of a prognosis. The substantial probability of a prognosis is not initially founded in that which someone expects. One can also expect the improbable. The probability of a forecasted future is, to begin with, derived from the given conditions of the past, whether scientifically isolated or not. The diagnosis has precedence and is made on the basis of the data of experience. Seen in this way, the space of experience, open toward the future, draws the horizon of expectation out of itself. Experiences release and direct prognoses.

But prognoses are also defined by the requirement that they expect something. Concern related to the broader or narrower field of action produces expectations into which fear and hope also enter. Alternative conditions must be taken into consideration; possibilities come into play that always contain more than can be realized in the coming reality. In this way, the prognosis discloses expectations which are not solely deducible from experience. To set up a prognosis means to have already altered the situation from which it arises. Put another way, the previously existing space of experience is not sufficient for the determination of the horizon of expectation.

Thus, space of experience and horizon of expectation are not to be statically related to each other. They constitute a temporal difference in the today by redoubling past and future on one another in an unequal manner. Whether consciously or unconsciously, the connection they alternately renew has itself a prognostic structure. This means that we could have identified a characteristic feature of historical time which can at the same time make plain its capacity for alteration.

## Historical Change in the Classification of Experience and Expectation

I come now to the historical application of our two categories. My thesis is that during *Neuzeit* the difference between experience and expectation has increasingly expanded; more precisely, that *Neuzeit* is first understood as a *neue Zeit* from the time that expectations have distanced themselves evermore from all previous experience.

This does not settle the question of whether we are dealing with objective history or only with its subjective reflection. Past experiences always contain objective conditions which enter as such into their reworking. Quite naturally, this has effects on past expectations. Even as future-oriented dispositions, they might have possessed only a kind of psychic reality. The impulses which they emit are not thereby any less effective than the impact of worked-over experiences, since the expectations have themselves produced new possibilities at the cost of passing reality.

Thus, to begin with, a few "objective" data will be nominated. It is easy to assemble them in the terms of social history.[7] The peasant world, which two hundred years ago comprised up to 80 percent of all persons in many parts of Europe, lived within the cycle of nature. Disregarding the structure of social organization, fluctuations in market conditions (especially those in long-distance agricultural trade), and monetary fluctuations, the everyday world was marked by whatever nature brought. Good or bad harvest depended upon sun, wind, and weather, and whatever skills were needed were passed on from generation to generation. Technical innovations, which did exist, took a long time to become established and thus did not bring about any rupture in the pattern of life. It was possible to adapt to them without putting the previous store of experience in disarray. Even wars were treated as events sent by God. Similar things are true of the urban life of the artisan whose guild regulations, however restrictive they might be individually, made sure that everything would remain the way it was. That they be felt restrictive already presupposes the new horizon of expectation of a freer economy.

This picture is oversimplified, of course, but it is clear enough for our problem: the expectations cultivated in this peasant-artisan world (and no other expectations could be cultivated) subsisted entirely on the experiences of their predecessors, experiences which in turn became those of their successors. If anything changed, then it changed so slowly and in such a long-term fashion that the rent between previous experience and an expectation to be newly disclosed did not undermine the traditional world.

This almost seamless transference of earlier experiences into coming expectations cannot be said to be true of all strata in exactly the same way. The world of politics, with its increasingly mobile instruments of power (two striking examples are the Crusades and later the annexation of distant lands); the intellectual world spawned by the Copernican revolution; and the sequence of technical inventions and discoveries in early modernity: in all these areas one must presuppose a consciousness of difference between traditional experience and coming expectation. "Quot enim fuerint errorum impedimenta in praeterito, tot sunt spei argumenta in futurum," as Bacon said.[8] Above all there, where an experiential space was broken up within a generation, all expectations were shaken and new ones promoted. Since the time of the Renaissance and the Reformation this vibrant tension affected ever more social strata.

As long as the Christian doctrine of the Final Days set an immovable limit to the horizon of expectation (roughly speaking, until the mid-seventeenth century), the future remained bound to the past. Biblical revelation and Church administration had limited the tension between experience and expectation in such a way that it was not possible for them to break apart. This will be briefly outlined here.

Expectations that went beyond all previous experience were not related to this world. They were directed to the so-called Hereafter, enhanced apocalyptically in terms of the general End of the World. None of the disappointments that arose when it once more became evident that a prophecy of the End of the World had failed could alter this basic structure of anticipation.

It was always possible to reproduce a prophecy that had not been fulfilled. Moreover, the error revealed by the nonfulfillment of such an expectation itself became proof that the next forecast of the End of the World would be even more probable. The iterative structure of apocalyptical expectation ensured that contrary experiences made at the level of this world would be disallowed. They testified *ex post* the opposite from what they had initially seemed to confirm. This then is a matter of expectations that no contrary experience can revise because they extend beyond this world into the next.

It is possible now to explain what today seems to be a state of affairs resistant to rational comprehension. Between one disappointed expectation of the End and the next passed several generations, so that the resumption of a prophecy concerning the End of the World was embedded in the natural generational cycle. To this extent, long-term, worldly, everyday experiences never collided with expectations that reached toward the End of the World. The contrary force of Christian expectation and worldly experience remained in relation without contradicting each other. Accordingly, the eschatology could be reproduced to the extent that and as long as the space of experience on this world did not itself change fundamentally.

The opening of a new horizon of expectation via the effects of what was later conceived as "progress" changed this situation.[9] Terminologically, the spiritual *profectus* was either displaced or dissolved by a worldly *progressus*. The objective of possible completeness, previously only attainable in the Hereafter, henceforth served the idea of improvement on earth and made it possible for the doctrine of the Final Days to be superseded by the hazards of an open future. Ultimately, the aim of completeness was temporalized (first by Leibniz) and brought into the process of worldly occurrences: *progressus est in infinitum perfectionis*.[10] As Lessing concluded, "I believe that the Creator had to make all that he created capable of becoming more complete, if it was to remain in the state of completeness which he had created."[11] Corresponding to the doctrine of perfection, the form *perfectionnement*, to which Rousseau assigned the basic historical sense of the "perfectibilité" of men, was made in France. Henceforth history could be regarded as a long-term process of growing fulfillment which, despite setbacks and deviations, was ultimately planned and carried out by men themselves. The objectives were then transferred from one generation to the next, and the effects anticipated by plan or prognosis became the titles of legitimation of political action. In sum, from that time on, the horizon of expectation was endowed with a coefficient of change that advanced in step with time.

It was not just the horizon of expectation that gained a historically new quality which was itself constantly subject to being overlaid with utopian conceptions. The space of experience also had increasingly altered its form. The concept "progress" was first minted toward the end of the eighteenth century at the time when a wide variety of experiences from the previous three centuries were being drawn together. The solitary and universal concept of progress drew on numerous individual experiences, which entered ever more deeply into everyday life, as well as on sectoral progress that had never before existed in this way. Examples are the Copernican revolution,[12] the slowly developing new technology, the discovery of the globe and its people living at various levels of advancement, and the dissolution of the society of orders through the impact of industry and capital. All such instances are indicative of the contemporaneity of the noncontemporaneous, or perhaps, rather, of the nonsimultaneous occurring simultaneously. In the words of Friedrich Schlegel, who sought to capture the *Neuzeitliche* in terms of history in the progressive mode:

The real problem of history is the inequality of progress in the various elements of human development [*Bildung*]; in particular, the great divergence in the degree of intellectual and ethical development.[13]

Progress thus combined experiences and expectations, both endowed with a temporal coefficient of change. As part of a group, a country, or finally, a class, one was conscious of being advanced in comparison with the others; or one sought to catch up with or overtake the others. One might be superior technically and look down on previous states of development enjoyed by other peoples, whose guidance was thus a justifiable task for their civilized superiors. One saw in the hierarchy of orders a static ranking which in the future would be superseded by the pressure of progressive classes. It is possible to extend these examples. What interests us here is that progress was directed toward an active transformation of this world, not the Hereafter, no matter how diverse the actual relationship between Christian expectation of the future and progress might be when registered by intellectual history. What was new was that the expectations that reached out for the future became detached from all that previous experience had to offer.

Even the new experience gained from the annexation of lands overseas and from the development of science and technology was still insufficient for the derivation of future expectations. From that time on, the space of experience was no longer limited by the horizon of expectations; rather, the limits of the space of experience and of the horizon of expectations diverged.

It became a rule that all previous experience might not count against the possible otherness of the future. The future would be different from the past, and better, to boot. All of Kant's efforts as a historical philosopher had as their aim the ordering of all objections based on experience, contradicting this axiom in such a way that they actually confirmed the expectation of progress. Kant strenuously opposed the thesis that, as he once summarized it, "things would always remain as they were" and that, consequently, one could not forecast anything which was historically new.[14]

This statement contains a reversal of all the usual forms of historical forecast customary until then. He who had previously become involved with prognosis instead of prophecy naturally drew upon the experiential space of the past, whose given entities were studied and then projected far into the future. Precisely because things would remain as they had always been, it was possible for someone to foretell the future. This was argued by Machiavelli: "He who wishes to foretell the future must look into the past, for all things on earth have at all times a similarity with those of the past."[15] Even David Hume argued in this way when he asked himself whether the British form of government tended more to absolute monarchy or to a republic.[16] He was still bound up in the network of Aristotelian constitutional forms which limited the number of possible variations. Above all , every politician dealt in these terms.

Kant, who may have been the originator of the term *Fortschritt* (progress), indicates the shift that concerns us here. A forecast which basically anticipated what had already occurred was for him no prognosis, for this contradicted his expectation that the future would be better because it should be better. Thus, experience of the past and expectation of the future were no longer in correspondence, but were progressively divided up. Pragmatic prognosis of a possible future became a long-term expectation of a new future. Kant conceded that "the task of progressive advance is not soluble directly on the basis of experience." But he added that new experiences, such as the French Revolution, could be accumulated in the future, in such a way that the "instruction of frequent experience" might secure a sustained "advance to the better."[17] Such a statement could only be conceived after history in general was formulated and experienced as unique; as unique not merely in the individual case, but in its entirety, as a totality opened toward a progressive future.

If the whole of history is unique, then so must the future be: distinct, that is, from the past. This historicophilosophical axiom, a result of the Enlightenment and an echo from the French Revolution, provided the foundation for "history in general" as well as for "progress." Both are concepts which achieve their historicophilosophical plenitude only with their lexical formation; both indicate the same substantive content; that is, no longer can expectation be satisfactorily deduced from previous experience.

The emergence of the progressive future was also accompanied by a change in the historical valency of the past. Woltmann wrote in 1799:

The French Revolution was for the whole world a phenomenon that appeared to mock all historical wisdom, daily developing out of itself new phenomena which one knew less and less how to come to terms with.[18]

The rupture in continuity was one of the generalized topoi of the time; thus, as Creuzer concluded in 1803, "didactic purpose is incompatible with *Historie*."[19] History, processualized and temporalized to constant singularity, could no longer be taught in an exemplary fashion. Historical experience descending from the past could no longer be directly extended to the future. As Creuzer continued, history had to be "considered afresh, newly explained by each new generation of progressing mankind." Stated differently, the critical reworking of the past, the formation of the Historical school, was founded upon the same conditions that had set progress free into the future.

This finding cannot simply be dismissed as modern ideology, although ideology and ideology-critique have taken up various positions and perspectives, stemming from the difference between experience and expectation. Our initial systematic reflections, whose historical background has in the meantime become evident, referred us to the asymmetry between space of experience and horizon of expectation as an asymmetry which could be deduced anthropologically. The first attempt to grasp *neue Zeit* as *Neuzeit* involved the restriction of this asymmetry to an irreversible progress and its one-sided construal as such. "Progress" is the first genuinely historical concept which reduced the temporal difference between experience and expectation to a single concept.

It was always a matter of assimilating experiences which could no longer be inferred from previous experience; and thus, accordingly, the formulation of expectations which could not have been nurtured previously. This challenge increased in scope during the whole of the period that is today called *frühe Neuzeit*. It sustained a potential utopian surplus, and it led to the cataract of events in the French Revolution. With this, the previous world of social and political experience, still bound up in the sequence of generations, was blown apart. "The more directly the history of succeeding occurrences is forced together, the more vehement and generalized will be dispute," as Friedrich Perthes, among many others, observed. Earlier epochs had only known changes of direction which took centuries:

Our time has, however, united in three contemporary, existing generations, the completely incommensurable. The monstrous contrasts of the years 1750, 1789, and 1815 dispense with all interim and appear in men now living not as a sequence but as coexistence, according to whether they are grandfather, father, or grandson.[20]

The one process of time became a dynamic of a coexisting plurality of times.

What progress had conceptualized—that, in brief, old and new collided, in science and in art, from country to country, from *Stand* to *Stand*, and from class to class—had, since the French Revolution, become the lived experience of the everyday. Generations did live in the same experiential space, but their perspective was interrupted according to political generation and social standpoint. Since then there has existed and does exist the consciousness of living in a transitional period that graduates the difference between experience and expectation in distinct temporal phases.

From the late eighteenth century, another finding joins the one we have just discussed: that of technoindustrial progress, which has an impact, albeit a varying impact, upon everyone. It became a general empirical principle of scientific invention and its industrial application that they gave rise to an expectation of progress that could not be calculated in advance. A future not inferable from experience released all the same the certainty of an expectation that scientific inventions and discoveries would bring about a new world. Science and technology have stabilized progress as a temporally progressive difference between experience and expectation.

Finally, there is an unmistakable indicator of the way in which this difference persists only through its constant renewal: acceleration. Politicosocial and scientific-technical progress change by virtue of the acceleration of temporal rhythms and intervals in the environment. They gain a genuine historical quality which is distinct from natural time. Bacon had to forecast that invention would accelerate: "Itaque longe plura et meliora, atque per minora intervalla, a ratione et industria et directione et intentione hominum speranda sunt."[21] Leibniz was able to endow this statement with experience. Finally, Adam Smith showed that the "progress of society" arose from time saved resulting from the increasing division of labor in intellectual and material production, as well as from the invention of machines. Ludwig Büchner, for whom "regress is local and temporary, progress however perpetual and generalized," in 1884 found it no longer astonishing "if today the progress of a century approaches that of a thousand years in earlier times"; the present produced something new practically every day.[22]

While it was an experience of established progression in science and technology that moral-political progress lagged or limped along behind, the maxim of acceleration also spread to this sphere. The idea that the future would not only change society at an increasing rate, but also improve it, was characteristic of the horizon of expectation outlined in the later Enlightenment. If hope evades experience, then Kant used the topos to reassure himself of the approaching organization of world peace, "since the times within which similar progress is made will hopefully become ever shorter."[23] The changes in social and political organization since 1789 did in fact seem to break up all established experience. Lamartine wrote in 1851 that he had lived since 1790 under eight different systems of rule and under ten governments. "La rapidité du temps supplée à la distance"; new events constantly pushed themselves between observer and object. "Il n'y a plus d'histoire contemporaine. Les jours d'hier semblent déjà enfoncés bien loin dans l'ombre du passée,"[24] by which he described an experience that was for the most part shared in Germany. Or, to take a contemporary witness from England: "The world moves faster and faster, and the difference will probably be considerably greater. The temper of each new generation is a continual surprise."[25] Not only did the gap between past and future become greater, but also the difference between experience and expectation had to be contantly and ever more rapidly bridged to enable one to live and act.

Enough of the evidence. The concept of acceleration involves a category of historical cognition which is likely to supersede the idea of progress conceived simply in terms of an optimization (improvement, *perfectionnement*).

This will not be discussed further here. The burden of our historical thesis is that in *Neuzeit* the difference between experience and expectation is increasingly enlarged; more precisely, that *Neuzeit* is only conceived as *neue Zeit* from the point at which eager expectations diverge and remove themselves from all previous experience. This difference is, as we have shown, conceptualized as "history in general," a concept whose specifically modern quality is first conceptualized by "progress."

As a control on the fertility of our two cognitive categories, two further semantic fields will, in conclusion, be outlined; and these do not, like "progress" and "history," have a direct relation to historical time. This will demonstrate that the graduation of social and political concepts according to the categories of "expectation" and "experience" offers a key to registering the shifts of historical time. The series of examples comes from the topology of constitutions.

First we will introduce the German linguistic usage associated with federal forms of organization and belonging to the necessary bases of human life and all of politics. The highly developed forms of association among the *Stände* in the Late Middle Ages led, but only after some delay, to the easily remembered expression *Bund*.[26] This expression was first formed (outside of Latin terminology) only when the shifting forms of association had found temporally limited but repeatable success. That which was at first only sworn verbally, that is, the individual agreements which for a specific period mutually bound, obliged, or associated the parties, was, as the outcome of its successful institutionalization, brought under the one concept, *Bund*. An individual *Bündnis* still had the sense of an active concept operating in the present. *Bund*, on the other hand, referred to an institutionalized condition. This is apparent, for example, in the displacement of the parties, when the *"Bund* of cities" became the "cities of the *Bund."* The real agent is hidden in the genitive. While a *"Bund* of cities" still placed emphasis on the individual partners, the "cities of the *Bund*" were ordered to an overall agency, the *Bund*.

In this way, the various activities of *Bündnisse* became retrospectively consolidated in a collective singular. *Der Bund* incorporated experience which had already been made and brought them under one concept. This is, therefore, what might be called a concept for the registration of experience. It is full of past reality which can, in the course of political action, be transferred into the future and projected onward.

It is possible to see similar developments in the expressions contained in the constitutional and legal language of the Late Middle Ages and early modernity. Without interpreting their meanings too systematically and thereby overlaying them theoretically, it can be said with respect to their temporal ranking that these are experiential concepts sustained by a contemporary past.

The temporal loading of three concepts of *Bund* that were first coined toward the end of the Holy Roman Empire—*Staatenbund, Bundesstaat, Bundesrepublik*—is quite different. These were minted around 1800 and were artificial words at first: *Bundesrepublik* was coined by Johannes von Müller, who almost certainly borrowed from Montesquieu's "république fédérative."[27] The three words are by no means based only on experience. Their purpose was to bring together in one concept specific federal organizational possibilities embodied in the declining *Reich* so that they could be used with benefit in the future. These concepts were not deducible in their entirety from the *Reich* constitution, but could nonetheless extract particular levels of experience that might be realized in the future as possible experience. Even if the Holy Roman Empire could no longer be conceived as a somewhat ill-defined imperium of Kaiser and Reichstag, at least the advantages of federal constitutional forms of semisovereign states could be saved for the new century: these advantages consisted in their intolerance of absolutist and revolutionary states. It is certain that this recourse to the experience of the old *Reich* anticipated the approaching constitution of the German *Bund*, even if the future constitutional reality could not yet be perceived. Within the *Reich* constitution longer-term structures were made visible and could already be sensed as coming possibilities. Because they concentrated obscure and hidden experiences, the concepts contained a prognostic potential which opened out a new horizon of expectation. This, then, no longer involves concepts that register experience, but rather, concepts that generate experience.

A third new term brings us fully into the future dimension: the concept *Völkerbund*, which Kant constructed so that he might transfer into a moral and political objective what had previously been expected on earth of the empire of God. More exactly, an anticipation (*Vorgriff*) was constructed out of a concept (*Begriff*). Kant hoped that the future would bring a republican *Bund* of self-organizing peoples at ever-shortening intervals, i.e., with increasing acceleration. Federative plans transcending individual states had been sketched before, but not a global scheme of organization whose fulfillment was a dictate of pracitcal reason. The *Völkerbund* was a pure concept of expectation that had no correspondence with an empirical past.

The index of temporality contained within the anthropologically given tension between experience and expectation provides us with a standard, by means of which we are also able to register the emergence of *Neuzeit* in constitutional concepts. When considered with respect to their temporal extension, the manner in which these concepts are formed testifies to a conscious separation of space of experience and horizon of expectation, and it becomes the task of political action to bridge this difference.

This is even more evident in a second series of examples. The Aristotelian forms of rule—monarchy, aristocracy, and democracy—which had until now sufficed in their pure, mixed, or decadent forms for the processing of political experience, were around 1800 reformed, both historically and philosophically. The three constitutional types were changed into a compulsory alternative: "despotism or republicanism," the alternative concepts gaining a temporal index in the process. The historical path led from despotism in the past to the republic of the future. The old political concept *res publica*, which until then had been able to cover all forms of rule, in this way assumed a restricted exclusiveness, which was, however, oriented to the future. While this process has been outlined only very briefly here, it had been developing for a long time. The result was perceptible at the time of the French Revolution. A concept of expectation developed out of a concept filled with experience that had been employed historically or theoretically. This perspectivistic shift can likewise be exemplified by Kant.[28] "Republic" was for him a defined objective, derivable from practical reason and constantly present for mankind. Kant called the path to it "republicanism," a new expression at the time. Republicanism indicated the principle of historical movement, and it was a moral dictate for political action to press it forward. Whatever constitution might be in force, it was necessary in the long run to displace the rule of men by men with the rule of men by law; i.e., to realize the republic.

Republicanism was therefore a concept of movement which did for political action what "progress" promised to do for the whole of history. The old concept of "republic," which had previously indicated a condition, became a telos, and was at the same time rendered into a concept of movement by means of the suffix "ism." It served the purpose of theoretically anticipating future historical movement and practically influencing it. The temporal difference between all previously experienced forms of rule and the constitution that was to be expected and toward which one should strive was in this way embodied in a concept which had a direct influence on political life.

This provides the outline of the temporal structure of a concept and which recurs in numerous concepts that followed it, whose designs for the future have since then sought to overtake and outbid. "Republicanism" was followed by "democracy," "liberalism," "socialism," "communism," and "fascism," to name only the most influential. All such expressions received in the course of their minting a modest amount (if any) of empirical substance, which in any case was not what was aimed at in the constitution of the concept. In the course of their terms' various constitutional realizations there naturally emerge numerous old experiences, elements that were already contained within the Aristotelian constitutional concepts. The purpose and function of concepts of movement distinguish them from the older topology. The Aristotelian usage placed the three constitutional forms, together with their mixed and decadent forms, in a cycle and rendered finite the possibilities of human organization, one form being deducible from the previous form. Concepts of movement by contrast open up a new future. Instead of analyzing a limited number of possible constitutional forms, these should promote the construction of new constitutional situations.

In terms of social history, these are expressions that react to the challenge of a society changing itself technologically and industrially. They served to reorganize under new slogans the masses, who have been stripped of *ständisch* structure; social interests and scientific and political diagnoses entered into them. In this respect they have the character of catchwords which promote the formation of parties. The entire sociopolitical linguistic domain is generated by the progressively emerging tension between experience and expectation.

All concepts of movement share a compensatory effect, which they produce. The lesser the experiential substance, the greater the expectations joined to it. The lesser the experience, the greater the expectation: this is a formula for the temporal structure of the modern, to the degree that it is rendered a concept by "progress." This was plausible for as long as all previous experience was inadequate to the establishment of expectations derivable from the process of a world reforming itself technologically. If corresponding political designs were realized, then, once generated by a revolution, the old expectations worked themselves out on the basis of the new experiences. This is true for republicanism, democracy, and liberalism, to the extent that history permits us to judge. Presumably this will also be true for socialism and also for communism, if its arrival is ever announced.

Thus it could happen that an old relation once again came into force; the greater the experience, the more cautious one is, but also the more open is the future. If this were the case, then the end of *Neuzeit* as optimizing progress would have arrived.

The historical application of our two metahistorical categories provided us with a key by means of which we could recognize historical time; in particular, the emergence of the so-called *Neuzeit* as something distinct from earlier times. At the same time, it has become clear that our anthropological supposition, the asymmetry of experience and expectation, was itself a specific cognitive product of that time of upheaval during which this asymmetry was progressively exposed. Our categories certainly offer more than an explanatory model for the genesis of a history in forward motion, which was first conceptualized with the term *neue Zeit*.

The categories also indicate to us the one-sidedness of progressive interpretation. It is evident that experiences can only be accumulated because they are—as experiences—repeatable. There must then exist long-term formal structures in history which allow the repeated accumulation of experience. But for this, the difference between experience and expectation has to be bridged to such an extent that history might once again be regarded as exemplary. History is only able to recognize what continually changes, and what is new, if it has access to the conventions within which lasting structures are concealed. These too must be discovered and investigated if historical experience is to be transformed into historical science.

# Notes

## Preface

1. J. G. Herder, *Metakritik zur Kritik der reinen Vernunft* (1799) (East Berlin, 1955) 68.

2. *Neuzeit*, literally, "new time." Modernity is not an exact translation here, but is appropriate to the extent that Koselleck is concerned with the varying historical constructions of "modernism." See also "Notes on Translation and Terminology." (Trans.)

3. *Geschichte*. See "Notes on Translation and Terminology" for the manner in which *Geschichte* and *Historie* are dealt with in this translation. (Trans.)

## Modernity and the Planes of Historicity

Koselleck's inaugural lecture as professor of history in Heidelberg in 1965. First published as "Vergangene Zukunft der frühen Neuzeit," in H. Barion, E.-W. Böckenförde, E. Forsthoff, W. Weber (eds.) *Epirrhosis. Festgabe für Carl Schmitt* (Berlin, 1968) Bd. 2, 549–66.

1. This is known in English as "The Battle of Issus." Points raised in a discussion with Dr. Gerhard Hergt are taken up in this essay. On the term *vergangene Zukunft*, see the use made of it by R. Aron, *Introduction to the Philosophy of History* (London, 1961) 39 ff.; and R. Wittram, *Zukunft in der Geschichte* (Göttingen, 1966) 5. On the interweaving of the three temporal dimensions, see N. Luhmann, "Weltzeit und Systemgeschichte," in P. Ludz (ed.) *Soziologie und Sozialgeschichte*, Sonderheft 16 of *Kölner Zeitschrift für Soziologie und Sozialpsychologie* (1972) 81–115.

2. Luther, *Tischreden* WA 678. On Altdorfer, see E. Buchner, *Albrecht Altdorfer und sein Kreis* (Munich, 1938); K. Oettinger, *Altdorfer-Studien* (Nuremberg, 1959); and A. Altdorfer, *Graphik*, ed. F. Winziger (Munich, 1963). For more recent work, see G. Goldberg, "Die ursprüngliche Schrifttafel der Alexanderschlacht Albrecht Altdorfers," *Münchener Jahrbuch der bildenden Kunst* 3 Folge, Bd. 19 (1968) 121–26; F. Winziger, "Bemerkungen zur Alexanderschlachts Albrecht Altdorfers," *Zeitschrift für Kunstgeschichte* Bd. 31 (1968) 233–37; and K. Martin, *Die Alexanderschlacht von Albrecht Altdorfer* (Munich, 1969); and finally, for other analyses of the painting, see J. Harnest, "Zur Perspektive in Albrecht Altdorfers Alexanderschlacht," in *Anzeiger des Germanischen Nationalmuseums* (Nuremberg, 1977) 67–77.

3. Luther, *Tischreden* 2576b (Addendum).

4. Robespierre, *Oeuvres complèts*, ed. M. Bouloiseau (Paris, 1958) t. IX, 495.

5. St. Augustine, *De civitate Dei* XVIII, c. 53; and XX, c. 7.

6. Luther, *Tischreden* WA 6893.

7. K. Zeumer, *Quellensammlung zur Geschichte der deutschen Reichsverfassung* (Tübingen, 1913) 346 ff.

8. Cited in R. Schnur, "Die französischen Juristen im konfessionellen Bürgerkrieg des 16.Jahrhunderts," in *Festschrift für Carl Schmitt* (Berlin, 1959) 186.

9. That is, religious confession was determined by and coextensive with the government of a territory by a ruler. (Trans.)

10. Grotius, *De jure belli ac pacis* (Amsterdam, 1670) 389, 398 (II:22, para. 15).

11. Approximately: "Objections to visions, based on biblical authority." (Trans.)

12. Regarding the above, see H. Grundmann, "Die Papstprophetien des Mittelalters," *Archiv für Kulturgeschichte* Jg. XIX (1929) 77–138; A. Hübscher, *Die grosse Weissagung* (Munich, 1952); A. Klempt, *Die Säkulisierung der universalhistorischen Auffassung* (Göttingen, 1960); W. E. Peuckert, *Die grosse Wende* (Darmstadt, 1966, 2 Bde); R. Taylor, *The Political Prophecy in England* (New York, 1911); and, fundamental for England, K. Thomas, *Religion and the Decline of Magic* (New York, 1971).

13. Guicciardini, *Ricordi* (Bari, 1935) II:58, 114.

14. Richelieu, *Testament politique*, ed. L. André, L. Noel (Paris, 1947) 334.

15. Leibniz, "Letter to Coste 19 December 1707," in *Leibniz — Deutsche Schriften*, ed. G. E. Guhraner (Berlin, 1838) II:48 ff.

16. D. Hume, "A Theory of Politics," in *Essays I*, ed. F. Watkins (Edinburgh, 1951) 162.

17. Barozzi, Berchet, *Relazioni degli ambasciatori Veneti nel secolo decimosettismo*, Ser. II: *Francia* (Venice, 1859) II. Cf. B. Nani, *Ein Venezianischer Gesandtschaftsbericht*, ed. A. von Schleinitz (Leipzig, 1920) 61, 72.

18. Lessing, *Die Erziehung des Menschengeschlechts, Gesammelte Werke*, Bd. 9 (Leipzig, 1858) 423.

19. Raynal, *Histoire Philosophique et Politique des établissements et du commerce des Européens dans les deux Indes* (Geneva, 1780) IV:488 ff. Dieckmann has proved in *Revue d'Histoire litteraire de la France* (1951) 431, that these passages are in Diderot's handwriting. Cf. Diderot, *Oeuvres politiques* (Paris, 1963) XXXIII.

20. Talleyrand, "Conversation in Erfurt, 9.October 1808," in *Mémoires*, ed. le Duc de Broglie (Paris 1891) I.

## Historia Magistra Vitae. The Dissolution of the Topos into the Perspective of a Modernized Historical Process

Based on Koselleck's faculty lecture, Heidelberg. First published as "Historia Magistra Vitae. Über die Auflösung des Topos im Horizont neuzeitlich bewegter Geschichte," in H. Braun, M. Riedel (eds.) *Natur und Geschichte. Karl Löwith zum 70. Geburtstag* (Stuttgart, 1967) 825–38.

1. F. von Raumer, *Erinnerungen* (Leipzig, 1861) I:118.

2. J. H. Zedler, *Universal-Lexikon* (Halle and Leipzig, 1732 f.) Bd. 13, 281 ff.

3. Diodorus Siculus, *Bibliotheca Historica*, ed. F. Vogel (Leipzig, 1883) I:1.

4. Cf. H. Friedrich, *Montaigne* (Bern, 1949) 246 ff.; and Jean Bodin, *Methodus ad facilem cognitionem historiarum* (Paris, 1572) chap. 3.

5. "History is the inexhaustible well from which everyone draws the water of example to wash away their filth." This was taken by K. F. Wander in his *Deutsches Sprachwörterlexikon* (Leipzig, 1867) I:1593, from Jassoy in *Welt und Zeit* (1816–19) V:338, 166, and III:80.

6. *The Histories of Polybius* (Bloomington, 1962) II:102, and I:40–41; see M. Gelzer, *Kleine Schriften* (Wiesbaden, 1963) III:115, 175 ff.; and A. Toynbee, *Greek Historical Thought* (New York, 1952).

7. "History indeed is the witness of time, the light of truth, the life of the memory, the messenger of antiquity; with what voice other than that of the orator should it be recommended for immortality?" Cicero, *De oratore* II:9,36 and 12,51.

8. "History is full of examples." Cicero, *De divinatione* I:50. See K. Keuck, "Historia, Geschichte des Wortes und seiner Bedeutungen in der Antike und in den romanischen Sprachen" (diss., Münster, 1934).

9. Manitius, *Geschichte der Literatur des lateinischen Mittelalters* (Munich, 1911) 478 ff.; and Zielinski, *Cicero im Wandel der Jahrhunderte* (Leipzig, 1908).

10. J. Fontaine, *Isidore de Seville et la culture classique dans l'Espagne wisigothique* (Paris, 1959) I:174 ff.

11. "The history of the world is not a burden to its readers insofar as what it says is useful. Many wise men have applied the past deeds of men which they have read in histories to their behavior in the present." Isidor of Seville, *Etymologianium sive originum libri XX* I:43. Cf. H. Friedrich, *Die Rechtsmetaphysik der Göttlichen Komödie* (Frankfurt, 1942), in which reference is made to Gregory the Great's toleration of expressly heathen examples (36).

12. "For if history records the good deeds of good men, the careful listener will be aroused to imitate this good; and if it relates the bad deeds of bad men, the devout and religious listener or reader will no less be stirred to avoid what is harmful and evil and to seek all the more carefully those things which he has learned to be good and worthy." Bede, *Historia ecclesiastica gentis anglorum, Proöm.* Cf. H. Beumann, *Widukind von Korvey als Geschichtsschreiber* (Weimar, 1950); and H. Grundmann, "Eigenart mittelalterlicher Geschichtsanschauung," in *Geschichtsdenken und Geschichtsbild im Mittelalter* (Darmstadt, 1961) 143 ff., 430 ff.

13. This is shown in Klempt, *Die Säkularisierung der universalhistorischen Auffassung* (Göttingen, 1960) 21 ff., 142. On Luther, see H. Zahrnt, *Luther deutet Geschichte* (Munich, 1952) 16 ff.

14. Machiavelli, *The Discourses* (Harmondsworth, 1970) 207–8.

15. Bodin, *La méthode de l'histoire* (Paris, 1941) XXXVIII:14, 30, 139.

16. See, for example, the *Lexicon Juridicum*, printed in several editions, of J. Kahl: "True history is an account of those things in whose doing the author played a part. But since the creation of the world, God has wanted history to be written in order that he might create before our eyes an image using examples from all ages, which we can follow when we are deliberating how we may best restore the state in times of crisis." See also G. A. Viperano, *De scribenda Historia* (Antwerp, 1569), where the task of the historian is described as "to tell of deeds which provide examples of how to act."

17. "A historical education consists of good practical examples which are to be gained from reading history. History is the theater of the whole universe, the mirror of time, a treasure chest of illustration, the eye of wisdom, the mirror of foolishness, weakness, and stupidity, the first principle of practical wisdom, the guardian and spokesman of the virtues, a witness to malice and wickedness, the prophet of truth, the mother city of wisdom, and a treasure house for posterity, and a κτγρα ιs αει [a possession forever]." J. H. Alsted, *Scientiarum omnium Encyclopaediae* (Lugdini, 1649) IV, Book 32.

18. De Mably, *De l'Etude de l'histoire* (Paris, 1778) chap. 1, which recommends the reading of Plutarch so that the ruler might choose his model.

19. "The teacher of future times." F. Wagner, cited by P. Moraw, "Kaiser und Geschichtsschreiber um 1700," in *Welt als Geschichte* (1963) 2:130.

20. Cited by T. Schieder in *Deutscher Geist und ständische Freiheit* (Königsberg, 1940) 149.

21. Cited by H. Haussherr in *Hardenberg, eine politische Biographie* (Köln, 1963) I:30.

22. Abraham de Wicquefort, whose work *L'Ambassadeur et ses fonctions* was repeatedly published after 1682, demanded that "the principal study of those who wish to be employed as ambassadors must be history." (Amsterdam, 1746) I:80. He named Tacitus and Commynes as teachers of equal standing for diplomats. See also V. Pöschl's introduction to Tacitus's *Historien* (Stuttgart, 1959) II ff. J. C. de Folard translated the *Histoire de Polybe* (Paris, 1727 ff.) and added a technical military commentary of contemporary standing. This work was so well regarded by Frederick II that he arranged for a section to be published, which was then translated into German (Leipzig, 1760).

23. Frédéric le Grand, *Oeuvres* (Berlin, 1846) 2: "Avant-Propos" of 1746 to the *Histoire de mon temps*, III ff.

24. "Whoever diligently reads history will see that sometimes the same scenes are reproduced, it being necessary only to change the names of the actors." Frédéric le Grand, *Oeuvres* 2:34. Cf. G. Arnold, *Wahres Christentum Alten Testaments* (1707) 1:5: "The same comedy or tragedy is played out in the world, with a constantly changing cast of actors." Frederick drew the conclusion that it was therefore preferable to follow the discovery of truths and progress in the enlightenment of intellect.

25. Frédéric le Grand, *Oeuvres* 9:166. The prognosis was deduced in 1770 as a consequence of Holbach's *Système de la Nature*.

26. Guicciardini, *Ricordi* (Bari, 1935) II:58, 110, 114, and, in contrast, I:114.

27. Gracian, *Criticón* (Hamburg, 1957) 179 ff.

28. "For it is a property of the human spirit that examples never provide a corrective for anyone; the follies of the fathers are lost on their children, and it is necessary that each generation commit its own" (written 17 December 1763). Frédéric le Grand, *Oeuvres* 5:233.

29. J. Burckhardt, *Weltgeschichtliche Betrachtungen* (Pfullingen, 1949) 31. See K. Löwith, *Jacob Burckhardt* (Stuttgart, 1966) 19, 53, 94.

30. G. W. F. Hegel, *Phenomenology of Spirit* (Oxford, 1977) 124.

31. "I go back from age to age to the remotest antiquity; but I find no parallel to what is occurring before my eyes: as the past has ceased to throw its light upon the future, the mind of man wanders in obscurity." A. de Tocqueville, *Democracy in America* (London, 1889) II:303. See H. Arendt's comments on this in *On Revolution* (London, 1963).

32. Cf. Heinsius, *Allgemeines Bücherlexikon (1700–1810)* (Leipzig, 1812) Bd. 2, in which the displacement of *Historie* by *Geschichte* is evident in the headings. This process is examined in detail by Koselleck in "Die Herausbildung des modernen Geschichtsbegriffs," in the article "Geschichte, Historie," in *Geschichtliche Grundbegriffe* Bd. 2 (Stuttgart, 1975) 647–717.

33. See J. Hennig, "Die Geschichte des Wortes 'Geschichte,' " *Deutsche Vierteljahrsschrift für Literaturwissenschaft und Geistesgeschichte* 16 (1938) 511–21; and H. Rupp, O. Köhler, "Historia—Geschichte," *Saeculum* 2 (1951) 27–38.

34. J. G. Droysen, *Historik* (Munich, 1943) 325, 357 para. 83.

35. H. Luden, *Handbuch der Staatsweisheit oder der Politik* (Jena, 1811) vii ff. The expression "history itself" forbids drawing the conclusion that an equivalence exists between the usage of Luden and the old topos, according to which the historian should only let the facts speak, or present only a mirror, or act as a painter reproducing the naked truth (an expression that continually reappeared from Lucian onward, through his reception and the Latin translation by W. Pirckheimer in 1514, and the German translation by Wieland in 1788). See R. Reichardt, "Historik und Poetik in der deutschen und französischen Aufklärung" (diss., Heidelberg, 1966). This self-conception of historians remains bound to a naive epistemology according to which the historical facts can and should be imitated as they are represented. Cf. Mosheim: History should "paint, but without colors. This means that it should adorn as little as possible the deeds and persons which it forms by comparisons, images, or fanciful turns of speech. Everything, if I might so express myself, should be shown and presented in the state of nature." *Versuch einer unpartheyischen und gründlichen Ketzergeschichte* (Göttingen, 1748) 42 ff. Here the bridge to Luden is provided by Möser, who demands in his preface to the *Osnabrückische Geschichte* (1768) (Berlin, 1843) I:vii that "in history, just as in a painting, it is only deeds that talk; impression, observation, and judgment must remain the part of the viewer."

36. Radowitz, *Ausgewählte Schriften* (Regensburg, n.d.) II:394.

37. "Die wahre Lehrerin ist die Geschichte selbst, nicht die geschriebene." G. von Mevissen, cited in J. Hansen, *Ein rheinisches Lebensbild* (Berlin, 1906) I:133. (This is from the year 1837 and is also directed against Hegel.) An early form of this critique may be found in Lichtenberg, *Gesammelte Werke* I:249: "That history is the teacher of life is a saying that is quite certainly used by many without further thought. One instead considers the source from which men, having raised themselves up through reason, draw this reason. It is found in affairs themselves; where things take place, and not where they are recounted." Lichtenberg does, however, resort to an old topos in maintaining that it was preferable for great men to write their own histories; Mevissen, by contrast, found even this to be without value, posing as a new task instead "the writing of the history of the reflection of history."

38. Droysen, *Historik* 354.

39. Ibid., 2d ed., Col. 386. [In modern German, *die Geschichte* (f. nom. sing.); plural, *die Geschichten*. (trans.)]

40. Benecke, Müller, Zarncke, *Mittelhochdeutsches Wörterbuch* (Leipzig, 1866) II:2, 115 ff.

41. In Zedler's *Lexikon*, there is still no entry for *Geschichte*. Adelung, who registered the displacement of *Historie* by *Geschichte* and sought in this way to promote this process, wrote: "Die Geschichte, plur. ut nom. sing. . . ." In its usual sense, he went on, history (*Geschichte*) constituted "a definite whole" and was true, i.e., not fabricated. "The history of this man is quite remarkable, that is, all that has occurred around him, his affairs. It is in this meaning that the word is frequently collective and without a plural: several affairs of one kind." *Versuch eines vollständigen Grammatisch-kritischen Wörterbuches der Hochdeutschen Mundart* (Leipzig, 1775) II:600 ff.

42. Bd. 34 (1778) 473. Anonymous review of C. F. Flögel, *Geschichte des menschlichen Verstandes* (Breslau, 1776).

43. "The principal perfection of history consists in order and arrangement. To attain such good order, the historian must embrace and possess all of his history; he must see it entirely as a single perspective . . . its unity must be shown." Fénélon, *Oeuvres complèts* (Paris, 1850) III:639 ff.: *Projet d'un traité sur l'histoire* (1714). I would like to thank H. R. Jauss for this reference; cf. his *Literarische Tradition und gegenwärtiges Bewusstsein der Modernität* (Göttingen, 1975) 173. For Germany, see Moser, who in his *Patriotische Phantasien* (Hamburg, 1954) IV:130 ff., outlines a plan for German *Reichsgeschichte* from the year 1495, writing that it would be necessary to lend it "the course and the power of the epoch." "As long as we do not elevate that plan of our history [*Geschichte*] to a unity, it will remain like the body of a snake which, flayed into a hundred parts, carries along each part of its body connected by the vestiges of remaining skin." A complete *Reichshistorie* can consist solely in the "natural history [of its] unification."

44. See M. Scheele, *Wissen und Glauben in der Geschichtswissenschaft* (Heidelberg, 1930).

45. *Einleitung zur richtigen Auslegung vernünftiger Reden und Schrifften* (Leipzig, 1742). Chladenius distinguishes between a *Geschichte an sich*, which is never completely apprehensible, and the idea of it; from this discrepancy he derives the points of view (para. 309), the compulsion for elaboration (para. 316), and the representation of histories in rejuvenated images. Cf. his *Allgemeine Geschichtswissenschaft* (Leipzig, 1752).

46. Cf. P. S. Jones, "A List from French Prose Fiction from 1700 to 1750" (diss., Columbia University, New York, 1939) (I owe this reference to H. Dieckmann); and H. Singer, *Der deutsche Roman zwischen Barock und Rokoko* (Köln, 1963). Singer's sources for the period 1690–1750 reveal far more *Geschichten* than *Romane*. For an overview, see W. Krauss, *Studien zur deutschen und französischen Aufklärung* (Berlin, 1963) 176 ff.; and H. R. Jauss, *Ästhetische Normen und geschichtliche Reflexion in der "Querelle des Anciens et des Modernes"* (Munich, 1964).

47. Aristotle, *De Arte Poetica* (Oxford, 1958) chap. 9, 1451b. For Lessing, see *Über den Beweis des Geistes und der Kraft* (Berlin, 1958) 8, 12; or *Hamburgische Dramaturgie* pt. 19 (3 July 1767). The traditional location of historical science did not prevent Lessing—as it did not prevent the Encyclopedists—from opening up new historicophilosophical paths, even if he did not use the concept *Geschichte* in this way in *Erziehung des Menschengeschlechts*. See H. Blumenberg, *Paradigmen zu einer Metaphorologie* (Bonn, 1960) 105.

48. Leibniz, *Theodizee* (Leipzig, 1932) Teil 2, 148, 149.

49. Kant, "Idea for a Universal History with a Cosmopolitan Purpose," in H. Reiss (ed.) *Kant's Political Writings* (London, 1970), Ninth Proposition. This antithesis was taken over by Köster in his article "Historie," in *Teutsche Encyklopädie* (1790) 15:652; it was first formulated by the Göttingen School.

50. B. G. Niebuhr, *Geschichte des Zeitalters der Revolution* (Hamburg, 1845) 41.

51. *Die Geschichte* "is of service not so much on account of individual examples to be followed, or to be avoided: these are often misleading and are seldom instructive. Its true and immeasurable utility in animating a sense of the treatment of reality and elucidating it is more a matter of the form taken by events, rather than the events themselves." W. von Humboldt, *Über die Aufgabe des Geschichtsschreibers* (1821), *Gesammelte Schriften* IV:41.

52. J. von Müller, *Vier und Zwanzig Bücher allgemeiner Geschichten besonders der europäischen Menschheit* (Stuttgart, 1830) VI:351. E. M. Arndt developed a similar transition from pragmatic instructiveness to the historical fulfillment of fate: "There is little instruction that we take as *Bürger* from the past, when we could take more, but . . . it is well that it is so. Only in the sense of totality can one pass from the past to the future; teachings, rules, and examples mean little on their own, for each era passes without pause according to its own spirit." *Der Bauernstand—politisch betrachtet* (Berlin, 1810) 109.

53. L. von Ranke, ed., *Sämtliche Werke* (Leipzig, 1867–90) Bd. 33, vi ff.

54. "Only too often do we in the present entertain the notion that our conditions are new and quite novel. We readily seize what our neighbor today thinks good; we seldom recall the teachings which past centuries provide. . . . The Book of History lies open; we can know the means by which nations become great, and why they decline; we have the concurrent examples of the ancient past and the freshest memory." *Historisch-Politische Zeitschrift* (Hamburg, 1832) I:375.

55. See, for example, K. von Rotteck, *Allgemeine Weltgeschichte* (New York, 1848) I:42 ff., paras. 70 ff.: "Uses of History."

56. Voltaire, *Philosophie de l'Histoire* (1765) (Geneva, 1963); reviewed by Gatterer in *Allgemeine Historische Bibliothek* (Halle) I:218; and translated and provided with a theological commentary in the following year by J. J. Harder, *Die Philosophie der Geschichte des verstorbenen Herrn Abtes Bazin* (Leipzig, 1768).

57. Cf. R. V. Sampson, *Progress in the Age of Reason* (London, 1956) 70 ff.; and H. M. Köster, *Über die Philosophie der Geschichte* (Giessen, 1775).

58. H. M. Köster, article on "Historie, Philosophie der Historie," in *Teutsche Encyklopädie* (1790) 15:666. Even in 1838, J. Schaller wrote in the *Hallische Jahrbücher* 81:41, that "History [*Geschichte*], as the representation of what has taken place, is in its realization necessarily at once philosophy of history."

59. Wherever Christian-theological interpretations of earthly events are placed in the genealogy of the modern concept of history, salvational history presupposes as a concept the decline of *historia sacra* and *historia profana* and the formation of an autonomous "Geschichte an sich." T. Wizenmann consciously took up the complete range of meaning of the modern concept of history in subtitling his history of Jesus, *Die Geschichte Jesu*, "On the Philosophy and History of Revelation" (Leipzig, 1789): "The time has finally come when one begins to treat the history of Jesus not simply as a repository for dogma, but as the higher history of mankind" (67). "I wished to confirm philosophy on the basis of history, rather than history on the basis of philosophy. History is the source from which everything must be drawn" (55).

His intellectual teacher, Bengel, was not yet able, as was Lessing, to make use of the modern concept of history in interpreting the succession of hitherto failed apocalyptic exegeses as a process of increasing exposure and consciousness, in which factual and spiritual *Geschichte* converge in a final and thus ultimately true prophecy (*Erklärte Offenbarung Johannis*, 1740). In this way, a theological model was set up for the *Phenomenology of Spirit* which made Kant remark in the "Contest of Faculties": "It is, however, a superstition to take belief in history as a duty and a part of blessedness" *Werke* VII:65. Only subsequent to the full development of idealistic historical philosophy was it possible for J. C. K. von Hoffman to coin in the forties the necessarily partial counterconcept of a salvational history. See G. Weth, *Die Heilsgeschichte FGLP* (1931) IV:2, and E. Benz, "Verheissung und Erfüllung, über die theologischen Grundlagen des deutschen Geschichtsbewusstseins," *ZKiG* 54 (1935) 484 ff.

60. "Natural history, improperly called history, and which is an essential part of physics." Voltaire, article "Histoire," in *Encyclopédie* 17, 555 ff. Adelung, *Wörterbuches* II:601: "In a very loose meaning, [the expression *Geschichte*] is used for the term 'natural history.' " On the historicization of the concept of nature, see Kant's *Allgemeine Naturgeschichte* of 1775 and his philological remarks in the *Critique of Judgement*, para. 82. See also L. Oken, *Über den Wert der Naturgeschichte besonders für die Bildung der Deutschen* (Jena, 1810). Marx's comment that history is the "true natural history of men" is discussed by Löwith in *Sinn der Geschichte* (Munich, 1961) 43.

61. Cf. Kant, *Anthropology from a Pragmatic Point of View* (The Hague, 1974) 62.

62. Hegel, *Lectures on the Philosophy of World History. Introduction* (Cambridge, 1975) 21.

63. R. Kornmann, *Die Sybille der Zeit aus der Vorzeit* (Regensburg, 1814) I:84.

64. Goethe, Reinhard, *Briefwechsel* (Frankfurt, 1957) 246.

65. D'Alembert, *Discours préliminaire de l'Encyclopédie* (1751).

66. "Was man von der Minute ausgeschlagen, gibt keine Ewigkeit zurück." Schiller, "Resignation," in *Sämtliche Werke* (Stuttgart, 1877) I:46.

67. Von Schön: "If one does not take time as it comes, seizing the good within it and promoting it in its development, then time punishes." "Woher und Wohin" (1840), in *Aus den Papieren des Ministers . . . Th. v. Schön* (Halle, 1875) III:239.

68. Diderot, article "Encyclopédie," in *Encyclopédie* 12 (1781) 340.

69. Sieyès, *Was ist der dritte Stand?* (Berlin, 1924) 13 (extract from literary remains).

70. Macaulay later said that in France, where "the gulf of a great revolution completely separates the new from the old system," the history of the period before 1789 could be composed in a sober and unprejudiced manner. "But where history is regarded as a depository of title deeds, on which the rights of governments and nations depend, the motive to falsification becomes almost irresistible." In England the events of the Middle Ages retained their force. Decisions frequently were not reached in Parliament until "all the examples which are to be found in our annals, from the earliest times, were collected and arranged." T. B. Macaulay, *The History of England from the Accession of James II* (New York, 1849) I:24, 25.

71. Sieyès, "Histoire," in *Nouveau dictionnaire historique* (1791).

72. Malchus, then *Staatsrat* to the Kingdom of Westphalia, 14 July 1808, cited in F. Timme, *Die inneren Zustände des Kurfürstentums Hannover 1806–1813* (Hanover, 1893) II:510.

73. Kant, "Der Streit der Fakultäten," *Werke* VII:79–80.

74. See H. Taine, *Les origines de la France contemporaine* (Paris, 1878–94). See also Droysen: "The highest commandments determine what history has really occurred." *Das Zeitalter der Freiheitskriege* (Berlin, 1917) 256.

75. C. T. Perthes, *Friedrich Perthes' Leben* (Gotha, 1872) III:271 (between 1822 and 1825).

76. B. G. Niebuhr, *Geschichte des Zeitalters der Revolution* (Hamburg, 1845) 41.

77. Cf. Luther, Tischrede September–November 1532 (WA *Tischreden*, 1913) II:636 ff., 2756b: according to Melanchthon, the world would last another 400 years, "But God would shorten these because of the chosen; the world is in a hurry, since in these ten years there has been almost a new millennium."

78. Cf. Lessing, *Erziehung des Menschengeschlechts* para. 90. See also Robespierre, "Sur la Constitution, 10 May 1793": "The time has come to call upon each to realize his own destiny. The progress of human reason has laid the basis for this great Revolution, and the particular duty of hastening it has fallen to you." *Oeuvres complètes* IX:495. "Perpetual Peace" for Kant "is not just an empty idea . . . for we may hope that the periods within which equal amounts of progress are made will become progressively shorter." *Political Writings* 130.

79. Chateaubriand, *Essai historique, politique et moral sur les révolutions anciennes et modernes . . .* (Paris, 1861) 249. Cf. Jauss, *Aspekte der Modernität* 170.

80. Kant, "Streit der Fakultäten" 2 Abschn. 7.

81. F. Ernst, "Zeitgeschehen und Geschichtsschreibung," *Die Welt als Geschichte* 17 (1957) 137 ff.

82. See the discussion between Perthes, Rist, and Poel over the planning of the "europäische Staatengeschichte" after 1820 in Perthes, *Leben* III:23 ff.

83. Droysen, *Historik* 300 ff.

84. Savigny, *Zeitschrift für geschichtliche Wissenschaft* (1815) I:4.

85. T. Mommsen, *Römische Geschichte* (Berlin, 1882) III:477.

86. "History [*Geschichtskunde*] belongs to the domains of science which cannot be acquired directly by teaching and learning. For this it is partly too easy, partly too difficult." "Rektoratsrede, Berlin 1874," in T. Mommsen, *Reden und Aufsätze* (Berlin, 1905) 10.

87. *The Education of Henry Adams, An Autobiography* (Boston, 1918) 497.

# Historical Criteria of the Modern Concept of Revolution

First published under the title "Der neuzeitliche Revolutionsbegriff als geschichtliche Kategorie," *Studium Generale* (1969) 22:825–38.

1. For the history of the word and concept the following can be consulted: H. Arendt, *On Revolution*; K. Griewank, *Der neuzeitliche Revolutionsbegriff, Entstehung und Entwicklung* (Frankfurt a.M., 1969); R. Koselleck, *Kritik und Krise* (Frankfurt a.M., 1975); E. Rosenstock, "Revolution als politischer Begriff," in *Festgabe der rechts- und staatswissenschaftlichen Fakultät in Breslau für Paul Heiborn* (Breslau, 1931); F. W. Seidler, "Die Geschichte des Wortes Revolution, ein Beitrag zur Revolutionsforschung" (diss. phil., Munich, 1955).
The following will not provide a complete survey of the sources, since these can be found in the article "Revolution," in *Geschichtliche Grundbegriffe*. From the more recent literature, the following might be consulted: R. Reichardt, *Reform und Revolution bei Condorcet (Bonn, 1973); C. Dipper, Politischer Reformismus und begrifflicher Wandel* (Tübingen, 1976); and K.-H. Bender, *Revolutionen* (Munich, 1977). For a summary of the state of current research that takes up questions of conceptual history, see T. Schieder, *Revolution und Gesellschaft* (Freiburg i.Br., 1973).

2. B. Hauréau, "Révolution," in *Dictionnaire Politique* (1868) 846.

3. H. Ryffel, *Metabolé Politeion* (Bern, 1949).

4. See Bender, *Revolutionen* 19–27, on Le Roy's concept of revolution and his hope, typical of the emergent consciousness of progress, that a renewed decline might be avoided in the future.

5. Hobbes, *Behemoth or the Long Parliament* (London, 1889) 204.

6. "Revolution, die Umwälzung, Veränderung oder Ablauf der zeit, Revolutio regni, die Veränderung oder Umkehrung eines Königreiches oder Landes, wenn nämlich solches eine sonderliche Änderung im Regiment und Policey-Wesen erleidet." Sperander, *A la Mode—Sprach der Teutschen oder compendieuses Hand-Lexicon* (Nuremberg, 1728).

7. L. S. Mercier, *L'An deux mille quatre cent quarante* (London, 1772) 328. The quote is one of the most pointed and is explained as follows: "The happiest of all revolutions has had its point of maturity, and we now (in 2440) are reaping its fruits." The notes refer to the year in which the book appeared: "In some states this is an epoch which has become necessary; a terrible, bloody, epoch, but nonetheless the signal of liberty. I refer to civil war."

8. C. M. Wieland, "Das Geheimnis des Kosmopoliten-Ordens," in *Gesammelte Schriften* (Berlin, 1909) Bd. 15, 223.

9. Reichardt, in *Reform und Revolution*, raises objections to this model (326); cf. Bender, *Revolutionen* 107 ff.

10. Leibniz, *Nouveaux Essais sur l'Entendement Humain*, Book 4, chap. 16 in *Philosophische Schriften* (Darmstadt, 1961) 3/2:504.

11. See above, "Modernity and the Planes of Historicity," note 19.

12. Haréau, "Revolution," in *Dictionnaire Politique* 846.

13. See above, "Historia Magistra Vitae," note 79.

14. *Dictionnaire de l'Academie Français* (Berlin, 1800) suppl. to vol. I, 411.

15. " . . . die Rechte marschiere immer links, aber die Linke niemals rechts." This is not fully translatable, containing as it does a play on "legal" right and right as opposed to left in the political domain. (Trans.)

16. " . . . aus der französischen Revolution eine Révolution sociale das ist, eine Umkehrung aller jetzt bestehenden Staaten zu machen." In the same year, A. F. C. Ferrand published in London *Considerations sur la Révolution Sociale*.

17. Marx, "Critical Marginal Notes on the Article 'The King of Prussia and Social Reform.' By a Prussian" (1844), in *Collected Works* 3:205.

18. H. Heine, *Französische Zustände* (article IX, 16 June 1832), in *Sämtliche Schriften* (Munich, 1981) Bd. 5, 215.

19. Robespierre, "Speech on 18 Floréal II" (17 May 1794), in Garaudy (ed.) *Les Orateurs de la Revolution Française* (Paris, 1940) 77.

20. K. W. Koppe, *Die Stimme eines preussischen Staatsbürgers in den wichtigsten Angelegenheiten dieser Zeit* (Köln, 1815) 45.

21. "The principle of movement presupposes as a given fact a preceding revolution, but it requires that the subsequent reorganization of the previously existing political system does not remain at the level of this fact, not merely restricting the restructuring of the totality to mere reforms which gradually enter political life with circumspection, caution, and effect. The principle of movement seeks rather to eternalize the actual revolution, declaring it actually permanent so that all the powers the revolution has promoted and extended to their utmost might bring about the complete 'rebirth' of the entire internal life of the state." (Here the old metaphor of the cycle reemerges.) K. H. L. Pölitz, "Die politischen Grundsätze der 'Bewegung' und der 'Stabilität,' nach ihrem Verhältnisse zu den drei politischen Systemen der Revolution, der Reaction und der Reformen," *Jahrbücher der Geschichte und Staatskunst* (1831) H. l, 534 ff.

22. On Proudhon and Marx, see T. Schieder, "Das Problem der Revolution im 19.Jahrhundert," in *Staat und Gesellschaft im Wandel unserer Zeit* (Munich, 1958) 37, 54; and H. A. Winkler, "Zum Verhältnis von bürgerlicher und proletarischer Revolution bei Marx und Engels," in *Sozialgeschichte heute, Festschrift für Hans Rosenberg* (Göttingen, 1974) 326–53.

23. Marx, *The Class Struggles in France 1848 to 1850*, in *Collected Works* 10:47.

24. Marx, *The Eighteenth Brumaire of Louis Bonaparte*, in *Collected Works* 11:106.

25. Marx, *Class Struggles* 127.

26. Kant, "Streit der Fakultäten" 88.

27. Condorcet, "Sur le sens du mot 'révolutionnaire,' " *Journal d'Instruction sociale* 1 June 1793, *Oeuvres* (1847) 12:615–23; see Reichardt, *Reform und Revolution* 358.

28. F. Schlegel, "Athenäums-Fragmente," in *Kritische Schriften* (Munich, 1964) 82.

29. W. Weitling, *Garantien der Harmonie und Freiheit* (1842) (Berlin, 1955) 79.

30. F. J. Stahl, *Die Revolution und die constitutionelle Monarchie* (Berlin, 1848) 1.

31. L. von Ranke, "Tagebuchblätter, Unterhaltung mit Thiers 19.8.1841," in *Weltgeschichte* (Leipzig, 1910) 4:729.

32. See H. Tetsch, *Die permanente Revolution* (Opladen, 1973).

# Historical Prognosis in Lorenz von Stein's Essay on the Prussian Constitution

First published in *Der Staat* 4 (1965) 469–81.

1. Lorenz von Stein, *Geschichte der sozialen Bewegung in Frankreich von 1789 bis auf unsere Tage* (1959) III:194.

2. Kornmann, *Die Sybille*; see above, "Historia Magistra Vitae," note 63.

3. Hegel, *Lectures* 21. Hegel's statement that no one can learn from history is not related, as was the case with many of his contemporaries, to the acceleration of history. The world spirit united in itself knows no acceleration of its historical realization.

4. For Stein, see *Sozialen Bewegung* I:84, 146, 502.

5. Ibid., I:65.

6. Perthes, *Leben* II:146 ff., III:23 ff.

7. Lorenz von Stein, *Die Municipalverfassung Frankreichs* (Leipzig, 1843) 68.

8. See E. W. Bockenförde, "Lorenz von Stein als Theoretiker der Bewegung von Staat und Gesellschaft zum Sozialstaat," in his *Staat, Gesellschaft, Freiheit* (Frankfurt a.M., 1976).

9. K. G. Specht (ed.) Lorenz von Stein, *Begriff und Wesen der Gesellschaft* (Köln, 1956) 21.

10. Stein, *Soziale Bewegung* III:216.

11. Lorenz von Stein, "Zur preussischen Verfassungsfrage," *Deutsche Vierteljahrsschrift* (1852). See also C. Schmitt, "Die Stellung Lorenz von Steins in der Geschichte des 19. Jahrhunderts," *Schmollers Jahrbuch* (1940).

12. Stein, *Sozialen Bewegung* I:139 ff.

13. Stein, "Verfassungsfrage" 24.

14. Ibid., 36.

15. Ibid., 4.

16. Ibid., 35.

17. Ibid., 30.

18. Ibid., 12.

19. See the evidence in my book, *Preussen zwischen Reform und Revolution* (Stuttgart, 1975) 258 ff.

20. Stein, "Verfassungsfrage" 14.

21. E. R. Huber, *Deutsche Verfassungsgeschichte seit 1789* (Stuttgart, 1963) III:635.

22. Stein, *Sozialen Bewegung* I:149.

23. Stein, "Verfassungsfrage" 23.

24. Ibid., 21.

25. For details, see my *Preussen zwischen Reform und Revolution*.

26. Stein, "Verfassungsfrage" 35.

## Begriffsgeschichte and Social History

First published as "Begriffsgeschichte und Sozialgeschichte," in P. Ludz (ed.) *Soziologie und Sozialgeschichte*, Sonderheft 16 of *Kölner Zeitschrift für Soziologie und Sozialpsychologie* (1972) 116-31.

1. Epictetus, *Encheiridion* c. V.

2. The following thoughts are based on work associated with the editing of *Geschichtliche Grundbegriffe*. Further elaboration of these points can be found in the introduction to Bd. I. For an account of the evolution and present state of *Begriffsgeschichte*, see H. G. Meier, "Begriffsgeschichte," *Historisches Wörterbuch der Philosophie*, ed. J. Ritter (Basel, 1971) I:788-808.

3. A clear and bibliographically comprehensive account of political semantics can be found in W. Dieckmann, *Sprache in der Politik* (Heidelberg, 1969). In the area of method and theory, special mention should be made of R. Koebner, "Semantics and Historiography," *Cambridge Journal* 7 (1953); M. A. Cattaneo, "Sprachanalyse und Politologie," in R. H. Schmidt (ed.) *Methoden in der Politologie* (Darmstadt, 1967); L. Girard, "Histoire et lexicographie," *Annales* 18 (1963), which is a review of J. Dubois, *Le vocabulaire politique et social en France de 1869 à 1872* (Paris, 1962); and R. Koselleck (ed.) *Historische Semantik und Begriffsgeschichte* (Stuttgart, 1978).

4. G. Winter (ed.) *Die Reorganisation des Preussischen Staates unter Stein und Hardenberg* (Leipzig, 1931) Erster Teil, Bd. I, 316. The original reads: "Überhaupt gehört eine vernünftige Rangordnung, die nicht einen Stand vor dem anderen begünstigte, sondern den Staatsbürgern aller Stände ihre Stellen nach gewissen Klassen nebeneinander anwiese, zu den wahren und keineswegs zu den ausserwesentlichen Bedürfnissen eines Staates." For the sociohistorical context, see my *Preussen zwischen Reform und Revolution* 158, 190 ff., and its App. II for the conceptual categorization of *Staatsbürger* and other related terms.

5. F. Meusel (ed.) *Friedrich August Ludwig von der Marwitz* (Berlin, 1908-13) II/1:235 ff., II/2:43.

6. Koselleck plays on the word *Recht* here: by writing *(Vor) Rechte*, running them together in the same way that Hardenberg does, he draws attention to the fact that the rights of the *Stände* were at the same time privileges. (Trans.)

7. See N. Chomsky, *Aspects of the Theory of Syntax* (Cambridge, Mass., 1965) 161.

8. Cf. E. W. Böckenförde, *Die deutsche verfassungsgeschichtliche Forschung im 19. Jahrhundert* (Berlin, 1961).

9. Cf. M. Riedel, "Gesellschaft, bürgerliche," in *Geschichtliche Grundbegriffe* (Stuttgart, 1975) 2:719-800.

10. Cf. H. Lübbe, *Säkularisierung* (Freiburg, 1965); and H. Zabel, "Verweltlichung—Säkularisierung. Zur Geschichte einer Interpretationskategorie" (diss., Münster, 1968).

11. Cf. my article "Bund," in *Geschichtliche Grundbegriffe* (Stuttgart, 1972) 1:582-671.

12. *Sachgeschichte* is "factual" or "material" history. (Trans.)

13. P.-L. Weinacht, *Staat* (Berlin, 1968).

# History, Histories, and Formal Structures of Time

First published in R. Koselleck, W.-D. Stempel (eds.) *Geschichte, Ereignis und Erzählung* (Munich, 1973) 211-22.

1. St. Augustine, *De doctrina christiana* II, XXVIII:44.

2. Herodotus, *Historia* 3:80-83.

3. See G. Rohr, *Platons Stellung zur Geschichte* (Berlin, 1932); and the review by H. G. Gadamer in *Deutsche Literaturzeitung* Heft 42 (1932) 1979 ff.

4. Plato, *Laws* 691 B, 692 B.

5. See A. Momigliano, "Time in Ancient Historiography," *History and Theory* Beiheft 6 (1966) 12.

6. Cf. K. Weidauer, *Thukydides und die Hippokratischen Schriften* (Heidelberg, 1954).

7. St. Augustine, *Confessions* II:14–27.

8. St. Augustine, *City of God* XIX:12.

9. Ibid., IV:14 ff.

10. Ibid., XIX:5, 7.

11. Bossuet, *Discours de l'histoire universelle* (Paris, 1681) pt. 3, chaps. 1, 2, 9.

12. E. Gilson, *Les métamorphoses de la cité de Dieu* (Louvain, 1952).

13. Bossuet, *Discours*, pt. 2, chap. 15.

14. A. L. Schlözer, *Weltgeschichte* (Göttingen, 1785) Teil I, paras. 36, 76 ff.; and Kant, "Idea for a Universal History," in *Political Writings*, Ninth Proposition.

# Representation, Event, and Structure

First published as "Ereignis und Struktur," in R. Koselleck, W.-D. Stempel (eds.) *Geschichte— Ereignis und Erzählung* (Munich, 1973) 560–71. It is based on discussions at a 1970 conference of the research group "Poetik und Hermeneutic."

1. This essay is based to a great extent on the contributions of Fellmann, Greimas, Jauss, Lübbe, Stierle, Stempel, Szondi, and Taubes. I would like to acknowledge the stimulation I drew from them.

2. St. Augustine, *De doctrina christiana* II, XXIX:45.

3. G. Simmel, *Das Problem der historischen Zeit* (Berlin, 1916) 29.

4. Kant, *Anthropology* (The Hague, 1974) 62.

5. Cf. K.-G. Faber, *Theorie der Geschichtswissenschaft* (Munich, 1971) 100 ff.

6. Montesquieu, *Considérations sur les causes de la grandeur des Romains et de leur décadence* (Paris, 1951) 475.

7. Here it seems that there is an analogy between historical event and the work of art which, in becoming an "event," contains at the same time more and less than what was included in its predecessors. This "at once more and less" defines the axiom of uniqueness. This does not, of course, exclude the possibility of an infinite number of factors actually entering unaltered into an event so that it might become reality: this is the domain of structural conditions, which

in the case of art, tend to be explained in terms of style. On the whole, I do not want to strain this analogy between event and the work of art, however much a hermeneutic frame might cover them both. On this, see the contribution of Jauss to this collection ("Zur Analogie von literarischen und historischem Ereignis," in *Geschichte — Ereignis und Erzählung*). Every historical event contains temporal qualities in its execution and in its reception: duration, periodicity, and acceleration; but these are not relevant to a created work of art. The habit of referring to a work of art as timeless has, in comparison with historical events, an inescapable meaning. If all history is the history of effect and reception, this does not mean that everything that has an effect is constituted in the same way.

8. Cf. my "Einleitung" to *Geschichtliche Grunbegriffe* Bd. 1.

9. Stein, *Soziale Bewegung* III:194.

# Chance as Motivational Trace in Historical Writing

First published as "Der Zufall als Motivationsrest in der Geschichtsschreibung," in H. R. Jauss (ed.) *Die nicht mehr schönen Künste* (Munich, 1968) 129–41.

1. R. Aron, *Introduction to the Philosophy of History* 16. According to context, "chance," "accident," and "coincidence" are used interchangeably here to translate the original *Zufall*. (Trans.)

2. E. H. Carr, *What Is History?* (Harmondsworth, 1964) 98 ff.

3. Cf. the work produced by the school around Hugo Friedrich; K. Heitmann, *Fortuna und Virtus* (Köln, 1958); and H. Jansen, in *Kölner Romanistische Arbeiten* N.F. Heft 9. See also F. P. Pickering, *Literatur und darstellende Kunst im Mittelalter* (Berlin, 1966) 112 ff.; and E. Köhler, *Der literarische zufall und die Notwendigkeit* (Munich, 1973).

4. "Where then is the definition of Fortune? How does she receive her name from chance circumstances? If she be Fortune, all worship is in vain. . . . " St. Augustine, *De Civitate Dei* IV:18.

5. O. von Freising, *Chronica sive Historia de duabus Civitatibus* (Darmstadt, 1960) 10, 92 (a rare case in which "worldly fortune," not *fortuitis casibus*, is at issue), 130, 210, 290, 446.

6. Cf. H. Löwe, "Regino von Prüm und das historische Weltbild der Karolingerzeit," and H. Beumann, "Widukind von Korvei als Geschichtsschreiber und seine politische Gedankenwelt," both in W. Lammers (ed.) *Geschichtsdenken und Geschichtsbild im Mittelalter* (Darmstadt, 1961) 123, 133, 154.

7. Zincgref, *Emblematum Ethico-Politicorum Centuria* (Heidelberg, 1666) XCIV. See also the summary of the tradition, which is given in Zedler's *Lexikon* Bd. 9, 1545 ff.

8. Gracian, cited in Jansen in *Romanistische Arbeiten* 191 ff.

9. Boethius, *De Consolatione Philosophiae* lib. 2 (Zürich, 1949) 80.

10. Gracian, *Criticón* 116.

11. Pascal, *Pensées* (Paris, 1948) 162.

12. Frédéric le Grand, *Oeuvres* VIII:151.

13. See J. H. Brumfitt, *Voltaire, Historian* (Oxford, 1958) 105 ff.

14. *Carl Duclos' geheime Memoiren* (Berlin, 1792) I:15.

15. Frédéric le Grand, *Oeuvres* VIII:149, and chap. 25 of his *Antimachiavell*.

16. Ibid., 285.

17. Von Archenholtz, *Geschichte des Siebenjährigen Krieges* (Halle, 1791) 2.

18. Ibid., 40 ff.

19. Isidore of Seville, *Etymologianium* I:40 ff.

20. While it has not been undisputed, the idea, which has existed since Aristotle, that inner probability is more convincing than reality, is an argument which rendered creative thought (*Dichtung*) superior to history. This is because the former concerned itself with probability and not with facticity. Von Archenholtz made use of this train of thought, which was made known to him through Lessing, to elevate history above creative thought with the classical arguments of poetics. This is one of the ways in which the revaluation of history with respect to poetry took place in the eighteenth century. Cf. Blumenberg, *Paradigmen* 96–105.

21. Von Archenholtz, "Eine Begebenheit, wie erdichtet," in *Geschichte* 254.

22. Montesquieu, *Considérations* 475. His dictum was well known in the eighteenth century (cf. Brumfitt, *Voltaire, Historian* 113). This train of thought was certainly known to von Archenholtz, since he introduced a variation according to which recent history provided no examples "which might connect the gain or the loss of a single city with the fate of an entire monarchy" (*Considérations* 342). Since Frederick's strategy was based on movement, it would have been possible for him to leave the most important fortress in his country, Magdeburg, relatively lightly defended. It was not possible for his enemies to force a conclusion to the entire war through a single encounter here. In his essay on the great powers, in *Historisch-Politische Zeitschrift*, Ranke argued that the Seven Years War distinguished itself from all previous wars between states in that "for such an extended period of time, the existence of Prussia was continually at stake." One bad day would have meant the end. In seeking to identify the general causes preventing the collapse of Prussia, Ranke suggested that Frederick was not a captive of the pleasurable philosophy of the French. Frederick "creates his own rules; he rests on his own truth." The primary cause was that he "upheld himself morally." Notwithstanding the accuracy of this observation, it can be said that for Ranke, the antithesis between general causes and chance is subsumed by the concept of individuality. The continued effectivity of Montesquieu's differentiation of general trends and chance occurrences is noted by Carr, *What Is History?* 101–2, with respect to Marx and Trotsky.

23. Von Archenholtz, *Geschichte* 241.

24. Ibid., 44, 98.

25. Carr, *What Is History?* 99.

26. Ranke, article "Friedrich der Grosse," in *Allgemeine deutsche Biographie*.

27. Von Archenholtz, *Geschichte* 350.

28. The extent to which the consequences of such chance events is excluded in the modern world is demonstrated by Roosevelt's death in 1945. This led the National Socialists to draw a propagandistic parallel with the death of the tsarina in 1762 so that a historical-ideological

escape from an inescapable situation might be found. Roosevelt's death could not influence the course of the Second World War. The role of the hero had by this time been denaturalized in favor of historical structures which left ever less space for fortune, not only as a means of representation but also de facto.

29. Von Archenholtz, *Geschichte* 47, 174, 328, 350.

30. Von Humboldt, *Geschichtsschreibers* 24, 18.

31. See the critical review by H. G. Gadamer in *Philosophische Rundschau* 18 (1971) 61.

32. Leibniz, in Holz (ed.) *Metaphysische Abhandlung* Abh. 13, 1965:86; cf. *Theodizee* paras. 3 ff., and *Monadologie* paras. 31 ff. On the prehistory of theodicy with respect to the exclusion of chance, see Boethius, *De Consolatione* lib. 5.

33. C. M. Wieland, *Über die Behauptung, dass ungehemmte Ausbildung der menschlichen Gattung nachteilig sei, Sämtliche Werke* (Leipzig, 1857) 29, 311.

34. Hegel, *Lectures* 28.

35. Novalis, *Heinrich von Ofterdingen, Schriften* I:259.

36. Ranke, "Über die Epochen der neueren Geschichte" (1854), in Hoffmann (ed.) *Geschichte und Politik* (Stuttgart, 1942) 141.

37. Droysen, *Briefwechsel* II:282.

# Perspective and Temporality: A Contribution to the Historiographical Exposure of the Historical World

First published as "Standortbindung und Zeitlichkeit. Ein Beitrag zur historiographischen Er-schliessung der geschichtlichen Welt," in R. Koselleck, W. J. Mommsen, J. Rüsen (eds.) *Objektivität und Parteilichkeit in der Geschichtswissenschaft* (Munich, 1977) 17-46.

1. Dilthey, *Gesammelte Schriften* 7:205. In this essay, "Standortbindung" is rendered variously by "perspective," "positional commitment" and "restriction to a particular position"; the term literally means "locational binding," but this rendering is not suitable for the different ways it is used by Koselleck. (Trans.)

2. Lucian, *How to Write History*, in *Works* 6 (London, 1959) chap. 39; and Cicero, *De oratore* 15:62.

3. Cf. C. Weymann, "Sine ira et studio," *Archiv für Lateinische Lexikographie und Grammatik* 15 (1908); and J. Vogt, "Tacitus und die Unparteilichkeit des Historikers," *Würzburger Studien zur Altertumswissenschaft* 9 (1936).

4. Lucian, *How to Write History* chap. 51.

5. G. J. Voss, *Ars historica* (1623) (Lugdunum Bat., 1653) V:27.

6. J. S. Halle, article "Geschichte," in *Kleine Enzyklopädie* (Berlin, 1779) I:522. Cf. Reichardt, diss.

7. Blumenberg, *Paradigmen* 47 ff.

8. Fénélon, "Lettre à M. Dacier sur les occupations de l'Académie," in *Oeuvres complètes* 6:639.

9. J. C. Gottsched, *Versuch einer critischen Dichtkunst* (Leipzig, 1742) 354.

10. Ranke, *Zur Kritik neuerer Geschichtsschreiber* (Leipzig, 1824) 28.

11. Blumenberg, *Paradigmen* 55.

12. Ranke, *Englische Geschichte* (Berlin, 1860) 2, 3.

13. Lucian, *How to Write History* chap. 41.

14. Ranke, *Geschichten der romanischen und germanischen Völker von 1494 bis 1514, Sämtliche Werke* (1874) 33/34, VII.

15. Cited by Vogt, *Würzburger Studien* 1.

16. G. G. Gervinus, *Grundzüge der Historik* (Leipzig, 1837) 93 ff.

17. Ranke "Einleitung zu den Analekten der Englischen Geschichte," *Sämtliche Werke* 21:114.

18. Ranke, *Deutsche Geschichte im Zeitalter der Reformation* (Leipzig, 1881) I, x.

19. See the article "Geschichte, Historie," in *Geschichtliche Grundbegriffe* 2:597 ff.

20. See Ernst, "Zeitgeschehen und Geschichtsschreibung," op. cit.

21. J. A. Comenius, *Das Labyrinth der Welt und das Paradies des Herzens* (1623), (Lucerne, 1970) 105 f f.

22. Zedler, *Universal-Lexikon* 13:286.

23. The following evidence does not pretend to present a strict chronology of the argument, which differs from country to country and from language to language.

24. Chladenius, *Allgemeine Geschichtswissenschaft.* See especially chap. 11, "On old and foreign *Geschichten,*" and chap. 12, "On things of the future."

25. Chladenius, *Einleitung zur richtigen Auslegung vernünftiger Reden und Schriften* (Leipzig, 1742, reprinted 1969) 185 ff., and *Geschichtswissenschaft* 74 ff., 152.

26. Chladenius, *Einleitung* 188 ff., and *Geschichtswissenschaft* 100 ff.

27. Chladenius, *Geschichtswissenschaft* 127.

28. Ibid., chaps. 6 and 7.

29. Chladenius, *Einleitung* 237.

30. Chladenius, *Geschichtswissenschaft* 166, 151.

31. Ibid., 161 ff.

32. F. G. Klopstock, *Die deutsche Gelehrtenrepublik, Sämtliche Werke* 12:78 ff.

33. Fénélon, "Lettre" 638: "Projet d'un traité sur l'histoire."

34. Abbt, *Geschichte* (Halle, 1766) I:219.

35. J. C. Gatterer, "Abhandlung vom Standort und Gesichtspunct des Geschichtsschreibers oder der teutsche Livius," in *Allgemeine historische Bibliothek* (Halle, 1768) 5, 7.

36. J. G. Büsch, *Encyklopädie der historischen, philosophischen und mathematischen Wissenschaften* (Hamburg, 1775) 12.

37. A. L. von Schlözer, preface to Mably, *Von der Art, Geschichte zu schreiben* (Strasburg, 1784) 7.

38. G. J. Planck, *Geschichte der Entstehung, der Veränderungen und der Bildung unsers protestantischen Lehrbegriffs* (Leipzig, 1781) I, VII, and *Einleitung in die theologischen Wissenschaften* (Leipzig, 1795) 2:243.

39. Bengel, *Erklärte Offenbarung.*

40. J. S. Semler, *Neue Versuche, die Kirchenhistorie der ersten Jahrhunderte mehr aufzuklären* (Leipzig, 1787) 1 ff.

41. J. S. Semler, *Versuch einer freiern theologischen Lehrart* (Halle, 1777) 9.

42. Semler, *Neue Versuche* 3.

43. Semler, *Versuch* 33 ff., 8.

44. Semler, *Neue Versuche* 101.

45. Goethe, *Materialien zur Geschichte der Farbenlehre, Werke* 14:93.

46. F. Gentz, preface to Mallet du Pan, *Über die Französischen Revolution und die Ursachen ihrer Dauer* (Berlin, 1794) 20 ff.

47. F. Schlegel, "Über Fox und dessen historischen Nachlass (1810)," *Kritische Ausgabe* 7:115 ff.

48. F. Schlegel, "Über die neuere Geschichte. Vorlesungen 1810–11," *Kritische Ausgabe* 7:129.

49. Schlegel, "Über Fox" 116.

50. Schlegel, "Neuere Geschichte" 129.

51. "Even to hear talk of a religious, Christian, Catholic party" gives rise to "inner uneasiness and embarrassment." F. Schlegel, "Signatur des Zeitalters (1820–23)," *Kritische Ausgabe* 7:519.

52. Hegel, *Lectures* 30.

53. Ibid.

54. Perthes, *Leben* 2:240.

55. Ibid., 3:24 ff.

56. F. C. Dahlmann, *Die Politik* (Leipzig, 1847) 291.

57. Stein, *Municipalverfassung* 68.

58. L. Feuerbach, "Todesgedanken (1830)," *Sämtliche Werke* 1:48.

59. Gervinus, *Grundzüge* 92 ff.

60. Ranke, "Georg Gottfried Gervinus. Gedächtnisrede vom 27.9.1871," *Historische Zeitschrift* 27 (1872) 142 ff.

61. It follows from this that wherever theoretical premises are pregiven party-politically, and are not themselves open to critical examination, even the criteria of the objectivity of source exegesis does not suffice for the scientific conduct of historical research.

## The Historical-Political Semantics of Asymmetric Counterconcepts

First published as "Zur historisch-politischen Semantik asymmetrischer Gegenbegriffe," in H. Weinrich (ed.) *Positionen der Negativität* (Munich, 1975) 65–104.

1. Kant, *Metaphysics of Ethics*, pt. 2, para. 36 n.

2. R. J. Sattler, article "Barbaren," in *Grundbegriffe der Geschichte* (Gutersloh, 1964) 33–35.

3. J. Jüthner, *Hellenen und Barbaren* (Leipzig, 1923) 1–13.

4. Cf. Ibid., 14.

5. Plato, *Politiea* 262 A.

6. J. Burckhardt, *Griechische Kulturgeschichte* (Stuttgart, 1939) I:284 ff.; and Plato, *Republic* 471 B–E.

7. Plato, *Meno* 245 C.

8. Plato, *Meno* 242 G, *Republic* 269 B.

9. Aristotle, *Politics* 1252 B, 1327 B.

10. Aristotle, *Nicomachean Ethics* 1145 A.

11. Aristotle, *Politics* 1252 B, 1285 A, 1329 A, 1330 A.

12. Plato, *Politiea* 262 A.

13. Aristotle, *Politics* 1254 B, 1327 B.

14. Jüthner, *Hellenen und Barbaren* 16.

15. Aristotle, *Politics* 1255 A, B.

16. Aristotle, *Nicomachean Ethics* 1161 B.

17. Cf. A. Rüstow, *Ortsbestimmung der Gegenwart* (Erlenbach 1950) I:84 ff.

18. H. Nicolson, *Die Herren der Welt privat* (Frankfurt a.M., 1933) 174.

19. Thucydides I:3; Plato, *Republic* 452 D; and Aristotle, *Politics* 1257 A, 1268 B, 1269 B, 1295 A.

20. Thucydides I:6.

21. Cicero, *De republica* I:58.

22. J. Burckhardt, *Historische Fragmente* (Stuttgart, 1942) 4. Here he registers caution with respect to the usage, since the "concepts fluctuate too much." "The use or nonuse of the word [Barbarism] ultimately becomes trying."

23. E. Troeltsch, *Der Historismus und seine Probleme* (Aalen, 1961) 4.

24. Diogenes Laertius 6:38, 63. See the critique by W. W. Tarn, "Alexander the Great and the Unity of Mankind," *Proceedings of the British Academy* 19 (1933) 125. He argues that the negation as used by Diogenes does not—contrasting here with the usual interpretation—involve a comprehensive community. *Kosmopolit* "is a horrible word, which he coined and which was not used again for centuries."

25. Jüthner, *Hellenen und Barbaren* 34 ff.

26. J. Burckhardt, *Griechische Kulturgeschichte* I:296; and ibid., 55.

27. H. Naumann, "Der edle und der wilde Heide," in *Festgabe Gustav Ehrismann* (Berlin, 1925) 80–101.

28. R. Gonnard, *La légende du bon sauvage* (Paris, 1946).

29. Plutarch, *Moralia* 329 D. This was directed against Aristotle, *Politics* 1254 B.

30. M. Pohlenz, *Die Stoa* (Göttingen, 1948) I:153 ff.

31. Diodorus, II:6–8.

32. Tarn, "Alexander the Great" 135 ff.

33. J. Bidez, *La cité du monde et la cité du soleil chez les Stoiciens* (Paris, 1932). M. Hammond, *City-State and World-State in Greek and Roman Political Philosophy until Augustus* (Cambridge, Mass., 1951).

34. Stobaios, cited in Tarn, "Alexander the Great" 128. M. Manilii, *Astronomicon* (London, 1930) 5:733 ff. Diodorus I:1, 3. Epictetus, *Discourses* 2;5, 4 (on mimesis).

35. Abbreviation of the contrast can be found in E. Gilson, *Les métamorphoses de la cité de Dieu* (Louvain, 1952).

36. Cicero, *De Officiis* I:53 ff. Cf. J. Vogt, *Orbis Romanus* (Tübingen, 1929).

37. "Some pay attention to both of these republics at once, the greater and the lesser one, some only to the lesser, and some only to the greater. We are able to serve this greater republic even when we are not engaged in politics—maybe even better when we are not engaged in politics." Seneca, *Ad Serenum de otio* c. 31.

38. Marcus Aurelius, *Commentaria* 6:44; cf. 3:11.

39. Epictetus, *Discourses* 2:5, 4.

40. Ibid., 3:13.

41. U. Duchrow, *Christenheit und Weltverantwortung* (Stuttgart, 1970) 59 ff. See also Tertullian's expression: "The Romans, that is the non-Christians...." (*Liber apologeticus* 35:9); and the interpretation of H. von Campenhausen, *Lateinische Kirchenväter* (Stuttgart, 1960) 21 ff.

42. Tertullian, cited in Jüthner, *Griechische Kulturgeschichte* 145, 93.

43. Cicero, *De republica* I:58.

44. Jüthner, *Griechische Kulturgeschichte* 60 ff.

45. H. Conzelmann, "Heidenchristentum," *RGG* (Tübingen, 1959) 3:128–41.

46. K. Barth, *Der Römerbrief* (Zürich, 1954) 59.

47. Cf. the linguistically nonparadoxical usage for the same idea in 1 Cor. 12, 13. The ideas advanced here stem from discussions with Jacob Taubes.

48. R. Bultmann, *Das Urchristentum im Rahmen der antiken Religionen* (Zurich, 1949) 200 ff.

49. H. Kantorowicz, *The King's Two Bodies* (Princeton, 1957); and W. Berges, *Der Fürstenspiegel des hohen und späten Mittelalters* (Leipzig, 1938).

50. J. Rupp, *L'idée de Chrétienté dans la pensée pontificale des origines à Innocent III* (Paris, 1939); and D. Hay, *Europe. The Emergence of an Idea* (Edinburgh, 1957).

51. See the many and varied references in Jüthner, *Griechesche Kulturgeschichte* 87–121.

52. S. Stein, *Die Ungläubigen in der mittelhochdeutschen Literatur von 1050 bis 1250* (Darmstadt, n.d.) 17 ff., 22; and Hay, *Europe*.

53. *Origines*, c. Cels. 2:14, 8:72. See also A. Miura-Stange, *Celsus and Origines* (Giessen, 1926) 43 ff.

54. St. Augustine, *City of God* 15:18, 19:17.

55. Ibid., 15:17.

56. Ibid., 19:13.

57. Ibid., 15:1.

58. Ibid., 19:7–9.

59. St. Augustine, *Letters* 185, 11. See also Duchrow, *Christenheit* 297 ff.

60. St. Augustine, *City of God* 20:19.

61. Ibid., 1:8.

62. Ibid., 1:8 ff.

63. J. N. Figgis, *The Political Aspects of St. Augustine's City of God* (London, 1921).

64. Dawson, "St. Augustine and His Age," in *A Monument to St. Augustine* (London, 1930) 70 ff.

65. R. Schäfer, "Wesen des Christentums," *Historisches Wörterbuch der Philosophie* 1:1008 ff. B. Bauer shares the same premises on the irreversibility of the historical process in doubting the ability of the Jews to emancipate themselves as such; see "Die Judenfrage," *Deutsche Jahrbücher für Wissenschaft und Kunst* (1842) 1093 ff.

66. "Where there is now paganism let there be Christianity." Cited in Hay, *Europe* 30.

67. "Let the love of the land of his birth delay no one, since for the Christian in different ways the whole world is exile and the whole world is his native land. Thus exile is home, and home, exile." William of Malmesbury, cited in Hay, *Europe* 32.

68. Thomas Aquinas, *Summa Theologica* II, sect. 2, qu. 10, art. 8.

69. H. Kamen, *Die spanische Inquisition* (Munich, 1969) 41. The Papal Bull of 24 September 1449 directed itself, without success, against the division of Catholic members of the Church according to "racial" criteria.

70. Verse 1015, provided by H. Gumbrecht.

71. Hay, *Europe* 29, 35; and Rupp, *L'idée de Chrétienté* 99 ff.

72. Hay, *Europe* 14, 41 ff.

73. Stein, *Literatur* 24, 39; M. Villey, *La Croisade, Essai sur la formation d'une théorie juridique* (Paris, 1942); A. Noyer-Weidner, "Farbrealität und Farbsymbolik in der 'Heidengeographie' des Rolandsliedes," *Romanische Forschung* (1969) 22–59.

74. Nauman, "Der Heide" 80.

75. Stein, *Literatur* 15.

76. Ambrosius, Letter 17. See also H. Lietzmann, *Geschichte der alten Kirche* (Berlin, 1950) 4:68; St. Augustine, *City of God* 5:24.

77. Cf. Figgis, *St. Augustine's City* 89.

78. 1 John 4, 6; and R. Hooker, *Of the Laws of Ecclesiastical Polity* (London, 1954) I:104 ff.

79. For the sake of accuracy and to enable the reader to observe the formation of terminology around *Mensch*, the original German terms are retained in this section. (Trans.)

80. Cicero, *De Officiis* 1:3, c. 28–32.

81. Lessing, cited in W. Stammler, *Kleine Schriften zur Sprachgeschichte* (Berlin, 1954) 82. See also Lessing, *Minna von Barnhelm*, Act 1, Scene 8: "No, there are no complete *Unmenschen*! We will stay together!"

82. "Alle Laster . . . sind inhuman, objektiv betrachtet, aber doch menschlich." Kant, *Metaphysics of Ethics* pt. 2 "On Virtue" para. 36 n. With respect to the dualistic formulation, the Christian-Stoic doctrine of the two persons is continued by Kant's philosophical anthropology, in which the concept of the *Mensch* is doubled; the empirical *Mensch* is subordinated to an inhering ideal *Menschheit*, the imitation of which is a postulate of historicophilosophical fulfillment.

83. St. Augustine, "Enarrationes," in *Psalmos* 68:6.

84. Kant, "On Perpetual Peace," in *Political Writings* 108.

85. Grimm, *Deutsches Wörterbuch* Bd. 6, col. 2077 ff.

86. Cited in Stammler, *Sprachgeschichte.*

87. Ibid.

88. Kotzebue, *Theater* (Leipzig, 1840) I:31.

89. A. Blumauer, *Gedichte* (1782) I:228.

90. Salzmann, *Carl von Carlsberg* V:316.

91. Moritz, *Anton Reiser* 3:220, cited in Stammler, *Sprachgeschichte.*

92. "Der Fürst sei Mensch, der Sklave frei, dann eilt die goldne Zeit herbei"; cited by Stammler, *Sprachgeschichte.*

93. Rousseau, *Emile* I:3. See also my *Kritik und Krise* 204 ff., 116 ff.

94. Friedrich der Grosse, "Denkwürdigkeiten," in *Werke* 5:51.

95. J. Harrington, "The Commonwealth of Oceana," in *Political Works* (Cambridge, 1977) 229.

96. A. Smith, *The Theory of Moral Sentiments* (Oxford, 1976) pt. I, section I, chap. 2.

97. J. Boswell, *The Life of Dr. Samuel Johnson* (London, n.d.) 198.

98. W. Blackstone, *Commentaries on the Laws of England* (Chicago, 1871) I:241.

99. Cited in O. Vossler, *Der Nationalgedanke von Rousseau bis Ranke* (Munich, 1937) 81.

100. C. F. D. Schubart, *Teutsche Chronik* 65.

101. R. Desèze, *Défense de Louis XVI* (Leipzig, 1900) 1.

102. St. Just, *Oeuvres* (Paris, 1946) 120.

103. In contrast to *Übermenschen*, the term *Untermensch* is only to be found in the German language from the end of the eighteenth century on. See Grimm, *Deutsches Wörterbuch*: "Übermensch" Bd. 11, 2 Abt., 417 ff.; "Untermensch" Bd. 11, 3 Abt., 1686 ff.

104. See F. Tricaud, " 'Homo homini Deus,' 'Homo homini lupus': Recherche des sources des deux formules de Hobbes," in R. Koselleck, R. Schnur (eds.) *Hobbes-Forschungen* (Berlin, 1969) 61 ff.

105. K. Burdach, "Rienzo und die geistige Wandlung seiner Zeit," in Burdach (ed.) *Vom Mittelalter zur Reformation* (Berlin, 1913) Bd. 2, T. 1, 1 Hälfte, 211 ff., 269 ff.; see also E. H. Kantorowicz, "Mysteries of the State," *Harvard Theological Review* 47 (1955); and E. Benz, *Der Übermensch* (Stuttgart, 1961).

106. Cited in Grimm, *Deutsches Wörterbuch* Bd. 11, Abt. 2, Col. 417.

107. H. Müller, "Vom Ohnmenschen, Kein Mensch/kein Christ," in *Geistliche Erquickstunden* (Frankfurt a.M., 1673).

108. "He is an anomaly, not a man; he is a great foe, in human form." Demonstration and interpretation in H. Lutz, "Zum Wandel der katholischen Lutherinterpretation," in Koselleck, et al. (eds.) *Objektivität* 178 ff.

109. C. Hohberg, *Theologia mystica* (1730), cited in Grimm, *Deutsches Wörterbuch* Bd. 11, Abt. 2, col. 1174.

110. Herder, "Briefe zur Beförderung der Humanität," *Sämtliche Werke* Bd. 17, 142.

111. R. M. Meyer, *Vierhundert Schlagworte* (Leipzig, 1901) 6-24, on the history of the word "Übermensch."

112. See D. Groh, "Cäserismus," in *Geschichtliche Grundbegriffe* Bd. I, 726 ff.

113. Herder, "Briefe" 17:115.

114. Cited in Grimm, *Deutsches Wörterbuch* entry for "übermenschlich."

115. Goethe, *Gesamtausgabe* Bd. 1, 8.

116. "Man, who looked for a superhuman being in the fantastic reality of heaven and found nothing there but the *reflection* of himself, will no longer be disposed to find but the *semblance* of himself, will no longer be disposed to find but the semblance of himself, only an inhuman being, when he seeks and must seek his true reality." Marx, "Contribution to the Critique of Hegel's Philosophy of Law. Introduction," in *Collected Works* 3:175.

117. Dostoevski, *Tagebuch eines Schriftstellers* (Munich, 1923) Bd. 4, 366.

118. Nietzsche, *Werke* Bd. 3, 628; Bd. 2, 279, 1166; Bd. 3, 440.

119. "Gesetz zur Wiederherstellung des deutschen Berufsbeamtentums vom 7.4.1933," para. 3, and "Schriftleitergesetz vom 4.10.1933," paras. 5, 3, in U. Broderson, I. von Münch, *Gesetze des NS-Staates* (Bad Homburg, 1968) 30, 165. The term "Aryan" later gave way to "German and associated blood" and (negatively) "Jews."

120. Cf. P. von Polenz, *Geschichte der deutschen Sprache* (Berlin, 1970) 169.

121. C. Schmitt, *The Concept of the Political* (New Brunswick, N.J., 1976).

122. St. Augustine, *City of God* 19:12.

# On the Disposability of History

First published as "Über die Verfügbarkeit der Geschichte," in *Schicksal? Grenzen der Machbarkeit.* Symposium der Karl Friedrich von Siemens Stiftung (Munich, 1977) 51-67.

1. J. C. Eustace, *A Tour through Italy, Exhibiting a View of its Scenery, its Antiquities and its Monuments; particularly as they are objects of classical interest and education: with an account of the present state of its cities and towns; and occasional observations on the recent spoliations of the French* (London, 1813) 31 ff. This essay deals with the "making" of history, the belief that one has the power of disposition over it. Koselleck consequently makes use of the term *machbar*, substantive *Machbarkeit*, which has no strict equivalent in English. Where it seems important, I have used the literal translation "makeability." (Trans.)

2. Cited in G. Bauer, *"Geschichtlichkeit." Wege und Irrwege eines Begriffs* (Berlin, 1963) 2.

3. "If history were an exact science, then we should be in the position to reveal the futures of states. But we are not able to do this; everywhere, historical science runs up against the

puzzle of personality. It is persons, men, who make history; men like Luther, Frederick the Great, and Bismarck. This great, heroic truth will remain true forever; and it will always be a puzzle to we mortals how these men appear, the right man at the right time. Genius is formed by the times, but is not created by it." Treitschke then noted—keeping a space open for possibilities and freedom—that the combination of external circumstances was insufficient for the determination of a necessary historical course. His theory, which is here based on von Humboldt, does not, however, become involved with the overworked partial citation. H. von Treitschke, *Politik. Vorlesungen* (Leipzig, 1897) I:6.

4. Cf. article "Geschichte," in *Geschichtliche Grundbegriffe* Bd. 2 647 ff.

5. J. T. Jablonski, *Allgemeines Lexikon der Künste und Wissenschaften* (Leipzig, 1748) I:386.

6. Böttinger, "Erinnerungen an das literarische Berlin . . .," in F. A. Ebert (ed.) *Überlieferungen zur Geschichte* (Dresden, 1827) 42.

7. F. W. G. Schelling, "Allgemeine Übersicht der neuesten philosophischen Literatur," *Philosophisches Journal* 8 (1798) 145.

8. Kant, "Idea for a Universal History with a Cosmopolitan Purpose," in *Political Writings* 42. (Slightly altered—Trans.)

9. Kant, *Anthropologie* para. 35.

10. Kant, "Idea for a Universal History" Seventh Proposition, and "Der Streit der Fakultäten" II:2, Abschn. 3c.

11. Kant, "Der Streit" 2, Abschn. 2.

12. Kant, "Über das Misslingen aller philosophischen Versuche in der Theodizee," *Werke* VIII:264.

13. Kant, *Anthropologie* para. 35.

14. Cf. R. van Dülmen, *Der Geheimbund der Illuminaten* (Stuttgart, 1975).

15. A. Weishaupt, *Geschichte der Vervollkommnung des menschlichen Geschlechtes* (Frankfurt, 1788) 29.

16. Ibid., 15, 27, 61 ff., 217. This text is the most sociohistorically accessible of Weishaupt's works and in theoretical terms is his best work, written during his emigration in Gotha. For his earlier position, see my *Kritik und Krise* 49 ff.

17. Perthes, *Leben* 23.

18. Ibid., 271 ff.

19. W. Schulz, *Die Bewegung der Production* (Zürich, 1843) 155 ff.

20. F. Engels, *Herr Eugen Dühring's Revolution in Science* (London, n.d.) 318. (Translation modified—Trans.)

21. Marx, Engels, *The Holy Family, Collected Works* 4:79.

22. Marx, Engels, *The German Ideology, Part One* (London, 1970) 67.

23. Marx, *Eighteenth Brumaire* 103. (Revised—Trans.)

24. See the text that is still today referred to in the Soviet world: Plekhanov, *The Role of Personality in History*. Cf. J. Kuczynski, "Der Mensch, der Geschichte macht," *Zeitschrift für Geschichtswissenschaft* 5 (1957) 1–17.

25. Bismarck, *Werke in Auswahl* 4:309.

26. Ibid., 330.

27. "Ansprache an eine Abordnung der Jenaer Universität, 20.7.1892," in H. Rothfels (ed.) *Bismarck und der Staat* (Stuttgart, n.d.) 86.

28. G. L. Weinberg (ed.) *Hitlers zweites Buch* (Stuttgart, 1961) 138.

29. Hitler, *Reden und Proklamationen 1932–1945* (Munich, 1965) I:1, 176. This is the text of his speech of 4 January 1933.

30. *F. D. Roosevelt: Public Papers and Addresses 1944–45* (New York, 1950), 616, 615. Message for 13 April 1945, written 11 April.

31. St. Augustine, *The City of God* 19:12. Cf. F. Fellmann, *Das Vico-Axiom. Der Mensch macht die Geschichte* (Freiburg, 1976). Despite a title which, from the point of view of conceptual history, is misleading, the book contains a systematic historicophilosophical analysis related to the points made here. This is likewise true for R. Specht, *Innovation und Folgelast* (Stuttgart, 1972). Cf. "Geschichte, Geschichtsphilosophie und ihr Subjekt," in Koselleck, Stempel (eds.) *Geschichte, Ereignis.*

## Terror and Dream: Methodological Remarks on the Experience of Time during the Third Reich

Not previously published.

1. Alsted, *Scientarium omnium encyclopaedia* (Lyon, 1649) table, 619.

2. See A. Seifert, "Historia im Mittlealter," *Archiv für Begriffsgeschichte* 21 (1977) 226–84, and "Cognitio Historica, Die Geschichte als Namengeberin der frühneuzeitlichen Empirie," *Historische Forschung* 11 (1976); and K. Heitmann, "Das Verhältnis von Dichtung und Geschichtsschreibung in älterer Theorie," *Archiv für Kulturgeschichte* 52 (1970) 244–79.

3. Blumenberg, *Paradigmen* 88 ff.

4. Aristotle, *Poetics* 1451 B, 1459 A.

5. Lessing, "Briefe, die neueste Literatur betreffend, Nr. 63," *Sämtliche Schriften* 8:168.

6. See the discussion of Chladenius in the essay "Perspective and Temporality," 136 ff. above.

7. Goethe, "Schreiben an Ludwig I von Bayern vom 17.Dez.1829," *Gesamtausgabe* 24, 316.

8. See 153 above.

9. Herodotus, *History* VII, c. 16 ff.; Cicero, *De divinatione*; and P. Burke, "L'histoire sociale des rêves," *Annales* 28 (1973) 329–43.

10. C. Beradt, *Das Dritte Reich des Traumes* (Munich, 1966) 25, 138.

11. For additional dreams which anticipated a coming situation not yet apparent at the time of the dream, see Beradt, *Dritte Reich* 29, 42, 45, 49, 61, 66, 72, 83, 85, 87, 90, 139.

12. G. Grosz, *Ein kleines Ja und ein grosses Nein* (Hamburg, 1946) 212–18.

13. Cf. V. von Wiezsacker, *Der Gestaltkreis* (Stuttgart, 1950).

14. J. Cayrol, *Lazarus unter uns* (Stuttgart, 1959).

15. B. Bettelheim, *The Informed Heart* (London, 1970); V. E. Frankl, . . . *trotzdem Ja zum Leben sagen* (Munich, 1977); M. Buber-Neumann, *Milena, Kafkas Freundin* (Munich, 1977) 286, 289 ff.; on 278 the dream of a guard at Ravensbrück which has the unambiguous political content of anticipation of the Allied victory is reported.

16. Beradt, *Dritte Reich* 56.

17. This was reported to me by P. E. Schramm, who was passing on an officer's expression, made in the witness box at Nuremberg.

18. Frankl, . . . *trotzdem Ja zum Leben sagen* 122.

19. J. Gabel, *Ideologie und Schizophrenie* (Frankfurt a.M., 1967) 123, 227.

20. Cf. F. Pingel, *Häftlinge unter SS-Herrschaft* (Hamburg, 1978).

21. T. Lessing, *Geschichte als Sinngebung des Sinnlosen* (Munich, 1921) 15.

22. See H.-U. Wehler, *Geschichte und Psychoanalyse* (Köln, 1971).

23. Bettelheim, *The Informed Heart* 98–99.

24. On the last section, cf. E. Coseriu, *Synchronie, Diachronie und Geschichte* (Munich, 1974).

# "Neuzeit": Remarks on the Semantics of the Modern Concepts of Movement

First published as " 'Neuzeit': Zur Semantik moderner Bewegunsbegriffe," in R. Koselleck (ed.) *Studien zum Beginn der modernen Welt* (Stuttgart, 1977) 264–99.

1. Schulz, author of *Die Bewegung der Produktion* (Zürich, 1843).

2. Grimm, *Deutsches Wörterbuch* Bd. 7, 689: "Neuzeit, die neue, jetzige Zeit, gegensatz zu vorzeit"; and Freiligrath, "ein kind der neuzeit, fiebernd und erregt. . . ."

3. Ranke, *Aus Werk und Nachlass* ed. W. P. Fuchs, T. Schieder (Munich, 1975) Bd. 4. Ranke distinguished "neuere" from "neueste" *Zeit* or *Geschichte*, the shift lying somewhere in the second half of the eighteenth century according to the problem at hand. He also uses *neue Zeit* as a way of marking the Middle Ages off, but does not use *Neuzeit*. *Neuzeit* appears once in a drafted afterword to *Epoche der Reformation und der Religions-kriege*, in Fuchs, Schieder (eds.) *Aus Werk und Nachlass* Bd. 2, 283–27; but the usage is not authentic.

4. Article "Geschichte," in *Brockhaus' Conversations Lexikon* 13th ed., 7:868; this distinguishes *neuere* (from 1492) from *neueste Geschichte* (from 1789), as had been done in the article of the

same name in *Allgemeine deutsche Real Encyclopädie* (Leipzig, 1820) 4:182. The division"Altertum—Mittelalter—Neuzeit" first appeared in the article "Zeitalter," in *Brockhaus*, 16 (1887) 854. The earliest example that can be found, to my knowledge, was drawn to my attention by Helga Reinhart and involves a translation from the French: "Journalism. The human spirit flies in idea from one end of the world to the other; it fills the past with memory, the future with hope; even our bodies are provided by industry with a right to uniquity; civilization seeks to disregard materiality and lend wings to intercourse, as with the ideas of men. For this reason the press, bringing all our intellects into contact and transforming our ideas and feelings with such enormous speed, is the achieved conquest of *Neuzeit*." This source, which is currently the earliest descovered, fulfills all the criteria which will be developed below, especially in Section II, characterizing the new concept as one of an epoch and as one of periodization open to the future. E. Alletz, *De la démocratie nouvelle* (Paris, 1837), translated under the title *Die neue Demokratie* (Karlsruhe, 1838) 23.

J. Voss has drawn my attention to another source that comes from historical writing: C. Wernicke, *Die Geschichte der Welt* pts. 3-5 (*Die Geschichte der Neuzeit*) (Berlin, 1865-66, first ed., 1855-57). Wernicke distinguishes the transitions of the three periods so that he might attain a criterion of *neue Zeit*. Antiquity came to an end because new peoples had initiated the Middle Ages. This was not, however, the case for the transition to *Neuzeit*. "All the more powerful, therefore, the new creations which, laid down for centuries before, have since the beginning of the sixteenth century been created within each people in all areas of life, in Church and state, in art and science, such that the time since the beginning of the sixteenth century has to be treated as genuinely new." (pt. 3, 2 ff.)

The following outline claims neither to be comprehensive nor novel. Reference should be made to the forthcoming article of J. Voss on *Zeitalter*, in *Geschichtliche Grundbegriffe*, Bd. 6.

5. See the detailed study of J. Voss, *Das Mittelalter im historischen Denken Frankreichs* (Munich, 1972) pt. I and the references 391 ff., which include non-French examples.

6. Until now, there has been no historical study of the term *Neuzeit*. On *Zeitgeschichte*, of interest in parts, but from this aspect inadequate, see O.-E. Schüddekopf, "Zeitgeschichte," in *Grundbegriffe der Geschichte* (Gutersloh, 1964) 413-27.

7. See Voss, *Dos Mittelalter* 40. See also T. E. Mommsen, "Petrarch's Conception of the 'Dark Ages,'" *Speculum* 17 (1942) 226-42.

8. C. Cellarius, *Historia universalis* (Altenberg, 1753). Cf. A. Klempt, *Die Säkulisierung der universalhistorischen Auffassung* (Göttingen, 1960) 78.

9. Ranke, *Vorlesungseinleitungen*, in Fuchs, Scheider (eds.) *Aus Werk und Nachlass* Bd. 4, 36.

10. See W. K. Ferguson, *The Renaissance in Historical Thought* (Boston, 1948); and B. L. Ullmann, "Renaissance—The Word and the Concept," *Studies in Philology* 49 (1952) 105-18; and F. Masai, "La notion de Renaissance. Équivoques et malentendus," in C. Perelman, *Les catégories en histoire* (Brussels, 1969) 57-86. Even in 1718, Nicolo di Castelli was unaware of the expression *renascità*; neither did he use it as a translation of *Wiedergeburt*: *Dizionario italiano tedesco e tedesco italiano* (Leipzig, 1718).

11. K. Burdach, "Sinn und Ursprung der Worte Renaissance und Reformation," in his *Reformation, Renaissance, Humanismus* (Darmstadt, 1963) 1-84.

12. See the dictionaries of early modernity. See also J. C. Adelung, "Reformation," in his *Versuch eines vollständigen grammatisch-kritischen Wörterbuches der hochdeutschen Mundart* 3 (1777) col. 1336, in which the general usage is first noted. But note: "This term is most often used for the ending, on the part of Luther and his assistants, of the misuses and errors which had entered Church and doctrine; some refer to this in German as the improvement in belief (*Glaubensverbesserung*); others more correctly refer to the purification of belief (*Glaubensreiningung*)."

13. Müntzer, "Auslegung des zweiten Kapitels Danielis" (1524), in *Politische Schriften* (Halle, 1950) 20.

14. W. Maurer, "Reformation," in *Die Religion in Geschichte und Gegenwart* (Tübingen, 1961) Bd. 5, 861.

15. Article "Zeit-Begriffe oder Zeitperioden," in Zedler, *Lexikon* Bd. 61 (1749) 832.

16. Cited in P. Meinhold, *Geschichte der kirchlichen Historiographie* Bd. I (Freiburg, 1967) 377. Further references to this usage are to be found in this work, but there seems to be no historical treatment of the term "Reformation."

17. A. Elkan, "Entstehung und Entwicklung des Begriffs 'Gegenreformation,' " *Historische Zeitschrift* 112 (1914) 473–93.

18. H. Grundmann, "Die Grundzüge der mittelalterlichen Geschichtsanschauungen," in W. Lammers (ed.) *Geschichtsdenken und Geschichtsbild im Mittelalter* (Darmstadt, 1961) 427.

19. W. Freund, "Modernus und andere Zeitbegriffe des Mittelalters" (diss., Münster, 1957); and H. R. Jauss, "Literarische Tradition und gegenwärtiges Bewusstsein der Modernität," in his *Literaturgeschichte als Provokation* (Frankfurt a.M., 1970) 11–66. See also Gumbrecht, article "Modern, Modernität, Moderne," in *Geschichtliche Grundbegriffe*.

20. Ernst, "Zeitgeschehen"; and Seifert, "Cognitio Historica."

21. ". . . to add to their work those new events which will have happened in the following ages until the end of the world." G. Melville, "System und Diachronie. Untersuchungen zur theoretischen Grundlegung geschichtsschreiberischer Praxis im Mittelalter," *Historisches Jahrbuch* 95 (1975) 313.

22. ". . . to epitomize history from the creation of the first man up to modern times." Melville, "System und Diachronie."

23. Alsted, *Encyclopaedia* Bd. 4, 37, 65, table on 619.

24. F. Bacon, *De dignitate et augmentis scientiarum* Book 2, chaps. 8, 9, in *Works* I:511–13.

25. J. Bodin, *Methodus ad facilem historiarum cognitionem* (Amsterdam, 1650) Prooemium, 4.

26. "Introduction to the Chronicle of Johann Carion," in H. Scheible (ed.) *Die Anfänge der reformatorischen Geschichtsschreibung* (Gütersloh, 1966) 15.

27. Chladenius, *Geschichtswissenschaft*.

28. Cited in T. E. Mommsen, "Petrarch's Conception" 163.

29. Quite confusing in the article "Neu, -er, -este," in J. C. Campe, *Wörterbuch der Deutschen Sprache* (Brunswick, 1809) 483, where he compiles the series "neue, neuere, neueste, mittlere, alte, ältere, und älteste Zeit" or also *Geschichte*.

30. "He kept all historical records; not only ancient ones, but also those both old and modern of the intervening time up to our own age." Cited in K. Borinski, *Die Wiedergeburtsidee in der neueren Zeiten* (Munich, 1919) 113.

31. "Because of this, holy men often call this age the last and the end of all ages." Expression of N. von Cues, cited in Borinski, *Die Wiedergeburtsidee* 112.

32. "Ideas of History during the Renaissance," in P. O. Kristeller, P. P. Wiener (eds.) *Renaissance Essays* (New York, 1968) 74-94.

33. See Voss, *Das Mittelalter* 422.

34. See Klempt, *Die Säkulisierung* 75 ff.; and the references in Voss, *Das Mittelalter.*

35. Article "Die Geschicht," in K. Stieler, *Der teutschen Sprache Stammbaum und Fortwachs oder Teutscher Sprachschatz* (Nuremberg, 1691) pt. II, col. 1746.

36. Article "Zeit [neue]," in Zedler, *Lexikon* 61 (1749) 797. In "Neue der Zeit [das]" Bd. 24 (1740) 139, there is an entry for *Novum temporis*, but this is only for the domain of the law covering questions about that which has been "Neither seen nor heard of by anybody" or has only been forgotten.

37. J. C. Adelung, *Versuch* Bd. 2, 488, on the other hand, uses *gegenwärtig* in the temporal sense, deriving it from the spatial meaning.

38. Article "Die Zeit, -en," in Campe, *Wörterbuch* Bd. 5 (1811) 831.

39. Article "Neuwelt," in Campe, *Wörterbuch* Bd. 3 (1809) 488.

40. Article "Welt," in Campe, *Wörterbuch* Bd. 5 (1811) 668.

41. Article "Neuerthum," in Campe, *Wörterbuch* Bd. 3 (1809) 484.

42. J. C. Gatterer, *Einleitung in die synchronistische Universalhistorie* (Gottingen, 1771) contents list, and pt. II, 3 ff. Here, *Epoquen* are described as "resting places" offering the opportunity to pause "so that at least from time to time, important parts of the whole might be surveyed." This is only possible with epochs "whose influence in the whole is of the greatest." The suggested four epochs are: the creation of the world in world-year 1, the origin of nations in world-year 1809, the migration of peoples in the fifth century A.D., and the discovery of America in A.D. 1492. In 1767, Gatterer inserted the reign of Charles the Great: "Vom historischen Plan und der darauf sich gründenden Zusammenfügung der Erzählungen," *Allgemeine historische Bibliothek* 1 (1767) 43 ff. On the theory and conceptual history of "epochs," see H. Blumenberg, *Aspekte der Epochenschwelle* (Frankfurt a.M., 1976); and M. Riedel, "Epoche, Epochenbewusstsein," *Historisches Wörterbuch der Philosophie* 2 (1972) 596-99.

43. Müller, "Wie sich der Übergang der mittleren Zeit auf die neue Gestaltung der Dinge nach und nach bereitete (1273 bis 1453)," and "Von denjenigen Revolutionen, welche die neue Ordnung der Dinge besonders veranlassten (1453-1517)," in *Geistliche Erquickstunden.*

44. H. M. G. Köster, "Historie," in *Deutsche Encyclopädie* Bd. 12 (1787) 657.

45. J. G. Büsch, *Encyclopädie der historischen, philosophischen und mathematischen Wissenschaften* (Hamburg, 1775) 128. Büsch shares the view of Gatterer on the epoch: it is the resting place for great world affairs, "and the time between two such epochs is a period." Considered from the point of view of the immanent course of history these are, without doubt, "the major events of the world, revolutions of great importance, which affect the human species as a whole, and which have gradually produced the present times and states." (538 ff.) The usage *Neuesten Zeit* in Morhof is nonspecific, standing in opposition to *mittlere Zeit*; see his *Unterricht von der Teutschen Sprache und Poesie* (Kiel, 1682) 277, 308.

46. A. H. L. Heeren, *Handbuch der Geschichte des Europäischen Staatensystems und seiner Colonien* (Göttingen, 1822) XVII.

47. Ranke, *Vorlesungseinleitungen*, see fn. 3 above.

48. Cf. my "Geschichte," in *Geschichtliche Grundbegriffe* Bd. 2 (1975) 647-91.

49. Article "Zeitgeschichte," in Campe, *Wörterbuch* Bd. 5 (1811) 833.

50. Kant, *Anthropologie* 62.

51. See the evidence for the seventeenth century in R. Eucken, *Geistige Strömungen der Gegenwart* (Berlin, 1920) 277. Also related is the programmatic statement by Clarendon that it is "more useful to posterity to leave a character of the times, than of the persons; or the narrative of the matters of the matters of fact, which cannot be so well understood, as by knowing the genius that prevailed when they were transacted." *Selections from the History of the Rebellion and Civil Wars* (London, 1955) 7.

52. See W. Krauss, "Der Jahrhundert begriff im 18 Jahrhundert. Geschichte und Geschichtlichkeit in der französisichen Aufklärung," in his *Studien zur deutschen und französischen Aufklärung* (Berlin, 1963) 9-40; and J. Burckhardt, *Die Entstehung der modernen Jahrhundertrechnung* (Göttingen, 1971).

53. H. M. G. Köster, "Historische Erkenntnis," *Deutsche Encyclopädie* Bd. 12 (1787) 670.

54. Cited in Burckhardt, *Die Entstehung* 88.

55. W. Wieland, "Entwicklung, Evolution," in *Geschichtliche Grundbegriffe* Bd. 2 (1975) 199-228.

56. J. G. Herder, *Metakritik zur Kritik der reinen Vernunft* (Berlin, 1955) 68.

57. On the following, see R. Koselleck, C. Meier, "Fortschritt," in *Geschichtliche Grundbegriffe* Bd. 2 (1975) 391-402.

58. "Not only a help and kindness, but also a model for comparison." Bacon, *Novum organum* I:29, in *Works* I:222.

59. Cited in Ullmann, "Renaissance" 268.

60. Article "Zeit," in Zedler, *Lexikon* Bd. 61 (1749) 725-34.

61. D'Alembert, "Discours préliminaire de l'Encyclopédie (1751)," and Diderot, "Encyclopédie," in *Encyclopédie* 5 (1755) 635-49.

62. Marx, *Contribution to the Critique of Hegel's Philosophy of Law.*

63. See, for the following, the essay "Perspective and Temporality," sect. II.

64. Abbt, *Geschichte*, I:219.

65. Gatterer, "Abhandlung" 7.

66. Büsch, *Encyclopédie* 12.

67. Goethe, *Farbenlehre* 93.

68. W. von Humboldt, *Das achtzehnte Jahrhundert*, in *Werke* I:401.

69. F. Ancillon, "Über die Perfectibilität der bürgerlichen Gesellschaft, ihre Bedingungen und Triebfedern," in *Zur Vermittlung der Extreme in den Meinungen* (Berlin, 1828) I:192. The social and political structure of this transitional period is summarized by W. Conze in his essay "Das Spannungsfeld von Staat und Gesellschaft im Vormärz," in W. Conze (ed.) *Staat und Gesellschaft im deutschen Vormärz 1815-1848* (Stuttgart, 1970) 207-69.

70. Humboldt, *Das achtzehnte Jahrhundert* 398.

71. G. G. Gervinus, *Einleitung in die Geschichte des neunzehnten Jahrhunderts* (Leipzig, 1853) 174; and Henry Adams, *The Education of Henry Adams* 489 ff.

72. E. M. Arndt, *Geist der Zeit* (Altona, 1877) 76, 55.

73. "Über einige der gewissen Vortheile, welche die gesammte Menschheit durch die itzige politische Catastrophe schon erhalten hat, oder noch erhalten möchte," *Schleswigsches Journal* St. 10 (October 1793) 222 ff., 242.

74. F. Schlegel, *Philosophie der Geschichte* (1828) *Kritische Friedrich Schlegel Ausgabe* 9:417.

75. Arndt, *Geist der Zeit* 53.

76. On a traditionalist's scale of guilt attribution: "Nowadays one allows world history no time for birth; it is not permitted to develop; all at once a present that is no daughter of the past has to be there. What might possibly be brought about by several centuries is anticipated, should be created in months, which raises the question of whether centuries will suffice. . . ." T. Aclines, *Recht und Macht des Zeitgeistes* (Schleswig, 1824) 5.

77. Planck, *Einleitung* pt. 2, 243. Barely a century later, Jacob Burckhardt on 2 July 1871 wrote to Bernhard Kugler: "First, I wish you well in rejecting the proposal for a new German history. Nothing is less needed by advanced knowledge; nothing is more destructive for scientific life as the exclusive concern with contemporary events. We live in times that are quite different from those of Thucydides, who was able to command an overview of the situation and its conflicts and was familiar with everything. He who today seeks to describe contemporary history risks being outdated by a few secret documents published later; he also has to compete with a whole collection of fabricators who, with their *feuilleton* style, repeatedly reduce his public status." *Briefe* (Leipzig, 1938) 355 ff.

78. Cf. G. G. Gervinus, *Geschichte der deutschen Dichtung* (Leipzig, 1871) I:8: "Since the dissolution of the *Reich*, we have more than adequately completed the older time of our people; this must be, despite the estrangement of the nation from its older history, sufficient notice and challenge for historical writers to devote their whole energy to those times with which we must now come completely to terms, whose conditions are becoming clearer to us, the more that we are distanced from them."

79. F. List, *Das nationale System der politischen Ökonomie* (Jena, 1928) 469.

80. F. Bacon, *The Advancement of Learning and the New Atlantis* (London, 1951) 86; and V. de la Popelinière, *L'Histoire des histoires* (Paris, 1599) 61.

81. Raleigh, *History of the World*, preface; cited in A. B. Grosart (ed.) *Choice Passages from the Writings and Letters of Sir Walter Raleigh* (London, 1893) 191 ff.

82. Büsch, *Encyclopédie* 123, 164 ff.

83. W. T. Krug, *Versuch einer systematischen Encyclopädie der Wissenschaften* (Wittenberg, 1796) pt. 1, 85.

84. J. S. Erhardt, *Philosophische Encyklopädie* (Freiburg, 1818) 52.

85. F. A. W. Diesterweg, *Beiträge zur Lösung der Lebensfrage der Civilisation* (Essen, 1837) XVIII:38 ff.

86. Perthes, *Leben* Bd. 3 (1872) 24 ff.

87. For example, see C. Strahlheim (i.e., C. Friederich), *Unsere Zeit oder geschichtliche Übersicht der merkwürdigsten Ereignisse von 1789–1830* (Stuttgart, 1826-30) 30 vols.; or Ernst Freymund (i.e., A. F. Gfrörer), *Die Geschichte unserer Tage* (Stuttgart, 1831–33) 8 vols. In his introduction (vol. I, 5–7), Freymund states: "Centuries in the political affairs of Europe have not brought about the changes that the single year of 1830 has effected. The spirit of the time has, like a torrent, broken its banks. . . . Liberalism and Royalism are the two magic words dividing European humanity into two camps . . . and this division is not just in the state; it divides civil life as well: society, literature and science. . . ." Further reference can be made to the "Gegenwarts-encyclopädien" of Brockhaus, which provide, for approximately the period 1830-40, a cross section, and which, after the Revolution, appeared in monthly installments.

88. In the conclusion to *Conversationslexikon der Gegenwart* Bd. 4 (1841) V ff., it is affirmed that "for the vast majority, it is impossible to follow the history of their time and clearly observe the course of events." It is just this, in the opinion of the reviewers, which the lexicon does: "Reducing all party opinion to the standpoint of rigorous objectivity, projecting and completing in advance the significant development of circumstances not yet concluded by means of analogous combinations, comprehending on the basis of various symptoms events apparently accidental, and, with the perspicuous prospect of the historical writer providing them with a new form, showing how various aspects of progress are in fact different parameters of the same single movement."

89. Cf. the entry on compounds of "Zeit," in Grimm, *Deutsches Wörterbuch*. Note that the list of suffixes to "Zeit" that Koselleck provides here has been translated suffix by suffix. They do not form actual elements of compound words, since this would alter the point that is being made. (Trans.)

90. "Zeit," in Zedler, *Lexikon* 749.

91. F. von Baader, "Über den Evolutionismus und Revolutionismus oder die posit. und negat. Evolution des Lebens überhaupt und des socialen Lebens insbesondere," *Sämtliche Werke* 6:101.

92. C. von Clausewitz, *Politische Schriften und Briefe* (Munich, 1922) 179.

93. See Koselleck, "Demokratie IV.1," in *Geschichtliche Grundbegriffe* Bd. 1 (1972) 850.

94. F. Schlegel, "Versuch über den Begriff des Republikanismus varanlasst durch die Kantische Schrift zum ewigen Frieden (1796)," in *Kritische Friedrich Schlegel Ausgabe* Bd. 7, 12 and 17.

95. H. Heine, *Sämtliche Schriften* 1:450.

96. Marx, Engels, *The German Ideology, Part One* (London, 1970), 56–57.

97. Cf. R. Vierhaus, "Konservatismus," in *Geschichtliche Grundbegriffe* Bd. 3 (1982).

98. J. Burckhardt, *Historische Fragmente* (Stuttgart, 1942) 201. See also T. Schieder, "Das Problem der Revolution."

99. K. G. Scheidler, "Emancipation," in *Allgemeine Encyclopädie der Wissenschaften und Künste* sect. I, pt. 34 (1840) 2. Prompted by the July Revolution, Immermann on 29 September 1830 stated skeptically: "The last great movement in history will certainly always present itself as a crisis of significance through which the world seeks its rebirth." He did not, however, believe that the "reaction" (that is, the temporary victors of 1830) would be able to create anything durable in place of the previous order. "I rather believe that it is only one of the elements which will ferment and produce a new form in the future. The mere majesty of the people as a principle of support will not suffice; this is partly a lesson of world history (the emancipation of great peoples and states has always ended in a new devotion), and partly a lesson about the Revolution itself. . . ." M. Beer, *Briefwechsel* (Leipzig, 1837) 216.

100. K. Frantz, *Louis Napoleon* (Berlin, 1852) 59.

101. Cf. C. Schmitt, *Die Diktatur* (Berlin, 1964) especially 146, n. 2.

102. Stein, *Geschichte* Bd. I, 453; III:213. Cf. also G. Diezel, *Deutschland und die abendländischen Civilisation* (Stuttgart, 1852) 109: In France it was customary that "socialist theories became the programs of parties or factions aimed at the future ministry, or better, at dictatorship of the party; these diverse programs agree on one point only: they propose a far greater extension of state power for their realization than what had previously ever been allowed the bourgeoisie. This increase of governmental power and its extension to relations of property and social intercourse renders these socialist systems into forms of transition to communism, the uttermost consequence of the absolutist state." See also Nolte, "Diktatur," in *Geschichtliche Grundbegriffe* Bd. 1 (1972) 900-924.

103. Adelung, foreword to *Versuch* I:xi.

104. See the article "Die Worte Rückschritte und Fortschritte in ihrer Anwendung im politischen Raisonnement," in *Ausserordentlichen Beilage zum Berliner politischen Wochenblatt* (1836) no. 3, 19 ff.

# "Space of Experience" and "Horizon of Expectation": Two Historical Categories

First published as "'Erfahrungsraum' und 'Erwartungshorizont'—zwei historische Kategorien," in U. Engelhardt, V. Sellin, H. Stuke (eds.) *Soziale Bewegung und politische Verfassung* (Stuttgart, 1976) 13-33.

1. F. Schlegel, *Kritische Schriften* (Munich, 1964) 51.

2. See my article "Geschichte, Historie," in *Geschichtliche Grundbegriffe*. The following reflections are based on work related to this historical lexicon of sociopolitical language in Germany. As a sign of my gratitude, they are dedicated to Werner Conze, without whose untiring encouragement the entire scientific enterprise could not have succeeded.

3. Novalis, *Heinrich von Ofterdingen* 258.

4. See St. Augustine's analyses in Book 11 of his *Confessions*, in which the three dimensions of expectation, realization, and memory are related to the intellect, to *anima*. See also the analysis in Heidegger's *Sein und Zeit*, especially chap. 5, "Temporality and Historicity," in which the temporal constitution of human existence is demonstrated as a condition of possible history. Of course, neither St. Augustine nor Heidegger extended their questioning to the time of history. Here it remains an open question whether the intersubjective temporal structures of history can be adequately adduced from existential analysis. The following pages seek to use the metahistorical categories of experience and expectation as indicators for alterations in historical time. The historical implications of all experience were disclosed by Gadamer in *Wahrheit und Methode* (Tübingen, 1960) 329 ff.

5. Goethe and Reinhard, *Briefwechsel* 246.

6. A. Drozdzynski, *Der politische Witz im Ostblok* (Düsseldorf, 1974) 80.

7. Cf. A. Gehlen, "Erfahrung zweiter Hand," in *Der Mensch als geschichtliches Wesen* (Stuttgart, 1974) 176.

8. F. Bacon, *Novum Organum* I:94, in *Works* I:200.

9. On the following, see the individual analyses in the articles "Fortschritt" and "Geschichte," in *Geschichtliche Grundbegriffe* Bd. 2.

10. Leibniz, "De rerum originatione radicali," *Opera philosophica* (Berlin, 1840) 150.

11. Lessing, "Brief an Moses Mendelssohn, 21.January 1756," *Sämtliche Schriften* 17 (1904) 53.

12. See H. Blumenberg, *Die Genesis der kopernikanischen Welt* (Frankfurt, 1975).

13. Schlegel, "Condorcets Esquisse d'un tableau historique des progrès de l'esprit humain' (1795)," in *Kritische Schriften* 236.

14. Kant, "Idea for a Universal History" 48–49.

15. Machiavelli, *Discourses* 3, 43.

16. Hume, *Theory of Politics* 162.

17. Kant, "Streit der Fakultäten," 2 Abschn., Abs. 4 and 7.

18. *Geschichte und Politik* Bd. I (1800) 3.

19. G. F. Creuzer, *Die historische Kunst der Griechen in ihrer Entstehung und Fortbildung* (Leipzig, 1803) 232 ff.

20. Perthes, *Leben* Bd. 2, 240 ff., 146 ff.

21. Bacon, *Novum Organum* I:108, *Works* I:207.

22. L. Büchner, *Der Fortschritt in Natur und Geschichte im Lichte der Darwin'schen Theorie* (Stuttgart, 1884) 30, 34.

23. Kant, "On Perpetual Peace."

24. Lamartine, *Histoire de la Restauration* (Paris, 1851) I:1.

25. J. A. Froude, cited in A. Briggs, *The Age of Improvement* (London, 1959) 3.

26. See my article "Bund, Bündnis, Foderalismus, Bundestaat," in *Geschichtliche Grundbegriffe* Bd. 1 (1972) 582 ff.

27. J. von Müller, *Teutschlands Erwartungen vom Fürstenbund (1788) Sämtliche Werke* 24:259 ff.; and Montesquieu, *Esprit des lois* 9:1.

28. Cf. the article "Demokratie," in *Geschichtliche Grundbegriffe* Bd. 1 (1972) 848 ff.

# Index